SABBATH SCRIPTURE READINGS II

RELATED TITLE FROM
SOLID GROUND CHRISTIAN BOOKS

Sabbath Scripture Readings
From the New Testament
by Thomas Chalmers

SABBATH SCRIPTURE READINGS ON THE OLD TESTAMENT
Spiritual Meditations
From Genesis 1 – 2 Kings 11

THOMAS CHALMERS

SOLID GROUND CHRISTIAN BOOKS
BIRMINGHAM, ALABAMA USA

𝔥𝔬𝔯𝔞𝔢 𝔅𝔦𝔟𝔩𝔦𝔠𝔞𝔢 𝔖𝔞𝔟𝔟𝔞𝔱𝔦𝔠𝔞𝔢.

SABBATH SCRIPTURE READINGS

BY THE LATE

THOMAS CHALMERS, D.D. LL.D.

IN TWO VOLUMES.

VOL. II.

𝔓𝔲𝔟𝔩𝔦𝔰𝔥𝔢𝔡 𝔣𝔬𝔯 𝔗𝔥𝔬𝔪𝔞𝔰 ℭ𝔬𝔫𝔰𝔱𝔞𝔟𝔩𝔢

BY

SUTHERLAND AND KNOX, EDINBURGH.
HAMILTON, ADAMS, AND CO., LONDON.

MDCCCXLVIII.

Solid Ground Christian Books
PO Box 660132
Vestavia Hills AL 35266
205-443-0311
sgcb@charter.net
www.solid-ground-books.com

SABBATH SCRIPTURE READINGS II
Spiritual Meditations on Genesis 1 - 2 Kings 11

Thomas Chalmers (1780 – 1847)

Taken from the 1848 edition by Sutherland and Knox, Edinburgh
Volume 5 of 5 Posthumous Works of Thomas Chalmers
Horae Biblicae Sabbaticae

Cover image is sheep grazing near Loch Linnhe,
In the NW Highlands in Scotland by Ric Ergenbright.
See all Ric's work at www.ricergenbright.com

Cover design by Borgo Design, Tuscaloosa, AL
Contact them at borgogirl@bellsouth.net

ISBN- 978-159925-192-9

CONTENTS.

SABBATH SCRIPTURE READINGS—OLD TESTAMENT—

	PAGE
GENESIS,	1-80
EXODUS,	80-139
LEVITICUS,	139-178
NUMBERS,	179-237
DEUTERONOMY,	237-291
JOSHUA,	292-329
JUDGES,	329-362
RUTH,	362-368
I. SAMUEL,	368-417
II. SAMUEL,	418-454
I. KINGS,	454-489
II. KINGS,	489-507

SABBATH SCRIPTURE READINGS.

Horae Biblicae Sabbaticae.

SABBATH SCRIPTURE READINGS.

OLD TESTAMENT.

GENESIS.

October, 1841.

GENESIS I.—Let me dwell in thought on God as Creator: let me try to realize it. Let me not be satisfied that hitherto I have made no question and felt no difficulty about it. We are too easily satisfied, dealing only with words and not with their archetypes. The thought of God as the Maker of me and all things is simple; but it is with the language or mere symbol, not with the object of the thought that we have been mainly conversant. As in algebra it is not with the *ipsa corpora* of quantity, but with its mere nominal representatives that we have to do—so it has been, but ought not to be, with theology.—My God, let the idea of Thee as my Creator come to me not in word only but in power. Give me to feel how passive, how subordinate, how prostrate and entire is the submission which I owe to the Mighty Sovereign who made me, and who is all in all.

And O may Thy Spirit, who caused this world of beauty and order to emerge from a chaos, operate with like effect on my dark, and turbid, and ruined soul. I pray for the light that shineth in the heart. (2 Cor. iv. 6.) Thou canst make it instantly to arise. May Thy Spirit so move and blow as to awaken me, and may Christ give me light. (Eph. v. 14.)

And may I forget not the likeness in which I was created; or that the great object of the economy under which we sit is to be restored to it now that it has been lost. Looking unto him, O God, by whom Thou madest the worlds, (Heb. i. 2,) may I be made like unto Him. (2 Cor. iii. 18; Col. iii. 10.) May I strive to recover the image of God, and to be perfect even as my Father in Heaven is perfect.

All things were good, very good, O Lord, when they came out, and as they came out of Thy hand. God made man upright, but they sought out many inventions. (Eccles. vii. 29.) Corruption springs from the creature: he is led away of *his own* lusts. Let me therefore look outwardly from myself, and upwardly to that quarter from whence alone cometh every good and perfect gift. (James i. 14-17.) Thou hast never changed. We would look therefore to Him who is the brightness of Thy glory and the express image of Thy person—that we may be transformed to thine own very image, by the study and imitation of the character of Jesus Christ, who is the same to-day, yesterday, and for ever.

GENESIS II.

Sabbath is old as the Creation. Let me feel the reverence due to an institution so originated and of such antiquity; and let me take an especial lesson from the use to which it was appropriated by God: He rested from the labours of the preceding week. O that I could make the day thus set apart, and for such a purpose, a day of holy rest from the secularities and cares of our everyday world. Thereby I should at once both sanctify and enjoy it—making it a day alike of pleasure and of profit to my soul. But for this end let my conversation be in Heaven—let my pleasure lie in communion with God. Quicken me, O Lord, into a sense and perception of the things of faith.

Another holy institution of this chapter is that of marriage. O how sadly I have perverted this ordinance by my glaring neglect of that higher fellowship which belongs to those who are heirs and expectants of the grace of life. And then there are the outbreakings of natural temper, the bitterness, the brooding—all of which are most woful infractions on the express admonitions as well as whole spirit of the gospel.—My God, Thou knowest my infirmities; and Thou knowest my desire to overcome them. Send forth Thy spirit to help me in this warfare. Give me wisdom, O God, and the meekness of wisdom. Let the power of Christ rest upon me. When I am weak then may I experience that I am strong. Teach me self-denial; and fill me with the charity which animates all, and endures all, and overcomes all. May I be made, O Lord, to know how to Christianize the converse of my family, and how to acquit myself of the duty which I owe to the souls of those who live with me.

GENESIS III.

The subtlety of the devil. We are not ignorant of his

devices; we are at this moment amongst his wiles. He is plying my heart with the cares and the provocations of my authorship.—My God, give me the victory; and let the wisdom and the meekness of wisdom which Thou alone canst inspire, carry me in safety through this sore warfare to a haven of peace.

O may Thy word, and the providences by which I am at this moment surrounded, be effectual instruments in the hands of Thy Spirit, for repelling the assaults and artifices of this cruel and skilful adversary. Resist the devil, and he will flee from you. Put on the whole armour of God. Be careful for nothing; but in everything by prayer and supplication, with thanksgiving, make your requests known unto Him. Satan is now bruising my heel; may the Captain of my salvation bruise his head, and fulfil the declaration that Satan shall be bruised under my feet shortly; for this end may I exercise myself, not in these vain, unquiet, restless, and ever recurrent broodings over my annoyances and my wrongs, but may I exercise myself unto godliness. And let the law of the Spirit of life in Christ Jesus free me conclusively and for ever from the law of sin and of death.

"And he shall rule over Thee." It is his part—nay, his duty to rule. It is a relinquishment of the place which God hath given him not to do it. And extending my regard beyond this particular case to the general principle, there is a fault in him who knows not his place and acts not up to it. There is a natural and fitting place for each man in the Church, in society, in little circles, whether of family or of neighbourhood,—and should that be a place of superiority, he ought to know this, and to comport himself therewith. I have to record it as one great error of my life that I have not done this—have not asserted my natural prerogative, which I should have done with the calmness of principle, and not suffered the delinquencies to accumulate till brought out to repel them with the energy of passion. O Lord, give me wisdom in this, and the meekness of wisdom. Let not a wrong humility or a wrong delicacy restrain me either from the testimony which it is mine to give, or the authority which it is mine to exercise. Keep me from the fear of man which is a snare.

The flaming sword at the east of the garden of Eden turns every way to keep man from the tree of life; and under our Christian economy it turns every way but one—but that way is open and accessible to all. No man cometh unto the Father but by the Son: He is the way, and He is also the life. Out of that way no man shall ever meet salvation; in that way no man shall ever miss it. Stablish my feet, O God, therein; and through the open door of Christ's Mediatorship may I find access to Thee as my reconciled Father and Friend.

GENESIS IV.

Give me, O Lord, an interest in that blood which speaketh better things than the blood of Abel. His cried for vengeance; Christ's for the forgiveness of all who trust in it.—My God, work in me this trust. Give me full assurance of heart in the blood of sprinkling. Let me have the same precious faith in a more excellent sacrifice, by which Abel obtained the testimony and the acceptance of a righteous person. Without faith, O God, it is impossible to please Thee—it being the first and greatest of those commandments which are pleasing in Thy sight; for this is Thy commandment, that we should believe on the name of Thy Son, Jesus Christ.

But the commandment goes further than this—that we should love one another. (1 John iii. 23.) It might be for Cain, the outcast of God's displeasure, to say—"Am I my brother's keeper?" but not for us, the reconciled children of God, whose part it is to walk in love, as Christ also hath loved us. My God, how deficient I am here—what impatience under the exposures and interruptions of a manifold society—what a disposition to shun and to hide myself from my own flesh! I have a strong constitutional tendency to keep by the one object that I am prosecuting, and an apprehension or antipathy almost nervous, and I fear overdone, to those numerous applications *ab extra* which threaten to break up or distract me from my own line of employment.—And yet the employment may be for a good object, nay, preferred and selected because of a man's own well-warranted conviction, founded on the experience or the consciousness of what he himself is fittest for, and therefore adopted in the very spirit of the injunction—"In every good work consult thine own soul." There is thus a competition of calls which, on the principle of being able to do only one thing, or to be only in one place at one time, necessitates the rejection of one of them. But give me wisdom, O God, and guard me against all selfishness and anger; and let me never forget the obligation of looking to the things of others as well as to my own things—of bearing their burdens, of loving others whom I do see, as well as the God whom I do not see.

Seth was appointed instead of Abel the head and

representative of a better family than that of Cain, who called upon, or upon whom was called, the name of the Lord.—Whatsoever others do may I and my house serve the Lord, having the power of godliness as well as the profession. Enable me to burst asunder the restraining delicacies which prevent me from appearing with my family on the Lord's side, and separating us from a world which lies in deep ungodliness.

GENESIS V.

Never, O Lord, let me forget the rock out of which I am hewn—that I was shapen in iniquity, and that in sin did my mother conceive me. Seth was born in the likeness, in the image—now tarnished and transformed—of fallen Adam; and that likeness has been transmitted to all his posterity. Thou, O God, who ordainedst this constitution, the rationale of which we are not able to comprehend, didst ordain another constitution, the rationale and juridical principle of which we may be alike unable to comprehend—even that, by the operation of faith in Christ the second Adam, we are transmuted into His glorious likeness, and invested with the everlasting righteousness which He has brought in. The one constitution should reconcile us to the other, as being analogous and parallel thereto; and what ought more to insure our full consent and acquiescence in the second, is its visible harmony with the darling attributes of the Godhead—with the love which is announced to us as the essence of the Deity, (1 John iv. 16)—with the mercy which rejoices over all His works and in the midst of all his perfections. In this confidence, O God, would I now partake of that

Sacrament which I am on the eve of celebrating,* and eat of the bread and drink of the wine in full reliance on the efficacy of that atonement whereof these are the appointed symbols.—My God, be with me; let me wash mine hands in innocency, and so compass Thine altar, O God. Enable me to pay my vows and to substantiate the good profession which I am now to make before many witnesses.

There is something to me very impressive in this antediluvian record of deaths; the long periods of life only make it all the more so. It tells me more forcibly of there being no escape from this law. The cadence of "and he died" recurs with the effect of a tolling bell upon my imagination; and the length of interval between them adds to the solemnity of the lesson so given forth. The great practical truths of religion are not educed by an ingenious process of inference, but lie before us on the surface of the Bible—on the surface of observation. We know them, but the thing wanted is that we should consider them; and this unvarying register of a mortality which no strength of endurance in the vital principle could exempt from, should speak powerfully home to the fears and the urgent interests of the men who now live in this era of puny and ephemeral generations.

But it is not altogether an unvarying record. Enoch did not die, for God took him; and he had this testimony—that he walked with God. May such, O Lord, be henceforward my walk in the world—not without but with God, and therefore not without Christ, (Eph. ii. 12,) through whom alone we have peace with the Father, and but for whom

* Castlebank, Morningside, October 31.

there could have been no such walk; for how can two walk together unless they are agreed? I have received the memorials of that atonement through which alone I look for acceptance with the Lawgiver whom I have offended:—"Uphold my goings, O Lord, in THY paths, that my footsteps slip not."

GENESIS VI.
November, 1841.

Not that He will altogether cease from striving; but He will not, as heretofore, so lengthen it out—He will curtail the period of it: henceforth the days of man shall be an hundred and twenty years. Threescore and ten years, or less, now sum up the earthly existence of the great majority of our species, or the season with each man of the Spirit's striving with him, for there is no such striving after death. We are then conclusively and for ever let alone—left to ourselves, to the inveteracy of our acquired habits, to the cruel tyranny of our own evil and tumultuous passions, to the wild misrule of that fierce internal anarchy which rages without and in the bosoms of the impenitent—an anarchy which conscience is unable to control, though it be still alive to upbraid, to exasperate, and to chastise, as if by the whip of a home tormentor, a worm that dieth not, a fire that is never quenched.—O my God, while the Spirit still strives with me let Him no longer strive in vain. I would invite Him to my bosom—let Him dwell there. I plead Thine own promise. I pray for this inestimable gift. May it be shed abroad in my heart, and I become a temple of the Holy Ghost. Without Him I am altogether evil, in every thought and in every imagination continually. Let me hold out no longer; let me cease all resistance to His further instigations—lest I so grieve Him as to quench Him—grieve Him even as God was grieved exceedingly by the wickedness of men before the flood; so that even before death He may be provoked to a final abandonment, leaving me an unreclaimed and irreclaimable outcast from the presence of God, from the hopes and joys of eternity.

Heavenly Father, may I find grace in Thine eyes.

That I may invite that grace, and that I may increase that grace, may I proceed on the gospel economy, that to Him who hath more shall be given. May I be faithful in that which I have, and so look and pray for more. The Holy Ghost is given to those who obey Him; let me make the right use of His first and lesser influences, that I may be led thereby to larger and ever brightening manifestations. He who is faithful in that which is least shall be counted worthy of a larger confidence, and entrusted *with*—as one who shall also be faithful in—*much*.

We now meet with the important word "covenant," of mighty use—if well pondered and proceeded on—in stablishing and settling and making steadfast the faith of believers—bringing in as it does the immutable truth of God as a guarantee for the fulfilment of all the hopes held out to us in the gospel. It was because of God's faithfulness to the covenant which He established with Noah (verse 18) that the ark into which he entered proved to him an ark of safety. Let us in like manner venture into our ark—venture our all upon Christ, our ark of safety, and in whom we have all the securities of a covenant between God and man, ordered in all things and sure. Let my heart be fixed, trusting in God, while

I think of those promises which are yea and amen in Christ Jesus.

GENESIS VII.

The righteousness which God saw in Noah was a personal righteousness, as well as that which is the righteousness of faith.—My God, give me to blend these, and no longer to dissociate or so oppose them to each other as I fear the systems and controversies of theology might lead us to do.—Faith is ascribed to this illustrious patriarch in the eleventh chapter of the Hebrews; but so also is obedience: "And Noah did according to all that the Lord commanded him." May I aspire to the doing, O Lord, of all Thy will; and give effect by Thy Spirit to these aspirations.

Noah and his family were saved by water. There may be an excess of figurative interpretation—but no danger of it surely, when we carry it no farther than the inspired writers of the New Testament. And Peter says that the like figure, even baptism, doth also now save us by the resurrection of Jesus Christ. We are buried with Him in baptism, even as Noah and his household would have been by the waters of the flood, had he not been borne upward and above them in an ark of safety. We desire to find a place in Christ our ark, who Himself rose from the dead, and who raises all His faithful disciples from their death in trespasses and sins to newness of life. O give me to be saved by water and blood. Sanctify as well as reconcile me, O God. I pray for the washing of regeneration, for the renewing of the Holy Ghost. Give me the baptism of living water, that I may die unto sin —that I may henceforth live unto righteousness.

But the same water which buoyed up the ark and delivered Noah, destroyed all who were left out; and so the same Gospel which to some is the savour of life unto life is to others the savour of death unto death.—O my God, may this Gospel prove the savour of life unto life to me and my family. Give me to bring them up with wisdom and grace, and in all gravity.

GENESIS VIII.

In the language of the Bible the history of the world is its history as God's world. He did not lose sight of His own; He remembered him whom He had reserved from all the other families of the earth again to people and to replenish it, after it had been desolated of the former generation. And Thy remembrance, O God, is as special of each as it is comprehensive of all. "I am poor and needy," says the Psalmist, "yet the Lord thinketh upon me." Heavenly Father, give me comfort as well as warning and holy fear, in the reflection that I am the object of Thy thoughts, and that Thou seest me. Above all, give me a place in Thy book of remembrance for good, even among those who fear Thy name.

We are warranted to view the ark, if not as an express type, at least as a *commodious*, it being indeed a *scriptural* illustration of Christ as our refuge and place of safety. It might be pushing the accommodation too far when we liken to the dove that sinner who, out of Christ, seeketh rest and findeth none: it supplies, however, a very good expression of his state when we speak of him as finding no rest for the sole of his foot till he finds it in the great Surety. O my God, may He at all times be my refuge and my resting-place, and let me take no rest to my soul till I find it in my Saviour. There is great fulness of sentiment in the concluding verses of this chapter, which present us with the account of Noah's sacrifice, and of its blessed effect in pacifying and propitiating the great Lawgiver—reminding us of that great sacrifice on the cross, with the incense of which God is well-pleased, as with the savour of a sweet-smelling sacrifice.—My God, as Thou art well-pleased with what He has done to satisfy Thine offended justice, may we be alike well-pleased with what He has done, as a sufficient basis on which to rest all our hopes and all our dependence before Thee. May we joy in Thee through Him by whom we have received the atonement; and do Thou through Him rejoice over us to bless us and to do us good. The reason assigned by God for not cursing the ground again is deeply interesting—even that the imagination of man's heart is evil from his youth: he was born in sin, he was shapen in iniquity. Sin is the inheritance of our race, the element in which they live and breathe from infancy upward; and on this consideration God founds His purposes of mercy. It is thus that I have often viewed the doctrine of our guilt and corruption by Adam as an argument for confidence in the righteousness of Christ—assured that He who instituted the relation, with all its consequences, between us and the first Adam, will give full effect to the blessings which He hath ordained on behalf of those who enter on the counterpart relation which subsists between the second Adam and all who believe in Him. Let me therefore take up with Thy Son as my resting-place, O God; and under the canopy of His Mediatorship may I delight myself in the abundance of peace. The present succession of the seasons will proceed without cessation or disturbance till the next catastrophe, in which the world will be destroyed by fire.

GENESIS IX.

God putting the fear and dread of man on the inferior creatures suggests an argument for a God from this as an observed fact. Let me recognise in all the relations between one part of nature and another, be they in the world of matter or in the world of life, the traces of a divine wisdom and a divine workmanship.

And a great lesson is to be gathered from the respect here expressed for man as being the image of God—extending to more virtues than one—not only to refrain from the defacement of that image by violence, but also from the defilement of that image by impurity. Keep me alike, O God, from anger and licentiousness, and let them not merely be repressed in the actings of the outer man, but by the establishment of holiness and charity in the heart, may their counterpart affections be overborne, if not eradicated, from the inner man.

The continuance of all things as they were from the flood, guaranteed by the laws and phenomena of nature, so far from ministering to infidelity or false security, should but enhance our confidence in the faithfulness of God. The covenants, ordered and sure, which He makes as the God of nature and providence, should serve to stablish and settle us all the more in the unshaken trust wherewith we cast all our dependence on that Covenant of Grace, ordered in all things and sure, which He has made as the God of salvation. Heavenly Father, may I rest on the immoveable foundation of that truth which never fails, whether it be committed to the maintenance of nature's laws, or to the fulfilment of the promises of the gospel. And what a token hast Thou given for these in Thy Son Christ Jesus! Verily in Him Thy promises must be yea and amen. Thou who hast spared not Thy Son, but given Him unto the death for us all, how shalt Thou not with Him also freely give us all things?

In the concluding passage of this chapter there occurs a narrative which should powerfully enforce one of the lessons in this day's second paragraph—respect for the image of God in man; and more especially, should restrain all unhallowed freedom between those of the same household, whether prompted by curiosity or corrupt inclination.—My God, give me not merely to abstain from that which is evil, but to abhor it—not merely that in my conversation and doings I might maintain the most strict and guarded decorum, but that in my heart I might be enabled to maintain an ethereal purity—glorifying the Lord with my soul and spirit, as well as body, which are the Lord's.

GENESIS X.

December, 1841.

Thou, O God, art the Governor among the nations as well as the families of the world. Thou appointest the bounds of the habitations of all of them. We can have no doubt that in the persons who bear the names recorded in this chapter, and who may be regarded as the primitive germs of the future nations of the earth, God bore a prospective regard to the coming history of our species, or history on a great scale. And what a wonderful prescience as well as power that could both foresee and direct movements of such complexity—and all the more wonderful that in point of experience the greatest events, and on which the state of whole continents for thousands of years has been determined, are often found to hinge on the minutest incidents in the life or fortunes of a single individual. How this consideration, if rightly pondered on and applied, enhances and gives multiple force to the evidence of prophecy, seeing that it is chiefly with nations rather than with individuals—save in the case of sacred and scriptural personages, as our Lord Jesus Christ—that prophecy is conversant.

The Church is so implicated with the world that we should not be inattentive to the great movements and revolutions of the latter on the pretence of its being altogether a field of secular contemplation. We should never forget that after all it is God's world. Nimrod was a mighty hunter *before the Lord*—probably a warrior and the founder of a dynasty; at all events, a great actor on the stage of profane history, yet before the Lord notwithstanding. If it be the characteristic of a worldly man that he desecrates what is holy, it should be the part of a Christian man to consecrate what is secular, and to recognise a present and a presiding Divinity in all things—referring them to Him who worketh all in all.

God evinces not merely an individual but a national respect to mankind—dealing with them not only as separate persons but as distinct aggregates, whether as inhabitants of the same land or descendants of the same ancestor. He fastens a brand or a blessing on them in their collective as well as their individual capacity—as we may see in the posterity of Ham upon the one hand, and of Shem upon the other. It is true that the children of Israel are now in temporary obscuration and disgrace; but when recalled from their dispersion a great and glorious pre-eminence is awaiting them. We pray, O God, for the building up of Thy Jerusalem, and for the speedy arrival of those grand fulfilments which will make it palpable to all—that verily there is a God who reigneth on the earth.

GENESIS XI.

The passage respecting Babel should not be without an humble and wholesome effect upon my spirit. I have been set on the erection of my Babels—on the establishment of at least two great objects, which, however right in themselves, become the mere idols of a fond and proud imagination, in as far as they are not prosecuted with a feeling of dependence upon God, and a supreme desire after His glory. These two objects are the deliverance of our empire from pauperism, and the establishment of an adequate machinery for the Christian and general instruction of our whole population. I am sure that in the advancement of these I have not taken God enough along with me, and trusted more to my own arguments and combinations among my fellows than to prayers. There has been no confounding of tongues to prevent a common understanding, so indispensable to that co-operation without which there can be no success; but without this miracle my views have been marvellously impeded by a diversity of opinions, as great as if it had been brought on by a diversity of language. The barrier in the way of access to other men's minds has been as obstinate and unyielding as if I had spoken to them in foreign speech; and though I cannot resign my convictions, I must now— and surely it is good to be so taught—I must now, under the experimental sense of my own helplessness, acknowledge with all humility, yet with hope in the efficacy of a blessing from on high still in reserve for the day of God's own appointed time—that except the Lord build the house the builders build in vain. In Thine own good time, Almighty Father, regenerate this earth, and gather its people into one happy and harmonious and righteous family.

He that believeth shall not make haste, but look unto God and be still. How many ages elapse from one era to another of His administration? Read over the many and to us apparently useless generations of this chapter, which intervened between Noah and Abraham, whose call formed the next great and noticeable step after the flood, towards that dispensation which was to be ushered in by a promised descendant of his family. All His schemes are carried forward gradually and by a progress; and can we doubt that there is as great wisdom in the rate and manner of the development as there is in the full and final consummation?

We feel now as if approaching the confines of evangelical light when we come to the end of that genealogy which terminates with Abraham—the father of the faithful—an example to all who should afterward believe, and in whose seed all the families of the earth were to be blessed. It is here that there is a perceptible brightening of the dim and early morning twilight of these patriarchal ages.

GENESIS XII.

My God, give me to rejoice in the light of that now risen day which made Abraham glad when he saw it from afar. May Christ be precious to me: He who is the Sun of righteousness, with healing under His wings. Instead of exclusiveness there was a most expansive liberality in this first call of Abraham. It was connected with a great purpose of mercy in behalf of mankind at large. It was for the sake of all the families of the earth; and let me, therefore, read in this the same extent of invitation, and so the same warrant for confidence, that is held out in the widely-sounding proclamation of—"Look unto me, all ye ends of the earth, and be saved."

And give me, O Lord, to walk in the footsteps of the faith of my father Abraham. He forsook all, and followed the voice of God.—My gracious Father, arm me with the like mind; show me, at all times, the path of duty; may I surrender all that is dear to nature whenever required by Thee to make the sacrifice. Give me the firm and honest resolves, and then shall I feel the sweets of an unreserved obedience. May Thy will, without limit and without exception, be my will, and then shall a glory from the Lord shine upon my ways; then shall I experience the fulfilment of the saying—"That if mine eye be single my whole body shall be full of light."

And as Abraham had his altars and his consecrated places, may I love the sensible ordinances as well as the more hidden services of piety. May I not forsake or despise the assembling of ourselves together, but rejoice when the particular call comes round, and it is said unto me, Go up to the house of the Lord.

Let me not forget the respect and affection due to the descendants of Abraham for his sake. Cursed is every one that curseth Thee. I look with complacency to the efforts now making for the restoration of their birthright to them—the land of their fathers, even though it should be anterior to their conversion.

I am called on not to walk in all the footsteps of father Abraham, but only in the footsteps of his faith. In this chapter he evinces a want of faith when instead of trusting to God for his safety he trusted to a device of his own. The God who delivered him in spite of this his perversity would surely have delivered him had he committed himself in all fearlessness and truth to His holy keeping. In the history of all the three patriarchs, Abraham, Isaac, and Jacob, and more especially in that of Jacob, may we observe the intromission of human diffidence and deceit with the proceedings and the purposes of the divine administration. Nevertheless, the counsel of the Lord that shall stand, unaffected alike by the opposition of enemies and the waywardness or misconduct of friends.

Let me never forget, O God, the simplicity and godly sincerity which become the discipleship of Christ, and that one of the specific fruits which spring from a renewal in the spirit of our minds is—that we should lie not one to another. Give me, O Lord, so to exercise myself as to have a conscience void of offence both towards God and towards man.

GENESIS XIII.

When Abraham revisited the holy place which he had himself erected, it filled him with holy recollections. May my desire, O God, be towards the sacred place where Thine honour dwelleth; and to prepare me for heaven, may I delight in Thine ordinances upon earth. May I be glad when they say unto me, Go up unto the house of the Lord. More particularly, may I enjoy and use aright Thy

Sabbath, loving it for its sacred opportunities, and counting all its services to be precious. Enable me, O God, to maintain throughout the whole of this day a close and confiding fellowship with the Father and with the Son. A day in Thy courts is better than a thousand elsewhere. But we are told to follow peace with all men as well as holiness, without which (either) we shall not see God. Abraham exemplified both; and give me, Almighty Father, to make peace my assiduous study, so that as much as in me lieth I may live peaceably with all men. O in and through Christ may I grow in each of these two master graces of the Christian character—holiness and charity. Let me follow the meek and yielding patriarch, in preferring others and seeking not my own. We know not if Lot was aware of the character of those among whom he chose to live; but certainly the fruit of his election was that he had to dwell in the tents of wickedness.

The juxtaposition of God's promise at the close of this chapter to the record before of Abraham's peaceable demeanour reminds us of the promise—"Blessed are the meek, for they shall inherit the earth;" the land—the land of promise—the heavenly Canaan, in the glories and privileges of which inheritance all the provocations and injuries of life might well be borne. Give me, O Lord, along with this hope the charity which endureth all things; and let me ever amid the collisions of society commit myself to Thee, who judgest righteously. Abraham built another altar in his new place of residence. While I bear respect unto the sanctuaries of Thine earthly worship, may I know what it is to sanctify the Lord God always in my heart, to call upon Thee in every place, and worship Thee, who art a Spirit, in spirit and in truth.

GENESIS XIV.

January, 1842.

This chapter affords ground for supposing that, beside the light of natural theism kept up at that period in sundry ways, there was also upholden a light of evangelical truth and evangelical piety. The family of Abraham, as well as himself, probably knew well of Melchizedek, the king of peace while the king of righteousness—so as to impress the faith and sentiment of the gospel on the minds of men in these particular ages.—My God, save me from the peace which is no peace; let me have no peace either without my Saviour or with my sins. Save me from moral lethargy, O God; and may remorse let me not alone till I am conclusively shut up unto Him in whom alone I am safe. And O do Thou, as the very God of peace, sanctify me wholly. Let me try the union of these two elements—peace and the prosecution of holiness—without the disquietude of the legal spirit, yet with all earnestness and honesty. May the law of the Spirit of life in Christ Jesus make me free from the law of sin and of death.

Let me walk in all the footsteps of father Abraham as recorded in this chapter. First, the alacrity wherewith he hastened to the relief of his friend. Let me bear the burdens of others; and save me, O God, from the selfish indolence which would repress my promptitude and my exertions in their service.

And like him may I be liberal in the support of all useful institutions, especially those which subserve the maintenance and extension of religion in the world.

But above all, let me imitate him in what some would call scrupulosity, but which had better be regarded as a holy abstinence from sin, even in the least appearances and degrees of it. He would not touch one article of the spoil. Let me not touch the unclean thing. It may not be my besetting sin to tamper with the limits of integrity; but O save me from tampering with all limits. I confess, O Lord, my grievous delinquencies from holiness of heart and life; I deeply feel my need of being washed in the blood of the Lamb—that pure and spotless thing which lays me under the most sacred and special obligation to be holy even as Christ is holy.

GENESIS XV.

Let me not forego the motive to good works which lies in the comfort and encouragement of their being acceptable to Thee through Jesus Christ. There is a certain orthodox antipathy to the very name of reward, and a certain forbidding glance cast at it by those in authority, and possessing the estimation of masters in Israel, which have practically the effect of an interdict, or at least a chilling influence on all obedience, even the new obedience of the gospel.—My God, release me from this bond; and walking in the footsteps of the faith of our father Abraham, let me believe in Thee not as a shield only, but as an exceeding great reward also, who wills my sanctification and rejoices over it, and finally rewards it. Let this consideration have its direct and natural impulse on all the springs of activity within me; and cause me to go forth with confident alacrity in Thy service—trusting in the Lord and doing good. The controversy between faith and works has had a deadening effect on gospel obedience; and by relaxing the affinity between faith and a good conscience, we fear it may have led many of their faith to make shipwreck. It has divided Christ and broken up the entireness of His system of doctrine, so as to give men but a partial and mutilated view of it.—And, O God, let me follow the faith of Abraham in believing Thy promise amid all the unlikelihoods of nature and experience. And in this faith would I pray believingly for Thy Spirit —that Christ may be formed in me, and I may emerge a new creature—born again, and made meet for the inheritance of the saints. What am I, O God, to be made the subject of so glorious a transformation! Nevertheless, let me believe, seeing Thou hast said that Thou wilt give Thy Holy Spirit to them who ask Him. I ask him, O God, at Thy hands, that I may be regenerated and sanctified wholly. But while I thus aspire after holiness of life, let me never forget that my justifying righteousness, a righteousness of faith, is that everlasting righteousness which Christ hath brought in, the same that was reckoned to Abraham and to all his spiritual posterity. Yet even as he did so would I, O God, supplicate at Thy hands a token of the coming fulfilment. And the token for which I pray is the earnest of Thy Spirit, that by His fruits I may be known; and that such a decisive work of grace might be done upon me here as shall be at once the pledge and the preparation of my glory hereafter.

GENESIS XVI.

My God, suffer me not to let go my hold of Thy providence. Thou who didst interpose sensibly and by miracle to deliver Hagar from her extremity, still interposest for delivery of Thy children as effectually as ever, in answer to the prayer of helplessness, though not in the same way of palpable and extraordinary manifestation. May Thy protecting angel extricate me from all my troubles, and more especially from all my temptations. O may one of those whose office it is to minister to the heirs of salvation shield me from the influences of an evil world. Not to him however, but to Thee, O God, I pray, that in whatever way Thou wilt Thou wouldst not suffer me to be tempted beyond what I am able, but with the temptation provide a way to escape, that I may be able to bear it. Leave me not, O God, unshielded and alone amid the perils of the dreary wilderness of this world; but cast the mantle of Thy protection over me, and give me to experience that though in the world I have trials and troubles on every side, yet in Christ I have safety and peace.

And let the sentiment, that Thou God seest me, not only minister a felt security in the hour of danger, but operate at all times as my warning and my restraint, when like to give way to that which is evil. I confess myself, O God, a helpless, poor, and degraded creature. Work in me, O God, both to will and to do, that I may ever walk as in Thy sight, and work out my own salvation with fear and with trembling.

GENESIS XVII.

Abraham, after that righteousness was imputed to him, did not therefore stand discharged from all service, but on the direct contrary was all the more bound and astricted thereto. It was his constant business to walk before God, and his constant aim was perfection—the mark for the prize of his high calling.—My God, enable me, having received the promises, to perfect my holiness in Thy fear—(2 Cor. vii. 1)—having received Christ to become and to walk as one of Thy children. (John i. 12.) Thine everlasting covenant includes this power and this sanctification. (Heb. viii. 10.) Put Thy laws, then, O God, in my heart, and write them in my mind, that I may be prepared for the heavenly Canaan, the everlasting possession, the Jerusalem which is above.

Give me the circumcision of the heart, O Lord. Give me the crucifixion of the flesh, with its affections and lusts, otherwise I shall be cut off.—My God, let me be effectually resolved by this thought against the evil propensities of this evil and corrupt nature. May I so exercise myself as to keep this vile body under subjection, and escape the awful doom of a castaway. And O my God, let me feel the solemn responsibility wherewith I am invested over my seed after me. Forbid that by my neglect they too should become outcasts from Thy kingdom. Let me bring them up as within the bond of Thy covenant, and may my children be Thy children, O God.

The laughter of Abraham may have proceeded from a sense of incongruity, though perhaps there was somewhat of incredulity in it too. Certain it is, however, that he must at length have got quite the better of this last, for against hope did he believe in hope, both in the matter of Isaac's birth, and more illustriously still, in the matter of his sacrifice; yet his prayer for Ishmael savours of a disposition to associate with him the fulfilment of God's special promises. Let me imitate that faith which could maintain its steadfastness in the face of nature's unlikelihoods; but let me also hope that as God heard the prayer of Abraham for Ishmael, even for him who was born after the flesh, so He will hear my prayer, first, for the spiritual wellbeing of my children; and not only so, but that He will also listen with favour and indulgence when, under the impulse of a parent's affection, I pray for their safety, their health, their comfort, and exemption from the ills of the present life—at least, O God, from such trials as might prove to be more than either they or I shall be able to bear. But let me seek first, both for them and for myself, the kingdom of God and His righteousness; and then as God blessed Abraham even in Ishmael, so will all other things be added unto me.

And, O my God, let me yield unto Thee an immediate and resolved obedience, both in the things of personal and of family religion; and let my cognizance extend not to children alone, but to servants and domestics, and visitors also. Let me adopt the holy purpose of Joshua—that whatever others do, I and my house shall serve the Lord.

GENESIS XVIII.

The circumstance of Abraham entertaining angels unawares is an argument for hospitality. Let mine be of a godly sort, and let me aim at the good of human souls in all my social intercourse with others. But the Lord Jehovah appeared on that occasion: the Angel of the Covenant was there. May His power rest upon me; may His strength be perfected in my exceeding great weakness.

Sarah's laughter was that of incredulity, as appears from the terms of the remonstrance—"Is anything too hard for the Lord?" My God, in the confidence of Thy power would I pray for Christ being formed in me—that

He may dispossess the legion of evil thoughts and imaginations within me. Pluck this thorn out of my flesh; or, if Thou wilt not eradicate, may Thy grace enable me to check those vile affections which war against my soul.

And, O my God, enable me to walk in the footsteps of Abraham as a father and the master of a household. May I know to rule well in my own house—else how shall I be able to rule aright in the Church of God? And what a noble escape from those degrading propensities which so torment and would fain tyrannize over me, did I give myself to prayer and exertion for the salvation from impending ruin of sadly degenerated Scotland. And it is a mighty encouragement that He who saves by many or by few has invested human agency with the power of so wide an operation, insomuch that one man has by his single voice decided the fate of nations. Ten righteous persons would have saved Sodom.—O my God, direct me as to the best way of rallying the friends of Christianity in our land around the standard of a great reformation. Bring good out of the evils which so harass and endanger my soul; and may the besetting temptations of my life be kept at bay while life continues, and till I emerge into that purer region where sin in its deformity and sin in its bitterness is unknown. So help me God.

GENESIS XIX.

O Lord, give me not over to vile affections, else it will be more tolerable even for Sodom and Gomorrah than for me. My God, arm me with resolute principle, that I may endure any suffering in the flesh rather than not cease from sin. Save me from self-deceit, and give me the wisdom both of keeping my own soul and winning the souls of others also. O deliver me from the blood-guiltiness of offending any of Thy little ones.

And let me not linger, O God, as Lot and his family did. Let me haste and make no delay to keep Thy commandments: and let mine be a total surrender of myself to Thy will, and so a total relinquishment of all that is evil. Let there be a clear and complete separation of myself, O God, without reservation, and without any tarrying at the confines of what is wrong or questionable. I would remember Lot's wife, and the danger of sending back one longing aspiration, or so much as a sigh of regret to those evil indulgences which I now desire to renounce, and that wholly and everlastingly.

Lot was delivered both for his own sake (2 Peter ii. 7-9) and also, as appears from verse 29 of this chapter, for the sake of Abraham. My God, Thou hast made promise to the children of the righteous.—O that my way and my walk were so perfect before Thee as to bring down not a curse but a blessing on my family.

To prepare Lot for the revolting enormities described at the close of this chapter he had to be plied with wine. Let me charge myself with the lesson of temperance. How watchful I need to be, O God! What dangers beset me: how unequal is my strength to cope with them.

GENESIS XX.
February, 1842.

Preserve me, O God, from the fear of man, which is a snare. Let me not be afraid of him who can only kill the body, and after that can do no more; but may I fear Him who can put both soul and body into hell. May I stand in awe and sin not, and be enabled promptly and effectually to meet every suggestion on the side of that which is evil by the reply—Shall I do this evil thing and sin against God?

God of mercy, pour upon me the washing of regeneration; create a clean heart, renew a right spirit, put truth into my inward parts, and may it prevail over the deceitfulness of this world's lusts—so that my prayer may rise with acceptance to Thy throne, whether for my own soul or for the souls of those of whom I must give account. The sin of Abimelech would have damaged His kingdom. O God, let neither my family nor the Church be damaged by any sin of mine. Give me to awake, O God, and to work out my salvation with fear and trembling. Save me from the waywardness of my own heart; save me from the great deceiver and destroyer of men. Keep me, Almighty Father, from all disingenuousness. We are called to walk, not in all the footsteps of our father Abraham, but only in the footsteps of his faith. What is recorded of him here proceeded from the want of faith. Let me ever trust in God, and not be afraid of what man can do unto me.

And yet Abraham's prayer for Abimelech was heard. O that my prayer may ascend unto Thy presence, and more especially for those to whom any of my doings might prove an offence and a stumbling-block. Hear me, O God, and deliver me from that most appalling of all enormities—the sin of soul-murder.

GENESIS XXI.

The promise was fulfilled, and ample proof given that

what was impossible to nature gave way before the power of Him to whom all things are possible.—My God, enable me to hope and to believe great things, that great things may be done unto me. I cannot regenerate myself—I cannot call the new man into existence, or form him within me; but I would call on Thee, O God; I implore Thy regenerating Spirit, I pray for that new birth—that new creation without which I can never inherit the kingdom of God; and O enable me to crucify the old man, that I may be conformed to Christ in His death as well as conformed to Him in His resurrection when He is formed within me the hope of glory.

However grievous, O Lord, the surrender of any object dear to nature may be, enable me, at Thy bidding, to cast it out—even to the cutting off of a right hand and the plucking out of a right eye. Translate me from bondage into liberty—the glorious liberty of God's own children. My desire is toward Thee, O Jerusalem, which art above, which art free, and the mother of us all.

And while I supplicate Thy grace, let me confide in Thy providence. In this confidence, O God, let me repress all sinful anxiety for the future—but let my heart be fixed, and not afraid of evil tidings, because trusting in the Lord. God will provide for me a table in the wilderness. As the day comes, the provision will come. Let me not then be thoughtful about the things of to-morrow, but cast my care on Him who careth for me.

Abraham at length came into favour with them who are without. Abimelech at length did him homage; and still if our ways please God, not only will He make our enemies be at peace with us, but men will take knowledge of us as being in the right, and so wisdom be justified of her children. Abimelech paid court to Abraham; and Abraham remonstrated in his hearing against an injustice which he had suffered. It is not right to retaliate for wrong, but right to give witness of the wrong; and God will not let us suffer from our forbearance. The meek shall inherit the earth. Give me, O Lord, to walk in wisdom and charity towards them who are without. But let me never cease, while I sojourn in this wilderness, let me never cease calling on the name of the Lord, the everlasting God. Thou endurest eternally; and while the world passeth away and the lust thereof, it is they who do Thy will that shall endure for ever.

GENESIS XXII.

O my God, may I yield myself unto Thee in all things. Strengthen and resolve me for the doing of all Thy will; nor let either the dearest affections, or most headstrong passions of nature prevail over any one duty to which Thou callest me. May I be in readiness to cut off a right hand, and pluck out a right eye; and whatever the word be which Thou givest, may I hold it my great my only business to obey. Let me walk in the footsteps of father Abraham; and surely I shall, after all, be walking at an humble distance from him, if when he, at the bidding of his Father in heaven, went forth upon the sacrifice of a rightly and well-beloved son, I at the same bidding shall make surrender of any inordinate affection which tyrannizes over me. And we shall lose nothing by thus presenting our bodies a living sacrifice, but receive an hundredfold even in this life—in the godliness which is great gain, in the life of the spiritually-minded, in the peace of those who love God's law. Give me, O Lord, to abound in spiritual sacrifices; and let me have comfort when making them in a sense of Thee as my approving Master, and exceeding great reward. Let not a false orthodoxy chill the encouragements of Thy divine word to a life of obedience. Abraham received Isaac back again in a figure; and Thy Son, O God, sprung back into life when He arose from the grave. Thou providest Him a Lamb for the sins of the world—an offering in our stead. Conform me to Him in His death; and conform me to Him in His resurrection—that henceforward I may die unto sin, with all my affections thereto subdued and mortified; and walk in newness of life with the holy and heaven-born tastes of a regenerated nature. Let us no longer spurn at obedience as a condition after the emphatic testimony of God's own approbation and promise to Abraham—" Because thou hast done this thing, because thou hast obeyed my voice."

The historian while he records the high walk and converse of Abraham with God, does not allow this to supersede his interest in the patriarch's earthly relationship; and O that I could combine with the most strenuous efforts of spirituality and self-denial the perennial operation within my heart of the law of kindness, specially to those of my own household and my own kindred, and generally to all men. Abraham, we doubt not, not only signalized himself by his transcendental deeds of obedience to God, having renounced a father's house, and been ready to offer up his son at Heaven's call—but added to the graces of his character, by the strength and tenderness of his domestic affections.

GENESIS XXIII.

March, 1842.

Let me charge my heart with the certainty of death. Let it be the theme of my frequent and solemn meditation; and when like to be tempted by pleasure or transported by injustice, or depressed by the threatenings of evil, let me escape from all these earthly feelings, by looking forward to the end of all living, and bethinking myself of that grave where the wicked cease from troubling, and the weary are at rest. Mixed with the sympathy felt for the mourners of a household death, there is often a respect awakened by it—a certain reverential feeling for those who are thus signalized—although apart from this, the greatness of Abraham's character and station would have commanded respect at any time. Yet in death itself there is a something fitted to draw out our more serious regards to the bereaved family—and even for the memory of him who has undergone this mysterious transition. Let us not reserve this feeling till the period when the event has happened, but anticipate the event and honour all men—holding them in a sort of awful reverence as subjects of the same mighty and unknown changes to which ourselves and all humanity are liable. There is something pleasing in the courteousness of the Hittites to Abraham, and inexpressibly affecting are the noble, graceful, and dignified returns of his obeisance. Let us imitate him even in this secondary propriety; and as still more indispensable, let us follow his footsteps in the cardinal virtues of disinterestedness and strict undeviating equity—scrupulously faithful in acquitting himself of all its obligations, and at the same time wisely observant of all its needful securities and forms. There was no lengthened procession on this occasion. The place of Sarah's death was the place of her burial. Rachel had to be buried off hand, on the way from Bethel to Mamre, near Ephrath. In those countries where the process of decay must be rapid, they could not keep the body long enough for Rachel to be carried to the family burial-place. The Egyptian art of embalming, however, enabled them to carry Jacob there; and Joseph, who after a very long interval was taken up for final interment to Canaan, was embalmed also.

GENESIS XXIV.

Seeing it was felt by Abraham of so much religious importance to shun an affinity with the idolaters of Canaan, may I, O God, feel the importance, now that my family affinities are fixed, of protecting all in my own household from the idolatry of the world. Give me in this to follow the footsteps of the father of the faithful, who brought up his children in the fear of the Lord.— And, Heavenly Father, let me recognise Thee in the outward providences of life, as well as in the operations of Thy grace in the inner man. Let me be religiously observant of events—whether they be the events of personal or of public history—in everything making my requests known unto God, and in everything giving thanks—so as to imitate the servant of Abraham both in the prayerfulness and the gratitude which are here recorded of him who seems to have combined fidelity to his master with fealty to his God. Let me commit myself at all times to Him who is the angel of Thy presence, O God—the angel of the covenant, who is both able and willing to keep in safety that which is so committed, and to prosper me on my way to everlasting life. Lead me, O Thou Saviour and Friend of sinners, in the right way; and enable me henceforth to abjure the wicked and wrong imaginations which have hitherto so lorded over me, and made war upon my soul. Give me to put this interpretation on all that befalls me *ab extra*—that the thing proceedeth from the Lord, so as to be grateful for all that is prosperous, and peacefully resigned under all that is adverse and calamitous. But may I never forget of every evil thing which cometh forth *ab intra*, that it proceedeth from myself—when drawn away of my own lust and enticed. In these great preparatory steps for ushering the Saviour into the world, let me look on Thy providence as the minister and handmaid of Thy grace—the steps of a process of many ages, and which at length terminated in the advent of Him in whom all the families of the earth are to be blessed. O that my meditations of God were more productive of a distinct and lasting benefit to my soul—that I could maintain a more habitual converse and fellowship both with the Father and the Son; and for this purpose ought I not to have more frequent, and withal fixed seasons, for the lifting of my soul to that sanctuary where Christ sitteth at the right hand of God.—And let not the sacred impede—let them rather strengthen and exalt the social and domestic affections of my heart—even as good Isaac had his seasons of high and heavenly contemplation, while his affections were so settled upon home.

GENESIS XXV.

Let me be mindful of my coming death; let me ever

count on the speed and certainty of its arrival. In the midst of present and of impending troubles, it is a contemplation which sometimes tranquillizes me, when I think of being gathered with my fathers, and of being laid in my quiet resting-place. But awaken me, O God, to a sense of the dread realities beyond—that I may bethink myself not only of the coming death, but of the coming judgment and coming eternity. Like the father of the faithful, let my desires and my hopes settle on the city which hath foundations.

And give me, O Lord, to be rightly impressed not only by the view of my own death, but by the death also of my relatives and friends. I forbear to speculate on the salvation of Ishmael. But it is not a speculation, it is a certainty, that he who is without the pale of the everlasting covenant—or, in other words, he who hath not Christ—hath not life. O may Christ be formed in each and all of my household: may I receive grace to watch over, and have wisdom to win their souls; and in fulfilment of the precept—to look not only on my own things, but on the things of others also—may I ever hold the first and foremost of these to be the things which belong to their everlasting peace.

And let me remember that there is an instinctive constitutional earthly love of offspring, one of the strongest of our affections; and under the promptings of which we, though evil, know how to give even good gifts to our children—but not gifts which conduce to the good of their immortality. It is not the benevolence of nature, but the benevolence of faith which is wanting—that benevolence which longs and labours to secure for them a birthright in heaven. Isaac and Rebekah had their respective favourites; but for aught which appears each felt towards them but the impulses of a blind partiality which came unbidden, and bore respect only to the enjoyments of the life that now is. Sanctify, O Lord, and elevate my family regards, that I may consult for their real and permanent, and not for a mere counterfeit good to them in the deceitful and fleeting interests of time, lest, after all, I shall be found to have given them not a loaf but a stone, not an egg but a scorpion, not a fish but a serpent.

It was a profane thing in Esau to despise his birthright, which therefore must have had relation to what was sacred—not, we think, the property to which his primogeniture might have entitled him, but the great family promise made to Abraham, which descended not to Ishmael, who was cast out from the inheritance, but to Isaac, in whom the seed was called. It seems to me that what Ishmael was ejected from Esau gave up by a voluntary renunciation. Let me not incur, O God, the guilt of profanation, either by bartering my own eternity for the worthless gratification of a moment, or the eternity of those who are dear to me, by a preference for them of the meat which perisheth to the meat which endureth unto life everlasting.

GENESIS XXVI.

It was because of his obedience that the blessing of Abraham descended to his posterity. Give me, O Lord, to know the value which Thou hast for the keeping of Thy commandments; and let not the artificial orthodoxy of men weaken or disturb my estimation of it. O that I had the comfort of knowing that my services as well as my person were acceptable to God through Jesus Christ, and that I was walking worthy of the Lord unto all well-pleasing. Let me taste the sweetness of self-crucifixion, and of merging my will into Thy will; and O that I could prove my own interest and part in the blessing of Abraham by walking in his footsteps.

And yet there are passages in the lives of these best and highest patriarchs which should serve as our beacons rather than our examples. As new born creatures we are called upon to speak the truth; and while we walk in wisdom to them who are without, let not deceit enter as an ingredient into our policy towards them. I would at all times cast my care upon Thee, O God—seeking to Thy protection as my unfailing refuge, and not to any dissimulation or artifice of my own. I pray for truth in the inward parts; and that with simplicity and godly sincerity—not with fleshly wisdom—I might have my conversation in the world.

God blessed Isaac with worldly abundance; and he is worthier of our imitation for those virtues which belong to a state of safety than for those which belong to a state of danger. While a man of prosperity he was pre-eminently a man of peace. On him was verified the blessing of the meek—he inherited the land, and was secured in the fruits of it, though as much as in him lay, and as far as was possible, he lived peaceably with all men. He strove not, and at length his enemies ceased to strive with him. If a man's ways please God, He will make even his enemies be at peace with him.—My God, whether Thou art pleased or not that I should dwell in the bosom of that tranquillity which Isaac loved, and after which I sigh, invest me with the mild graces of his character; and if it be Thy blessed will, let my setting sun descend in peace—at least in charity with all mankind. This history is pregnant with lessons. The Lord made room for Isaac in the midst of his enemies—saying unto him, Fear not; and Isaac did not repudiate their advances, but held convivial intercourse with them under his own roof. And he was a man of piety as well as peace—calling on the name of the Lord. Let me follow after peace and godliness; let mine be the conjunct virtues of the saint and the citizen, having my conversation in heaven, and at the same time useful in the world while unspotted therefrom.

And O let it be my distinct—Heaven grant that it may be my successful—effort to conquer the alienation of my household from the truth as it is in Jesus. Give one and all of them fully to receive the gospel of Jesus Christ into their hearts. Purge out all that is worldly—that freed from the spirit of this earthly Canaan ours may be a united and unanimous Christian family, where the prayers and the praises of Thine own people are ever heard—even the melody which dwells in the tabernacles of the righteous.

GENESIS XXVII.

April, 1842.

Isaac's love of savoury meat reminds me of one of age's infirmities, and that an infirmity which I should watch against and pray against, even till I prevail over it. Let not my heart, O Lord, be overcharged with surfeiting, but may I put a knife to my throat rather than give myself up to the cravings of appetite, or give way to the temptation of such dainties as are set out before me. Through the Spirit may I mortify this deed of the body and live;

for it is an indulgence most adverse to that spiritual-mindedness which is both life and peace. Yet Thou art not the severe Master of a family: Thou permittest the use of Thy creatures, and hast said that nothing is to be refused if it be received with thanksgiving. Let me know what it is to use without abusing. Let me avoid every gratification wherein there is excess; and O may Thy will be the object of my distinct consideration, and distinct conscientious regard at all times. Herein may I ever exercise myself.

Favouritism in families is the fruit, in general, of a merely instinctive regard. What I stand in need of is a spiritual regard for my children—an affection for their souls—a higher care than for this world's blessings—a deep practical concern for the good of their eternity. He who despised the birthright was afterward disinherited of the blessing. Let me seek first the kingdom of God and His righteousness; and this is the most effectual way of having all other things added unto me. But let me not seek these by an unfair policy; and neither let me fret because of the unfair, and at the same time successful policy of others; for thus it is often, as in the chapter before us, that God fulfils the high purposes of His own pleasure. Let me under every provocation be still, and acquiesce in the sovereignty of Him without whose permission there can no accomplishment take place.

There is a wisdom that we are called upon to observe. but surely it must be of a different style and principle altogether from the craft and reticence and whole management of Rebekah. Let mine not be a fleshly wisdom, but that of simplicity and godly sincerity, by the grace and under the guidance of God.

GENESIS XXVIII.

There may be gathered from this chapter a lesson of principle and caution in the forming of family relationships; and should the time for this have gone by, it may well be extended into a lesson for charging ourselves with the character and spirit of all who are under our roof, that they may be turned from the secularities of this earthly Canaan, and spiritualized into the frame and temper of God's own Israel. I again pray, O God, that Thou wouldest enable me to acquit myself aright of what I owe to the immortality of those under my roof. Give me the happiness of a Christian family, that whatever befalls in this world we may possess the only true riches, and be all prepared for an inheritance of glory in the heavens. Then shall I indeed have the blessing of Abraham, having God Himself for the everlasting portion of me and mine.

What a solemn representation of God's overruling providence, and of the high sovereignty and superintendence which belong to Him—at the top of the ladder reaching from heaven to earth, with His ministering angels ascending and descending thereupon! O that I felt as I ought the relation in which I stand to the designs and the doings of that exalted upper sanctuary, and that as the heir of salvation, even as Jacob was of the promised land, the events of my history were all made to subserve my schooling for an abundant entrance upon the land of eternal rest. Keep me, O God, whithersoever I go, and so preserve me as to present me faultless before the presence of Thy glory with exceeding joy. Give me, O Lord, so to behold Thee in faith as to awaken in me the solemnized feelings of the patriarch. It may be said of Him who is everywhere present—" Surely the Lord is in this place" —and of the world, that it is the gate of eternity. O may it be to us a school of preparation for heaven—for that house not built with hands—for those mansions of the just which never fall nor decay. My God, Thou knowest my infirmities, and with what undue earnestness I set my aims and affections on a house that is built with hands, and wherein I would fain dwell and repose myself as in an earthly paradise. I have had some trials and conflicts hitherto in my attempts to realize it, and for aught I know there may be further exercises of patience and principle required of me in the prosecution of this object. In connexion therewith I do not vow, but I will pray, that should God be pleased to settle me there in peace, and to grant me there an abode of security and comfort, O may it be an abode of piety; and may I be enabled to consecrate the remainder of my days to the delights of a calm and contemplative solitude, with such labours of Christian usefulness as I have strength for. May the Lord be my God. May I have a heart for Jacob's vow; and if it please the sovereign Disposer of all events, may I have the ability to discharge it. But prepare me for the whole of Thy blessed will. Enable me to sit loose to the world, and not to set my affections thereupon. Give me to feel that here I am but a stranger and a pilgrim; and may my doings plainly declare that I seek a country on the other side of death. To all this help me, good Lord.

GENESIS XXIX.

There is a lesson of providence in this chapter, in the very movements of Jacob, by which he was conducted to a meeting with Rachel; and I desire to recognise God in all, even the minutest events of my history. O that I could discern His hand and will in everything, and deal with all occurrences as the exponents of that power and of those purposes which are given forth from above. In the character of Laban there is another lesson—a beacon against both avarice and duplicity. Save me, O God, from the idolatry of wealth, and may all my transactions with men be in the spirit of simplicity and godly sincerity. There is a third lesson, and wherewith I should like to be charged. I am too much alive to the coldness of my fellows; and God has been pleased in some degree, though far below my evil deservings at His hand, to exercise me with the desertion and calumny of friends, and if not the positive hatred of many, at least such a want of cordial and congenial sympathy as sometimes makes me marvel at the very small number of habitual or confidential intimacies which I enjoy. But God can amply make this up to me, even as He did to Leah, who was hated, and who at each visitation of His goodness to her acknowledged the hand of Him who looked upon her affliction, and who did her all this kindness because He saw that she was hated. Let me then be patient under a similar adversity, seeing that He who could cause that Leah should be loved by her husband, and the two to be joined in affection with each other, that He can turn at His good pleasure the hearts of enemies towards me. Meanwhile let me acquit myself with all forbearance and gentleness; and O that I could take the wrongs of injustice and unmerited alienation, not quietly alone, but thankfully. He at His own right time can interpose in my favour; and indeed though I have not yet the evidence of a returning positive affection in those who at one time heaped their reproaches upon my head, God at least has silenced the voice of obloquy, not perhaps of my opponents in the strife of party, but of those with whom I at one time took counsel together.—My God, perfect that which concerns me. Give me an entire patience; and when Thou seest meet let me, in peace and charity with all men, say with Leah—" Now will I praise the Lord."

GENESIS XXX.

Save me, O God, from that $\epsilon\pi\iota\theta\upsilon\mu\iota\alpha$ which, in its more general acceptation, signifies the setting of one's mind, or of one's whole desire, on any terrestrial object, or any mere creature comfort, of whatever kind—as Jonah on his gourd, and Rachel on children. Let Thy will be done on earth as it is in heaven; and never let me take an unlicensed or unwarrantable way for the accomplishment of any object that my heart is set upon.

And forbid, Lord, that the ruder practices of the earlier should be suffered to vitiate our conceptions of the high and spiritual morality of our later dispensation. Enable us to bless Thee for the pure and perfect ethics of the New Testament, and thus to give thanks at the remembrance of Thy holiness.

In old times Thou manifestedst Thyself in an extraordinary way, even to those in the humble and domestic walks of life—as to Rachel and Rebekah, whom Thou endowedst with a certain measure of prophetic illumination.—My God, manifest Christ unto me. May Thy Spirit take of His things and shew them unto my soul. Give me a token of the blessed fulfilment of His gracious promise—that He will cause me to abound in much fruit. May He be formed in me the hope of glory—such a hope as might purify and reach its blissful and glorious consummation in eternity hereafter.

But let me never forget that Christianity germinates something more than a mere hope; it commences and sustains a new life. More especially they who are thus born lay up their treasure in heaven, and lie not one to another. (Col. iii. 9.) O Lord, save me both from the deceit and avarice of which we read in this chapter. Let me be effectually warned by the record, whether of the vices of the ungodly or the infirmities of the righteous. More especially let me not be lulled into a false and fatal security by the recorded delinquencies of good men—as Jacob and David and Peter—far less by what we hear or observe of the foulest delinquencies even of the inexplicable defects and blemishes of the reputed and, let us hope, real and earnest professors of godliness in the present day. I have recently heard of an eminently spiritual minister, who died but a few months ago, that his daughter had said of him, that he never once had spoken to her of her soul. Save me, O God, from such a denial of Christ within the limits of my family; and grant me the tongue of the courageous and the wise, that I may never be silent when I ought not, but speak at all times aright of the great things He has done, and the greater things He offers to one and to all of us.

GENESIS XXXI.

May, 1842.

To Thy wisdom and to Thy providence, O God of Bethel, would we commit all our ways. Teach us to conduct ourselves aright amid the oppositions of evil men; and if not to disarm at least to escape the hostility of those who are the enemies of Thy Church, because the enemies of truth and righteousness. Yet let us not be partakers of other men's sins; let us not try to overmatch our adversaries in the game of a deceitful policy. May ours be the simplicity and godly sincerity of men who, not in flesh, but by the grace of God, have their conversation in the world. My God, teach me the way in which I should walk, for the advancement of Thy cause in the world. Open up such a way for me. And if I have done rashly or wrong in so much as hinting at the likelihood of a movement to London for the public explanation of our Church's question, forgive the waywardness, O Lord. Overrule all to Thy glory, and to the good of Thy Church in Scotland. Save me from the counsel of mine own heart, and from the sight of mine own eyes. And let me realize this property of a genuine faith, that he who believeth shall not make haste but wait for the guidance of Thine own blessed directions—whether these are given by illuminations of Thy word and Spirit, or by the manifestations of Thy providence. And Thou, O Lord, art not only the conductor and the shepherd of Thine own children, but Thou canst change the hearts or turn from their purposes the deadliest of our adversaries. Let us place therefore our unbounded confidence in Him who has the command of infinite resources for the deliverance of His faithful worshippers and servants. Let us trust in God, and not fear what man can do unto us. We will not trust in princes, nor in the sons of man, but make the God of Abraham, and Isaac, and Jacob our only refuge—committing every thought of our hearts unto Him, and leaning not to our own understanding. And teach me, O God, to live peaceably; teach me the wisdom of conciliation, but only within the limits of integrity and faithfulness. May I be first pure, then peaceable. And O if I could only mingle more of piety in all my transactions with others, and not be ashamed of a direct reference by joint prayer to God, on the event of journeys or separations or any other notable transactions whatever, between friends or with my family.

GENESIS XXXII.

Even as Jacob met a host of angels may I be enabled to discern the messages and manifestations of God in the thickening events which are before and around me. And O send me in these momentous times encouraging tokens of good to the Church of my fathers. Let me do all that in me lies to propitiate our enemies, even as Jacob did to propitiate his brother Esau. But let me further imitate his example by adding to prudence prayer. O deliver the Church of Scotland from the hand and power of her adversaries. Interpose, O God, for her safety in these days of menace and approaching trial. Turn the hearts of those who are opposed to her; and grant, if it be Thy blessed will, that there may be peace as well as truth and righteousness in our day. Enable us, O God, to devise aright, and to order aright, for the best possible effect on the minds of those who would usurp for Cæsar the things of God, and make human law paramount to divine, even in those matters which are purely ecclesiastical. And this we would ask with all importunity and perseverance, even till we receive. Ever blessed be Thy name, O Lord, for the lesson that men ought to pray always, and not to faint. We would ask till we receive, we would seek till we find, we would knock till the door is opened to us. Like Jacob of old, we desire, O Lord, to wrestle and to prevail. Blessed be Thou, O God, for having put into our mouth an all-prevailing name and an all-prevailing argument—even the name of Thine only beloved Son, and the argument of His all-sufficient power, and all-perfect righteousness; a Priest upon His throne, and whom Thou hast set a King on Thy holy hill of Zion. O the exceeding greatness and preciousness of the promise, that whatsoever we ask in His name we shall receive. Pour forth the spirit of prayer on Thy Church's ministers, O Lord. Furnish them richly with grace as well as with wisdom. May the eyes of all our Church's friends be towards Thee, and let there not be wanting a full dependence upon Thee, along with all diligence both in counsel and in action. We are smitten with infirmity, and have long gone halting among the half measures, and between the two opinions which the vain attempt at a compromise and amalgamation of elements, now found to be incompatible, has served to germinate in our views of ecclesiastical polity. Give us freedom and enlargement, O Lord; and by Thy power resting on us may we henceforth—yet trusting all the while in Thee and not in ourselves—carry, even in the sight of our enemies, the erect air and confident step of men walking at liberty. O may Thy presence and power be sensibly felt in the General Assembly of our Church. Be a wall of defence round about her—be the glory in the midst of her.

GENESIS XXXIII.

Give me, O Lord, both the charity and the wisdom that

might disarm an adversary. Let me forget not that though the first property of the wisdom from above is that it is pure—the second is, that it is peaceable. Let me never transgress the courteousness which I owe even to an enemy; and when that enemy is one in authority, save me from the sin which so easily besets me, of railing against or speaking evil of him. I have much to learn, O God, in this department of the Church's warfare. Let me do my part; and who knows but that God, who can turn the hearts of all men—even as He did that of Esau—will cause even the deadliest of our adversaries to be at peace with us! To make way for this promise, let the ways of the Church and my own ways please God. Let my language towards the civil Government of the country be that of benediction and respect. And let us endeavour to make it palpable to them that we could not do otherwise than we are doing, in not acceding to their proposal. Let us labour to assure them that our non-compliance with their Erastian propositions is not because of any hostile or disrespectful feeling towards them, but because of that most uncontrollable and imperious of all necessities—the necessity of principle. God can do great things for us. He could even, in return for our firmness, dispose the very party with whom we are at variance to be more generous and helpful than they ever were before. Let it be our care first to be pure, and then may He not only cause our enemies to be at peace with us, but may open their hearts for such an enlargement and endowment of the Church of Scotland as we have laboured in vain of late to realize. Do enable us, O Lord, to multiply Thine altars over the whole length and breadth of our land. Let there not be even one solitary fragment of our population beyond the reach of gospel opportunities and gospel ordinances. Plant an effective ministry everywhere; and O grant that, as the fruit of our contendings with the powers of this world, the earth may be made to help the woman, and our National Church continue to be upholden in all her present immunities. In the exercise of her functions may she become the instrument of a great revival—so that our land might be a land of righteousness, a country which the God of Jacob shall be pleased to signalize as the place of His special habitation.

GENESIS XXXIV.

Teach me circumspection, O Lord. Give me to shun every exposure, and make me abstain from the least approaches to that which is evil. The curiosity of Dinah ended in her lamentable corruption. Lead me not into evil, but deliver me from him who is the prince of evil —the evil which sin and Satan have brought on the degenerate race of mankind. In carrying on Thine own righteous and moral administration, the instruments of Thy holy discipline are often the wrath and wickedness of men—which Thou, O God, canst cause to praise Thee by employing them as the ministers of vengeance. But let us not, therefore, look on wickedness otherwise than with deep abhorrence. Save us from unbridled anger; and let both deceit and cruelty be spurned away from us. Even from the most revolting narratives of crime may I derive a benefit—looking not only to the examples which are to be followed, but at the beacons which should be shunned—making use of those records of earlier times as written not for their admonition only, but for the warning of those on whom the latter ends of the world have come.

To complete the lesson of this chapter we should take in the blessing of Jacob—or rather, the curse which he pronounced on Simeon and Levi from his deathbed. O my soul come not thou into the secret, and mine honour be not thou united with the assembly of bloody and deceitful men, who began their iniquity with a lie, and, after a dread process of fierce and fell cruelty, finished this tragedy by giving way to base avarice, and adding the guilt of robbery to murder.

GENESIS XXXV.

Remind me effectually, O God, as Thou didst Jacob of old, of the duty under which I lie to worship Thee in public and in the solemn assembly; and O may it be a pure worship in spirit and in truth. O maintain Thine altars in our land; and bringing our Church out of her distress and difficulties, do Thou enable us henceforth to consecrate our all to Thy service, and to give up all for the advancement of Thy name and glory in our world. Overcome our adversaries, that they may abstain from all further molestation and be at peace with us.

Give me to be kind and respectful to all under my roof. O that I felt a more solemn responsibility for their souls; and not only viewed but treated them as dying, and withal immortal creatures: and give me to act the part of a Christian master as well as a Christian father and husband.

Thou art a promise-keeping God. O give me a part and an interest in the exceeding great and precious promises of the gospel. I would take my place, O God, in the covenant of peace. Give me an intelligent and realizing view of Thy gospel overtures, and dispose me to an instant and practical compliance therewith. O may I ask till I receive, and thus wrestling with God, may I prevail in my desires after the grace and righteousness which are held out even to the chief of sinners. Make me to abound in the fruits of righteousness; and may I and my children and my whole family become meet for heaven.

It is a touching remembrance when we bethink ourselves of dead and departed relatives. Thou hast long spared me, O God. O that I felt the evil of having so neglected the ample opportunities which Thou hast so amply held out to me. Let me haste and make no delay whatever, while I and my wife and my children are still in the body, to treat them as the possessors of so many imperishable spirits, and thus to train them for eternity. But, Lord, help me in this great undertaking; and let me intercede in behalf of them all, that they may come to the knowledge of the truth and be saved.

O for such a mild, benignant, and patriarchal old age as was enjoyed by Isaac.—But this as Thou pleasest, O God.—May I meet him in heaven; and when the earthly house of this tabernacle is dissolved, be translated to those mansions where be the spirits of the just made perfect.

GENESIS XXXVI.

June, 1842.

Let me not put forth of all regard and attention what are usually called profane studies. God has been pleased to admit within the limits of His own Bible what in one view might be termed profane history. We are here presented with the genealogies of profane Esau; but the nation of which he was the founder stood related to Israel; and civil history has its influence and bearings on the history of the Church, and other studies beside those which are directly sacred may nevertheless minister to feelings and point to conclusions of sacredness. Thy works, O Lord, are great—sought out of all them who have pleasure therein—and all are Thy creatures.

There was a tolerated polygamy in these days.—Let me cherish in heart as well as maintain in habit the ethereal purity of our better and nobler dispensation.

The distinctions of rank seem inseparable from the state of humanity in all countries and ages. Let me bear respect to this arrangement of Providence. From Jude we learn that these two moral delinquencies went often together—defiling the flesh, and despising dominion. Let me not speak evil of dignities.

These brief notices of successive generations should remind us of our own, as having its place and passage, too, in this line of ever-flowing continuity, and soon to be numbered among the periods of bygone history.

The children of Esau inhabited the land of Seir by the ordination of that God who not only determines the times before appointed, but the bounds of every habitation. (Acts xvii. 26.)

As we read of kings and dukes let us acquiesce in the gradations and varieties of government as established in different countries of the world. Our plain duty is to hold in reverence those whom God hath made our superiors in station and power. Rank as rank is held up as being of itself a rightful object of human respect—a principle this which is not to be abrogated, because rank may and often is associated with a profligacy in virtue of which it forfeits in every such individual the estimation which natively and properly belongs to it.

GENESIS XXXVII.

Save me, O God, from partiality in my affections towards my children—or rather, let me have one and the same, and that a very intense and withal a practical affection for their souls. At the same time, give me so to love them and be kind to them that I may win both their gratitude and their confidence. But, at all events, let me abstain from such preference as might stir up heartburnings or jealousies betwixt them.

Give me to adore Thy providence, and furthermore, to trust in it, while I peruse this, one of its most striking records: and though now Thou mayest have withdrawn Thy supernatural revelations from the world, still guide me aright, and inform me of all that is needful for the regulation of my conduct; and give me if not such a knowledge at least such a judgment of futurity as that I shall walk wisely through the world.

And cause me to be observant of the signs of the times. Let me not look heedlessly on the events that are passing around me, and let me treasure up all the premonitions which might be gathered from the sayings of men. There is still a certain light cast by experience, and still more by the Scriptures, on things which are to come. Let me at least read the words of Thy prophecy, O God, and keep in mind the things which are written therein.

Let me recognise Thy finger, O God, even in the slightest movements of Thy creatures here below. If not a sparrow falleth on the ground, so not a fellow-man walketh on the highway but by Thy appointment and ordering. Give me to see a providence even in what are termed little things; for on these dost Thou often, amid the intricacies of this world's mechanism, make the great events and evolutions of history to turn.

In the conduct of Thy providence the passions and the wickedness of men are often the instruments of Thy holy purposes—the wrath of man Thou makest to praise Thee. The cruelty, and avarice, and injustice of men are but parts of that instrumentality which is in the hands and under the entire and absolute direction of an altogether good and righteous God. How interesting to see in embryo, and to mark the rudimental steps of that process which runs throughout the fortunes and history of the children of Israel.

One evil perpetration leads to another—an act whether of violence or impurity to an act of deceit for the purpose of its concealment.—My God, let me walk in the light: let all I do bear the exposure of open day; and let me apply this principle not to actions only, but to the regulation of my thoughts. Let not my deeds—nay, let not my very desires and imaginations be such as that I should blush were they made known. O what a busy and watchful cultivation were required to cleanse from all vanity and from all filthiness of the spirit. O God, may I ever live as in Thy sight, and under the felt control of Thine omniscient eye. Thou hast wonderfully spared me, O God, from the sorrows of family bereavement: Thou hast given me a long season of grace and opportunity for cultivating the souls of my children.—How shamefully and sinfully have I neglected them! May God forgive, may

God amend and rectify, and withal counsel and sustain me in the work of their education for heaven.

GENESIS XXXVIII.

Let this record of licentiousness lead me all the more to shun and to detest it. My moral sensibilities are not nearly so alive to the sinfulness even of the grosser carnalities as they are to that of injustice or inhumanity. Let me, nevertheless, hold it enough that God has given His express testimony to the evil of both; and let me, in resolute obedience to the authority of Scripture, so exercise myself as to keep my body under subjection. Create a clean heart, renew a right spirit; and let me never forget that unless there be a purity of the inner as well as the outer man I cannot see God.

It was probably after an excess of festivity that Judah was led to the more heinous excess that is detailed in this chapter. Let me be temperate in all things. Let me live soberly as well as righteously, and godly as well as both. What scope for the exercise of a holy watchfulness and holy discipline; and how experience testifies to the suitableness and necessity of the precept—Work out your salvation with fear and trembling. Give me, O Lord, to fear always, that I may remember Thy commandments to do them. O that this body of mine were a temple of the Holy Ghost, so as that through the Spirit I might mortify the deeds of the body and live. But my most frequent delinquencies are of a spiritual nature, which, though not followed up by outbreaks, are hateful in the sight of God—for the very thought of foolishness is sin; and how vile then that heart which is a brooding chamber of such thoughts, insomuch that it becomes—in being a crowded repository of these—like a cage for every hateful and unclean bird.

What a wonder-working God art Thou! Verily, Thy ways are not as our ways, nor Thy thoughts as our thoughts. Our Saviour according to the flesh descended from the progeny of a most revolting wickedness. Truly Thou bringest good out of evil; and at the end—the final landing-place of all the transmigrations which take place in this created universe—when time shall be no more, and the mystery of God is finished, will it be seen that holy art Thou in all Thy doings, and that just and true are Thy ways, Thou King of saints.

GENESIS XXXIX.

Rostrevor, June 26, 1842.

Give me, O Lord, ever to recognise the hand of Thy providence as manifested in the narrative here given, and which presents us with one of the most striking and affecting of its specimens. What a mighty improvement on our spiritual education did we, by the hourly habit of such a recognition, convert the whole of human life into a school of faith.—Make me, O God, an apt disciple of this school; and so as that among the events of my history I may be ever looking beyond the secondary and the sensible, and day after day be always found walking with God. "A man's goings are of the Lord." Give me, O Lord, to proceed on the truth of Thine own saying; and O let me consecrate my present evolution, in having been brought to Ireland, to Thy glory, and the Christian good of my family and friends. What reality it gives to religion when one can read the finger of the unseen

Governor of all things in the familiar movement and occurrences of one's journey through the world, and thus be a learner in the Book of Providence as well as in the Book of Revelation. Let me exercise myself more than I have ever yet done in the former of these volumes— assured as I am that both volumes will throw light on each other, and that both will be found to harmonize. In the practical and truly important sense of the term, Thou temptest not any man—although Thou ordainest the circumstances under which, or in the midst of which, man suffers himself to be tempted, and to be drawn away of his own lust and enticed. Lead me not, O God, into temptation; or if, in the course of Thy providence, I am placed in a dangerous exposure—dangerous from my own negligence of circumspection and prayer—then, O Lord, interpose with Thy grace to deliver me from evil, by bringing what is right and holy to my remembrance, and impressing it upon me with power. Save me from thinking that I stand. Give me to take heed lest I fall. Let the memorable sentence of Joseph sink deep into my heart, and be my preserver—I had almost said my amulet or charm—in every hour of temptation, "Shall I do this great wickedness and sin against God?" And let me not hold it enough to be kept from evil deeds; keep me, O God, from evil thoughts. Let me remember that not only is there a forbidden territory of action, but also a forbidden territory of thought. Enable me not only to turn away my sight and eyes from viewing vanity, but my mind from dwelling on it. Give me a sensitive recoil from the very imagination of licentiousness, and deliver me from all speculative as well as actual impurity—seeing that without holiness of heart as well as life, I shall never see God. Neither let me think it strange if for welldoing I should suffer wrongfully. God knoweth how to deliver the godly out of their temptations. No present if necessary support will be wanting; and there will be a full and final deliverance at the last.

> " The trials which afflict the just
> In number many be;
> But yet at length out of them all
> He'll set them safe and free."

Give me a right practical sense of my weakness, that I may betake myself to watchfulness and prayer. Let not what ought to be my daily exercise be forgotten. And O save me from blood-guiltiness—from the wo that lies upon those who give offence to any of Thy little ones. Whether to sustain my faith in Thy providence, or to guard and discipline my own heart in the grace of celestial and heaven-born purity, let me remember Joseph, and not, like Pharaoh's butler, forget him.

GENESIS XL.

Rostrevor Quay, July 3, 1842.

Let these further evolutions of Thy wise and righteous providence bring the lesson home of Thy presiding agency in the affairs of our world. What a complicated machine is human society, made up of the many thousand wills and states of its various individuals, yet all under the perfect view of Thy divine intelligence, the perfect control of Thy divine policy and pleasure. Let me stand in awe when I think how wholly I am in the hands of the all-regulating God, who could bring me either weal or wo from so many quarters altogether beyond the sphere of any present cognizance or observation of mine.

But let me also feel a comfort and a confidence in this contemplation—though for that I should have the trust or the knowledge that God is my friend. Let me have but faith in the Lord Jesus, so as to become one of God's reconciled children, and all things will be mine—all things will work together for my good. The bad and good passions of our nature are alike instruments in the hands of Him who is Supreme in the armies of heaven, and among the inhabitants of earth. Both the wrath of Pharaoh and the sympathy of Joseph bear a part in this chapter of the history now going forward; but there is something more than an ordinary providence here, as indicated alike by the dreams that were sent from heaven, and by the faculty of interpretation which also came down thence. Let me, however, in the absence of the extraordinary, still look up both in desire and dependence towards God, as to Him who worketh all in all. Yet seeing that even the consciousness of immediate gifts and guidance from on high did not supersede in Joseph the use of those expedients which were likely to effect his deliverance—for he attempted to enlist the human instrumentality of the butler on his side—let me, too, combine prudence with piety—doing as much as I ought for myself, yet depending as much as I ought upon God. I would provide for the lawful good both of me and mine, yet would cast all my care on Him who careth for all His children.

Though it be God's overruling will which assigns evil as well as good to man, yet our acquiescence in His adverse disposals to others should not preclude our compassion for the unfortunate. We cannot but pity the case of the poor baker.—Let me weep with those who weep as well as rejoice with them who rejoice. O that I had a heart more alive to the sympathies, and a hand more ready for the services of the second great law.

Let me also observe the rule of patience under the ingratitude of those who have been served by me—and above all, patience under the postponement of my disappointed hopes. God's time is not our time; and life is a school of discipline. Let me arm myself with the mind of Christ, that I may be able to cast in my lot with the saints and the holy sufferers of other days. But what a self-willed creature have I all along been—like a bullock unaccustomed to the yoke; and how impatient under the crosses and disappointments of life—more especially if due at all to the perversity or neglect of others. Where have been my self-denial and submission to the awards of Providence? Prepare me, O God, for the preferments of a coming eternity—compared with which this world is a dungeon. Let me sit loose to earth: let my conversation be in heaven.

GENESIS XLI.

God knoweth how to deliver the godly; and the time of their deliverance comes at length. At the end of two full years did He interpose and enlarge Joseph out of his distresses. This may have been in the way of a supernatural visitation—although in these dreams of Pharaoh, and the consequent proceedings, there is nothing decisively miraculous till we come to Joseph's gift of interpretation. But miraculous or not, we know how to harmonize the control of God's special providence over all history with the uniformity of visible nature. But let me not be satisfied with the knowledge of this in theory: let me have a practical, prayerful, believing sense of it. Let me ever be looking, and that beyond the secondary and the sensible, to God—so as in everything to see His hand—in everything to make known my requests—in everything to recognise and trust and adore Him.

The butler, after a profound sleep of forgetfulness, was at length awakened to the remembrance of his faults.— My delinquencies are followed up by the remorse of a very few days; and many thousands have been the faults which have vanished altogether from my remembrance. O God, remember them not against me; awaken not to judgment, lest, revisited by the consciousness of all which is now forgotten by me, I be overwhelmed under the load of my grievous and accumulated guilt. Blot out as with a thick cloud my transgressions; cleanse me with hyssop; and let my iniquities be all washed out in the blood of the Lamb. I believe, help mine unbelief. Enable me to lay a confident hold on the great propitiation made for us by Thy dear Son; and do Thou for His sake, O Lord, forgive all and forget all.

And God not only renders forgiveness to them who fear Him, He giveth liberally of the gift of wisdom to all such as ask it in faith. It was He who not only endowed Joseph with the faculty of interpretation, but who enabled him to found thereupon a right and judicious advice. The Spirit of God was in him; and it was God who shewed him all this—what the dreams portended, and what was to be done in consequence. So, O Lord, may wisdom still be justified of her children. Thou hast been pleased, O Lord, that we should be involved in difficulties —Thou hast hedged up our way: O abandon us not to the counsel of our own hearts, or to the sight of our own eyes.

May the wisdom that is from above direct and regulate all our movements. Give us to calculate aright on futurity, and to provide rightly against it. Should the Church of Scotland be cast out of favour and support by the powers of this world, may she still abide in the strength that is from on high, and be a precious repository of truth and a pure Gospel, for the spiritual interests both of our own people and of the people of other lands. O enable her ministers to hold fast their integrity, and to be wise in counsel as well as firm in purpose; and may she at length shine forth in the respect of the nations of Christendom.

Certain it is that in the largeness of the Divine superintendence, the individual and the national histories are intimately blended; and that in determining the fortunes of a single person, God often has respect to the state of kingdoms and to the state of the world for centuries to come. To Thy grace and Thy guidance, O Lord, would I commit myself: do unto me what seemeth to Thee good —whether as an object of persecuting violence, or as an humble instrument in Thy hand for the accomplishment of Thine own gracious though at present inscrutable purposes. Thou knowest the circumstances wherewith I am beset, and the prospects which at present are before me. If —— —— follow out his hostility, let me be enabled to meet his proceedings with charity and wisdom; but ward off, if it be Thy blessed will, a controversy, O Lord. If called to the metropolis to give my testimony, O enable me to do it faithfully, intelligently, and impressively. Let not mine enemies triumph over me; and extending as I ought my regards from the personal to the public, do Thou, in Thine own good way, prosper our cause, that its prosecution may be in all wisdom and integrity, and its termination be the triumph of truth and righteousness.

GENESIS XLII.

The comprehensive and well-laid scheme of Providence reaches at length to Jacob—sets him in motion—brings him down from his dwelling-place in Canaan to the land of Egypt, which settles his family there, where they expand into a nation, and so gives rise to a lengthened stage in the history of the varied fortunes of this singular people.—Strengthen, O Lord, the habit within me of referring all to Thee, and of recognising Thee in all things.

Here begins the record both of the fulfilment of the Divine vision vouchsafed to Joseph, and also of the chastisement inflicted on the other sons of Jacob, for the great transgression committed by them a number of years before. There is no forgetfulness—no falling away from His wise and holy purposes, on the part of God. To Him the obliterating influence of time is unknown. He keeps steadfastly to the execution both of His designs and also of His discipline—in virtue of which the evil deeds of men meet with their punishment, either in the way of their adequate and final retribution at the last, or in this life for the correction and instruction in righteousness of His wayward and rebellious children. Let us hope of Jacob's family that they are now in heaven, and that God forgave them, while He took vengeance on their inventions.—O God, let me stand in awe and sin not. Fill me with the love that worketh no ill—the reverence and the godly fear in which I might serve Thee acceptably.

The consciences of these evil-doers recalled their sins,

which they saw in their punishment now coming upon them; and thus it is that when judgment comes upon an offender the justice of God will even to him be made manifest. How affectingly do these tears of Joseph, as mixed with the severities which he at that time was inflicting on the fears and feelings of his brethren, remind us of our Saviour weeping over Jerusalem, even while He pronounced the doom that He would not recall of its approaching desolation.—Verily, O God, judgment is Thy strange work, and mercy Thy darling attribute; yet Thou canst not undermine the pillars of that throne, whereof justice and judgment are the habitation. Let me never forget that the forgiveness with Thee is a forgiveness that Thou mayest be feared.

The fears of Jacob's sons were enhanced by their evil consciences.—My God, how much have I to be afraid of! Give me, O Lord, a sound, thorough, practical repentance for all mine enormities; and may I so watch over and so withstand my besetting tendencies, that in reference to the evil doings to which they have heretofore led me, I may sin no more.

The sufferings which the sons now underwent were communicated to the father, who through life had been the subject of many vicissitudes and many trials.—Prepare me, O God, for the troubles of age, if Thou art pleased to inflict them. I deeply feel how mild Thy treatment of me hitherto has been, when compared with the heinousness and frequency of my offences against Thy holy law. To Jesus I flee for refuge—in Him to be safe —by Him to be sanctified.

Though Jacob partook in the sufferings now felt by his children, he was no partaker in that great transgression to which in their own consciences they referred the evils which they now feared, and which had in fact already befallen them; but he had fallen into other and grievous sins against the law of God. His gross injustice to Esau, and the gross deceptions which he practised for carrying it into effect, were sad delinquencies in his early life. He deceived his father, and was himself made the subject of a most cruel deception by his sons, under the influence of which he mourned—and for many long years—the imagined loss of the best loved of his children.—Spare me, if it be Thy blessed will, the infliction of Thy chastening hand. Deal not with me according to my deservings; yet prepare me for the full enjoyment of Thyself in heaven, and may I be presented faultless and without spot before the throne of God.

GENESIS XLIII.

The processes or ways of God are in long periods, and consist of many stages. He sees the end, however distant, from the beginning. Man has but a brief and limited perspective of that which is before him, and is ever looking for immediate results, or looks and longs for them impatiently at some such short interval as his own puny optics can apprehend. How many a weary season of disappointments and trials had poor old Jacob to abide ere he attained to the rest and satisfaction which he arrived at in the closing years of his life—during which, however, he still calls himself a stranger and a pilgrim, away from the land of final rest. It is well to abide God's time, and brace our spirits to the possibility of yet many new and hard inflictions, ere God's purposes in regard to us shall be finally accomplished. Let us hope that as our day is so our strength shall be. Let us, in the spirit of prudence, suit our measures to every new occasion—yielding, as Jacob did, to the necessity which pressed upon him, and not obstinately standing out by aught which might be imperiously required by the urgencies of the moment. It is well, however, to imitate him farther, by adding to the spirit of prudence the spirit of prayer, and in this spirit committing every way to God—invoking God's blessing on every enterprise, and resigning one's self to His gracious disposal in all things, whether the final issue be success or a heavy and affecting bereavement of that which is dearest to us. A farther discipline and exercise of conscience had still to be gone through with Joseph's guilty brethren; and for himself we can ascribe his lengthening out of their perplexities and terrors, in opposition, we should imagine, to the current of his own natural feelings, which, meanwhile, he kept in abeyance—we can ascribe it to nothing else than that, under the control of a superior wisdom, he spoke and did as he was moved by the Holy Ghost. O that the same beneficent and gracious power were ever to interpose for the regulation of all my movements. Save me, O God, from the impulses of my own wayward nature; let me ever know what it is to ask for Thy counsel, both among the critical difficulties and the everyday occurrences of life—that Thy Spirit may mingle His influences with my own spirit's desires, and designs, and deliberations, and effectually overrule them for that which is best. What I need to be most shielded from is my own headstrong self, with its headlong propensities and passions. Thou knowest my frame, O God. Thou, who weighest the secrets of every spirit, art intimately acquainted with all my grievous infirmities, and the consequent errors which flow from them. In everything let me make request unto God. In ways unknown to myself, and by influences on my heart—of which at the time I am perhaps insensible, Thou canst order all my goings, and so as that amid ever-changing circumstances they may be well and rightly ordered. With this mighty power and wisdom above me, in waiting for my call let me always be looking upward, and let it ever be my habit to pray without ceasing. My desire is toward Thee, O God; and most earnestly do I pray for Thy presence being ever with me, and for a presiding influence from on High over all my movements and all my ways.

GENESIS XLIV.

Whether this desire of Joseph was prompted by direct inspiration, or he was left to the counsel of his own heart in it, and so only permitted to frame and to follow it—the providence of God has as much to do with it in the one way as in the other. We are not called on to vindicate the integrity of Joseph in this matter; and would only pray to be kept in the spirit of simplicity and godly sincerity—so that all which is deceitful in human policy may ever be the object of our avoidance and aversion. Yet God can make the falsehood of man, as He does the wrath of man, to praise Him.

Both what Joseph deliberately planned, and what his brethren were suddenly surprised into, are made alike subservient to the purposes of God. It is interesting to trace the hand of His controlling power, and to observe that what is so capricious and so much beyond the reach of any prescience of ours—as the thoughts, and feelings, and precipitate utterances of man—should lead to the accomplishment of the Creator's designs, by as determinate a series of footsteps as if by a mechanism of blind and unconscious forces, with nought but the dynamics of the material world in operation. It remains our duty, however, to maintain at all times both a moral and a prudent circumspection in our sayings and doings. O Thou great upholder of the goings of men, and from whom alone come both the preparations of the heart and the answer of the mouth—do Thou at all times work in me both to will and to do of Thy good pleasure. The presence and power of God in all that now befell them were recognised by Judah, who felt in their misfortunes the punishment of their great transgression, or the retributive justice of Him who presided in a high government of truth and righteousness over the affairs of men. His iniquity had found him out, for God had found out his iniquity. Let me stand in awe and sin not; let me take cognizance of God as a God of judgment. Thou knowest, O God, the delinquencies of my heart and life, and none of my sins are hidden from the all-searching eye of Him with whom I have to do. Save me, O God, from the temporal, but above all, from the spiritual and eternal inflictions which I so fully and richly deserve. Deal not with me, O Lord, according to mine offences, but may all be washed out in the blood of the Lamb: and may I—not counting this blood an unholy thing—abjure and cast aside all the evil tendencies which so easily beset me, and walk henceforth as becometh one of God's own reconciled children. What a well-ordered argument is that of Judah, and it prevailed. Give me, O Lord, if it be Thy blessed will, to order my cause aright in the presence of those whom Thou hast been pleased to invest with pre-eminence and power in this world. Enable me to come forth with such a representation as might disarm the wrath or dissipate the prejudice of adversaries. I would commit myself, and the care of our Church, to Thee, O God; and from these, the records of Thy providence, may I assure myself that at length and in Thine own good time all will be well.

GENESIS XLV.
Last Sabbath at the Quay of Rostrevor, August 7, 1842.

One mark of deep corruption is to be without natural affection. In Joseph we have a beautiful example of this virtue, and in this I desire to resemble him. I lie under defects herein which I should labour to remedy; and may the Giver of all grace enable me, in whatsoever things are lovely and of good report, to think of these things. And with what humanity and feeling does he seek to comfort his brethren, and restore them from the confusion into which he had thrown them by the discovery of himself. I am miserably apt to be precipitated into such expressions as hurt the sensibilities of others. It is true that this in general is immediately followed by compunction, and a desire to repair the severity; but how infinitely better to put a guard on my lips, and maintain such a tenderness for the feelings of other men as shall prevent, rather than redress, the violence which I may have done them. Beside the conscience there was the shame of their great delinquency, which operated on the brethren; and let me no more think that the hurt felt by myself for having hurt others is an atonement, than that the shame on this occasion atoned for the transgression into which these culprits had fallen.

We should take a lesson, even from natural men, in what is seemly or amiable. One likes the sympathy felt by Pharaoh on this occasion, and which prompts the generosity wherewith he acted. I enjoy too the interest felt by the domestics. The injunction of Joseph to his brethren, that they should not fall into controversy or quarrel by the way, carries in it a moral lesson also. There was danger lest they should get into criminations and remonstrances on the respective shares which each had in the unnatural outrage inflicted by them upon their brother. But God turned it to good; and let me ever recognise and do homage to that providence and power which can make instruments of all, and has unlimited sway over the forces both of the moral and material world.

In reading of Jacob and the preservations of his family, let me not forget the goodness and longsuffering of God to myself. Three days ago I completed the thirtieth year of my married state, and during the whole of that time there has been no death in my immediate family. What have my returns been, and what the use I have made of this lengthened season of grace and opportunity? What have I done for the souls of those over whom it is my especial duty to watch as one that has to give an account? May God forgive my indifference for the spiritual wellbeing of my wife and children. It forms indeed a most convincing proof that the element of faith is not the element of nature. But O that I could feel more, as well as reason on this sad insensibility to eternal things. Open mine eyes, O God, to the magnitude and reality of this great interest, that henceforth I may both feel and act as a Christian parent. I pray for the effectual visitation of Thy grace both in my own behalf, and that of all who are dear to me.

GENESIS XLVI.

Let me commit myself to God in every movement which I take, and with a full reference to the sacrifice of Christ as my alone plea for His favour and protection. It seems as if some great though yet unknown transition were before me, from the Church of my fathers, long in a state of external security, to the Church in a state of suffering. Let me not be fearful, but trust that God in His good time will recall me if not to the blessings of an earthly Canaan, at least to a place in His own heavenly and everlasting kingdom.

And O that throughout every stage of my spiritual life I could take my family along with me: they will share in my temporal hazards, and, if so be, in my temporal calamities. O that I hungered and thirsted more after righteousness; and that they shared in this spiritual longing for grace here and for glory hereafter. I pray, O God, for one and all of them, expressly and particularly—my dear wife, Anne, Eliza, Grace, Margaret, Helen, and Fanny, and last, for my only grandchild, dear little Tommy. During the remainder of my pilgrimage I would never cease to pray for them and to watch over them. May each and all be translated from the walk of sight to the walk of faith, that henceforth they may be my fellow-travellers to Zion; and we, the parents, walking together as heirs of the grace of life, may be the Christian heads of a Christianized family.

And God, if He see meet, can prepare for us an earthly

Goshen, desirable to nature. Let me at least not quit my natural affections, though it be my duty to love God and His cause more than wife and children and all possessions. And who knows but that a common adversity may draw us nearer together, and make us happy in each other's confidence and good-will, while an offence, perhaps an abomination, to them who are without? Yet He can provide us with an earthly Pharaoh or protector; and if not, He can make us supremely blest in the direct possession and enjoyment of Himself. He can shed the love of Himself abroad in our hearts, and so give us a part and interest in the gracious declaration that all things shall work together for good to them who love God.—This should have been written at Londonderry, in the house of Mr. Denham, and on the day I preached for him. Let the recollection of all my pleasurable feelings there, both in the landscapes and society of that charming town and neighbourhood have the effect of strengthening my confidence in that God who has such an infinity of resources at command, and can open up a refuge for me and mine, either in this or a thousand other places of His goodly and unbounded creation; or, failing all, can make good to me the promise of the life that is to come, and as to the life that now is, can at all times enable me to say, that God is my helper, and I will not fear what man can do unto me.

GENESIS XLVII.

He who maketh the earth to help the woman can dispose even worldly and unconverted men not only to be at peace with but even to bear in their hearts a liking for His own saints and children. We know not the character and state of Pharaoh in the sight of God, but certain it is that God made him the instrument of large and liberal benefactions to Jacob and his family.

And here we may learn a lesson of courtesy to them who are without—such courtesy and reverence as Paul showed to Agrippa and even Festus, and such as we observe in the similar homage which Jacob rendered to Pharaoh. Let me not confine this to benefactors, but may I know how to acquit myself rightly in the presence of rulers and judges, even though they should be the persecutors and enemies of our Church.

And enable me also, like Joseph of old, to do liberally and aright in respect of the obligations which I owe to all my kinsfolk.

And if called to devise, and for a whole country, make me rich in sound devices as Joseph was. Let me be helpful by Thy strength and in Thy wisdom, O God, for planning and carrying into effect a right ecclesiastical system for Scotland. The present economy may perhaps be broken up: I pray for the guidance from on high of those who may be called to substitute another in its place. There may be a removal of many of our clergymen into cities from their country parishes. Do Thou preside over the coming changes, O Lord; and may they prove subservient to the revival of a good work of faith and repentance in our land. May Thy Church be extended: may Thy cause be established and prevail over the whole earth.

But earth is not our resting-place: it is spiritual Egypt —the land of our exile from a better and enduring home —a land in which we are only the sojourners of a day—

strangers and pilgrims who look for another country wherein there is a city which hath foundations. Let not my affections, O God, settle, neither let my prospects terminate here. I would look away from and beyond the world, even as Jacob looked out of Egypt to a more kindred and congenial land. I would join in heaven those fathers in Christ who have gone before me. Give me, O Lord, to realize the coming death, and set my house in order for the coming judgment and eternity. And what a worthless thing the world is to take up with as our alone portion; for, as was impressively said by the patriarch after he had nearly doubled the age which old men now attain to—few and evil the days of the years of the oldest of us are.—This should have been written at Belfast, on the day I preached for Dr. Hanna; and the recollection suggests the prayer of my heart for the interests of the Presbyterian Church in Ireland.

GENESIS XLVIII.

I am now approaching not to the age of Jacob, but, in the now reduced scale of human longevity, to that season of his earthly existence when he took him to the bed of his last sickness, and sent for his children that they might hear his last words, and receive his prophetic blessings. Ere my time comes, O Lord, may I be confirmed in the faith, and have the unspeakable comfort of seeing all of my household established in the good way, that I might tell them with all confidence of the everlasting possession of the land of many mansions, where we shall together spend our eternity. And enable me even now, O God, to speak, not with the affection alone but with the authority of a parent. Give me to rule mine own house well; and as the best preparation for this, give me that strength of serious principle which will make it visible to my family, that the good of their souls is what mainly and most intently I have at heart.

And let this seriousness of purpose and feeling extend to my dear grandchild. Let my natural ripen into a sacred affection. May I henceforth make the state of his soul an object of thought and care; and give me the wisdom of winning over all who are near and dear to me to Christ and His salvation.

I may well share with Jacob in a grateful retrospect of God's goodness to me: Hitherto Thou hast preserved me, O Lord. O preserve me faultless even unto the end, and for this purpose keep my heart and mind in Christ Jesus, that the sad and shameful delinquencies of my bygone life may all be passed over, and that henceforward I may be kept from falling into them, because kept by the power of faith unto salvation.—This should have been written five weeks ago, or on the 28th of August, when I was at Belfast, and preached for Dr. Cooke. The recollection of a brief interview with Mr. Emerson Tennent, suggests a prayerful aspiration to God for the Church of Scotland. Thou turnest the hearts of men whithersoever Thou wilt. Overrule, O God, the rulers of our land. Appear for the defence and glory of the Church of our fathers. Save us alike from faithless friends and open enemies. Give right and resolved principle to our ministers; and O make all redound to the speedy revival of serious and spiritual religion in the towns and parishes of our beloved land.

GENESIS XLIX.

September, 1842.

Jacob here delivers a series of prophecies, and from some of them a moral is to be drawn.

The first is the blasting effect of licentiousness on all other pretensions of dignity or excellence. Reuben had irretrievably disgraced himself by a crime which his dying father had not forgotten: let purity of heart and life be strictly and resolutely guarded.

The second we gather from the forcible denunciations of the patriarch on the cruelty and deceit of his two sons Simeon and Levi. Let me ever hold in utter abomination the foul dispositions and deeds of these brethren in wickedness.

Judah was evidently a person of weight in the family, yet we know more of his transgressions than of his virtues; yet that Saviour who let Himself down to the lowest depths of humiliation for our sakes, condescended to be of his offspring in the flesh; and in the sublime prophecy which was now delivered, one cannot help a certain sense of elevation, in contemplating the venerable seer when he looked from afar on the day of Christ and rejoiced.

What follows is, as far as we can see, the mere prediction of futurities, all of which we doubt not were realized; and from which, though we may not be able to draw any practical lesson, yet we doubt not that it would in the fact of its various fulfilments serve to uphold the faith of the children of Israel when settled in their own land.

We cannot resist the impressiveness of the beautifully interjected exclamation by the patriarch—I have waited for Thy salvation, O Lord! So let me wait, O God, till

Thou bring me out of spiritual darkness, and in the light of Thy salvation cause me to rejoice. Meanwhile let me give earnest heed to the word of Thy testimony, till the day dawn and the day-star arise in my heart.

Solemnize me, O God, by the view of my coming death. —Prepare me, O God, for the approaches of this last messenger. May I be wise and consider my latter end; and O may that Spirit, who is the earnest of a glorious inheritance, be vouchsafed in rich abundance to myself, and wife, and children, whom Thou hast given me.

GENESIS L.
At Wishaw House.

Give me, O Lord, to indulge, in the measure and degree which I ought, all the right affections of nature—though not to be swallowed up of over-much sorrow, when even the nearest and dearest of all earthly relatives are taken away from me. O prepare me for all Thy dispensations; and give me, O Lord, both a pious deathbed and a peaceful grave. May I imitate the example of Joseph, so as best to fulfil the precept of the apostle, when he enjoins— "Whatsoever things are lovely." Give me a proper sensibility to the death of others, whether kinsfolk or acquaintances; and, what is still more important, give me a proper delicacy and feeling for the living, as well as a proper respect and tenderness for the memory of the dead. How beautifully tender was Joseph of his brethren under the shame and distress of their penitent and fearful emotions. Give me, O Lord, to cherish more and more the sympathies and the forgiving disposition by which he was actuated: and not only pardon, but rectify my tendencies to an abrupt displeasure, or a rough and regardless treatment of those who stand before me. O that principle had the entire sway over all my sensibilities and all my movements; and may I add the practical to the pathetic when called to join at funerals with the mourners who have assembled to carry a neighbour to his last resting-place. Let it be my aim to charge my own heart, and to press on others the wisdom of considering our latter end, and of so numbering our days that we may apply our hearts to the work of preparation for eternity. And give me, O Lord, to recognise thy providence in all the changes of my own personal history, as well as in the eventful history of the world at large. And in the consideration that it is Thy wisdom which regulates and Thy will which determines all, may I so far forget the injuries of my fellow-men as to feel Christianly and considerately towards them.

Thou hast spared me, O God, to see my children of the third generation. In regard to the further continuance and prosperity of my earthly life, Thy will be done. Let me die in faith and hope; and, O Lord, do Thou cheer me with the bright anticipations of a grace and a goodness still in reserve for the Church of Scotland. It is my confidence and comfort that the Lord reigneth.

EXODUS.

Fairlie.

EXODUS I.—The disappearance of whole generations should solemnize our hearts, and bring home to us the incommutable law of death. And the contrast between our state when consigned to the silence and forgetfulness of the churchyard, and the state of the world's living population, as numerous, and busy, and instinct with life and thought, and the sense of human interests and passions as ever, just serves to deepen all the more the lesson of our mortality. May God endow me with the practical wisdom of considering aright, and acting aright on the consideration of my latter end.

Let me not think that any strange thing has happened to us if we receive the treatment which the true Church has received from the hands of persecutors in all ages. Let me not trust in the gratitude or fidelity of princes, but lay my account with the enmity which ever obtains between an unregenerate world and God's spiritual family. Prepare me, O God, for such seasons of adversity and trial as Thou mightest see to be good for us; and if days of restraint and rigour are coming on, let the true seed—the spiritual Israel—be multiplied thereby, so that while the outward man of the Church perisheth, its inward man might be renewed day by day. Add daily, O Lord, to the Church such as shall be saved; and the more we are oppressed the more may we multiply and grow. Our enemies may deal wisely in their generation, and form their deep-laid devices against us. Give us the wisdom that is from above, that the children of light may at length prevail over the children of this world, and that the adversaries of what is good may not have the final triumph over us.

And it is also by a preventive process that our rulers of the present day are proceeding against the Church established in these lands. They are replacing her vacancies with men of whom there is too good reason to fear that they will prove to be unfaithful. They are casting off the good from stations of preferment and usefulness, and are setting the bad in high places. They meditate by this process of exhaustion the extinction of that party who stand up for the prerogatives of Christ's government over the Church of which He is the alone Head. Disappoint their machinations, O God, so that Thine own people might multiply and wax very mighty even under the attempts which are made to subvert and to destroy them. But let us act with simplicity and godly sincerity in the midst of a crooked and perverse generation. Let there be perfect integrity in all our doings—no cunning, no artifice, and, at the same time, no indiscretion, and none of that folly which Solomon charges on those who speak for the mere pleasure of discovering their hearts.

EXODUS II.
Inverary.

God raised up a deliverer for the children of Israel in Moses; let me hope that He will do the same by the Church of Scotland. Let me not despair when I think of the infinity of His resources. What a providence appears even in the minutest incidents of history; and looking to the concatenations and manifold influences of one event upon another in the moral world, all under the absolute direction of Him who reigneth over all, let me cherish a hopeful feeling as to days of triumph, and safety, and prosperity, yet to come. I am now at Inverary, under the same roof with the Duke of Argyle and the Marquis of Lorne, whose family have signalized themselves on the side of the Scottish Church, and whose present heads have already given demonstration of such an interest in her preservation as we fear to be slightly and rarely felt among the nobles of our land. O my God, pardon all that has been amiss in my spirit or deportment here. Heaven knows that the cravings of my heart are for a life and a society of godliness. O strengthen more and more my aversion to the mere world, whatever might be its fascinations or its splendours; and give me to be freer, O God, in my testimonies for Thee and for the truth of Thy gospel among men. I have my misgivings on this most difficult and delicate of all trials; and I pray for light, and wisdom, and moral courage, in regard to the conduct I should observe towards them who are without. It was Moses, cradled in adversities, who in God's hand was the instrument for the deliverance of Israel. Can we, through any other ordeal than this, expect release and enlargement for the Church of Scotland?

O God, interpose in Thine own good time for our Church, even as Thou didst in other days for Thy people in the land of Egypt; but let that time be waited for, and meanwhile prepare us for the whole of Thy will. O for patience to suffer all that Thou wouldst have us to endure, and wisdom to direct us in the paths Thou wouldst have us to walk upon. We would ask counsel of Thee at all times, and most earnestly pray for the grace of Thy Spirit both to enlighten and to strengthen us.

EXODUS III.
October.

This is one of the most wondrous manifestations of the Deity recorded in holy writ, and such a manifestation as identifies God with the Angel of the Covenant—even with Him who afterwards became God manifest in the flesh, and made atonement for the sins of the world—the second person of the glorious Trinity. Let me honour the Son even as I honour the Father; and when I think of the divinity of my Saviour, and of such a sacrifice for all my violations of the Divine law, let the dread of its penalties no longer agitate my bosom; but let the peace of God, which passeth all understanding, keep my heart and mind in Christ Jesus. Yet though now brought nigh, let us forget not that it is upon holy ground—ere we enter upon which we must cast off all our defilements. God is holy; and the forgiveness that is with Him is a forgiveness that He may be feared.

But God also is love. Thou art full of compassion, O Lord, having respect unto Thine heritage. O interpose for the delivery of Thy Church in Thine own good time; and may our Church in these lands ever acquit herself as part of the true Israel of God. Save us from our enemies, if it be Thy blessed will, or arm us for the battle.

What a depth of mystery lies in this name of God. Thou art the self-existent Jehovah, the everlasting Now, from eternity to eternity—the same (Jesus Christ) yesterday, to-day, and for ever. O that I had the light and the grace adequately to feel and adequately to adore. Let me be humbled under a sense of my own littleness, as I bethink myself of the inaccessible and incomprehensible Deity—the great I AM—the essence and fountain of being.

But God is not only to be viewed as He is in Himself, He is also to be viewed in relation to us. He who had just proclaimed His mysterious name, also proclaims Himself in the endearing and more intelligible character of the God of Abraham and Isaac and Jacob. And He is the God and reconciled Father of all who walk in the footsteps of the faith of Abraham. Let us draw nigh with the confidence and the love of children, yet with awe and humble submission; for not only is He mysterious in His own unfathomable nature, but mysterious in His dealings with the children of men. He foreknew the wickedness of Pharaoh—for whom He will He hardeneth. Yet has He set a plain path for our feet: He is accessible to our prayers, and not only can, but will, in answer to these, convert our hearts of stone into hearts of flesh. O God, take my heart such as it is—make it such as it should be.

EXODUS IV.

It was long, and after a struggle, ere the difficulties of Moses were overborne. The want of a due sense of one's own personal fitness for a given work may often be resolved into a want of faith. After the demonstrations made to Moses he became the object of God's rightful displeasure in standing out. Let me in my humble sphere learn a lesson from this passage, and more especially, let me be less careful of how I shall speak in the public assembly; but in a good cause, and with full integrity of purpose, let me trust more fearlessly in the promised aids of the Holy Ghost. And I have the aid of others in conducting the business of the Church—men who are ready speakers, as Aaron was; but let me not give up my own principles or my own views into their hands.

Moses seems to have kept up from Jethro the real, or rather, the main purpose of his mission to Egypt. There are a wisdom and a wariness required in the conduct of all business; but save me from all deceitful reticence, O God: let there be perfect simplicity and godly sincerity in all my conversation.

Let me be fearless and unfaltering in the performance of every required duty—and this in the face whether of one's own natural feelings, or of the remonstrances of those who are dear to me. Let me fear not the opposition of man, but fear Him who alone is able to cast both soul and body into hell. Prepare me, O God, for all the trials and adversities which Thou mayest be pleased to lay upon me.

There is something very affecting in the interview between Moses and Aaron, and still more in their interview with the people. One can imagine the sensation that would be amongst them when the signs and miracles were done before their eyes, and that to confirm their belief in the tidings of a great coming deliverance.—And the people did at the time believe. There is great force of sympathy in the general and manifested feeling of a multitude; and I have seldom been made more alive to this than when reading in the last clause of this chapter that the children of Israel, when they heard that the Lord had visited them in their affliction, "bowed their heads, and worshipped."—My God, give me, too, the belief that Thou lookest down upon me with compassion; and give me the right and responsive gratitude, that henceforth I might serve Thee acceptably with reverence and godly fear.

EXODUS V.

We have here the first interview and the first exhibition of Pharaoh's hardness of heart. Do Thou, O God, who art the author of every good and perfect gift, bestow upon me a heart soft and tender. Take the heart of stone out of me, and give me a heart of flesh.

Then follows the reaction upon the prophet's message on the part of this lordly oppressor—his aggravated cruelty to the children of Israel. Save us, O God, from the tyrant's wrath—save us from the hands of the persecutor; and, if it be Thy blessed will, turn the hearts of our rulers in peace and kindness to the Church of Scotland. Ours, too, is a matter of collision between the Divine and an earthly power—between the jurisdiction of Christ in the Church and that of the civil ruler: and for aught we know, hardships and ills are awaiting us because of the part we take in asserting the sole lordship of Him who is our Head over things ecclesiastical. Let not the cruelty and wrath of man prevail over us; and as it seems good unto Thee do Thou spare us the trial, or prepare us for the whole of Thy will. Our evil case may only have begun—O that wisdom from on high may descend upon us. Do Thou guide, O Lord, the deliberations and measures of that Convocation of ministers now on the eve of assembling; and save me, in particular, from all that is rash and unwarrantable, when engaged with the counsels or propositions that are before it. Moses did incur the displeasure of his own disappointed people; but then he had a clear warrant for all that he had done. Let not me, O God, without an adequate warrant, be the instrument in any way of disappointing or misleading my brethren. I pray for a right and a discerning spirit in this matter, O Lord.

The remonstrance of Moses had more to explain, though not to justify it, than ever I shall have in the way of reason, or even the semblance of it, to murmur against God. Let me not repine, O God, although our trial should be protracted, or whatever be the fresh and unlooked for infliction which Thou mayest suffer our enemies to inflict upon us. We cast ourselves upon Thy care; and on Thee do we devolve our cause.

EXODUS VI.

The Lord arises in vindication of His own faithfulness, as a God mindful of His covenant, and who had not forgotten His promises to the fathers. They knew Him by a name which indicated His power: His children were made to know Him by a name which indicated His necessary and eternal existence. Is not this progress from the less to the more transcendental, an indication to us that we should go on and increase in the knowledge of God? and that we are not unworthily engaged when we reverently contemplate, though at a distance which is infinite, the mysteries of His uncreated and incomprehensible nature? And this does not supersede but, in the passage before us, is mixed up with the more accessible and lovelier of His attributes as a compassionate God, who heard the groanings and was moved by the piteous cries of the children of Israel.

What a call on sympathy was the condition of the poor Israelites whom the iron-rod of the oppressor had reduced to a sad and sullen despair.

But God hath said it, and shall He not do it? The incredulity of the people, and in which Moses himself somewhat shared, did not divert Him from the execution of His purposes; and so He gives forth His authoritative command to His messengers, Moses and Aaron.

The genealogies of Moses and Aaron are here given, preceded by briefer descriptions of the families of the two elder tribes; cognizance, too, is here taken of Aaron's but not of Moses's children. The former were in the lineage of the priesthood.—O God, may the record of successive generations impress upon me the rapidity wherewith time and all its busy interests and concerns will pass away.

It is marvellous how Moses persevered in his diffidence. We are no judges, however, and never were able to test by observation the strength of human incredulity against the actual exhibition of miracles. Let me in the strength of the Lord, and by faith in Him for the preparation of the heart and the answer of the mouth, struggle against my own diffidence of my own extemporaneous powers; and O may I be enabled to declare His mind and will in the hearing both of rulers and of the great congregation.

EXODUS VII.

Moses as the vicegerent of God made known to Pharaoh the judgments that were awaiting him, as though God did denounce him by the prophet. Paul in making known the mercies of God to the Corinthians, speaks in the character of a vicegerent from God too, as though God did beseech them by the Apostle. (2 Cor. v. 20.) Lord, let us not after our hardness and impenitent heart despise the riches of Thy goodness and forbearance and long-suffering —for if he who braved the menaces of the Almighty's displeasure came to such an end, what shall our end be if we stand out against His offers and entreaties of reconciliation?

As the rod of Aaron swallowed up all the rods of the magicians, so let the right and heavenly affection within us overbear all the inferior appetencies of our corrupt and earthly nature. May the fear of God supplant every other fear; may the love of God subordinate every other love. I pray, O God, for this miracle of grace in my soul.

Pharaoh's heart seems to have undergone a progressive hardening. The greater and greater demonstrations of Divine power seem to have called forth a more sullen and determined resistance against the exhibition of it. Let me know the deceitfulness of the inner man, and beware of being further hardened by the deceitfulness of sin. There is a law of our nature in virtue of which the insensibility of our conscience grows apace with every act of defiance to its suggestions; and in virtue of which, too, if the warnings of one adverse providence have failed to impress, another and another, each more fitted to appal and to arrest than the former, may fall short of its moral efficacy for turning us from the evil of our ways. The semblance of Divine power by the magicians seems to have contributed in upholding the stout and resolute ungodliness of the king of Egypt. The analogous influence to this in ordinary life seems to lie in the usurping and dispossessing power of natural or secondary causes, by which the attention is diverted from Him who sits behind the elements He has formed, and gives birth and movement and continuance to all things. Let us recognise Thy power and Thy providence always; and save us from that evil heart of unbelief by which we depart from the living God.

EXODUS VIII.

November, 1842.

God keeps up and reiterates His manifestations, and Pharaoh still maintains a stout-hearted resistance. His refusal to the call with its accompanying threat, though not expressly mentioned, must have taken place, for the threat was executed, and frogs were made to swarm over the land of Egypt.

Here we have the first relenting of Pharaoh. He asked for Moses's intercession that the plague might be removed. The request was complied with, and the prayer of the prophet prevailed. In the day of adversity we consider and humble ourselves before God, but in the day of prosperity we forget.

And so did Pharaoh. When he saw that there was a respite he fell from his promises and professions, and relapsed into his former hardness, and—as is the case with all backsliding—into a greater hardness than before. The magicians could not imitate this next miracle, and told Pharaoh that now the hand of God had been undoubtedly stretched forth; yet he hearkened not unto them, and stood proof against more unequivocal demonstrations from on high than had yet been brought to bear upon him.—To-day, while it is called to-day, may I harden not my heart.

Then follows another and more remarkable sign, because accompanied with a most miraculous circumstance—the exemption of the land of Goshen from the flies which overspread the rest of Egypt. There is no barrier in air to the diffusion of flying insects; and how striking the supernatural power which restrained them within the limits assigned by God, and kept them from breaking forth on the land of Goshen!

Accordingly, this miracle seems to have had a more urgent and instantaneous effect on Pharaoh than any of the preceding ones. He not only promises to let Moses go, but bids him go; yet when the plague was withdrawn, Pharaoh again hardened his heart, and again dealt deceitfully.—My God, let me make the right use of all Thy visitations; and when in sickness or adversity I form the right purpose and lift the humble prayer, let not these be forgotten when restored to health or delivered from the evil thing which had grieved or solemnized me.

EXODUS IX.

These repeated appliances on Pharaoh are still kept up. The message given is in the name of the Lord God of the Hebrews, who claims them as "my people." The distinction that was maintained between the Egyptians and the Israelites certainly enhanced the miracle, though not so strikingly as in the miracle of the flies, when by a supernatural force these winged insects were restrained from entering the land of Goshen. There seems to have been no impression made at this time on the heart of the king.

In the next passage the obduracy of Pharaoh's heart is again assailed, and with as little effect as before. The hardening process seems to be advancing. Formerly there was at times a sort of momentary giving way, but even this is not observed in either of the two last miracles. —Heavenly Father, save me from being hardened by the deceitfulness of sin.

In the next visitation, as the former attempts fell short of the resistance, there looks as if a gathering and greater force of demonstration was now to be applied in order to exceed and overbear it;—a more formal and solemn message is sent than heretofore, accompanied with larger threatenings. The declared and the secret purposes are both made to appear in this part of the narrative. God raised up Pharaoh to make His power known by his destruction; yet not without many warnings and chastisements and remonstrances to turn him from the evil of his way. There comes in here a verse quoted by Paul in his argument on predestination. The hail came down on all the land of Egypt save Goshen; and it is described as one of the greatest of the plagues. Some of the Egyptians took warning, and—what is marvellous after such recent and striking exhibitions—others not. Lord, when Thy judgments are abroad in the world, let me learn righteousness.

And there was a transient impression made at this time on Pharaoh; but it was known to God, and known even to Moses His prophet, that it would not endure, and accordingly he sinned yet more. Sin is a growing malady, fostering and strengthening itself with every new act of resistance to the arguments whether of conscience or fear, till at length it stands its ground against the most emphatic denunciations and judgments.—My God, save me from this sad moral and spiritual degeneracy. Hearken to my prayer; and do Thou who, in compliance with the intercession of Thy prophet, didst withdraw Thy miracle of judgment, O do Thou work a miracle of mercy and grace to my soul.

EXODUS X.

Here is another remarkable exhibition of the declared, in juxtaposition with the secret will of God. He expressly tells Moses that He had hardened Pharaoh's heart, and yet He commissions Moses to remonstrate with Pharaoh, and tell him to humble himself before God.—Let us not be of the number of those who wrest the things which are difficult and hard to understand to their own destruction.

The threat of the next miracle seems to have told somewhat, first on Pharaoh's servants, and then through them on Pharaoh himself; but his relentings were soon arrested, and at this time he held forth not a dogged only but a passionate resistance; and he drove Moses and Aaron from his presence. He was growing apace in the school of reprobacy, till he so hardened his neck that destruction came upon him suddenly.

It disguised not the miracle, nor the part which the hand of God had in it, that it was brought on by an east wind, or that a secondary cause was employed for the purpose of making it good. No more let the constancy of visible nature intercept from our view nature's God: let not the instrumentality hide the agent from our perception; but let us acknowledge ever that though there be a diversity of operations, God is all in all.

Pharaoh, again visited with a fit of terror, promises for a moment to give up his obstinacy. He is more importunate, and makes larger concessions than ever; and again the Lord spared him, and employed the west wind—a reverse secondary cause from the former one—to drive back the locusts from the land of Egypt. Their being cast into the Red Sea is with me a monumental evidence for the truth of the history.

The distinction in point of darkness and light between Egypt and Goshen ought to have been a most impressive demonstration. But all was ineffectual; and yet it did tell to a certain extent on Pharaoh, and for aught which appears, it might have proved effectual, but that Moses rose in his demands. It was this which seems to have enraged Pharaoh at the time that the locusts were threatened, and it is this also which seems to have confirmed his obduracy in the last interview which he held with Moses. There is a mystery which we cannot comprehend, for it is part of the mystery of God not yet finished, in the alternations of the objective and the subjective which took place during the whole of the disciplinary process between God and Pharaoh—larger and louder denunciations brought to bear upon him from without, but, to overmatch these, a temper of greater and greater hardihood forming on the mind within. This does not foreclose duty, and more especially the duty of prayer.—Take the heart of stone out of me, O Lord, and give me a heart of flesh.

EXODUS XI.

The consummation of this process on the heart of Pharaoh now approaches; and to provide for it the Lord lays a special direction on Moses—the very speciality of which vindicates the charges which have been alleged against the morality of Scripture grounded on this passage. The Proprietor of heaven and earth issues an order for the distribution of that which belongs to Him; and it is the interposal of His express and rightful authority on this particular occasion which sanctions and sanctifies the whole proceeding—leaving the general laws of truth and justice and fair-dealing in full obligation and effect, save in those rare and extraordinary instances when God Himself comes forth and gives the word for such a disposal whether of lives or properties as may seem unto Him good.

—Let not these instances, O God, shake or disturb the influence over me of those eternal and immutable rectitudes which make up the perfection of Thine own character, and which Thou hast ordained for the government of Thy creatures. Put truth in my inward parts—and prepare me for the land of uprightness by enabling me to maintain the most entire simplicity and godly sincerity in all my words and in all my ways.

Moses, who by this time had risen to prodigious estimation both with the Egyptians and his own countrymen, at length announces the last and most appalling of these signal visitations. They ought to have had a preventive effect on the mind of Pharaoh; and it is his condemnation that they had not. O my God, let the threats and denunciations of Thy holy word have their right preventive effect upon my soul; and let me with all speed and diligence proceed on this irreversible saying—that unless we repent we shall perish.

And it should make us all the more heedful and earnest that if not persuaded by these terrors of the Lord we shall be hardened by every new declaration of them. What an instructive example we have of this in Egypt's king—he being often rebuked, hardened his neck; and in the end was suddenly destroyed, and that without remedy. (Prov. xxix. 1.) Let not the higher part of this mystery—the consideration of its being God who hardened the heart of Pharaoh—let not this have any darkening influence on the part which belongs to man in the matter of his own salvation, which is, that to-day while called to-day he should harden not his heart, seeing that now is the only accepted time he can count upon—that now is to him the only day of his salvation.

EXODUS XII.
December, 1842.

The institution of the Passover should remind us of Christ, our Passover, who is sacrificed for us—a Lamb without blemish. O God, may the blood of sprinkling be upon me, that my sins may be passed over, and the destroying angel may not touch me. Let me cherish that faith in the great propitiation which applies the virtue of it to my soul, and causes God to be at peace with me. And this fruitful institution has a significancy in it that tells of my required sanctification as well as of my assured justification. I must not only act faith on the great sacrifice, but I must eat the unleavened bread of sincerity and truth. Let me beware of all forbidden leaven, O Lord —that of the Pharisees and Sadducees, and of Herod; but to speak more plainly, let me purge out the old leaven of the old man, and more especially the leaven of malice and wickedness.—O my God, sanctify me wholly, and let not sin any longer have the dominion over me.

It was by the bunch of hyssop that the blood was sprinkled on the door-posts; and this has been regarded as the type of that faith in virtue of which we receive the atonement. Teach me, O God, to appropriate therewith the benefit of my Redeemer's sacrifice; teach me to draw water therewith out of the wells of salvation. O let not the impunity which this gracious dispensation ensures encourage me to sin. The forgiveness of the gospel, O Lord, is a forgiveness that Thou mayest be feared. Let me have grace, then, to serve Thee reverently, and that I may bow the head and worship before Thee all the days of my life.

When Thy judgments are abroad may I learn righteousness. Let not Thy visitations be thrown away upon me, or work in me, as their only effect, that terror which evaporates when the occasion has gone by.

In the name of Him who is our true Passover, and of whom not a bone was broken, do we again pray for all the blessings of His great redemption being fully realized upon us. Blot out my transgressions, O Lord, in the blood of the Lamb who was sacrificed for the sins of the world; and enable me henceforth to present myself to Him in soul body and spirit as a living sacrifice.

EXODUS XIII.

O God, let me keep the feast with the unleavened bread of sincerity and truth. Sift me and try me, O God, and whatever wicked thing is in me, separate and sanctify me therefrom, that freed from the carnality of this earthly and accursed nature—if not from its presence, at least from its fermenting and operating power—I may purge out the old leaven—that so, entirely renewed and purified, I may be remoulded in Thine own image of righteousness and true holiness.

Guide me, O Lord, in the way of family instruction. —What I aspire to myself let me show my children. Let Thy law be not in my heart only, but in my mouth. Let Thy word dwell in me richly in all wisdom, yet dwell not in safe only but in profitable custody; and when with the Psalmist I have hid Thy law in my heart that I may not offend Thee, let me remember that this hiding was a keeping, not a concealment. Let those of my own household be the partakers of whatever wisdom the Father of lights may be pleased to endow me with. Let the candle of the Lord not be placed under a bushel but on a candlestick; may it give light to all who are around. And give me liberally, O Lord, that which I mainly lack—the wisdom of winning souls—so that all my children may become Thy children, all redeemed by the blood and sanctified by the grace of the Saviour. Let me henceforth be mindful of the assiduities of constant and regular observation; and let what ought to be my constant observation be also my constant theme.

God leads His people by a way that they know not. Let us follow the leadings of Thy providence, O God, as shone upon and interpreted by the applications of Thy word. Thou mayest seem to lead us about, because not in that direct path on which our own wisdom, or perhaps our own impatience, would set us immediately; yet let us go harnessed; nor let us by a presumptuous tempting of Thee neglect aught that is lawful in the way of preparation, and which nature or experience tells us to be desirable. But let us not go when Thy presence goes not along with us.

In these troublous times there lie a charm and a quietude in the contemplation of the grave. My bones will soon be laid in their final resting-place; but meanwhile let me walk and work while it is day; and may I never, O God, be forsaken by such indices of Thy will as might serve to guide me in the path both of prudence and of uprightness.

EXODUS XIV.

The history by Moses lends illustration and support to the theology of Paul—" I will harden Pharaoh's heart, and I will be honoured upon Pharaoh." "What if God, willing to show His wrath, and to make His power known," thus deals "with the vessels of wrath fitted to destruction?" It is with the proximate and not the transcendental that we have immediately to do; it is with the duties of prayer and watchfulness, and the conscientious observation of all that is right. Save me therefore, O God, from the deceitful and the hardening influences of sin. Take the heart of stone out of me, and uphold my goings in Thy paths, lest like other transgressors who, being often reproved, have hardened their necks, I shall suddenly be destroyed, and that without remedy. And what a lesson here for God's own people, whose strength it is so often to be still—to stand still and see the salvation of the Lord.

Yet there is a time for everything; and now it appears was the time for the children of Israel going forward. Guide me, O Lord, that I may know when to wait and when to work—when to lie down and when to rise up. In the affairs of Thy Church may I be enabled rightly to divide the word of truth; and may such too be Thy dealings with her in our day that all may be made to see Thy glory, and when Thy judgments are abroad in the world, to learn righteousness.

It is thus that God acts diversely with His friends and His enemies. The same cloud which darkened the vision and lowered upon the one, shone brightly, and so as to give both direction and encouragement to the other. We know of no sentence more memorably impressive in the Bible than that which tells us that God looked out of the pillar of cloud and of the fire, and troubled the Egyptians. Such is the difference between the light of His countenance and the rebuke of His countenance. How fearful to have the eye of God turned in displeasure towards us! and O henceforth may I stand in awe and sin not, but ever feel how dread a thing it is to fall into the hands of the living God. Thou knowest how to deliver the godly out of their temptations: Thou knowest how to provide a way of escape. Heavenly Father, deliver out of her troubles the Church of Scotland. Open up for her an exit of freedom and honour from the place where she is now hemmed in. Above all, let her trust be in the Lord, and not in an arm of flesh. Save her, O God, from the perversities of Thine ancient people, while under a humbling sense of her manifold deficiencies and misdoings she walks in faith and penitence before Thee.

EXODUS XV.

Imbue me, O Lord, with the spirit and sentiment of this lofty song. Become my salvation, O God, and with salvation as Thy gift, let service—entire and devoted service—be my return. Let me help to prepare my Deliverer a habitation in this land. Save our beloved Church from her enemies; and may she become a Church of the living God, reared it may be anew by human hands, but more specially blest and beautified by the graces of the Spirit from on high. Make demonstration of Thy might, O God, in the midst of us, and let Thine own right hand obtain for us the victory. Let us remember what Thou hast done of old, and let us put our confidence in Thee, glorious in holiness as ever, fearful in praises, and always doing wonders. Thou wilt still be the Redeemer of Thy people, and be the conqueror of Thine enemies, and guide Thine own to a quiet habitation, even a habitation of holiness. With Thee as the strength of our hearts, and the Captain of our salvation, may we be enabled to maintain Thy righteous cause in the midst of all our adversaries; and let not their numbers nor their force cause us to falter from the way of Thy commandment. And O give forth a certain sound to the leaders and counsellors of Thy people, that they might be led by the way in which Thou wouldst have them to go, and that all united under the banners of truth and righteousness may have the light of the wisdom that is from above to direct their footsteps. While the cloud of a judicial blindness seems to hang over the minds of the rich and powerful amongst us, be Thou a pillar of fire before the eyes of Thy devoted followers, and bring them, O Lord, to the mountain of Thine inheritance, to the sanctuary which Thine own hands have established.

Fill the hearts of our families with encouragement and holy resolution, O God: let them, too, join in the high resolves of Christian patriotism, and put the song of triumph in their mouth when Thou hast compassed them about with songs of deliverance.

Yet trials may await us—trials of faith and patience. O strengthen and prepare us. May ours be the joyful resignation of a willing and obedient people; and save us from the murmurs of disaffection to the cause, or the heart-burnings of controversy among ourselves. May we experience at all times Thy healing hand; and let us ever cling with full assurance of heart to the promise—that as the day comes the provision will come. May it never be our discontent or our regret that we have left the flesh-pots of Egypt.

Thou wilt provide for us a shelter in the wilderness—

places of rest and refreshment along the dark and now uncertain futurity which lies before us.

EXODUS XVI.
January, 1843.

Save me, O God, from all sinful regrets when looking back on the pleasures of a world which it is my duty to renounce; and should I have to separate from a corrupt Church, let me submit not with murmuring but with joyfulness to every consequent privation. Let me always remember that man liveth not by bread alone, but by every word which proceedeth out of the mouth of God. Search me and try me, O God; and O may the result of the proof be, that there is truth in my inward parts—a thorough disposition in my heart to walk in Thy law. Let that law be my delight, and then nothing will offend me.—Let me, O God, at all events and in all circumstances, sanctify Thy Sabbaths; let no imagined necessity lead me to break in upon their sacredness; and neither let me look prospectively forward with sinful anxiety about the sustenance of myself or of my family through the days that are to come. Let me cast this burden on the Lord, and He will sustain it—causing that as the day comes the provision will come.

Incline me, O God, to make Thy Sabbath at all times a day of rest and a day of holiness. On this first day of the year I would purpose and resolve for a higher pitch of observance than heretofore—though more in the way of animating than of multiplying the services. Give me, in particular, to be more spiritual in my secret prayers, more attentive at church, more earnest, and O Thou Giver of all grace, more successful with my children.

Thou art slow to anger and a long-suffering God.—
Forgive my manifold violations of Thy law, and more
specially, of Thy Sabbath commandment. Thou hast
borne long with me, and hitherto hast Thou preserved
me, O God. Truly, it is of Thy mercies that I am not
consumed, and because Thy compassions fail not. How
many an Ebenezer might I raise along the path of my
journey through the wilderness of this world! Thou hast
spared me to another year; and I desire, O God, that
throughout the whole of my future life there might arise
to Thee the incense of a perpetual memorial. I am as the
fig-tree let alone. Let me henceforth abound in fruit, lest
I be cut off as a cumberer of the ground. Strengthen me,
O Lord, to fulfil my vows; and let not the purposes of the
season turn out to have been but empty aspirations, the
mere effluxes of emotion and not of principle.

EXODUS XVII.

The children of Israel hazarded the displeasure of God
—made, as it were, a fearful experiment on His long-
suffering, by the cries and complaints which they uttered
against Moses. They were based on incredulity; they
proceeded on the doubtfulness that was in their minds,
whether the Lord was among them or not; they forgot
the signs of His presence, and lapsed into ungodliness and
infidelity, and this, too, in the face not only of all the
wonders He had wrought in Egypt, but of the most recent
—which was the last and greatest demonstration He had
given of His power, by the destruction of Pharaoh and all
his hosts in the Red Sea. And the miracle of quails, and
the daily miracle of manna, were all thrown away upon

them. When now in straits they should have made their requests known to God, and not fretted against Moses—stopping short at the mere human, or secondary instrument, and betraying the utter insensibility and unthankfulness of their hearts towards the unseen Power in the heavens, yet seen in His mighty works, if not in Himself, to be a friend and a father to them. Moses, on the other hand, directed his application to the right quarter, and cried unto the Lord, from whom deliverance came as heretofore to the children of Israel. There is a lesson to be gathered here, and which I would do well to learn—a lesson that might be practised not in the greater calamities alone, but in the petty and familiar crosses of human life. The sentiment that all is of God, might convert even these occasions into the means of a godly discipline; and our meek acquiescence in His disposals, though they should be our own disappointments, might, by our perennial recognition of Him, be helpful to uphold that peace of God in our hearts which passeth all understanding. Teach me, O God, to behold Thine overruling Providence in all things.

There was no inherent virtue in Moses' arms—yet God required of him this co-operation. And as little is there aught of inherent virtue in aught that we can do, yet God admits us to the high honour of being fellow-workers with Him. Let us be as diligent as if we did all; let us be as dependent as if God did all. Nevertheless not me, but the grace of God that is in me, said Paul of all his successes in the Christian warfare. Let Jehovah-nissi be inscribed upon all our victories; and, O God, let ours be an unsparing and mortal warfare, even to extermination, against all sin. Let us give that hateful thing for which Christ died no quarter and no countenance. Let us put on the whole armour of God to fit and to prepare us for the contest—so as that sin may be cast down from its mastery, and we may never cease from our vigilance till it be finally destroyed.

EXODUS XVIII.

Let me trust that God whom Jethro blessed in the wilderness when he heard of the great deliverance which had been wrought for the children of Israel—let me trust that the same God will, in His good time and way, deliver our Church from all her adversities. Let me remember that not only is He a God of goodness, but that He is greater than all gods, and therefore greater than all the potentates of this world. Let us not be afraid what man can do unto us, for God is the helper of all who fear him. O may our ways please Thee, and then shall our enemies be at peace with us.—And do Thou, O Lord, who guidedst Thy people of old, be the guide and deliverer of Thy people now. Cause the wisdom that is from above to descend upon us, and stablish us on sure ground—leading Thy Church into a secure and wealthy place where she might be in safety from the world.

Raise up, O God, a sufficient agency for the service of the Church of Scotland. Take pity on her overburdened ministers, and let them be willing to devolve much that now lies upon them on others: and do Thou provide qualified men to relieve them of much of their present charge, so that they may neither be overworked nor secularized. Let theirs be the wisdom to order and ordain aright; and to others do Thou give the diligence to do. For the prosperity and good working of a Church there is a call for many services and many servants. Do Thou put the spirit of true Christian patriotism into the hearts of all her friends, that nothing might be wanting to the full equipment and effectiveness of a Church directed by Thy word and animated by the grace that is from on high. Send forth labourers to the harvest; and let ministers and elders and deacons be had in sufficient numbers for the duties and the wants of the Church of Scotland.

And give us, O Lord, competent advisers as well as agents—men fertile in devices, and such as may conduce to the great object of a well-planned and productive economy for the whole of our land. O pour down a blessing upon us, and enable us, in dependence on the showers of Thy grace, to turn our beloved country into a well-watered garden. Reclaim her waste places, and multiply her schools and churches, so that ours may become a Christian and intelligent population.

EXODUS XIX.

We are altogether unworthy, O Lord, to be thus signalized; yet as Thy children through the faith that is in Christ Jesus, may we claim the privilege—gratefully and confidently claim it—of being held as Thine own peculiar treasure, the people of God, a holy nation, a kingdom of priests, whom Thou bearest as on eagle's wings through the wilderness of this world, and guidest in safety to the land of everlasting rest. But, O God, may we keep fast by Thy covenant, and never forget that the way thitherward is a way of holiness. Let us maintain the sacredness of the Christian character, and henceforward hold ourselves separate from all sin and all ungodliness. Thou art exercising me at this moment by the illness of dear Mrs. Chalmers. Spare me once more, O God, if it be Thy blessed will. Restore her, O Lord, to the opportunities and calls of Thy gospel ere she and I go hence; and from this moment may we be Thine devotedly and Thine wholly.

And let me no longer accumulate on myself the guilt of vain and deceitful promises. What I have spoken, if agreeable to Thy will, enable me to do—to fulfil my vows, and ever live under a solemn sense of God, and of the awful and august sanctity of His nature. Ever blessed be Thy name, that we are now invited to draw nigh with boldness; but it is to a throne of grace, and of grace reigning through righteousness—and it is by a consecrated way, even a way consecrated by the blood of a Divine sacrifice. O let me not count this blood an unholy thing; but while laying hold of Thine offered forgiveness, may we never forget that it is a forgiveness that Thou mayest be feared.

What a fearful representation is here given of the Divine majesty and power; and how emphatic is the application made of it by the apostle—an application coming home to the subjects of our later dispensation. The grace of the gospel does not supersede all this state and majesty; for to those who either reject or abuse its privileges, God is still a consuming fire. The grace held out to us from heaven is a grace that enables us to serve God acceptably, with reverence and godly fear. O let me not go on in carelessness or sin, till at length there is no place for repentance. And now that since I penned the last page I have entered my dear wife's sick-room, and learned that she is better, O grave—and that in characters indelible—grave on my heart and memory the vows which I have made;

and may she and I walk together as heirs of the grace of life, that our prayers may not be hindered. Take the guidance of me henceforth, O Lord, lest I fail of Thy grace, and fall short of that holiness without which no man shall see the kingdom of God. Save me, O God, from all cowardice and false shame; and in the hearing of my children and acquaintances let my tongue sing aloud both of Thy mercies and Thy righteousness.

EXODUS XX.

Let me address myself to the work of obedience in the faith, O God, that Thou art my God. I pray for an evangelical outset in entering upon Thy service, that it may be the service of affection and not of constraint, and that I may go forth in the peace of those who love Thy law. And Thy commandment, O Lord, is exceeding broad; O incline and strengthen me for the work of keeping it. Save me from the love of the creature more than the Creator. May I think of Thee by the word and not mine own imagination; may I hallow Thy name; may I delight in Thy Sabbaths; may I honour my superiors—not speaking evil of dignities; and do Thou forgive the impatience I felt with my own parents. Save me from the feeling of hatred towards any living creature. May I be faithful even in the things which are least; and give me to be as scrupulously honourable in words as in actions. Finally, may I be content with such things as I have; and free me more especially from the covetousness that would trench on the possessions or the rights of other men. O put these laws in my heart and write them in my mind; transfer them from the place which they once held on tablets of stone to the fleshly tablets of my inner man, that it may prove no longer the ministration of death, but be unto me the ministration of righteousness; and that the law of the Spirit of life in Christ Jesus might make me free from the law of sin and of death.

God talked with the children of Israel from heaven—yet on earth. O may we not refuse Him who speaketh still. O give me grace to serve Thee acceptably with reverence and godly fear. May I prove the faith that is in my heart by the works of my history. May Thy law be my delight and my observance all the day long; and grant that my light may so shine before men, that others seeing my good works may glorify my Father who is in Heaven.

EXODUS XXI.

February, 1848.

Let the will of God be the predominating influence which reigns and regulates throughout all the transactions of my life. These provisions of His law fully indicate that the relations of human society and the duties annexed to these are of high account in the counsels and jurisprudence of heaven. In particular, we observe a sanction here to the place and the privileges of rank and station and property in the commonwealth. Let me not in the tumultuous swellings of a proud democratic spirit forget the deference to superiors which both the good order of society and the promptings of human nature, as well as the repeated declarations of God's word, require of all men; and grant that I may be more careful than I have always been not to speak evil of dignities.

The reigning spirit both of humanity and faithfulness actuates alike the Jewish and the Christian dispensations.

The toleration of polygamy to the former, we are told, was owing to the hardness of their hearts. Let the purity as well as benevolence of our highest economy be aspired after in all their highest characteristics, that we may be perfect and entire in the whole will of God.

Let these ordinations of the Jewish law raise my attention to the corresponding ordinations set forth in the sermon on the mount, where we are presented with those larger and higher developments of principle which now form the lessons for our heart and conduct in the law of the gospel. Let me not only refrain from violence but from hatred. Let me not only be rigidly just but largely and diffusively generous—insomuch as to forbear the prosecution of my own claims, and not only give way before the iniquity of others, but do them good and pray for them. In particular, let me be considerate of the feelings as well as rightful expectation of all inferiors, and all the more so because of their helplessness. And when I think of parents, of the duty and tenderness which are owing to them—how much, O Lord, have I to answer for. Let me wash out all the sins of my youth in the blood of the Lamb, and be henceforth filled with the charity which worketh no ill, and not only abstains from every outrage on the persons, or property, or freedom, or feelings of other men, but rejoices in all the acts of positive beneficence, and that too in the face of injuries and provocations.

How these regulations of the Divine polity in the familiar incidents which occur throughout the neighbourhoods of men living closely together, and in the habits of daily converse as well as hourly exposure to the waywardness of each other's tempers, or the untowardnesses of a thousand sorts which are perpetually breaking out—how the condescension of God in letting Himself down to the adjustment of such matters should sanctify in our estimation the whole of human life, and impart to our hearts a felt sense of obligation to God, that should never cease to follow us through all, even the minutest passages of our history, and mingle a grace and a godliness with all things.

EXODUS XXII.

In this chapter we have the farther enactments of a code where both the civil and the criminal are intermixed. We believe that the more theocratic the spirit of a government is, the less will be the distinction between these two branches of jurisprudence. What monstrous iniquities might be perpetrated by men who might be found right in law, and who because of their legal acquittal hold up their face in society, though guilty of the greatest moral enormities. Let me, on the other hand, O God, have equal respect to the whole of Thy will; and may a sense of Thee as my Heavenly Judge, make me studiously abstinent of all delinquencies. Save me from a covetous or revengeful spirit, and put truth in my inward parts, so as that I might clear my way honourably, and if possible without offence in the world.

Some of the injuries for which redress is here instituted are the effects of carelessness, and not of malice or dishonesty. There is a lesson here too, that I should be as careful of my neighbour's interest as my own. At present there is a particular call on me for the utmost vigilance, as in these days of controversy, and perhaps of approaching persecution, every slip might be magnified, and perhaps the most cruel and unjust advantage taken of it by enemies.

But let me be scrupulously right not only for wrath, but also for conscience' sake.

Let me be as observant of integrity in the minutest things as if the solemnity of an oath were upon me. Let principle, and sacred principle too, reign over all my transactions. I have at present been exposed to some such violence in a small way as marks certain of the cases here specified.—Give me wisdom and temper and the required forbearance in the prosecution of these cases. Be my shield and my counsellor, O God. Save me from the fear of man; and let the fear of Thee subordinate every other fear.

Give me to abhor that which is evil. Let me be kind to strangers; and in this I need Thy guidance and grace amid the multitudinous applications of those whom I do not know. Let me be generous and compassionate in all cases of ascertained helplessness and distress. Let me observe the mind of the Lord in all things—that what He loves I may love, that what He hates I may hate also.

EXODUS XXIII.

Enable me, O God, to fulfil these laws not only in the letter but in the spirit of them, even that Spirit of life which is in Christ Jesus, and which shines forth in greater distinctness and with fuller development in the New than in the Old Testament. Put truth in my inward parts, (verse 1); save me from conformity to the world, (verse 2); give me to have that thorough uprightness which is without partiality and without hypocrisy, (verses 2, 3); let me love and do good to my enemies, (verses 4, 5); let me not be just only but overflowingly generous to the poor, (verse 6); let me utterly abhor all deceit and violence, (verse 7); let me abstain from all covetousness, even though it might be indulged without dishonesty, (verse 8); and, finally, let me be alive to the helplessness of the desolate and the unfriended and the distant from home.

Though the miracle of the Sabbatical year is no longer before our eyes, let me never cease to observe, as of perpetual obligation, the Sabbatical day—that I may rest therein from all the cares and harassing cogitations of that weary world in which I fear I shall have tribulation. O that I took heed when spiritual idolatry made its encroachments, so that I might beware of loving the creature more than the Creator. Let me not make a god of anything in nature. (verse 13.) And surely though now liberated from the restraints of the ceremonial law, it were well still to set apart seasons of special intercourse with God. Let all be done with unleavened sincerity; and O God, do Thou at a time so eventful as now to the Churches of Christendom, put into our own hearts and those of many others, the spirit of liberality for the support and sustentation of a gospel ministry in our land.

And let the angel of Thy covenant, O God, be ever my guide and my tutelary guardian; and while I rejoice in the consciousness of safety under His mediatorial protection, let me rejoice with trembling, lest by only hearing His words and not doing them, He should withdraw from me here the light of His countenance, and lest on that awful day, when men will flee to hide themselves from the wrath of the Lamb, I shall be found to have built on a hollow foundation, and great will be the ruin of my final overthrow.

EXODUS XXIV.

I have long aspired to nearer and higher manifestations of the Godhead; but God in His wisdom may think fit to withhold from me this desire of my heart, and retaining me in the position which He sees to be best, may appoint me a longer period of dimness and distance from Himself, during which I shall have to worship afar off. For a season He may not permit me to draw so nigh as others on whom He confers the privilege of a closer intimacy. Now my allotted station may be still more remote than that of the elders of Israel, even among the people, who still, however, had their part and propriety assigned to them, and it will be well if with them I can say truly and in an honest spirit—" All the words which the Lord hath said will I do." He may not yet be pleased to bestow upon me a lively or exhilarating conception of Himself; but in the absence of this let me cherish and charge myself with the conviction that He is, and that the words of the Bible are His words, and that they are true. I cannot bring down the Father of Spirits from above—I cannot lift up myself even in thought to the place where His honour dwelleth; but let me give myself up to the plain work of the commandments, and holding immediate converse with the word that is nigh unto me, say—but with honest determination and dependence on the enabling grace of God—say, as did the children of Israel—" All that the Lord hath said will we do and be obedient." And O how sustaining the thought that there is the blood of an everlasting covenant by which both our persons and our services are made acceptable to God.—Enable me, O Lord, to lay hold of Thy covenant, and give me strength to fulfil my own part of it—that receiving from Thee both pardon and grace I may render to Thee myself as a living sacrifice, and walk before Thee all the days of my life in the new obedience of the gospel. And let me while I thus work also wait upon the Lord—seeing that if we keep His sayings to us will He manifest Himself.

And what a wondrous manifestation do we read of here —"the body of heaven in its clearness"—the sight of the God of Israel, and paved work that was under His feet. With the people He held converse by a law, by commandments which He Himself wrote, and which Moses was to teach them. Let ours be the work of obedience so long as we live in this lower world, in this outer court as it were of Thy glorious sanctuary. And beholding Thee as God in Christ, do Thou no longer appear to us as a devouring fire, but as a reconciled Father, that actuated henceforward by the perfect love that casteth out fear, we may serve Thee free of terror, yet in righteousness and holiness, all the days of our lives.

EXODUS XXV.

March, 1843.

Give a willing heart to Thy people, O God, in this the day of Thy Church's visitation. By the united liberalities of the people of Scotland may a sanctuary be built in which Thou mayest dwell, even a habitation for the mighty God of Jacob. And let ours be a Church framed according to the true and Scriptural pattern; and give us the wisdom by which to combine a definite government, and definite forms, and definite articles, with the right liberality to all who love the Lord Jesus Christ in sincerity and truth.

And first and foremost let ours be the article of a standing or falling Church—even the imputed righteousness of Christ made ours by faith alone—an article of which the mercy-seat, that could not be approached without blood, might well be regarded as an expressive emblem—setting forth as it does the doctrine of a propitiated forgiveness, or of acceptance through a Redeemer, and the merits of His obedience even unto death for us.

And by this Church let the bread of life be freely and plentifully dealt forth on all our population. May the souls of many be nourished up unto life everlasting. May pastors be raised up who shall feed the people with knowledge and understanding—even pastors, O Lord, according to Thine own heart, and under whose ministrations a rich spiritual blessing might descend on the families of our land.

May the future Church of Scotland be one of the Lord's own chosen candlesticks, supplied with oil from the upper sanctuary, whence an unction from the Holy One is made to descend on all those honoured vessels which are fit for the Master's use, and which, though of earthen material, may yet receive the treasures of grace from above, whence alone all power and all excellency do come. Let not Thy ministers, O Lord, walk in sparks of their own kindling; but may the light which they give forth be the pure light of Scripture, and the light of Thy blessed Spirit—these being not two, but one and the same light. Give them to be diligent in the study of their Bibles, and devout in supplication that their eyes may be opened to behold the wondrous things contained in the book of Thy law. And may they so meditate on these things, so give themselves wholly to them, that their profiting may appear unto all. Give them to look well that what they say to the people is in all things conformable to what Thou hast said in Thy word—speaking to their congregations not in the words which man's wisdom teacheth, but in the words which the Holy Ghost teacheth.

EXODUS XXVI.

The wisdom of God presideth over all things; and so in all things we should make our prayer unto Him—He who gave directions so minute and manifold for the framework of the tabernacle, He it is who endows men of all crafts and callings with the requisite skill both for devising and doing aright that which belongs to their own peculiar handiwork. May houses of Divine service, fit for use, and of the best design and construction, be raised everywhere for the accommodation of all true worshippers, and the services of a pure worship throughout our land. Give counsel and harmony and effect to the operations of all our Committees; and more especially may the proceedings of our Architectural Committee be conducted with sound judgment, and so as to enlist in the prosecution of their special objects both the willing liberalities of the public, and the important contributions of that advice and aid which are rendered by professional men. And though there be no authoritative pattern for our Churches, as for the Jewish tabernacle, still there is a directing and inspiring wisdom from on high which can guide the builders to all that is most suitable, both in appearance and real conveniency for a solemn house of prayer. And for this guidance to them, as well as for the grace of liberality to all our people, would we make our requests known unto God.

And I see no such contempt for ornament in the directory here given as was felt by the fanatics of other days. And if a needful economy should restrain us from greatly adorning our places of worship, let us at least strive that they should be of seemly appearance, and in proper keeping with the houses of cedar which we ourselves occupy. Above all, O God, may they prove to be places of real approach to the seat of Thine own holiness. There may the heart of many a worshipper enter into that within the veil, so as to carry them upward in faith from the holy to the most holy, from their house of sacredness on earth, to that house in the heaven, that upper sanctuary, to which in heart and in hope they are aspiring. May theirs be a substantial intercourse with the invisible above, and with our great Forerunner who has prepared for us a mercy-seat on high—even with Him who has opened up for all His true followers a clear and confident way of access unto God.

EXODUS XXVII.

Let me here be reminded of Him whom God did provide as the Lamb for a burnt-offering—even the Lamb slain from the foundation of the world—on whom my sins were laid; and who nailing them to the cross as being against us and contrary to us, there made an end of them. Let me take the full comfort of the thought, that they are now as if consumed in the death of the great expiatory victim, and so brought to nothing. O that I could lay all the stress on this great sacrifice, and give to it all the force and significancy which do in fact belong to it. Let me not live beneath the privilege of him whose sins, as if now burnt up and destroyed, are no more made mention of.

Only let me keep in mind that to be conformed to that death which absorbed all the penalties of a broken commandment, my own lusts and affections must be crucified with Christ, that the body of sin in me might be destroyed, and that henceforth I should not serve sin. O that spiritually I might die with Christ, and rise again with Him.

And let me so live in the world that to me it may be the outer court of heaven. Here we see through a glass darkly, and can but faintly image the light and glory which are on high. But there is a light without the veil— even that word hung down as it were from the upper sanctuary to be a light unto our feet and a lamp unto our paths—a light which if we follow here will usher us into clearer and brighter manifestations even on this side of death, till at length on the other side of death we shall see face to face, and know even as we are known. May I ever walk by this word; and do Thou uphold me, O God, in the paths which are prescribed for me there, that my footsteps slip not. Thou hast settled Thy word fast in the heavens—Thou hast exalted it above all Thy name.

EXODUS XXVIII.

I would consider Him who is the High-Priest and Apostle of my profession—Jesus Christ my High-Priest in the heavens; and in the contemplation of Him in the glories of His exaltation, and as altogether lovely, I would rejoice with joy unspeakable and full of glory.

And more especially would I regard Him as my Advocate and Intercessor, bearing my name in memorial, and pleading for my acceptance before the throne of God. O let me cast all my care and all my confidence upon Him, and place the whole of my reliance on the efficacy of His mediatorship. Truly I have nothing else on which I can lean; and henceforth let the daily experience of my infirmities with the recollection of all my grievous and accumulated sins shut me up unto the faith. Work in me this faith with power, O God—that while my name is graven on the heart of my Redeemer the remembrance of Him and of His name may never depart from me.

And let me not forget that the followers of our great High-Priest in the heavens are said to be themselves a "royal priesthood." They are made kings and priests unto God.—Enable me, O God, to sustain this high character, and in a way which becomes the dignity and gravity of such a designation. Let my habitual and constitutional levities give way before the power of a consideration so weighty and solemnizing as this—that I may adorn Christ's doctrine, and that others seeing my works and my ways, may glorify my Father who is in Heaven.

Above all, let me forget not that we are designated a "holy nation and a peculiar people." On every action and every footstep then let there be inscribed, "Holiness to the Lord." Let me be holy even as Christ is holy. And O Thou great Surety and ransom for the sins of the world, do Thou bear the iniquities of my holy things, that in Thee the beloved I may obtain full and perpetual acceptance with the God whom I have offended. And let me have an investiture worthy of this high calling—the graces of the Spirit and the robe of my Redeemer's righteousness.

EXODUS XXIX.

April, 1848.

Aaron had not only for the people but also for himself

to offer for sin—seeing that he too was compassed about with infirmity. And it was provided that the victims should be free of blemish. And so Christ the unspotted Lamb of God—unlike to Aaron who offered for himself as well as for the errors of the people—expiated our sins, not by the blood of bulls and goats but by His own blood. In this blood, O my Lawgiver in the heavens, but now my reconciled Father, let me wash out my sins. I feel the heavy burden of these grievous relapses and of this perpetual earthliness. I am in heaviness, O God. Give me to be temperate, O Lord. Let this and all the other fruits of Thy Spirit abound in me. Let me present my body a living sacrifice, and glorify the Lord with my body as well as my soul and spirit. I again pray for forgiveness. And O let me look not to my own things, but to the things of others also—and so more especially let me not give up either my labours or my importunities at the throne of grace, till Christ be formed in the hearts of my children.

And as in contemplation of the efficacy of Christ's blood I have been led to reflect on the magnitude of my sins— so let my experience of their frequent and daily recurrence ever lead me day by day to have recourse to that sacrifice, the virtue of which was shadowed forth by the continual burnt-offering, so that I might meet God at all times with acceptance, and He might speak peaceably to me. Thus will God, Emanuel, dwell in the midst of us, and without disparagement to His glory or His holiness. And O that He, the very God of peace, would sanctify us wholly, and so as that this alternate process of sinning and sorrowing might not lead to a confirmed Antinomianism: with my current and perennial faith in the atonement, let there be a progressive sanctification. Let me know God as my deliverer from an evil world, as well as my deliverer from the wrath that is to come. Bring me conclusively forth, O God, from the land of Egypt— from earth and earthlings; and let my delights be with Thine own people, even those among whom it is Thy delight to dwell. O more especially take up Thine abode in my own dwelling-place, and among my own family— that to me there might be given the exalted felicity of saying, "Here am I, O God, and the children whom Thou hast given me."

EXODUS XXX.

The ascending incense suggests to our minds ascending prayer. But our prayers ere they can rise with acceptance must be perfumed with the incense of a Saviour's merits. The people prayed without the temple while the priest was burning incense within. It was a sweet and a perpetual incense—to typify the acceptable intercession of our Saviour who ever liveth, and abideth a Priest continually.—My God, let me seek to no other incense, no other intercession than that of Christ the one mediator— all other is strange incense, and all other sacrifice—as of the mass or in any other form—is forbidden, seeing that we must now place our exclusive confidence in that great offering which was made once for the sins of the world. And the altar of incense had to be sprinkled with blood— even as it is the atonement made by Christ on earth which gives prevalence and power to His intercession in the heavens. This altar of incense was put before the vail, and before the mercy-seat. In all our prayers let us recognise the mercy of God as propitiated by the blood of

Christ. Let it not be the general but the gospel mercy in which we trust; and while still without, let these prayers be lifted up in the name of our great Forerunner who is within the veil.

My God, ever blessed be Thy name, that now when Christ has given His precious life a ransom for many, we may draw nigh without money and without price. Christ died for all; and it is their own fault if all—whether rich or poor—who are within reach of the gospel sound do not obtain an equal interest in that atonement which, by the decease accomplished at Jerusalem, has been made for souls.

And give me, O Lord, the washing of regeneration and the renewing of the Holy Ghost. Christ came by water as well as blood. Wash me thoroughly from the pollution of sin by the living water which cometh down from the upper sanctuary, even as Thou hast washed me from the guilt of sin in Thy blood. Make fast my sanctification with my justification, these two great gospel blessings which are linked inseparably together, and form the constituents of salvation in every man who has part or lot therein. "Purge me with hyssop and I shall be clean; wash me and I shall be whiter than snow."

Give me an unction from the Holy One—the anointing which remaineth. Thou who hast promised Thy Holy Spirit to them who ask Him wilt not give me a serpent for a fish, nor a stone in place of bread. Thou wilt not put me off with the counterfeit of that which I ask of Thee, but cause me to walk in the genuine light of Thy Spirit-illumed word, and not in sparks of my own kindling, else I shall lie down in sorrow, and be cut off from Thy people.

Let mine be the sterling and not the spurious—my

virtues be the graces of the Spirit, my grounds of confidence the merits of my Saviour.

EXODUS XXXI.

It is the inspiration of the Almighty which giveth understanding, and from Him proceed alike the gifts of nature, and the endowments of grace and spiritual discernment. It is well to recognise His power and wisdom, not alone in the mechanisms which proceed directly from His own hand, but in the skill which He imparts to the minds of those, who by a secondary wisdom derived from the great Fountainhead of all light and knowledge are enabled both to devise and to execute the various workmanships of utility and taste. O my God, do Thou endow the builders up of our Free Church with the requisite judgment for their arduous enterprise—and this not alone for the erection of its fabrics, but for the far higher achievement of framing its polity aright, and directing the administration of its various and complicated affairs. We lack wisdom. Upbraid us not, O God, but give us as we have need, and give us liberally.

We now live under the glorious law of liberty; yet being the liberty of the children of God, we as His children must love His Sabbaths—love the opportunities of converse with our Father—and what we do in love is done in the perfection of liberty. These awful sanctions and severities of the Jewish law are all the more emphatic testimonies to the respect which God has to this institution, and of His desire for its observance; and if we love God we shall will what He wills. Our liking for the Sabbath is a practical test of the state of our hearts, whether they are more set on the world or on God—on the affairs proper to the six days of the week, or on the special business of that one day which is set apart for Divine worship, and for fellowship by prayer and meditation with the Father and with the Son.

But that we may thus enjoy the Sabbath, and be qualified for its holy exercises, a great moral and spiritual change must take effect upon us. That law which was at the first graven on tables of stone must be graven on the fleshly tablets of our hearts, and then shall our affections be enlisted on the side of obedience. I will run in the way of Thy commandments when Thou hast enlarged my heart: then will it be my meat and drink to do Thy will. To do Thy will I would take delight, O God. Incline my heart, O Lord, to keep Thy testimonies; and in the very act of keeping them may I find a present and a very precious reward. Let such be my experience of this blessed day that I may identify Thy Sabbath with heaven, and have a foretaste in Thy Sabbaths upon earth both of the joys and exercises of the Sabbath of eternity. O may that whole law—and the Sabbath was part of it—which was written by the finger of God on tables of stone, be now written by the same finger on the tablet of my inner man—" not with ink, but with the Spirit of the living God."

EXODUS XXXII.

This lapse into idolatry seems truly marvellous amid the miracles and manifestations of that extraordinary period. Yet let us not have the imagination of there being no similar perversity in ourselves, and that our headlong tendency to idolize the creature and the things of earth is not as cleaving and inveterate as was that of the Israelites. I am here reminded of my own miserable alternations between the purposes and feelings of the closet when placed as it were at the gate of heaven's sanctuary, and the utter abandonment of myself to the influences of sense and of the world, so soon as the transition is made to the concerns and the companies and the festal parties of everyday life. My God, humble me, and also exalt me above these downward and degrading pronenesses. No wonder that the wrath of God should have waxed hot on such a provocation. But let me again remember my own sins of idolatry, and that God is angry with sinners every day : and let me have daily recourse to the Mediator, the daysman betwixt us, and who ever liveth to make intercession. O let not my enemies triumph over me, by exultation in my fall. Save me from such a humiliating overthrow; and suffer not me, who in their eyes have come out from amongst the companionships of the ungodly, suffer me not by any flagrant enormity to disgrace the holy name by which I am called ; or cause the scorner to revile conversion and sanctification and all the peculiarities of Christian discipleship as so many hypocritical and unreal things. I have done many things to injure my Christian reputation ; but, O my God, preserve me from these in all time coming, and in virtue of Christ's sacrifice and all-prevailing name, let Thine anger be turned away.

Moses as a good man and like unto God hated what God hated, and so his anger, too, waxed hot against the children of Israel. Yet there was a human infirmity mixed up with his indignation—a something of his own spirit that diluted and so tarnished the influences of the Spirit from above. Save us, O Lord, from our own waywardness; and whilst abhorring that which is evil teach us to know what it is to be angry and sin not.

Yet Moses had a warrant for his anger; it was by authority from the Lord that he armed the Levites against their brethren, and inflicted upon them so signal a chastisement. And yet how beautifully tempered with a relenting spirit was his righteous indignation, and how well he proceeded on the discrimination that to chastise was not to destroy; and so he gave way to compassion; and in the vehemence of his importunities for mercy, uttered a sentiment akin to that of the Apostle, who could wish himself accursed for his brethren's sake, his kinsmen according to the flesh. God would not, in His compliance with Moses' prayer, violate the equity of making each man responsible for himself and not for another. He does not thus transfer His severity from the guilty to the innocent; yet in the exercise of mercy, His darling attribute, He remits of the severity and punishes in measure. Still He punishes; and even though the angel of His presence has been set forth evidently before us, we must still expect that, in the administration of His holy discipline, He will correct the errors and iniquities even of his own children. He is a God who forgiveth, yet taketh vengeance of our inventions. Let me despise not the chastening of the Lord, but profit thereby

EXODUS XXXIII.

Was this not the angel of His presence whom the Lord Jehovah sent before Him—Himself the Lord Jehovah? and did any other than this angel appear before to guide or to hold converse with them? Was there any change here announced of conduct or procedure? or did God, on the occasion of this flagrant delinquency, make known the universal truth, that all our dealings with Himself must be by a Mediator? Let us ever be clothed with humility. May I at all times feel as a sinner, divested of all vain-glory.—My God, give me to be meek and lowly of heart, and may the Son of Thy love be all my desire and all my dependence. O that I had a profounder sense of my own emptiness, and drew more habitually and more largely out of the fulness that is in Christ Jesus. In His blood I would wash out all my sins, therewith to blot out mine iniquities; and that the sad delinquencies, the abominable idolatries into which I have fallen, might no more be made mention of.

The tabernacle seems on this occasion too to have been farther removed from the people. When Moses went to it the people rose up and looked out from a distance. He transacted with God for them, and became thereby a type of Christ. He spake with the Lord Jehovah face to face, while they only saw the manifestations or tokens of His presence—the very presence it may be which was sent *before* them, (verse 2,) while it was promised to be with Moses. (verse 14.) O my God, let me ever join in Moses' prayer, that I may go nowhere, that I may venture on no undertaking, that I may engage in no business without Thy countenance and blessing. Be with me—intimately and ever with me, throughout the whole of my proceedings in the guidance and future history of our Church. And whatever manifestations Thou art pleased to make of Thy glory, let me ever have at least the guidance of Thy word, and of its promulgations respecting Thy character and ways. O be gracious unto me, and shew mercy both to myself and to the beloved Church and country of my fathers. I cannot dive farther into the mysteries of this passage, or the profound mysteries of the Godhead. Was it God the Son with whom Moses spake face to face as in verse 11? and is it now God the Father who says—(verse 20)—"Thou canst not see my face; for there shall no man see me and live?" However this may be, give us, O Lord, the light of the knowledge of Thy glory in the face of Jesus Christ. Let me clearly apprehend the things which Thou hast been pleased to reveal, and feel a submissive and revering acquiescence in regard to the things which Thou art pleased to reserve—keeping them still in secrecy, or in a light that is inaccessible; for in Thee there is no darkness at all. Blessed be Thou, O God, that Thou hast bestowed upon us a word which Thou hast exalted above all Thy name.

EXODUS XXXIV.

Devon Iron Works, May 7, 1843.

O my God, do Thou renew the impress of Thy holy will on the fleshly tablets of my heart. I am a miserable defaulter; and times and ways without number have I, up to this moment, broken the commandments of God. There is not a company which I join, nor a feast I partake of, in which I do not depart from the living God. O pity me, and sustain me in those holy exercises of separate and sacred communion with Thyself, which may at length, on the promise of—ask and ye shall receive—obtain for me a part and an interest in that covenant which God makes with His people—"I will put my law in thy heart, I will write it in thy mind."

And as preparatory to this work of renovation give me

faith in Thine own blessed announcement of Thine own name—more especially in Thy graciousness, O Lord; and though Thou hast said, O Lord, that Thou wilt by no means clear the guilty, yet enable me to rejoice in that my guilt has been reckoned for with Him whom Thou madest to be sin for us, though He knew no sin, that we might be made the righteousness of God in Him. Thus art Thou a just God and a Saviour—thus art Thou just whilst the justifier of him who believes in Jesus. I believe, help mine unbelief.

But let me not forget, that if God is to be a Father unto me, and I am to be admitted among His sons and daughters, I must touch not the unclean thing, and hold no fellowship with evil, and come out from a world lying in wickedness—so as to make a clean escape from its corruptions and its follies. Save me, O God, from the ensnaring pleasures of the table; and turn my sight from viewing vanity. Save me from the lust of the eyes and from the lust of the flesh. Give me to keep the Passover, rejoicing in Christ my Saviour, with the unleavened bread of sincerity and truth; and to reverence Thy holy Sabbaths; and to honour the Lord with my substance; and to forsake not the assemblies of the saints, but to bear this evidence of my having passed from death unto life— even that I love the brethren.

And O remove that vail which so grievously and so long has obstructed my spiritual discernment. Manifest Thyself, O God, and fill me henceforth with a practical sense of the living God. Thou knowest the darkness and the blindness under which I labour, and the monopolizing influences of sense and of time. Give me, O Lord, with open face, to behold as in a glass the glory of the Lord—

that looking unto Him I may be made like unto Him, and be changed into the same image from glory to glory, even as by the Spirit of the Lord.

EXODUS XXXV.

Let me keep Thy Sabbaths, O Lord, in the newness of the Spirit, and according to the glorious law of liberty; but let me not use this liberty as an occasion for the flesh. Give me to love Thy Sabbaths, which I shall do if I love to breathe in the element of sacredness; and the law of love is the law of liberty.

Give, O Lord, willingness to the people, and give wisdom to the office-bearers of Thy Church in these our days. May the former contribute liberally of their means—may the latter be endowed with the requisite skill for the right construction both of an ecclesiastical plat and an ecclesiastical polity. We pray, O Lord, for more of unity to the counsels of our leaders; and direct me in particular to such measures and expedients as might prove of greatest efficacy for extending and sustaining the free-will offerings of the people of Scotland.

What a lesson might be here drawn from the respective parts which authority, on the one hand, and free-will, on the other, had in this matter of offerings for the tabernacle—or from the length and no further to which the commandment went, and the liberty that was left for the spontaneous inclinations of the subscribers themselves. The Lord commanded an offering to be taken—He ordained this way of raising the means; but still they were raised not as an exaction but as an offering. Every man whose own heart stirred him up, whose own spirit made him willing, gave of his own substance what seemed unto him good. O that our rulers but knew how far and no further they should push their legislation—and were restrained from so pushing it beyond its rightful boundaries as to lay a freezing interdict on those generosities which refuse dictation, and ought not to be tampered with.

We pray for more of Bezaleels and Aholiabs than we yet see to be engaged in the construction of the Free Church of Scotland. Give us, O Lord, the wisdom that is from above—and as we lack this greatly, give us liberally. And we pray more especially for the moral characteristics of this wisdom—its purity first, then its peaceableness, and gentleness, and meekness, and facility, and mercy, and fruitfulness of all that is right and good, and lastly, its freedom both from partiality and hypocrisy. The partiality that we most dread is that of favouritism, or even compassion, in the disposal of the Church's remunerated offices. Save us alike from the hypocrisy of unworthy applicants for these, and from the operation of all private considerations whatever on the part of the dispensers.

EXODUS XXXVI.

O that the Free Church of Scotland might prosper in the wisdom of her counsellors, and by the free-will offerings of her people. I pray, O God, for a skilful and clear accountantship. As in everything so in this thing would I make my requests known unto Thee: Thou knowest the complication of our affairs: Thou canst teach men how to reduce and to evolve it. I pray for a well-concerted scheme of accounts, which all may admire, and which may prove satisfactory to all.

And do Thou pour such a spirit of liberality on our people as Thou didst on the Israelites of old. There is much to be done. There is much land to be possessed. Speedily, O God, may there be more than enough for the sustentation of our present ministry, and the accommodation of our present worshippers. Nor would we restrain the people till there was more than enough for filling up with churches and schools the whole length and breadth of Scotland—and not even then—not till the knowledge of the Lord did cover the earth even as the waters cover the sea. It may be long, therefore, before we have to make proclamation of a superabundance in our treasury. O may the liberalities of the people abound more and more; may a right mechanism be framed for the ingathering of their gifts; and then let there be a right and vigorous working of that mechanism—and then let there be a right scheme of distribution adopted. Let all selfishness and all emulation give way before the patriotism that shall animate all and harmonize all. May we not on this question fall out among ourselves. Guide me aright, O Lord, in my meditations and studies on the platform and economics of our Church; and enable me, if it be Thy blessed will, to propose such a model as might unite the suffrages of all for its adoption.

There are differences, and I fear, injurious delays, in the matter of our Church's buildings. May there be a right and prosperous outgoing in this matter also. Direct us to such fabrics as shall combine economy with adaptation. These, no doubt, are but the outer things of the house of God—yet should they not be neglected, or left undone. All Scripture is profitable—nor is it without design, and a design too of infinite wisdom, that the construction thereof has been set before us in such manifold detail and particularity. Let us beware of despising as insignificant any part of that sacred volume which has been given for the admonition of the Church in all ages.

EXODUS XXXVII.

There was a Holy of Holies in the Jewish tabernacle, and corresponding to this there are in the Christian Church the glories of the inner temple. Chief of these is the mercy-seat in the heavens—the great propitiatory there, even of the true tabernacle which God pitched, and not man. Do Thou elevate my thoughts, O God, to the realities and archetypes of the upper sanctuary; and more especially to Him whom Thou hast set forth as the great propitiation for the sins of the world. Let my faith be ever fixed on that mercy-seat on high which is sprinkled with the blood of a satisfying atonement; and where, because of the law now magnified and made honourable, there sitteth a halo of all the attributes of the Divine nature. The sacrifice of Christ is to God like the incense of a sweet-smelling savour, and the blessed name of the Saviour is as ointment poured forth to those who love Him—even to those who believe, and to whom He is precious. Let the holy anointing oil also suggest to our minds what is of significancy and substantial weight in our new and spiritual dispensation; and may it not well suggest an unction from the Holy One, the anointing which remaineth, the living water from above, of which we are expressly told that it is the Holy Ghost given to them who shall believe! O let not our graces be of a counterfeit and spurious description; let them be the genuine work of Thy

Spirit in our souls—not our own work, or sparks of our own kindling, but the real product of fire from heaven. Thou who givest not a stone for a loaf, and who givest not a serpent for a fish, save us from being deceived by the mere semblances of natural virtue. Let what we offer be according to the work of the apothecary. Let ours be the genuine fruits of the Spirit's operation in our souls.

EXODUS XXXVIII.

June, 1843.

The laver being made of the looking-glasses of the women reminds one of what is now taking place for the rearing of a free and pure Church in these lands, when ornaments are parted with to be sold for the necessities and expenses of that great apparatus which is destined, I hope, under the blessing and countenance of God, to be the instrument of a great extension and revival of Christianity in the present day. O Heavenly Father, do Thou open more and more the hearts and hands of the Church's friends, that it may be adequately supported for the great end of providing the lessons of Thy blessed gospel to all the families of Scotland. But the most interesting application made of the laver is when viewed as the type of our regeneration. It was erected for washing the priests; and unless we are washed we have no part in Christ, and can never be admitted among those whom He has made priests and kings unto God.

But the wisdom and wealth of Israel were put into requisition that a suitable and seemly tabernacle might be raised to the God of Israel. And let us not spare either workmanship or costly materials in the erection of our churches. It is true that the highest object is a sufficient accommodation for the people, and if at the expense of this, all ornament ought to be discouraged. But we do not necessarily promote the one end by discouraging the other; and should the taste of any locality or any individual lead to a special offering for the adornment of a church, there may be an error both of policy and principle in looking hardly or forbiddingly thereupon. Save our counsellors, O Lord, from every wayward deviation whether on the right hand or on the left.

EXODUS XXXIX.

Let me not count it a matter of indifferency that on Sabbaths, and in the service of God, I should be studious of at least decency in my apparel. The Levitical law provided for more than this, and garments were appointed to the officials in the priesthood so as that they should be arrayed in glory and in beauty. Let me not, therefore, give in to the vulgar antipathies on this subject. It is easy for me to tolerate, because I approve, and have a taste for, professional costume. I will not, therefore, quarrel with these things in themselves, however much I might quarrel with the authority which would impose them, and utterly abjure the policy that would force an acquiescence in them on the reclaiming consciences of others. But there is one thing here beyond the reach of controversy—the holiness unto the Lord inscribed on the crown of gold that was placed on the head of the highpriest. O that this holiness of heart and of life were mine; and that I stood apart from the world and signalized above it by all those graces which separate and distinguish one from the men of a secular and ungodly generation. O let me be as a devoted and dedicated thing for the Master's use—set apart unto Thy service, and sanctifying Thee at all times in my heart. Let me be a temple of the Lord; and let this saying be ever present with me—" If any man defile the temple of the Lord him will God destroy."

The tabernacle was at length finished—both done and paid for by the children of Israel.—Put it, O God, into the hearts of Scotchmen to go and do likewise for the Free Church now set up in these lands. I pray for liberal hearts and ever-doing hands—for the willingness to communicate on the part of givers, for the habit of assiduous labour on the part of visitors and agents. Thus may our fabric of a Church be completed in all its parts and all its workings—that on viewing this goodly consummation its ministers and its people might rejoice together; and even as Moses blessed the children of Israel, a blessing might go forth from our Church on all its adhering families.

EXODUS XL.

When all the parts of this great apparatus were prepared then they had to be put together. The tabernacle was set up; and in the contemplation of its goodly structure may we recognise all that is most precious in our own dispensation: the laver to signify the washing of our regeneration—the altar our atonement for sin—the priest who ministered in holy things, and who shadowed forth our own great High-Priest, Himself the offering for our transgressions, and now living to make intercession for us. May we rise from these symbols of an everlasting priesthood to the view of its substantial and sublime realities; and when we think of all as anointed and ordained of God, may we bless ourselves in the abundance of that peace and perfect security which are certified to all who take refuge in the hope set before them in the gospel.

And if the things without the tabernacle remind us of what taketh place on earth, the altar of burnt-offering of the atonement made for us in Jerusalem, and the laver of the regeneration which is effected on the faithful below—the things which be within alike remind us of that part of our mediatorial economy which has place in heaven—of the great Forerunner within the vail mixing His own supplications with our prayers, and perfuming all our services with that odour of His own blessed sacrifice which rises at all times to God like the incense of a sweet-smelling savour.—O may the ministers of our Church be made altogether holy and fitted for Thy service. May Thy presence, O God, be in all our tabernacles; and may a well-qualified officiating servant be provided for each of them. Remove all those obstacles which retard the progress of our great work, and give us the comfort of beholding it in full progress towards a great and glorious accomplishment. Our want is that of labourers. O God, who providedst such a number of ecclesiastics in the form of priests and Levites for the people of Israel, do Thou, O Lord of the harvest, send forth a sufficiency of labourers for the plenteous harvest of our general population.

LEVITICUS.

Leviticus i.—The Book of Leviticus is full of evangelism; and we may there behold the doctrine of the new in the drapery of the old dispensation. It was

Matthew Henry who, in his Commentary, first made this portion of Scripture attractive to me; and now I can see that much is to be learned, and much that is new and delightful might be felt, in the study of the Mosaic ritual, and contemplation of the precious truths which are bodied forth there. The first of the sacrifices here described is, we are told, of a male without blemish—thus signifying the unspotted Lamb of God, even Him who was holy, harmless, undefiled, and separate from sinners. The sinlessness of the victim was indispensable to the efficacy of its offering for sin; and thus let my trust in Christ be all the more established as I view Him in the purity and perfection of His untainted holiness. And in the case here before us, it was a voluntary offering made on the part of a private person of his own free-will, and for his own benefit, too, seeing that when he put his hand upon the head of the burnt-offering it was accepted *for him*, and it made atonement *for him*. Thus, too, our will has to do with the great sacrifice; and an individual benefit to us is appropriated thereby. The Saviour's charge against those who not having the Son had not life, was—that ye will not, or are not willing, to come unto me that ye may have life. (John v. 40.) Our will is concerned in the act of confessing over the head of Him who is set forth as our propitiation, and whereby we wash out our sins in His blood. The name of the Saviour is to believers as ointment poured forth; and their utterance of that name in prayer ascends on the wings of acceptance to Him who sitteth on the throne, like the incense of a sweet-smelling savour. And though nothing done or suffered by man can add to the virtue of that great expiation, yet let us not imagine that we are therefore exempted from all personal sacrifices on our part. It was the death of Christ which gave their efficacy to all the offerings of the law; and still we have offerings to make, spiritual sacrifices of no value apart or by themselves, but acceptable to God by Jesus Christ our Lord. In coming to Christ for the benefits of His redemption, we have to forsake all that He requires us to forsake. The Israelite who brought a ceremonial offering brought it at his own cost to the door of the tabernacle, and at such a cost as was proportioned to his ability. The Christian who comes to God by the new and living way, who places himself at the door of the true tabernacle in the heavens, and cries for mercy in the name and through the merits of Him who is the minister of the true sanctuary, he also must consecrate of his own to the Lord who bought him. —May such be our services and such our surrenders for His sake, that He who lays upon His disciples no more than they are able to bear—He who required of the poor a less expensive offering, may say of me in the day of reckoning—He has done what he could. O how short of this, how miserably short!

LEVITICUS II.
July, 1843.

The offerings of this chapter are not sacrificial—they are thank-offerings; and with the exception of the first-fruits they are all offerings of free-will. When any *will* offer a meat-offering unto the Lord, (verse 1;) and again, *if* thou bring an oblation, (verse 4;) *if* thy oblation, (verses 5 and 7;) the conditional and the dependent marking it to be voluntary, whereas the oblation of the first-fruits is prescribed and authoritative—as for the oblation of the first-fruits ye *shall* offer them unto the Lord. No doubt there is a something prescribed concerning all these offerings, as that whether voluntary or not they shall, if to be done, be done in a certain way and with certain accompaniments. And we too have the counterparts of free-will offerings and thank-offerings in the Christian dispensation. The great sacrifice does not supersede our sacrifices—spiritual sacrifices acceptable to God by Christ, through whom the incense of them ascends like the frankincense of the meat-offering, of a sweet savour unto the Lord. It is remarkable that the voluntary offerings are all burnt on the altar, and that it is the altar which communicates to them their sweet savour—for of the required offering it is said, that it shall not be burnt on the altar *for* a sweet savour. Does not this point to the connexion between the great propitiatory sacrifice on the one hand, and the acceptance of all our services on the other; and though our offerings are not sacrifices in themselves, any more than the Jewish meat-offerings of the law, yet as theirs had to be brought to the altar, so ours must be in and through Him who bowed down His head unto the sacrifice. This forms an essential condition of the acceptance of our services, which like our persons are accepted only in the beloved. This forms an indispensable salt for the seasoning of all our works, for it is only labour in the Lord which shall not be in vain. Yet the salt may mean something personal in ourselves, even as the freedom from leaven does—for we must purge out the old leaven of malice and wickedness, and keep the feast with the unleavened bread of sincerity and truth; and as the willingness of our services does—for what we do unto the Lord should be done from the heart and cheerfully without a grudge, even as what arose with sweet savour was not only laid on the altar, but done with free-will. Lord, may I receive the truth as it is in Jesus into a good and honest heart, and then shall I be sanctified by that truth, and it shall make me free. May the law of the Spirit of life in Christ Jesus make me free from the law of sin and of death.

LEVITICUS III.

But though thank-offerings are not sacrificial, peace-offerings are. It is an offering for a sacrifice of peace-offering. (verses 3, 6, and 9.) Jesus Christ is the great peace-offering. We have peace with God through Jesus Christ our Lord. It is by the blood of Christ that we are made nigh unto God—for He is our peace, having broken down the middle wall of partition, having abolished in His flesh the enmity, having reconciled us unto God by the cross, and so as to make peace and furnish a sure warrant to the heralds of salvation, when in the fulfilment of their commission they proclaim peace on earth, or preach peace both to them who are afar off, and to them who are nigh. (Eph. ii. 13-17.) And the victim offered must be without blemish. Let this remind us of Christ, carrying us forward from the type to Him who is typified— even to Him who was holy, harmless, undefiled, and separate from sinners. We are redeemed by the precious blood of Christ, as of a lamb without blemish and without spot. (1 Peter i. 18, 19.) And there is another analogy between the sacrifices of the law and the great sacrifice— in that as under the former dispensation the offerer laid his hand on the head of the victim, so under our present dispensation, may we lay our hand on the head of Him who is the propitiation for the sins of the world. In those days each offerer offered for himself, and by the imposition of his hand transferred his own sins to the head of the substitute. And so is there still a channel or a way by which the sins of each in particular might be transferred to Christ, by which he might wash out his sins, his own sins in the blood of the Lamb, and cast his burden on the Lord who alone is able to sustain. Let us not lose ourselves in the generalities of the doctrine of our atonement, or miss our hold of that appropriation by which Christ becomes specially ours and the blood of expiation is sprinkled on our own souls, so as to bring the peace of a full assurance to our own hearts and consciences. O give me to trust in Christ for myself, and to lay my confident hold on Him—as the bunch of hyssop dipt in liquid takes it up and cleanses therewith, let my faith be such, O God, as to take up the blood of Christ wherewith to cleanse my soul. Purge me with hyssop and I shall be clean, wash me and I shall be whiter than the snow. Let such be my believing utterance of Christ's name, that in the calling of it I may be saved, and that the mention thereof might ascend to heaven's throne like the incense of a sweet-smelling savour.

LEVITICUS IV.

Who can understand his errors? Cleanse Thou me, O Lord, from secret faults. I judge not mine ownself for I know not mine ownself; yet am I not hereby justified—for He that judgeth me is the Lord who knoweth all things. Sins are nevertheless sins though I may not be aware of them. There might be a direct sinful tendency in my heart, which still is sinful though it may have escaped my own reflex observation. Many might be the movements whereof I have taken no cognizance, of vanity, and envy, and sensuality, and earthliness of all sorts within me; but God who pondereth every heart, and weigheth the secrets of every spirit, discerns all, and so far as His law taketh effect on the sinner himself, will reckon with him for all. It is His estimation of our state, not our own, that fixes our real character and the desert of all our actions. Let this consideration—the consideration of our many unknown delinquencies both in spirit and in conduct, humble us—greatly humble us, over and beyond all that by our own searching examination we may have discovered of ourselves; and let it also cause us to draw more largely on the blood of Christ, and to feel more deeply our need of the great atonement, in which there is all the virtue typified by all the sacrifices of the law—among which there are the sin-offerings of ignorance. Out of the fountain opened in the house of Judah for sin and for uncleanness, there proceedeth a virtue both to pardon and to purify beyond all that we can ask or think—beyond all the pardon we have ever asked for, and all the purification which we think ourselves in need of.

If the people of Israel were required to perform expiatory rites for their sins as a nation, are no spiritual sacrifices required of nations still? Can nothing be done religiously, or nothing be done by them for religion in their national capacity? Save me, O God, from rushing headlong or heedlessly into the Voluntary principle.

And in our sacrifices of thanksgiving for the benefits of that great sacrifice which has superseded all its prefigurations, let us give cheerfully, up to the extent of what God hath enabled us. Save me, O Lord, from grudging avarice, nor let me in particular be parsimonious of aid to the Free Church of Scotland.

Thou art an indulgent Father, laying on no man beyond what he is able to bear. Thou exactest no more from the widow than the widow's mite, on which at one time when given with self-denial and in faith, Thou didst confer the most illustrious of all testimonies.

LEVITICUS V.

The sins of ignorance seem to be mixed up in this chapter with sins done knowingly, and sacrifices are ordained for both. In my perusal of this Book let me drink deeper and deeper into the precious doctrine of our atonement. We cannot read the exposition of any sound author on such passages as these without feeling how deeply it is that the whole of the Mosaic ritual is impregnated with evangelism. This I felt long ago, when reading Matthew Henry on Leviticus, and more recently when reading Outram on Sacrifices. But we need go no farther than Scripture itself, and in such expressions as—the priest making atonement for him, and for his sins which he hath sinned and it shall be forgiven him, we recognise the very essence of the gospel. Let this study then go to enhance my faith in the great sacrifice, marking at the same time how, under the law, confession went before the offering. In like manner let us confess our sins in the very act of washing them out by faith in the blood of the Lamb: and O let me be more watchful, lest grievous and damnable sins should escape my observation. It is good to note the particularity of the confession—" It shall be when he shall be guilty in one of these things, that he shall confess that he hath sinned in *that* thing." Let me not lose myself in generality, but be observant of my special delinquencies, and confessing each in particular, bring it to the blood of atonement, that its guilt in particular might be washed away. And O grant, Almighty Father, that not counting the blood of the Covenant as unholy, each particular confession may be followed up by as particular a reformation. Forgive this, O Lord—rectify and reform *this*, O Lord; and may the grace for doing so, and for which I now supplicate, not be received by me in vain, but actually turned to the purpose for which I now ask it. Thus may I attain to a close walk with God in every one thing, and all the day long.

The sins of ignorance in holy things demand a costlier sacrifice; and so if I have fallen short in my religious charities, let my deficiency in these be followed by a larger compensation. And also solemnize me the more when engaged in sacred exercises; and let my conscience be more tender of all that is criminal or remiss in matters appertaining to the services of devotion and of religious study, whether public or private. This chapter concludes with a distinct assertion of the moral culpability of sins of ignorance. There is a guilt in them, and a guilt the principle of which we have repeatedly expounded.

LEVITICUS VI.

The sins of this chapter are done wittingly, and yet are expiable—a matter of the most urgent personal importance, seeing that there are sins of presumption, for which no sacrifice is provided ; and that however unable we may be to state or to define it, there is a degree of wilfulness beyond which if we carry sin, we are told even under our own dispensation that there remaineth no more sacrifice for sin, but a certain fearful looking for of judgment. Well may we join the Psalmist not only in praying that God would cleanse us from secret faults, but also that He would keep us from presumptuous sin. It is well too to remark, that in the case of an injury done to a neighbour, whether by fraud or falsehood, the reparation did not supersede the trespass-offering, neither did the offering supersede a reparation. The offender had to restore more than the amount of injury which he had done. And so in turning to Him who is the great sacrifice, we must turn from our iniquities. Our amendment does not discharge us from the need of a part and an interest in the propitiation of Christ, neither does the propitiation do away the need of repentance and amendment.

O God, may a fire be kindled in our hearts from heaven itself, and let it be ever kept burning there, so that we may never walk in sparks of our own kindling, but in the light of Thy Divine countenance, and the perpetual glow of that love which Thyself hast awakened.

It is this love, this sense of God's love to us calling forth our love to Him back again,—it is this which prompts to such thank-offerings as are fitly represented by the meat-offerings of the Old Testament—not sacrificial, though termed the sacrifices of thanksgiving, and so corresponding to the spiritual sacrifices of gospel obedience. There is no leaven in them ; and O that ours was a holy love, love without lust—not the love or the liberty which is for an occasion to the flesh.

No part of the priests' meat-offering was eaten by the priests. The liberalities of the people were in part allocated to the maintenance of the Church's ministers. The liberalities of the ministers themselves should not in any part come back to them, but form an entire surrender or entire sacrifice.

If what the sin-offering touched was holy, let us learn the enormity of our counting the blood of the Covenant that is sprinkled by faith on the souls of believers unholy. O God, let us ever bear in mind what the characteristics are of that which redeemed us—even the blood of Christ, as of a lamb without spot and without blemish; and grant that I may be holy even as Christ is holy. O give me to coalesce with the whole of the gospel salvation; and let me be ever intent on that which is the end of all and the object of all—even that I may be renewed in the spirit of my mind, and created again after the image of God in righteousness and true holiness.

LEVITICUS VII.

August, 1843.

A sin-offering I should conceive to be for sinfulness or sin in general; a trespass-offering for a particular sin. How manifold have been my transgressions, O Lord—my acts of disobedience! O treat me not as one of the children of disobedience. If Satan has at times—nay often had the advantage over me, O let me not be his slave. I pray to be released from the bondage of corruption, and translated into the glorious liberty of one of God's children. Meanwhile, O God, admit me anew into peace through Him who made His soul an offering for sin. May He see in me of His seed, and may Thy pleasure prosper in His hand, even Thy will, which is my sanctification. If any man sin we have an Advocate; O let our confidence in Him be such that we sin not.

These peace-offerings, these sacrifices of thanksgiving, these voluntary gifts and services, may represent the spontaneous and free-will character of our new obedience. But how emphatic a warning is also here set before us, in that if our peace-offerings be vitiated by uncleanness, we shall be cut off from the Lord's people.—My God, save me from delusion. Let me not lose my hold of the grace of God; but O save me from the awful doom of those who turn that grace into licentiousness. Let not sin have dominion over me.

Let me not pass over those injunctions in regard to meats. Whatever other rules may be now superseded, there is one of standing importance and obligation given by our Saviour Himself—and this is, that our hearts shall not be overcharged with surfeiting, lest the adversary should at any time come upon us unawares. Enable me, O God, to be temperate in all things, and to keep this vile body under subjection.

Give me to be more liberal, O God; and incline to liberality the hearts of many for the support of a gospel ministry in these lands. Pour out a spirit of generosity even to overflowing, that the few rich may give largely of their abundance, and that all may give according to their ability.

It is Thy will that the ministers of religion should receive an adequate maintenance. Enable me, O God, to devise and to carry into effect the right measures for securing this object. Let a wise and righteous law be framed for the accomplishment of it—enough to divide, and a proper method of division.

LEVITICUS VIII.

Ours is a holy priesthood, and the feeling of all who belong to it should be, that theirs is a high and holy service. What a rebuke does the sacredness of my profession lay upon the levity of my practice; and in particular, how awful is the responsibility should a minister of religion so act as to cause men to think lightly of its solemn obligations! Let me ever bear the sense in my heart that I am set apart in a peculiar way to Him for whose glory I ought to shine forth as a light in the world. When I think of the weight and multitude of my duties I cannot fail to be impressed with the weight of my manifold debts and deficiencies. Verily my iniquities are too heavy for me; and I must look unto Him upon whom, O Lord, Thou hast laid the burden of them all. And O that naming His name I should henceforth live to the praise of Him who calls out of darkness into marvellous light. There are two words in this chapter of distinct import, but each of capital importance—reconciliation and consecration. The blood of the bullock for the sin-offering was sprinkled upon the altar, by which it was sanctified, and the sacrifices made thereon were of effect for the reconciliation of those in whose behalf they were offered. But it was upon the head of this bullock that Aaron and his sons laid their hands, signifying the transference of their sins to the offered victim; for atonement behoved to be made in behalf of the priests as well as of the people. The ram of consecration was also slain in sacrifice, just as the bullock for the sin-offering was; but the blood of the ram was not, like that of the bullock, put on the horns of the altar for its sanctification, but upon the ears and thumbs and great toes of Aaron and his sons, for their consecration. In each of these sacrifices there was a transference of guilt—for Aaron and his sons laid their hands upon them both; but to be consecrated as well as reconciled, the blood was sprinkled upon their persons; and let us hence see how intimately blended the reconciliation and sanctification are with each other. And O that I experienced both the purifying and the peace-speaking power of the blood of Jesus. Save me, save me, O God, from the awful profanation of counting that blood an unholy thing. May I henceforth look upon myself as consecrated unto God, and so live a life of devotedness to His service. It may appear a little thing, yet God hath respect unto it, and made it the subject of authoritative regulation: He ordained special garments for the priesthood.—Let me not despise externals in matters of religion, and let me be more studious than heretofore of decency of apparel. It is unphilosophical as well as unscriptural to have a contempt for materialism. There is a character and expression in vestments as well as in other things; and there is a way of glorifying God in these just as there is a way of glorifying Him in our bodies as well as in our souls and spirits.

LEVITICUS IX.

The Jewish high-priest had to offer for himself as well as for the people—he, too, being compassed about with infirmities. Not so with the Apostle and High-Priest of our profession—He being holy, harmless, undefiled, and separate from sinners. The victims offered in sacrifice for the former behoved to be without blemish; but Christ was Himself without blemish. We are redeemed with the precious blood of Christ as of a lamb without blemish and without spot. Give us, O Lord, to act faith in Him as our propitiation, so that we may be placed in the situation analogous to that of those for whom the actual sacrifice was made in the days of the Old Testament. And O let the analogous effect described in this chapter be also realized. The glory of the Lord appeared unto those who made the representative sacrifice. Let the glory of the Lord appear unto us as we put faith in the real sacrifice. Give us to behold the glory of the Lord in the face of Jesus Christ. Give us to discern the character of God in the work of our redemption. And O that thus looking unto Thee I were made like unto Thee; and that beholding with open face the glory of the Lord, I were changed into the same image from glory to glory, even as by the Spirit of the Lord. O that the doctrine of salvation took possession of me as a living and a governing principle—not in the form of an inert and barren dogma, but of a living and operating power. Thou knowest my great want, O God. Call me, O Lord, effectually call me to glory and to virtue, and let the Spirit of glory and of God rest upon me. I cannot familiarize myself with the details of the Jewish ceremonial—and yet all must be profitable. I read again and again the procedure of these various offerings, but the steps and successions of that procedure take no hold of me—slipping as it were from my regard and my memory. Should I make an intense study of them;—or viewing them as things that might now vanish away, may I count it enough though I should know nothing but Jesus Christ and Him crucified, counting all things but loss for the excellency of this knowledge; and forgetting the types in the great Antitype, finding a sufficiency in that direct contemplation of Him by which I am made wise unto salvation.

LEVITICUS X.

The strange fire of Nadab and Abihu tells us that we must not serve the Lord with sparks of our own kindling, else we shall lie down in sorrow. O that I might be enabled to serve Him in the feeling and with the faith which His own Holy Spirit works in me, and not with any factitious or counterfeit fervours of my own. But our protection against all counterfeits is prayer; for in connexion with the promise that He would give the Spirit to them who ask it, do we read that He will not give a serpent in place of a fish, nor a stone in place of a loaf, nor a cockatrice in place of an egg. He will not put us off with the semblance, but give us the substance and reality of the thing itself. Thus, O God, may I be enabled to render unto Thee a genuine obedience, and with the genuine sentiment and principle of one of Thine own children.

Aaron, softened and humbled under the weight of this visitation, listened with the submissiveness of a weaned child to his brother, who laid still other directions upon him, and accompanied it with the solemn warning—all the more impressive from the exemplification which had just been given—lest ye put no difference between the holy and unholy, as Nadab and Abihu had done by offering strange fire instead of fire from the altar. Do not this other thing, neither thou nor thy sons, lest the like vengeance come upon you, and ye die.

He prosecuted his directions still further, but without

the awful sanction which accompanied the former one—illustrating the distinction between the sin which is unto death, and those sins which are not unto death. But save us, O God, from all sin. Give us to have that native abhorrence of it which is irrespective of threatened penalties and of all consequences. Let me be jealous of myself, and shun the least appearances or least approaches to evil. Deliver me from the mere utilitarianism of religion; and let it be my meat and my drink not so much to reap Thy wages as to do Thy will.

And yet let me take the comfort of the apostolic saying, that there is here a sin not unto death—such a sin as Aaron fell into; yet when he pleaded the infirmity of his sorely afflicted spirit, Moses was content. Thou art an indulgent Father—Thou knowest our frame—Thou knowest how much or how little we are able to bear—Thou hast compassion on our infirmities, yet let us not presume on Thy lovingkindness, on the tenderness of Thy mercy to the erring children of men; but give us, O Lord, to combine with the security of the Christian faith the diligence of the Christian practice—so that while rejoicing in hope we may at the same time be earnest in Thy service, working out our salvation with fear and trembling.

LEVITICUS XI.
September, 1843.

The children of Israel were separated from the idolatrous nations around them by such observances as we read of in this chapter. And there is a separation still enjoined on the people of God, though not in the matter of carnal ordinances, yet in the matter of those great moral and spiritual characteristics which distinguish the children of light from the children of this world. We must no longer walk as the Gentiles do, in lasciviousness, lusts, excess of wine, revellings, banquetings, and abominable idolatries. We must run not with them to the same excess of riot, however strange they may think it, or however much they may be provoked thereby to speak evil of us.

There must have been a restraint of their natural appetites on the part of the Israelites in complying with some, at least, of the injunctions here given. And though we should be absolved from some of their particular acts of self-denial, yet the habit of self-denial is still an essential part of our Christian education. We should deny all worldly lusts; we should put a knife to our throats if given to appetite; we should resist the temptations and pleasures of the table when they either tend to surfeit or to intoxicate us; and whenever any kind or excess of indulgence has the effect of making us wayward in passion or forgetful—then, with as great a repugnance as ever a Jewish devotee looked on forbidden meats, should we hold the indulgence in utter abomination. Make me watchful, make me temperate, O God.

Holiness is separation, and its essence lies in our being separate from sin and sinners. What an endearing and evangelical motive to holiness is here set before us! It differs from the motive proposed by Peter—" Be ye holy, for I am holy." It is—" Be ye holy, for I am your God." I am the Lord your God, ye shall *therefore* sanctify yourselves, and ye shall be holy. This motive is paramount and prior to the other, also propounded here, and reiterated by the apostle in the New Testament, (1 Peter i. 16); but the other presupposes that we have appropriated God as our God. He sets Himself forth to us as ours:

He is ours in offer; and we have only to believe Him as such that He may become ours in possession. O give us this appropriating faith; let us cleave to Thee as indeed our own; let us take up with Thee and depend on Thee as such; and then shall we feel the force of the consideration—that we should be like unto Him, whose we are, and whom we also claim as ours—for we are Christ's, and Christ is God's. Give us, O Lord, to feel this consideration in all its power and all its preciousness.

LEVITICUS XII.

There is a strong counteractive disgust associated with, or rather placed in opposition to the strongest of nature's propensities, which serves greatly to mitigate and restrain it, and which operates as an habitual check upon its outbreakings in place and time which are either not convenient or not lawful. This shame and this recoil from the loathsome accompaniments wherewith the indulgence is so closely beset, as if meant for preventions or guards against the excesses of an appetite which, for its own special object, required to be powerful, have been alleged both as indications of design in the constitution of our frame, and also as testimonies, by its great Author and Architect, to the evils of unbridled licentiousness. In as far as the ritual observances of this chapter imply a ceremonial as emblematical of moral guilt, they bespeak a nature pervaded with deep sinfulness, and serve to confirm the lesson of the Psalmist, that we are born in iniquity, and that in sin did our mothers conceive us. In as far as the purifications here prescribed imply uncleannesses—which even nature loathes and seeks for the removal of—

we doubt not that they would strengthen those antipathies of which we have already spoken as operating with a wholesome and beneficial antagonism against one of nature's most urgent inclinations.—This chapter derives a peculiar interest from a portion of New Testament history which relates to the birth of our Saviour, when Mary underwent the purifications of the law, and gave evidence to the poverty of her household by giving the humbler offering here specified in adaptation to the humbler circumstances of those in the lower walks of society. O may such sacred associations as these serve to guard and to sanctify my else impure and wayward imagination. May I shun the thought of evil, or let it be supplanted and overborne by other and better thoughts. Whatsoever things are lovely, and honourable, and of good report, may I think of these things, and not of things opposite to them, and which I ought to nauseate. May I abhor that which is evil, may I cleave with intent and holy determination to that which is good. Having received the promises of the gospel, let me cleanse myself from all filthiness of the flesh and spirit, and perfect my holiness in the fear of God May Thy Spirit help, O God, my manifold infirmities.

LEVITICUS XIII.

The physical defilement here so largely treated of has been spiritualized into that moral defilement by which our whole nature has been so deeply tainted and pervaded. Sin has been compared to a leprosy—to cleanse ourselves from which we must be diligent to be found without spot and blameless; and Christ is said to purify the Church so as that it shall be without spot, or wrinkle, or any such thing. And certain it is that there are many similarities between the natural and the spiritual disease—enough on which to found not only a plausible but an instructive analogy—as first there may be the semblance of sin without its reality; but let us do what we can to avoid the semblance—let us shun to our uttermost even the appearance of evil. But how often, alas! does the semblance turn out to be a reality either in the form of a revival of some old and virulent habit, or of a new sin in new circumstances and under new temptations? Then there is the spreading of this hateful and evil thing—so as that the whole man, his thoughts and his emotions, nay, his time and history, come to be altogether charged with it.

And besides, such is the infectiousness of its nature, that not only does it overspread all the habits and affections of the individual, but flows over upon others by contamination; and hence the necessity of secluding him for their sakes, as is done in the exercise of discipline, by which a stigma is fixed upon an offender, and he for a time is made an outcast from society.

The very description of the natural disease is loathsome and disgustful to our mere animal sensibilities. Let us think of the recoil which beings of an angelic nature must experience when their moral sensibilities are offended by the spectacle of sin. Above all, let us think of the pure and holy child Jesus, and of the infinite repugnance which in His immaculate nature He must have suffered when brought into contiguity and fellowship with the depraved children of men; and which must have formed at least one of the agonies which entered into His sore endurance. O that He, the merciful High-Priest, would minister unto our exceeding sinfulness—that He would pour upon us the washing of regeneration—that He would thoroughly cleanse, and sanctify, and restore, so as to make us meet for re-admittance into the company of the unfallen, and reinstate us as members and fellow-citizens in the household of God.

LEVITICUS XIV.

In the cleansing of the leper there were both an atonement and an anointing. The blood of the trespass-offering was put on certain parts of his body, and on the very same parts the anointing oil was put afterwards, even above the blood. And this is the blood of Christ's propitiation, first sprinkled upon our souls that we may be reconciled and have peace, and then the unction of the Holy Spirit—the anointing which remaineth—that we may be regenerated, and go forth on the way of progressive holiness. They who first trusted in Christ, after that they believed were sealed with the Holy Spirit of promise. (Eph. i. 13.)—O God, let me share in the whole of this twofold salvation; may I be saved not by water only but by water and blood—the blood to cleanse me from guilt, the living water to cleanse me from pollution. Thus may I be washed and sanctified as well as justified, in the name of the Lord Jesus, and by the Spirit of God.

But leprosy is a disease not of persons only but of things: and so inanimate matter has been made to share in the consequences of sin—a curse was laid upon the ground because of it. The elements became more intractable than before; and lovely as is the material creation, yet somehow or other has it been smitten and suffered by the inroad of moral evil into our world. And so at the time of the restoration of all things, a regenerating process will take effect on the outward universe as well as on the spirits of men. There will be a new heaven and a new earth wherein dwelleth righteousness.—O prepare me for this renovated system by the renovation of my own heart and character; make me meet for that glorious inheritance; may I be counted worthy to stand before the Son of man at His appearance and coming; may I be among the children of a blessed resurrection; and with my body discharged of all the polluting vices which now make it a vile body, but then transformed into the glorious likeness of the body of Christ, may I be transplanted into the paradise of God, and there serve Him through all eternity without frailty and without a flaw.

LEVITICUS XV.

October, 1843.

There is a strong feeling of loathsomeness called forth by these descriptions—emblematic of the abhorrence wherewith those of a pure and holy nature must look upon sin—even that sin from which we are saved not by water only but by water and blood, like as the uncleanness here had to be removed not by a washing alone, but also by a sacrifice.

There is the perfection of wisdom in all Thy ways, and more especially in the counteractive which Thou hast provided against the unruliness of human desires, by the method wherewith the allurements of passion, and the disgusts attendant on its indulgence, are so strangely and mysteriously blended. Thus it is that the fascinations of a loveliness the most exquisite and overpowering are tempered by accompaniments of a revolting character; and we may learn from these that the testimony of God's natural as well as of His revealed law is against all the excesses of licentiousness. Cleanse me, O Lord, and I shall be whiter than the snow. Create a clean heart, renew a right spirit within me.

LEVITICUS XVI.

The evangelism of this Book is now standing forth more palpably. Leviticus and the Epistle to the Hebrews both give and reflect back again their lights to each other. We have here the dread effect of approaching God's sanctuary on earth without an expiation; and so the high-priest when he did enter the holy place within the vail had to enter it with blood. And may we, O God, in all our approaches to the true sanctuary come before Thee in the name of our great Forerunner even of Him who hath entered for us—and also not without blood, even that blood which He shed, not for His own sins—as did the Jewish high-priest—but for the sins of the world. Neither let me forget, that beside the sacrifice which had to be effected in order to prepare for his ingress to the holiest of all, there had to be an investiture, and not an investiture only, but an ablution. And thus, O God, would we at all times appear before Thee clothed upon with the righteousness of Christ which we are invited to lay hold of; and more than this, cleansed from our pollutions by the washing of regeneration and renewing of the Holy Ghost. I pray for Thy sanctifying Spirit, O God. But not only do we read here of the preparations made for himself, and by which he typifies the incumbent preparation of those who under our more advanced economy are kings and priests unto God—we read also of the sacrifice that had to be made for the sins of the people; and we have a most interesting representation of the truth as it is in Jesus, both in the slain goat and in the scapegoat—the one being the type of the crucified, and the other of the risen Saviour. But ere Aaron proceeded to this part of the holy ritual, he, in effecting the sacrifice for himself, had also to burn incense within the vail that he die not; and thus, O God, in appearing before Thee, would we not only have our sins washed away by the blood of the everlasting covenant, but we would have the incense of our Saviour's merits mingled both with our prayers and our services, that they may ascend with a sweet-smelling savour before God. And as Aaron confessed the sins of the people over the head of the live-goat, so would we confess our sins in the name of Christ, now risen to that place where He lives for evermore, and through whom it is that our sins are not imputed, not made mention of, not reckoned against us—even because He took them upon Himself; and they are now as little held in remembrance as if borne away to a land that is not inhabited.

And let not, O Lord, all the safety and impunity which have thus been purchased for us—let not these discharge us from the work of repentance or from any of its befitting sensibilities. We would afflict our souls, we would mourn and be in heaviness because of our manifold iniquities. O may we henceforth put out from amongst us that hateful thing for which Christ died. Give us to rejoice with trembling—give us to aspire after the rest which remaineth, and to labour that we may enter therein. Not only was an atonement made for persons, but an atonement was made for the sanctuary in various of its parts. All had to be consecrated with blood. May all serve to enhance our sense of the holiness of God, and the augustness of that sanctuary where His honour dwelleth.

LEVITICUS XVII.

Some think that the law here given forth compelled the killing of every animal—even though for ordinary food, to take place before the door of the tabernacle; but the greater number would restrict this law only to the animals killed in sacrifice. Yet let all we do be sanctified—so that whether we eat or drink or whatsoever we do may be done to God's glory. The sacrifice behoved to be made at the appointed time and place, and not privately or at altars of their own.

How shall I know whether this eating of blood (verse 10) be a temporary or a perpetual law? I confess my difficulties in regard to this question, and that it is much aggravated by the apostolical decree in the Book of Acts, where the particular things forbidden or disallowed are not all of a ceremonial nature, one of them being distinctly an infraction of the moral law. Beside this, it is not the first time that this injunction is given; it was given to Noah, and seems to have been in force during the whole of the Patriarchal economy. What I know not, O Lord, teach Thou me. This were a good controversy for studying—were it only for the general principles of the casuistry which it must necessarily call forth. Guide me, O Lord, in the paths of wisdom and of all righteousness. Enable me rightly to divide the word of truth, that I may distinguish between the things which differ, and know how I shall betake myself to the more excellent way. It is a very striking reason given here of the prohibition to eat blood—even that it is the blood which maketh an atonement for the soul. Let me forget not the moral which lies in the ablutions that were laid on the children of Israel. There must be a washing undergone by all those who shall be admitted to God's spiritual sanctuary in the heavens. We are saved by the washing of regeneration—unless ye be washed, says our Saviour to Peter, you have no part in me.

LEVITICUS XVIII.

The appropriation of God as our God is the commencement and the ground of evangelical obedience; it forms the outset of the Decalogue in Exodus, and is also the point of departure at the beginning of this chapter—" I am the Lord your God." "Ye shall therefore keep my statutes and my judgments." O enable me to say unto God, Thou art my God. "Do this and live" seems a different proposition from—" If a man do these he shall live in them."* The one savours of the legal economy, which holds out a reward after the keeping of the commandments; the other of the gospel economy, under which we are told that not after but in the keeping of the commandments there is a great reward. Give me to experience the truth of this saying, and most of all in the pleasure and the beauties of holiness. Give me, O Lord, to win and maintain the elevation, the dignity of self-

* Yet it must not be omitted that verse 5 of this chapter is quoted by Paul in Gal. iii. 12, as illustrative of the legal economy, though to live by them, as in Rom. x. 5, seems a better English method of expressing the legal, while life in them is as accordant with the evangelical, as the declaration that to be spiritually-minded is life and peace.

command; and turn away not only my sight and eyes, but my very thoughts from vanity. Let mine be a spiritual contest for the ascendency within me of all that is pure and virtuous and holy. It is well that the testimonies of God in Scripture are so clear and loud and frequent; for in the light of natural conscience the sins of this class are not so reclaimed against as the sins of inhumanity and injustice. In defect of this let me hearken and be impressed by the reclaiming voice of God, when He tells us what it is that He holds to be an abomination. Let me flee those lusts which war against the soul; let me crucify the flesh with its affections and lusts.

LEVITICUS XIX.

The outset saying of this chapter is quoted in the New Testament, and forms a weighty and comprehensive rule, giving also the reason of the rule—that of being holy because the Lord our God is holy. Enable us, O God, to perfect our holiness both in its generality and in its details—honouring our superiors as well as parents, keeping Thy Sabbaths, refraining from all idolatry, as of wealth or fame or power—offering willingly unto the Lord, and also unto the poor, who are His peculiar care—abstaining from all falsehood and fraud—reverencing God's sacred name, and observing with considerate humanity as well as justice the convenience of our helpless dependents. Save me, O Lord, from the impatience I am too apt to feel at the infirmities of others, in the converse I hold with them; and O let me remember that the spiritually blind may be sadly stumbled, may have the greatest moral injury done to them, by the misleading example of those who have a name in the Christian world. Let me keep my judgment unwarped by all external influences, and neither let my adulation of the rich, nor my sympathy with the poor, turn me from the righteous sentence in aught that comes before me. Save me from idle or mischievous tale-bearing, and from all heart-hatred of others. Give me the courage and the honesty to rebuke what is sinful; and instead of vengeance or envy teach me what is here proved to be no new commandment—to love my neighbour as myself. And though some of the observances of this chapter have become obsolete, do Thou grave all its indelible moralities on my heart and practice—its bidden purity, its bidden sacredness, its bidden reverence for age, its bidden humanity to strangers, its bidden scrupulous and exact integrity. Let me not neglect its lessons on the way of forgiveness by an atonement, nor yet the delicacy of its recommendation to sympathy on the ground of our own felt experience as to the need of sympathy when ourselves in a like situation to those for whom our succour or our sympathy is required. There are in this chapter the beamings both of the advanced doctrine and advanced morality of the New Testament.

LEVITICUS XX.

Does not he who brings up his children so as that they value aught more than the true God—be it wealth, or fashion, or learning, or any other of the good things of this life—does not he give his seed to Moloch? does not he offer them up in sacrifice to idols? Save me from this dread and foul atrocity, O God. Give me practically to feel a love for the souls of those who are dear to me; and O let all my works, and words, and ways, prove one consistent testimony to the worth of spiritual and eternal things. Thou settest apart the children of Israel to be a people unto Thyself. Do Thou so separate and sanctify me, O God, that I may break loose from all sinful conformity to a world lying in wickedness, and be holy, even as Thou art holy. It strikingly marks how resolute a design it was in the policy of the Divine administration—that the sentence of excommunication, and even of death, by stoning or otherwise, here appended to a flagrant breach of clear and undoubted duty, should also at times have been pronounced and put into execution against the violations of what we hold to be merely ceremonials, but which served to peculiarize the Israelites, and so to fortify the distinction between them and the other nations of the earth. But most of the prohibitions of this chapter are not of a ceremonial character. When I recollect my impatience with the infirmities of my parents, into which very infirmities I myself am now falling, great is the call upon me to repent, and be humble, and pray for forgiveness. They have long been removed from me; but others are with and around me who might, not by their fault but through the sensibilities and instigations of my own corrupt nature, turn out to be provocatives to that which is evil.—It is because God had separated the Israelites from other people that (verses 24, 25) he put a difference between clean beasts and unclean, and the non-observance of this made their souls abominable.

LEVITICUS XXI.

Give me to feel, O Lord, the sacredness of the priestly and ministerial office; and if all ceremonial distinctions have been abolished, let me at least aspire to the distinction of a far higher devotedness and more thorough spirituality than are yet attained even by the more serious professors of the present day. As we are engaged in the solemn and peculiar services of the house of prayer, O let us be holy, so as to keep ourselves from all profanation. —And O let me aim at the same signalizing and peculiar sacredness as the characteristic of my family. I stand much in need of Thine inspiring guidance, O Lord, that I might walk in wisdom at home, and that my conversation may be with grace—seasoned with salt, and to the use of edifying. Let the purity of an unspotted holiness never cease to adorn my household, and may it extend beyond its limits to the whole circle of my relationship.

Let not the value manifested for externals under the old dispensation now vanish and disappear under the new, as if things outward and visible went for nothing. I fear that I have been too inattentive to dress and person, and the decencies of a fitting exterior. May all connected with the public service of God be in right keeping; and let not testimonies on this matter of the earlier legislators and prophets in the true Church be thrown away upon me.

LEVITICUS XXII.

What a solemn importance is here ascribed to the way in which we approach unto God—whether by the acts of worship or by the services of obedience. In worship no man cometh (with acceptance) unto the Father but by the Son; and our services, also termed spiritual sacrifices, are acceptable to God only by Jesus Christ. O give me heart and energy for these services; and let not a freezing orthodoxy lay its narcotic or paralyzing influences on the work of faith and labour of love—only let it be labour in the Lord. Let all we do be brought as an offering to the door of the true tabernacle in the heavens, and be presented there in the name of Him—the incense of whose merits alone can so perfume our feeble and broken and imperfect doings, as that they shall arise in grateful remembrance and with a sweet-smelling savour before the throne of God.—And O that all my sacrifices, whether in the way of effort or liberality, were unto God only, and not unto idols. Let me lay myself out for His glory and the advancement of His own kingdom, both in my own heart and in others also—and not for my own fame or fortune, or any of those frail and earthly goods which perish with the using, else I sacrifice unto devils, and not unto God.

Blessed be Thy name, O God, that we now live under a brighter and better dispensation; and where all are invited to be the members of a holy priesthood. He who, to try the Syrophenician woman, said, "It is not meet to cast the children's meat unto dogs," admitted her to the full privilege because great was her faith. And all now are the children of Abraham—nay, joint-heirs with Christ, who truly believe in His name. O that our faith were as large as the promises of the gospel, and then should we experience the fulfilment of the saying, Open thy mouth wide and I shall fill it.

Let me honour the Lord, not with the first only but with the best of my substance; and O let it be not grudgingly, but of hearty good-will. God loveth a cheerful giver; and therefore save me from the reluctances of selfish feeling. Enable me to dismiss and get above these;

and withal save me from ostentation, lest instead of a sacrifice to God mine be a wretched sacrifice to my own fellow-mortals, and thus I incur the guilt of a most worthless and degrading idolatry.

There was an urgent moral principle which lay at the bottom, as it were, or constituted the proper motive force of all these ceremonial observances. They were commanded by God, and it is the clear and imperative duty of every creature to obey God. For each and all of them there could be alleged this consideration—*Therefore* shall ye keep my commandments and do them; I am the Lord. Whatever others do, ye shall be hallowed and separated from all others by doing all that I have enjoined upon you; and whatsoever I will you ought to do in grateful return for all my goodness, whether, as in the old dispensation, it be that I brought you out of the land of Egypt; or as in the new, that I brought you out of darkness into the marvellous light of the gospel—and in order, under both economies, that I might be your God and reconciled Father. Teach me then, O Lord, to know all Thy will concerning me, and both incline and enable me for the doing of it.

LEVITICUS XXIII.

That there were festal as well as fast-days tells us of gladness being a part and an accompaniment of the true religion. May I know what it is to rejoice in the Lord, and may I richly experience of this joy that it is my strength. O that I could attain to this blessed spiritual temperament: it is a fruit of the Spirit, and like all His other fruits much to be prayed for, but in conjunction with an earnest attention to the words to which we are required to hearken diligently, and in the believing of which we shall obtain peace and joy to our souls. In the faith of Christ may we enjoy a perpetual sunshine of the soul—a festival both of gladdening hope, and of all good and gracious affections.

Let me know what it is to honour the Lord with the first-fruits of all my substance. Thou hast hitherto dealt liberally with me: Give me, O Lord, the blessing of a grateful heart, manifesting itself both in the desires and the deeds of liberality, for the good more especially of human souls, and the extension of Thy kingdom throughout our country and the world. The poor in this world's comforts have also been committed and commended to our care by the common Father of us all. To do them good, and with them also to communicate let us forget not, for with such sacrifices God is well-pleased. O my God, forgive and reform my deficiencies of service and aid, more particularly to strangers, whom I am too apt to rid myself of in too summary a way, without that patience of inquiry or that complaisance and civility of manner which are so incumbent on the professors of the blessed gospel.

O may my Sabbaths be both holy and happy Sabbaths, true spiritual festivals, and foretastes of a blissful eternity.

My God, let my faith in the atonement, and my full purpose of new obedience, though to the affliction and utter extinction of the old man, let these two, my faith and my repentance, go inseparably hand in hand.

Let me know what it is to rejoice, but to rejoice with trembling. Let me know what it is to follow up my acceptance of Christ's sacrifice by such spiritual sacrifices as are acceptable to God through Him. O that I combined with the security of the Christian faith the diligence of the Christian practice—serving God without the fear of terror, yet serving Him with fear and trembling notwithstanding—not the fear of Him as an enemy, but the fear of myself, lest in my own waywardness and weakness I should ever let go my hold of Him as my strengthener and my friend.

LEVITICUS XXIV.
December, 1848.

There is here provision made for light without the vail, and also for an offering to be placed there before the Lord. Blessed be Thy name, O God, that even in this lower world Thou hast not left Thyself without a witness, but given us to see, though as through a glass darkly. Open our eyes that we may behold all which is competent and necessary for us to know of those revealed things that belong to us and to our children. Let us make the most of our present opportunities; and though ours be still a light shining in a dark place, may we be guided thereby to that place of everlasting blessedness and glory where we shall know even as we are known. And teach us not only what we should know here, but what we should do here, or what the offerings of gratitude and service which are acceptable in Thy sight. Loose our bonds, O God, that we may break forth on the services of the new obedience of the gospel with the love and the liberty of Thine own children; and may all our services be rendered in the name of our great High-Priest, that they may prove acceptable to God through Jesus Christ our Lord.

Though free from cursing and blasphemy in words—yet in our hearts there may be despite and enmity. Let us sanctify the Lord God in our hearts, and cherish to the uttermost of our feeble and limited powers a high and holy reverence for the infinite majesty and august sacredness of the Godhead.

The sentence pronounced on blasphemy is in itself a strong demonstration of God's intolerance for the great master sin of enmity to God—it being in truth the most monstrous violence on all the principles of what is right and good which the creature can fall into.

And He makes provision not only against all violence done to Him, but if done to man whom He made in His own image—ordaining life for life in the case of man, property for property in the case of beasts. And the law comprehended strangers as well as Israelites—as if in recognition after all of man as man, and of the one blood of which He made all the nations that be on the face of the earth.

Let us here observe how pointedly and rigorously the sentence against blasphemy is followed up by the execution of it. Let us not deceive ourselves, O Lord, or think lightly of Thy judgments. It seems as if it were to guard against this that all the congregation were required not only to acquiesce in the ordained punishment, but to be themselves the inflictors of it.

LEVITICUS XXV.

How stupendous a miracle the Sabbatical year was; and yet had there been faith enough among the people for the observation of it, there would have been no lack of faithfulness on the part of God. They should not have been suffered to want, though the land had been permitted to rest every seventh year. O may our faith be commensurate to Thy promises. Let the institution of the jubilee teach us to honour all men. It was fitted to prevent those accumulating masses of wretchedness made up of such ever increasing families as are presented in our day and country, who have no resources for the present, and no prospect of restoration or recovery for the future. Prosper, O God, our measures for the moral and also for the economic elevation of the common people; may they be framed in wisdom, may they be executed with zeal and vigour. And O that our fear of God were such as to make us fearful of injuring those who are around us: and let me not think that oppression is confined to palpable acts. I may oppress and overbear, specially those of my own household, by impetuous and intolerant speeches on the side of my own will and my own way. Forgive, O Lord, these hasty and hitherto ungovernable effusions, and while enabled to rule well in my own house, let mine be a mild and paternal sway: and let this fatherly character be felt also in the relation which I have to servants and dependents. There are times when the people whom I employ provoke me by their unfaithfulness, whether as to the time or quality of their work. Let me be merciful and courteous and observant of that property which is ascribed to God—even His being slow to anger. What I do either in generosity or indulgence to those beneath me, let it be done, O God, unto Thee, and not merely under the impulse of a liberal or compassionate nature. Let the provision made for the natural freedom of the children of Israel—let it teach all who share of the spiritual, to stand fast in the liberty wherewith Christ hath made us free. In spiritual things let us call no man master. Save me, O God, from the influence of human authority in matters of religion; and let not an intolerant systematic theology warp my views of Scripture, or deafen the impression whether upon my mind or heart of any of its sayings. Let me derive all my Christianity, whether its *credenda* or its *agenda*, direct from the fountain-head of inspiration; nor suffer the portly volumes of the erudite masters in our science, nor even the confessions and formularies of any of our Churches, to stand between me and the Word of God.

LEVITICUS XXVI.

Heavenly Father, give me a part in the blessings of Thy covenant; and to ensure these, let not Thy soul abhor me, but do Thou have respect unto me, and be my God, walking and dwelling in me, and giving me power to walk as one of Thine own children. Save me from all heart-idolatry; and teach me both to reverence and to keep—not Thy Sabbaths alone but all Thy statutes. O that my conception were more lofty and powerful, and so as more adequately to realize and vividly apprehend the glories of Thy character. Let me seek first Thy kingdom and Thy righteousness, and then will all other things be added. The temporal blessings which were placed before the eyes of the children of Israel as the foreground promises of the older dispensation, have the place of supplements and additions assigned to them in our present and more advanced economy. Under that gospel which has brought life and immortality to light, grant, O Lord, that we may look beyond the things which are seen and temporal to the things which are unseen and eternal. Save us from all entanglements and from all degrading anxieties as to the things of this life; and make us to go upright, after having translated us into the glorious liberty of Thine own children. And let me learn in the curses of this chapter God's hatred of sin and His severity against it. Let me not forget that still He is a God of judgment; and that tribulation, and anguish, and wrath are in reserve for all who do evil. Save me with compassion, O Lord, and, if this will not do, save me with fear—that knowing the terrors of the Lord, and the terrors of the law, I may be persuaded to embrace the gospel. Let me not walk contrary to God, lest God should walk contrary to me. But even here and in the midst of all those tremendous judgments, there do break forth the lovingkindness and tender mercy of God. Let me never relinquish my confidence in these, manifested as they now are by the gift of God's own Son—after which will He not freely give us all things? But let me confess my sins over the head of the great sacrifice, and be humbled because of them: and let me not only confess but forsake, lest God should destroy me utterly. And God will not forget His covenant; He will not nullify His blessed gospel; He will fulfil to the last iota every word and declaration that He has uttered there. And calling as I now do on the name of the Lord His Son, as both the Lord my righteousness and the Lord my strength, let me look confidently up both for the mercy that pardons and the grace that sanctifies. On the whole what a striking display in this chapter both of the goodness and severity of God!

LEVITICUS XXVII.

When a thing was devoted to the Lord, either it, or an equivalent for it, was the Lord's. If it was a beast which might be offered in sacrifice, then the sacrifice thereof, I presume, was made; if not, it was put to holy uses, or redeemed. And so a house or a field was put to holy uses, say for the maintenance or accommodation of the priests, provided that they were not redeemed. I can imagine, too, that if a person was thus devoted and not redeemed he behoved to be set apart for something sacred and peculiar all his days. But whether we can speak intelligently or not of these details, we may at least feel and cherish the obligation of cleaving to the Lord fully, and of being wholly His. O my God, form me to Thyself that I may show forth Thy praise. May I be one of Thine own peculiar people—a devoted thing, not mine own, but His who bought me. Surely I am His property by whom it is that I am redeemed; and let me therefore glorify the Lord with my soul and spirit and body, which are the Lord's. And O do Thou pour forth a spirit of religious liberality on the members of our Free Church. Put into the hearts of her friends all wise and generous devices, whether in making over houses, or lands, or endowments of any sort for her more full equipment. Enlarge her borders, O Lord, without attenuating her provision and her means in that part of the land which is already possessed. O that we had more the feeling that neither ourselves nor ours were our own, and that we acted more as the stewards of Thy bounty and Thy beneficence. Teach us to open our hands liberally; and while on the one hand ministers are willing to undergo privations, on the other may the hearts and hands of the people be alike open to them. Whatever we do, or whatever we give, may it be done or given as unto the Lord. Enlarge our desires; and let all the straitenings of selfishness and avarice be done away.

NUMBERS.

Numbers i.—Thou art the Lord of Hosts, and at the same time the author not of confusion but of order. Number, and arrangement, and division, and the relation of part to part, as well as of each section to the whole, and all rightly marshalled under their respective governments and sub-governments—these are all exemplified in this chapter, and the wisdom which can devise and preside over these is mainly wanted in the administration of our Church's affairs. Supply that which is lacking, O God. Give, and give liberally. We ask this of Thee, and would ask it in faith; and meanwhile let me dismiss all vain and harassing anxieties, but be still in the thought that Thou reignest. And guide us to the right men who might take charge of their several departments—men qualified for their tasks, and having right tasks put into their hands. But, my God, while the constant tendency of my thoughts leads me to write thus, let me be calm—nay, charitable as well as fixed and determined, on the side of what is best for the interests of Thy Church upon earth. Save me from the paltry ambition of seeking to signalize myself, and alike save me from the fear of man, which is a snare. Thus, Lord, may we be guided in right order through this dreary wilderness, and be at length admitted to the full enjoyment of peace and love in our eternal home. Enable us, O Lord, rightly to discriminate between things sacred and things secular, between that which pertains to the spiritual service and that which pertains to the outward business of the house of God; and send forth efficient labourers to our harvest—men who are Levites indeed—men of faith and of prayer, whom others may support while they are engaged in the affairs of their higher ministry. O let them not be secularized; and grant, Almighty Father, that ours may be a better marshalled, and withal more harmonious body of office-bearers than heretofore. May there be more of peace and unity in the midst of us; and let each know how to keep by their own department, and to mind the affairs of their own allotted business, without interference or conflict with others. Look down with pity on the chaotic and unruly state of matters in which we are now involved; and enable me to set my face as a flint when violence would offer to threaten or overbear us into what is wrong. May it ever be our aim to do according to all that Thou hast commanded. I close the year in heaviness because of the Church's internal troubles. If spared, O God, to another year, may I witness a better spirit throughout the whole agency of its councils and committees, and a wiser system of operations.

NUMBERS II.

January, 1844.

He who is the author not of confusion but of order, both in the Church and in the world, here prescribes for the tribes of Israel the order of their encampment and also the order of their march. He does not confide this matter to the discretion and skill even of Moses, but Himself gives immediate directions upon it; and so all the more emphatically attests the importance of all having severally their right places and right movements assigned to them. We cannot look for the guidance of a direct inspiration in the regulation of our Church and the distribution of its various offices, but let us at least pray for the wisdom by which our counsellors might be qualified to devise in the most effectual manner for the prosperity of our Institute, whether for its own internal government or as having yet to make progress towards a safe and happy settlement of itself in society. And let us never forget the central and presiding superiority which the spiritual should have over the secular in the management of its concerns—bestowing our first attention on the services of the sanctuary, without despising or neglecting the outward business of the house of God. May the tried and glaring insufficiency of the ecclesiastics for this latter department lead us to seek about, and may we be directed to find men for deacons of such practical talent as might defend us from the evils of want, and enable us to uphold the fabric of our Zion against both the danger and the desertion to which she is exposed, whether from a careless or a hostile world. Then may we force the exclamation from our adversaries to which Balaam gave utterance when surveying the hosts of God's chosen people from one of the hill-tops of Moab —" How goodly are thy tents, O Jacob, and thy tabernacles, O Israel!" O give me wisdom and perseverance, and withal charity and temper, for helping onward so blissful a consummation. I am sadly deficient in that patience and that meekness which are fruits of the Spirit of God. Perfect, O Lord, that which is lacking in me; and give me the requisite grace and wisdom in every time of need.

NUMBERS III.

Let me not walk, O Lord, in the light of the sparks of

my own kindling. Give me to serve Thee with a pure heart fervently; but O may it be a fervency kindled by Thine own Spirit, and not be a strange fire lighted up or fed from any other sources than from the sanctuary of God. And O let me keep more closely to the Bible than heretofore; let not the heat of controversy raise up in me any false or exaggerated view so as to go beyond or beside the Scripture in anything; neither let me suffer myself to be overborne by the intolerance of controversialists, nor give way to the authority of great names; but, calling no man Master, let me defer to my own Lord, even Christ, and take my lesson from Him as laid before me in that word which shall never pass away.

What a goodly arrangement of offices in the Jewish Church; and how clearly is the distinction kept up between priests and Levites—between the higher and lower services, between the inner and outer things of the house of God. Thou knowest, O God, the sad difficulties and trials which now lie upon me because of the confusion that obtains among the offices and office-bearers of our Church. The various classes of Levites had their allotted departments, and they kept by them; but, alas! with us all is complicated and inextricable.—Give me wisdom, give me temper, O Lord. I have great infirmities: O may Thy Spirit help them. Enable me to see and impressively to say what ought to be done, but without violation of the law of Christ. O that I could testify with calmness; and enable me, O God, to say all I ought, but to say it in the right spirit and right manner, and if it be Thy blessed will, with beneficial effect.

These Levites were set apart from the rest of the children of Israel, and devoted to the Lord; and let me feel the sacredness of the employment when engaged even with the outward and subordinate things of His house. And O that in the management of these things I could be more godlike—that is, slow to anger, seeking not mine own things but those of my heavenly Master, less fretful at the perversities of others, while resolute to do all to point them out and to restrain them—but ever remembering that the wrath of man worketh not the righteousness of God. I pray both for Thy preventing and Thy directing grace, O God. Be with me in the hour of conflict; put the right words into my mouth—the answer of the lips, as well as the preparations of the heart. And O give me the comfort at length of seeing that all goes on smoothly and prosperously in the conduct of our Church's affairs, that when turned into an effectual instrument for the moral and spiritual regeneration of our people, I may be enabled to say—Lord, now lettest Thou Thy servant depart in peace.

NUMBERS IV.

The general principle that there shall be distinct classes of office-bearers in the Church, and that each class shall have its own distinct task, its own appropriate burden laid upon it, has been abundantly sanctioned and exemplified under the Jewish economy. Lord, Thou hast heard my prayer of Sabbath last; and let me here record my grateful sense of the guidance I obtained in converse with my brethren, and the peaceful—let me hope prosperous—result of it. There is still much before me; and in the very work of assigning their right place and performances to our various orders of functionaries we stand pre-eminently in need of wisdom and direction from on high, so as at once to preserve the sacredness of the ministerial character, and to secure the needful services of those who have stations in the Church, yet are not in the ministry. Enlighten me, O God, in the respective duties of the elders and deacons, so as that between the one and the other there might be a well-ordered economy; and more especially so as that the two shall be kept apart, to the effect that what is spiritual may not be desecrated by an unseemly admixture with it of the Church's secularities.

What a sensible demonstration is here given of the Divine holiness, in that the Kohathites, on pain of death, were not to intrude, not even to look on the holy things. Their office was to bear them, but without prying into them; and thus may we be satisfied with the plain doctrines and bidden duties of the gospel, though not able to scan its mysteries—nay, discharged from the presumptuous attempt to be wise above what is written.

The services of the Levites are variously apportioned; but beside the lesson of a right distribution of employment, let me repeat the lesson given to us by the immense number in the Jewish dispensation of ecclesiastics and ecclesiastical men. What a reproach to us for the small number both of our clergy and other office-bearers! This is a good argument for a large rather than a small number both of elders and deacons. Assist me, O God, in making a good selection of men for their respective offices; and more especially do I pray for a right and prosperous regimen for the Free Church of Morningside.

NUMBERS V.

Let all I read of the ceremonial uncleanness of the

Mosaic law and of the methods for its removal, lead more and more to the maintenance of a strict and guarded purity. All must be holy in the midst whereof the Lord dwells; and so these bodies of ours, which, if we be indeed the children of light, are the temples of the Holy Ghost. And accordingly how dread the sanction of the Christian and New Testament law—that if any man defile the temple of God him will God destroy. And the taint impressed on others by the foulness of our example and our doings is also another and truly a most emphatic consideration. Let me think of the denunciation that even the meek and gentle Saviour utters against such as offend one of these little ones, dwellers in the camp along with us—and for their sake let not a look or word escape from us, nor a salutation be given which can lead in the remotest degree to a wayward licentiousness either in our own minds or in those of others.

Let me act at all times not as the proprietor of what men call my own but as the steward thereof. So far from encroaching on the rights of others, or withholding that from the use and service of the Church which I ought to give, let me strive whether to win or to economize that I may have to give more abundantly for the supply whether of the temporal or the spiritual wants of men.

Some men's sins are open beforehand, going before to judgment, and some they follow after. In these days of miracle and of a sensible theocracy, the former was more frequently realized than now; and let me never forget that, whether it be fulfilled upon myself or not, the latter alternative is at least awaiting me—for all sin unrepented and unturned from. O that I had a more constant and practical respect to the day of judgment which is coming.

Thou, O God, knowest all my infirmities and all my errors. Give me from this time forward the victory over them. Let not sin have dominion over me. May all the guilt of the past be washed out in the blood of the Lamb; but may I henceforward enter on a holy warfare against all that polluteth, and never, never again return to foolishness.

NUMBERS VI.

February, 1844.

Let me in the spiritual sense of the term be a Nazarene indeed—breaking off from all forbidden conformity with this world, and devoted unto God. Let me never forget that we are told of the all which is in the world that it is not of the Father but of the world—and that if we love the world the love of the Father is not in us. And though not now the subject of those literal observances which were peculiar to the older dispensation—though no longer absolutely prohibited from the use of wine—yet let me always recollect and consider how hurtful all the indulgences of the table are to a vigorous spirituality, and to the mind's most healthful and productive exercises. And another injunction laid upon the Nazarene was, that he should not mourn for the dead as other men. The analogous thing to this in the spiritual Nazarene is that the mourning for the actual, nay even the likely approaching death from sickness of those who are the nearest and dearest to him, should be modified and restrained by the faith of immortality.—My God, there is one threatening appearance wherewith now Thou hast been pleased to exercise me. O may I know what it is to sit loose to this vain and evil world; familiarize me with death, and give me a realizing and quickening sense of that fulness of joy which there is in heaven. In this believing contemplation may my affections be weaned from earth and I become a true Nazarene—a Nazarene in heart. The death of dear Mrs. Parker is well fitted to enforce this lesson upon me, as breaking one tie to earth and adding another tie to heaven. But let no purposes, however strong, and no performances, however high, exonerate me from a felt dependence on the great sacrifice that has been made for the sins of the world. It is only at the altar of Christ's atonement that the spirituality of the soul can be sustained and kept alive.

And the heart which renounces the world, and can give up at the will and bidding of our Heavenly Father its dearest and best loved objects, is not therefore desolate. What a rich compensation for all which we thus resign when filled with the fulness of the Godhead—when we have the blessing and protection of Him who is on high —the light of His countenance, with all the grace and mercy and peace of the apostolic benediction to the Christian Churches, and in almost perfect identity with which is the benediction of Moses to the children of Israel. May Thy name, O God, be upon me; may Thy Spirit be in me—that henceforward I may renounce the devil, and the world, and the flesh, and live as a pilgrim on my way to the Jerusalem that is above.

NUMBERS VII.

The tabernacle was set up and anointed and sanctified, and so were all its vessels, ere that the princes offered their offerings. It seems to have been the offerings of these on so many successive days that constituted the dedication of the tabernacle. Who can doubt that the progress of the work helped on these offerings, and that the very circumstance of its being brought thus far stimulated the liberality of the princes? May we not look for something analogous in the Free Church of Scotland? Our present offerings are very inadequate to our impending wants; but will not this liberality and these wants keep pace with each other? We settle ministers before that the local associations have done what they ought and what they easily might for their maintenance; but then we are told that after the services of the gospel have been fully set agoing, these will become much more productive. Grant that it may be so; and, O God, do Thou not only disarm the hostility of the upper classes, but do Thou convert it into an exuberant and sincere benevolence for the great object of a universal Christian education in our land.

The offerings of the princes consisted partly of what was consumed for a present service, and partly of implements which might have lasted for centuries, and been currently used all the while in future services. And in like manner we distinguish between the maintenance of our Church on the one hand, and its fabric and furniture on the other. May a liberality be awakened adequate to a full provision for both. The silver and gold are the Lord's, and He can call them forth at His own good pleasure.

When I read of these various offerings I cannot but feel how much I stand in need of that which is typified and set forth in those of them that are expiatory—even the sin-offerings and the burnt-offerings. My God, may the blood of Christ cleanse me from all sin; and rather than count this blood an unholy thing, may I be saved from my hateful lusts, even though it should be by the spirit of judgment and burning, and so be saved even as by fire.

Thus and thus alone can I expect that God will speak peace to me from the mercy-seat. Pardon, Heavenly Father, and purify. Lift on me the light of Thy reconciled countenance. Heal my backslidings, and purge me wholly, O God. I desire to lie low in the dust under a sense of my manifold infirmities. Keep me, O Lord, from the great transgression. Keep me from all presumptuous sin; and let me not, by my example or my doings, incur the enormous guilt of offending any of Thine own little ones.

NUMBERS VIII.

May Thy word, O God, be a light unto my feet and a lamp unto my paths. Give me to be renewed in knowledge, and save me from those passions which war against the soul, and which, as being works of the flesh, are works of darkness. O that I walked as do the children of the light and of the day.

We are saved not by water only, but by water and blood. It did not complete the purification or cleansing of the Levites that they underwent ablution—an atonement also behoved to be made for them. And so too we must be justified as well as sanctified, have a part and interest in the great expiation, as well as in the washing of regeneration and renewing of the Holy Ghost. O visit me with a deep and humbling sense of my need of both; and enable me to give up myself as a devoted thing, a living sacrifice unto God. Give me not up, O Lord, to vile affections; enable me to crucify the flesh with its affections and lusts. Blot out my transgressions, and give me this best evidence that my sins are forgiven, even that I am delivered from the power of them, and have been made dead unto the world and alive unto God. O Lord, in thine own good time give me my dismission from the outward service of the Church; and enable me to give up a concluding season of retirement to the great work of a preparation for heaven. O Lord, let not my hope of this glorious inheritance be darkened or overthrown by any deed of impurity; may I remember and act on the apostolical test for the strength and reality of this hope, even that I may purify myself as God is pure. What an humbling thought for me, that perhaps I have been implicated with the manifold urgencies of a service mainly external and economical, because I could not be trusted with myself, and because the attention, now forcibly taken up with the calls of outward duty, would have spontaneously gone forth on corrupt and tempting objects, to the power of which, with a fuller command of my time, and freer opportunities, I might have given way. O may this consideration drive me both to watchfulness and prayer. Put truth, O God, into my inward parts, and let me not swerve from Christian integrity of purpose, lest I should lapse at length into the melancholy and irrecoverable state of those who, after they have received the knowledge of the truth, sin wilfully, and have their hearts fully set in them to do that which is evil.

NUMBERS IX.

And let me ever observe the Christian Passover both sacramentally and spiritually. Christ is my Passover, and in Him do I desire to abide constantly. He who eateth His flesh and drinketh His blood shall never die.

Let me feed upon Him by faith. Let the blood of His atonement be sprinkled upon me, that my grievous and multiplied transgressions may be passed by. And let me not forget the unleavened bread and the bitter herbs wherewith the Jewish Passover was followed up, that I may purge out from my heart the old leaven of malice and wickedness, and renouncing all the hurtful and forbidden sweets of natural indulgence, may present my body to God a living sacrifice. He who followeth after Christ must deny himself daily; and it is by repeated acts of mortification that our repentance is perfected.

Let nothing separate me from Christ, nor any other disqualification than unrenounced and unrepented sin keep me back from His holy sacrament. And more especially let me be reconciled to all ere I approach His altar. Let me carry no uncharitableness or grudge against my neighbour there; but in faith unfeigned, and love unfeigned, let mine be a pure offering. So would I compass Thine altar, O Lord, with a heart in which there was no guile, and hands washed in innocency.

I pray, O God, for the perpetual guidance of Thy word and providence. May I never want the indications of Thy will concerning me, nor be at a loss for the path whether of duty or of wisdom, even as if I heard at all times a voice behind me saying—This is the way, walk thou in it. Thus may I be directed aright through the intricacies of this dark and difficult wilderness, and be made to know when I should move and when I should be still. The indices which have been held out from time to time for the guidance of our Church have been abundantly clear and satisfying hitherto. O enable me on every question of her future movements to counsel as I ought and to do as I ought. And steer me right, also, among the perplexities of my more private and personal affairs. I would trust in God, and lean not on my own understanding. In all my ways I would acknowledge Thee, that Thou mayest direct my path. Do Thou establish all the thoughts and purposes of my heart; and looking upward to Thee, may I be made to discern the signals of Thy will, whether in the openings of Thy providence, or the testimonies of Thy word.

NUMBERS X.

March, 1844.

In the Bible great stress is laid on the conjunct and the social. It is a department of duty of which I have never adequately felt the obligation or the importance—and that though expressly enjoined to "forsake not the assembling of ourselves together." The church-bell performs the same function for this especial object that the trumpets did for other and more general purposes. Let me cultivate social religion more; let me know what it is to have fellowship one with another. In church let me advert to the community of feeling which there is among the pious and good of a congregation; and let it be such a sympathy as both to excite a livelier devotion in my own heart, and to give scope and exercise for the second as well as the first law.

And thus let all the movements of the Church—of the general ecclesiastical body—be both done in order and according to our conscientious understanding of God's will. Restrain us from either doing or going towards any consummation of any sort if Thy presence and blessing go not along with us. Let us not at the same time neglect the adminicles of human help and human counsel. Let us avail ourselves of the peculiar knowledge and fitnesses of all who are friendly, that we may have the benefit of such services as each can best render. And let me in particular feel the duty of self-sacrifices for the general advantage, nor decline, because of my preferences for home and quietness, any contribution or effort to which the Lord obviously calls me. But on this I would seek direction from on high. Is it better that I should still be distracted from the business of my class by the public business of the Church, or that I should give myself wholly for the direct religious benefit of my students and of the public for whom I write, to the work of spiritual and literary preparation? Forgive, O Lord, all my excursions into other paths than such as have been sanctioned or indicated by Thee. Let me share in all the blessings of a Church regulated as Thou wouldst have it, and acting as Thou wouldst have it. Discomfit all our enemies, O God, and deliver us from the hostility of those who bear a hatred to the cause of truth and righteousness. But let Thy countenance rest upon us for good; and do Thou so prosper our own Israel—do Thou so guide and nourish and strengthen the Free Church of Scotland, that it may prove the dispenser in Thy hand of blessings of the highest order to many thousands of our families.

NUMBERS XI.

Save me, O Lord, from inordinate affection of all sorts. Having food and raiment let me therewith be content—even such food and such other accommodations as Thou seest to be necessary and meet for me. Save me, O God, from the thraldom of such lusting or such appetency as that into which the people fell; and save me also from that impatience under the burden of those public duties which Thy providence hath assigned to me, whereunto Moses had well-nigh given way. However desirous of retirement, however much in want of leisure and quiet for the perfecting of my work as a professor, let me nevertheless seek for Thy counsel and be guided thereby—taking the right directions from Thy word, and putting the right interpretation on the events and leadings of Thy providence. More especially, O Lord, give me to bear with the perversities of men. O that I had the spirit of Him who did not strive, neither did He cry. Let me know what it is to be gentle unto all men—in meekness instructing them that oppose themselves. And, O God, send labourers to our harvest. Raise up men, not merely that I might be relieved, but that Thy work might be done. Provide, O Lord, a sufficient agency, and give wisdom and vigour and withal the most perfect disinterestedness and devotion to our great cause—even that of planting an adequate gospel ministry in Scotland. And in a work so sacred, so purely and highly patriotic, let all wretched jealousies be unknown. Let us rejoice in every accession and from whatever quarter, to this great service. Put an end to all such aims as are merely personal; and on the altar of our country's good, and most of all for the sake of a larger salvation of human souls, let us make the surrender of our every bye-interest or affection, and of all honour to ourselves. Send the spirit of Christian usefulness in all strength and purity forth among the friends of our Free Church; and instead of each man seeking his own things, let all seek the things of the Lord Jesus, and the advancement of His blessed kingdom in our land. From this chapter let me learn not to set my desires on any mere earthly or created good. God can bless me without it; or if I will make it the object of my overweening fondness, He while granting me my heart's wish can turn it into a curse, and thus fill me with the bitter fruit of my own ways. Let me then submit in all things to the wise and righteous disposals of my Father in heaven. To Him would I commit all my interests and all my cares. Do, O God, what Thou seest to be best for me; and let me give myself up with entire and unreserved confidence to Him who afflicts not willingly, and has promised that as the day comes the provision of all that is needful for the body will come along with it.

NUMBERS XII.

We are forbidden to speak evil of dignities. Let me repress my aptitude to depreciate public men when I condemn public measures. "Thou shalt not revile the ruler of thy people." Let not this be forgotten even in the midst of all those provocations and injuries which our Church has gotten at their hands: "Vengeance is mine, I will repay, saith the Lord."—O that I had more of the meekness of the Jewish legislator. How much he had to bear, and how well he bore it—even though he did give way at times to the complaints of impatience. I pray for a like grace under my humbler trials—that I may know both how to suffer and how to act under all the perversities to which I may be exposed. What a state of hazard and exposure was that of Moses in the wilderness—with the caprices and resentments of a wayward multitude ever breaking forth against him, and all that was hostile and envious rankling in the hearts even of his own near relatives. But how promptly and seasonably did God at all times interpose in his behalf, and prove Himself to be indeed a very present help in trouble. Verily it needed all these special demonstrations to maintain both the public authority and personal safety of this illustrious servant of God; but he earned them by the fidelity wherewith he acquitted himself of the charge that had been given to him: he was faithful in all God's house. And every parent has at least a household made over to his care. And besides there are other managements which might fall into one's hands, whether providentially or by obvious destination. Enable me, O God, to be faithful to my Church and to my College and to my children. As I am drawing nearer to eternity, may its great realities take a firmer and more practical hold upon me. On this day let me resolve to be more free and faithful in my dealing with human souls. Open my mouth henceforward; and let me no longer be ashamed of Thy testimony. Let me cast away these subtle dislikes and delicacies in the way of a full converse upon spiritual things. Guide and strengthen me, O God, in this high walk of duty and of difficulty, and suffer me not to be tried therein beyond what I am able to bear; but with the trial provide a way to escape, that I may be able to bear it. I am not worthy, O God, even of Thy faintest and most distant manifestations; but let me never cease to pray for what is so precious. Give me at all times to have a clear understanding and make a right application of Thy word; and if it be Thy blessed will, favour me with such other and higher views of Thyself as might serve for cordials, and foretastes, and encouragements in this the land of my pilgrimage. Thou chastenest whom Thou lovest, and Thou chastenest in measure, O God. Be very favourable, O God, to me and mine; and though Thou hast been pleased to hold out some threatening appearances in the health of some who are near and dear to me, O while solemnized and admonished by these, if it meet with the designs of Thy holy providence, let them speedily pass away.

NUMBERS XIII.

The all-foreseeing God, and who could have ensured the victory of His people without any preparation on their part, yet sent so many of them on a tour of observation that they might have a certain knowledge of the enemy's country before that they invaded it. The end was frustrated for the time, yet doubtless with the prescience and predetermination of God, and yet as doubtlessly by the fault of man. For the accomplishment of any given object, even though God should desire it as well as we, it is not for us to fail in the requisite means or the required obedience; for God's own purposes must be carried into effect by God's own processes; and should it be, as it often is, by a process of human agency that He would compass His designs, the condemnation is ours if we withhold this, even though for the making of it good there should be the fearful exposure of our own persons or the busiest exercise of all our faculties and powers. —Let me walk in Thy prescribed path, O Lord, if I want to reach Thy promised landing-place. Even now let my conversation be in heaven—that blessed land of promise, and abounding in good things, with fulness of joys and pleasures for evermore—that even from my distant glimpses of it on earth I may know what I am to do and how I am to acquit myself. And let not my heart fail because of the obstacles which lie in the way of my settlement therein. Thou, O Lord, alone art mighty in the pulling down of strongholds, even the strongholds of my own corruption and inveterate carnality. May they, by the aids of Thine all-conquering and all-subduing Spirit, may they be levelled to the ground, so that with a stronger than him who is god of this world now in possession of my heart, a universal holiness might henceforth take full occupancy and have the entire rule over me. And let me not be discouraged by the difficulties or terrors of the way to the spiritual Canaan—the inheritance that is above, but commit my soul unto Thee that Thou mayest keep that which is so committed, and I may be at length presented faultless before the presence of Thy glory with exceeding joy. Let me be of good courage, and pray in all faith and firm assurance for that blessed Spirit whose first-fruits may be to me the foretastes of my coming felicity and glory. Dissipate, O Lord, the enchantments of sense, that neither its fears nor its flatteries might cause me to falter from the onward course which leadeth to immortality and honour.

NUMBERS XIV.

Let me fear lest I should fall short of the heavenly Canaan after the same example of unbelief. Let no terrors stop me on the way of clear and commanded duty, nor restrain me from an upright testimony in the hearing of others, even though it should call forth their hostility and violence to the uttermost. See how promptly the Lord interposed to save His faithful servants Caleb and Joshua from the fury of the people; and He is still a very present help in the time of trouble. Let me not be afraid then, but go simply and evenly forward in what is right, yet without uncharitableness and without either contempt of others or resentment towards them.—What a lesson and example are here held forth in the conduct of prayer—Moses expostulating, I had almost said redarguing, with God, and so as seemingly to avert Him from His first purposes. The processes of the Divinity are at all times immutably right—as in this instance the displeasure and the audible proposition made to Moses, and the forbearance grounded on a regard to the glory of His name. But the very train whether of sentiment or proceeding which becomes the Deity should be harmonized with by man, whether by prayer beforehand or by submissive resignation afterward—so as to hasten onward the resemblance of the creature to the Creator. This intromission, in fact, of requests and supplications on the part of man, is so interwoven with the administration of God as to supply some of its essential steps; and thus we are allowed to plead the faithfulness of God, and to intreat that, for His own glory—the glory of His grace and truth, He would pass by our transgressions; and, in short, to urge the very considerations which, if righteous as felt and expressed by us, are also righteous as carried into effect by the sovereign Disposer of all things. And let us ever remember, both of His declarations and attributes, that so far from superseding prayer they form the groundwork of prayer—the plea on which to prefer its suit with confidence before God.—To the apprehension of man Thou seemest slack or slow concerning Thy promises, yet lengthened out as the changeful periods of the Jewish history have been, the time is yet coming when all the earth shall not only see but shall be filled with the glory of the Lord.

What views are here presented of the Divine policy! The promise in all its fulness will at last be accomplished, not on the generation of transgressors, but on their children. The chastisement of offenders must be carried into effect, and relatively to them the promise is not made good; so that all which they personally are made to feel is not the accomplishment but the breach of it.

The spies, as the foremost in this rebellion, are singled out to view as having died of the plague, while Caleb and Joshua were preserved as manifestations of the faithfulness of God.

Here follows an instructive history—the embodiment of a great principle. Had they gone forth against their enemies when the commandment of God was with them, they would have prevailed; but going out as they did, not only without but against that commandment, they were scattered, though by a small part or handful of their adversaries. Let me encounter temptation or danger when in the way of duty; but when the movement is not thus sanctioned let me consult the mediocrity of my powers, and learn that my strength lies in standing still.

NUMBERS XV.

April, 1844.

Many of these offerings which were a sweet savour unto the Lord were partly eaten both by the priests and the offerers—at once acceptable to God, and grateful both in the way of sustenance and enjoyment to man. Christians are said to be priests unto God, and they are called upon to offer spiritual sacrifices—and if like their great Head, it will be their meat and their drink to do God's will. O that we had the comfort of knowing that our labour in the Lord is not in vain, but is indeed well-pleasing to Him. Orthodoxy has so overdriven her demonstrations as to give forth the impression that nothing we can do is acceptable to God; and while it has been abundantly strenuous in urging the all-momentous truth that through Christ alone we can find acceptance for our persons, it has not been so earnest or so decided in its avowals that through the same channel we find acceptance for our services also—thus divorcing Christianity from human life, instead of leavening with her own essential spirit all the business and all the doings of men. Enable me, O God, to make effectual head against this misleading tendency; and let me do so in the exercise of that very faith which many would place in antithesis to works; but in the full exercise of which we should have comfort and confidence in the performance of them. Let even the very meat and drink-offerings of the law help me to this better habit and understanding of the matter. Give me to rejoice in the sense of a mutual satisfaction between me and God in the affairs of my personal and practical Christianity—He, on the one hand, well-pleased by my keeping of the commandments; and I, on the other, having the grateful experience that in the keeping of these commandments there is a very great reward. Our dread of the legal has been scattered away by the delight we ought to feel in the evangelical obedience. Who can understand his errors? Cleanse Thou me, O Lord, from secret faults:

keep me back also from presumptuous sins. Let them not have dominion over me, and may I be innocent of every great transgression.

And let Thy Sabbaths be my delight and my reverence. Save me from the guilt of profaning them. Give me a clear conscience on the subject of all its particular observances; and while aware that the law under which I now live is the glorious law of liberty, let not this liberty be an occasion for the flesh, nor let me indulge in any freedoms to which I am not prompted by the love of God and man, or which I cannot venture upon in faith.

May Thy Spirit bring all things needful to my remembrance, and so as to suit and to provide for every occasion of my history. Let me never forget Thy precepts. Guide me to such expedients and such memorials as might instrumentally be useful for this end. Save me from the counsel of my own heart and my own eyes. Recall me at all times to a sense of Thy presence and Thy will; and let me ever be arrested in my headlong tendencies to that which is evil by the prompt consideration—Shall I do this wickedness, or this folly, and sin against God?

NUMBERS XVI.

This is a remarkable passage in the history of God's people—from Egypt to Canaan. It is true that Moses was ordained of God in a more express and extraordinary manner than the existent rulers of this world; and it implied, therefore, all the greater hardihood in Korah and his fellow-mutineers to revile and rebel against him as they did. Still we are told that the powers which *be* are ordained of God, and also, that we ought not to speak evil of dignities—so that the transaction recorded here is not without admonition to us on whom the latter ends of the world have come. And it is an admonition of which we stand greatly in need in the peculiar circumstances of our own time. It is true that we have not deferred to the authority of rulers in a matter where God has not only not conferred it, but has expressly denied them any authority; but let us have a care lest the spirit of contempt or resistance in other things should insensibly take hold of us. As we have imitated apostles in withholding from Cæsar the things which are not his, let us imitate them also in giving with all conscientiousness and promptitude all that really belongs to him ; and O may loyalty, and respect to civil superiors, and the love of peace and order, and, in short, all the virtues of sacred and sober conversation ever characterize and adorn the ministers and members of the Free Church of Scotland.—And let us not only not be partakers with the turbulent and disaffected in their evil deeds, but let us avoid all fellowship with them—keeping aloof from them as well as from their practices, lest we share in the consequences of that vengeful reaction, which, though coming immediately from the governments of this world, has been instituted by God Himself for the maintenance of society. And let us observe that in this notable history a demonstration is given not only against all inroads on the civil, but against all inroads also on the ecclesiastical authority. Give us always to have respect unto them both; and give us also to understand and have most sacred respect to the line of demarcation between them.

What terrible demonstrations had God to make both of His presence and His power to keep these people right.

O let us not be stout-hearted, but fear. When the judgments of God are abroad in the world, or in any way made manifest to us, let us learn righteousness; and let the threatening appearance which overhangs the health of my own family lead me to walk softly and to fear. May we be taught by the ordinary providences of our day as well as by the extraordinary events and miracles of the days that are past. May we have grace to serve Thee acceptably with reverence and godly fear, and grace both so to teach and so to enable us as that we shall deny all ungodliness and worldly lusts, and live soberly and righteously and godly in the world.

NUMBERS XVII.

There is a beautiful analogy between the miracles recorded in this chapter, and the miracles of grace. He who can make a piece of inert wood effloresce into fruit and blossom, can also cause these dead and barren souls of ours to yield the fruits of righteousness—and that under the same external treatment with others immediately around us who remain unconverted. There may be hundreds of formal worshippers along with us who present themselves before the Lord in the house of His own ordinances; but it is only such as He discriminates who become trees of righteousness and the planting of the Lord that He might be glorified. It is by a power not our own that we are made kings and priests unto God; and they are only His priests, His selected ones, whom He has evoked from a world lying in wickedness, that He thus signalizes. And yet there is an instrumentality concerned in this operation, even as there was a process to the event of the rod's blossoming. Moses was commanded to lay up the rods before the Lord in the tabernacle of witness. And we too are commanded to assemble ourselves together in that place of sacredness where testimony is given to the blessed truths and promises of the gospel. But, alas! on how many do these fall unproductively and without effect —although we must put ourselves in the way of them ere we can look for that transforming influence by which the dead or the corrupt is turned into a good tree, yielding the good and pleasant fruits of righteousness. Let us therefore not forsake the attending upon ordinances, nor let us cease from devout and depending prayer. Neither let us forget that though the buds and blossoms and almonds which grew on the rod of Aaron did not germinate from seeds planted there by human hands—the fruits of righteousness in regenerated man, those good things which come out of the heart made good and new by the Spirit of God, do arise from seeds which have been previously deposited there, and that these seeds are the truths of God's holy word, whether as scattered abroad from the pulpit on the hearers of a congregation, or as gathered by each man for himself from his carefully perused and pondered Bible. In this great concern let us be fellow-workers with God. Let the word of Christ be made to dwell in us richly, though this we cannot expect without our own readings and our own hearings, and let us look up for light from above, that it might be made to dwell in us in all wisdom. It is for us to deposit the seed, but the dew of heaven alone can fertilize it. It is for us to give earnest heed unto the word; but that its entrance may give us light, the day must dawn and the day-star arise in our hearts.

NUMBERS XVIII.

The priests had their peculiar and sacred territory on which the Levites dare not enter on the pain of death. And the Levites also had theirs on which the children of Israel dare not enter but on the same penalty. There is a Church order too amongst us of the present day, though its several provinces and their lines of demarcation are not so authoritative, or guarded by such awful sanctions as under the Mosaic economy. All true Christians are now kings and priests unto God; yet this character does not lighten or extenuate, but rather enhances their every obligation, if not to the ceremonial proprieties of other times, at least to all the weightier matters of God's eternal and unchangeable law. Of how much sorer punishment shall we be judged worthy if we violate these? The family of Aaron were to bear the iniquity of the sanctuary and the priesthood, or were made responsible for these. Let a sense of our priesthood lay upon us all the deeper feeling of our solemn and high responsibility, that we may count not the blood of the covenant an unholy thing—that we may be holy even as Christ is holy. And let it not be the tendency of these reflections to obliterate that more strict and special sense of duty which attaches to those who hold offices of influence and distinction in the Church. There is an incumbent gravity and devotedness which lie upon ministers because of their being ministers; and so also of all the inferior functionaries—the Levites of our Christian economy. Any transgression of these official proprieties ranks in a more emphatic manner among the sins of our holy things; and grant, O Lord, in behalf of our Free Church, that all its elders and deacons, as well as ministers, may know their respective callings, and so acquit themselves as to uphold the character of our Institute, and cause it to be a light in the world, blameless and without rebuke in the midst of a perverse and crooked generation. Thou, O Lord, didst provide liberally for the ecclesiastical labourers of other days. Do Thou pour a right spirit of liberality on our Church, and that extending both to givers and receivers—so that while there shall be the utmost generosity on the one side, there may also be the utmost disinterestedness and moderation on the other. Thus may the two ends be made to meet; and thus may the outward business of God's house be made to prosper in the midst of us. But O, above all, let the spirit of grace and supplication be poured forth upon us. Let ours be mainly and pre-eminently a spiritual Church; and while it is well that we see to her towers and her bulwarks, her abundant provision, and goodly proportions, let it ever be her most distinguishing, as it would be her highest characteristic, that she was all glorious within.

NUMBERS XIX.

May, 1844.

We are saved not by water only but by water and blood. The water which sprinkled the children of Israel from their uncleanness was pervaded by the ashes of a heifer which underwent a death which bears in all its circumstances the character of a sacrifice. The sins of the people were laid upon her—insomuch that none could handle any relic or part of her dead body without being contaminated by the now sinful subject wherewith they came into contact, and so contracting a ceremonial defilement thereby. Thus the priest who took of her blood, and he that burnt her, and he that gathered the ashes, were all made unclean for a time; and yet there is a mystery in this—that these same ashes when they entered into the water of separation had the virtue of ceremonially purifying the unclean on which it was sprinkled, and at the same time of defiling those who sprinkled or touched the water of separation—for by so doing they became unclean. It is thus that we are checked in the prosecution of these analogies, and are often when spiritualizing the Mosaic rites all the safer the more general we are. Let us therefore keep by the generality of our being saved by water and blood, reminding us both of our atonement and sanctification—while no one can miss the application to our beloved Saviour of the red heifer being without spot and having no blemish—even to Him whose precious blood was as that of a lamb without blemish and without spot. Neither can we miss the application which the apostle made of it—" If the ashes of an heifer sprinkling the unclean sanctifieth to the purifying of the flesh, how much more shall the blood of Christ who offered Himself without spot to God, purge our consciences from dead works to serve the living God!" Give me a part, O God, in this blood of sprinkling—even the sprinkling of the blood of Jesus Christ. And O may it evidence its twofold property of being at once an atoning and a sanctifying operation—or, not only for cleansing me from my guilt, but for the washing of regeneration and renewing of the Holy Ghost.

Neither let me overlook the special application of this purifying water, this water of separation which separates, and sets apart, and sanctifies—do not let me forget its special application by means of a bunch of hyssop to each unclean subject that was purified thereby. If the bunch of hyssop denote faith, it must be an applying and an appropriating faith, which it ever will be if indeed a real and an intelligent faith. O Heavenly Father, work in me this faith with power. Enable me to say with the apostle —that Christ loved me and gave Himself for me; and may I henceforth give myself up unto Him. Let Him be peculiarly mine, and let me be one of His peculiar people— He mine, and I His. And O enable me through Thine all-purifying Spirit to realize this indispensable test of my indeed being one of Christ's own—even that I have crucified the flesh with its affections and lusts.

NUMBERS XX.

These frequent relapses of the Israelites into unbelief and murmuring—and that on the back of the most signal manifestations, and with the daily miracle of manna from heaven before their eyes, are apt to excite our wonder, as if they were anomalous to human nature, or at least such as we ourselves should not have fallen into. But let us only recollect our own cleaving and constant ungodliness, the dominion over us of things seen and present, the outbreakings of wilfulness and passion by which we are so often hurried into transgressions of the Divine law—and these, too, alternating at short intervals with a solemn and affecting sense of Divine things, awakened, if not by outward yet by inward manifestations, and we shall find much in ourselves that is quite in counterpart and keeping with the perversities of that stiff-necked and rebellious generation—much in our own deceitful hearts experimentally at one with the saying of our Saviour—

"That if we believe not the Scriptures, neither should we believe though one rose from the dead." Let us therefore not be high-minded but fear, lest we too fall after the same example of unbelief, and so fall short of the heavenly Canaan. And he that believeth shall not make haste. Let ours be a calm and confident faith, and free of that vitiating flaw which the great Discerner of hearts detected and discriminated, upon this memorable occasion, in the faith of Moses.

Let me take a lesson of rebuke to myself from the example of the inhospitable Edomites. How quickly do I resent, and how often do I repel the intrusion of others upon my own convenience! Give me, O Lord, the charity which endureth. Give me the wisdom from above that is easy to be entreated, and perfect within me all the graces and virtues of Thy second law.

Give me, O Lord, a serious and practical and effective sense of my coming death. How often, but for Thy forbearance and long-suffering, might I for this one and that other specific transgression have been cut off from the land of the living. But Thou hast spared me hitherto; and O let me not treasure up wrath against the day of wrath, but throughout the remainder of my pilgrimage walk in studious observance of the whole will of God. Let it henceforth be my care to lay up treasure in heaven by the perfecting of my holiness. May I consider my latter end, and so familiarize myself with the thought of it, as not to harden, but habitually to keep alive in my heart the sense of that great and eternal interest which lies on the other side of the grave, and to which I may now direct all my hopes and all my preparations.

NUMBERS XXI.

Give me strength, O Lord, to war against those worst of enemies—even the lusts that war against the soul—and let it be my vow to crucify and to destroy them. O that I had a sufficient strength of desire for this, and a sufficient strength of faith to prompt my supplications and gain acceptance for these! there would be no want of grace from on high to ensure my success and perfect that which concerns me.

What a precious passage is the next in order—quoted by our Saviour Himself in illustration of the most precious of doctrines—even that whosoever looketh believingly unto Him shall be saved. There is no soundness in me; but I am full of wounds and bruises and putrifying sores. Let me therefore fix my eye upon Him who was lifted up upon the cross for my offences, and experience the healing virtue of this great sacrifice. It has been well said, that the children of Israel did not look at their wounds but at the serpent. They felt their wounds, they knew of them, and this made them turn their eyes towards the proposed remedy. Neither did they seek if they had faith in their hearts ere they lifted their eyes; it was enough that they had as much faith as led them to make the movement; enough that it actuated them directly whether it was seen by them reflexly or not. And so let me but look unto Jesus—let me fasten my regards upon Him as an object of contemplation without and above me. Let me take my comfort from Him at first hand by believing, and not wait till I can get it at second hand from the consciousness of believing. O reveal Christ more and more to my soul. May He be all my desire and all my salvation.

And, O Christ, Thou Prince and Thou Saviour, to whom I look for deliverance from guilt, but look also for something more—even the washing of regeneration, do Thou give me of that water whereof Thou spakest to the woman of Samaria, that there may be struck out in my sanctified and renewed heart a well of water springing up into life everlasting.

In the days of old Thou deliveredst Thy people from all their foes when they trusted in Thee. Thou knowest, O God, my conflicts and difficulties and fears. To Thee I would flee for refuge, and implore Thy blessed guidance throughout the remainder of my work in connexion with the Free Church of Scotland. Enable me to clear my way aright among the opposing elements, and to trace a path in skilfulness and with safety through the labyrinth of misconceptions which are on every side of me.—And let me never forget that however essential her outward business might be, her strength lies in her spirituality. O give grace as well as guidance to all her ministers; and grant that I may be enabled to cast my care and my confidence on the God who careth for me, and so in patience to possess my soul.

But let me not forget that God's assistance was suspended on a condition—even that the children of Israel should destroy all and spare none whom it was His holy will to exterminate. O my God, let the old man be destroyed within me, and no quarter be given to the evil affections of my evil and accursed nature.

NUMBERS XXII.

The character of Balaam is a most profitable study, if

studied with application. There was obviously a strong and secret desire in his mind for the riches and honours of this world; and yet contemporaneously and along with this a sense of obligation to compliance with the will of God. In the struggle between them we are presented with a most instructive moral history, on the contemplation of which we may well cry out—Who can understand his errors? cleanse Thou me from secret faults. At one time the good influence prevailed, and he gave way to the impression of it; at another, the bad influence, especially when strengthened in any way by fresh appliances—as when Balak sent a second time to him with larger offers of preferment than before. Even then there was a conflict of forces; and it had been well if what he said in verse 18 under the operation of the right force had been simply and decisively adhered to; so as that he had not under the operation of the wrong force made the proposal of verse 19—hopeful of a chance that the Lord might still let him go, might still sanction his compliance with the proposals. And the Lord was pleased to try him, gave him up so far to his own heart's wishes, yet left him not without a sense of duty and without a prescribed duty which he was still to observe. The Discerner of the thoughts of the inner man saw the latent progress of the iniquity within him, and His anger was kindled. The strength of this iniquity was manifested by the prompt acquiescence of Balaam in the proposal of Balak's messengers, by his eagerness to get forward, by the resentment he felt at the obstacle which his poor ass interposed in the way of his progress. He yielded to the good influence when the angel of the Lord stood evidently before him; and under a conviction of his having sinned offered to return. But God further tried him; and he gladly availed himself of the Divine permission to accompany the princes of Balak. He who seeth not as man seeth espied the whole progress of the temptation and its effects; and there seems a very close accordancy between the successive steps of Balaam's descent toward the consummation of his wickedness and the ordinary stages which are traversed by backsliders along the path of human degeneracy. A lingering sense of duty, but ever becoming feebler in its operation, keeps its ground for a time, but offers a weaker and weaker resistance onward to the ultimate and irrecoverable. Along this fatal career there occurs a presumptuous exposure to temptation, with perhaps the honest resolution—or at least the semblance of it—to withstand its allurements. But God resisteth the proud and giveth grace unto the humble; and so Balaam is suffered to expose himself more and more since he would have it so, till it ends in the melancholy catastrophe of his ruined and undone soul. Lord, search me and try me. Put truth into my inward parts. Save me from the instability of double-mindedness; and give me that singleness of eye which sees clearly the path in which I ought to go; and which, intent on doing Thy will, receives strength for the performance of it.

NUMBERS XXIII.

June, 1844.

Balaam is now in the very thick of those temptations which he himself courted, and which he did wrong in adventuring himself upon, even though God permitted him; and in so doing, gave him up to his own heart's lust—a regimen this, a moral regimen, of which we have many traces and examples both in experience and in Scripture. And his peradventures that God might allow him to say what was pleasing to Balak, all indicate a bias towards the earthly king, and against that first manifestation which the King in the heavens made in favour of the children of Israel, by which Balaam should have abidden, and upon which he should peremptorily have rejected all the future overtures of Balak. His hope—rather his wish—that God would yet change His already expressed determination in favour of the Israelites, evinces a doubt in his mind of the Divine truth and Divine unchangeableness, and so a want of faith as well as a want of right inclination on the side of God and of His declared will. In short, there was enough in the waverings of Balaam's mental history to furnish the great Discerner of all our thoughts and intents with matter for that condemnation which he incurred, and that consequent punishment which befell him afterwards. Save me, O Lord, from double-mindedness. Deliver me from the operation of those subtle and perhaps unconscious tendencies which may well be denominated secret faults. Put truth in my inward parts; and give me henceforth to prosecute an unfaltering and single-hearted course in the way everlasting, so that when the time of my exit from this world comes, I may die the death of the righteous, and my latter end may be like his. This, too, was Balaam's aspiration, and at the time of its utterance it may have been an honest one; but he was unstable—and I pray for that fixity of principle which alone cometh from the unction that remaineth. Balaam ought to have acted from the first on the principle that God is not a man, or could lie, and that what He had said He would do; nor was it enough that he should have spoken this sentiment, or even felt it, under the influence of a recent communication, so as to counteract for a time the preferences and partialities of his own corrupt nature. It was obviously a matter of regret and disappointment to him that God had blest Israel, and he could not reverse it. He prophesies by constraint—the involuntary organ of benedictions on the people of God, which his own heart did not go along with. He spake as he was moved, while self was on the side of Balak and the Moabites.—And so he lent himself willingly to the fresh and further attempts which were proposed to him for a counter deliverance to any which he had yet given. Let me not walk in fleshly wisdom, O Lord, but in simplicity and godly sincerity let me have my conversation in the world.

NUMBERS XXIV.

It is obvious that Balaam's desire was set on the reversal which he failed in accomplishing. He had gone to seek for enchantments, but now desisted from them; and spake as he was moved by the Spirit of God. There is something highly picturesque in the whole representation; and the effect is in the highest degree poetical both of the scenery and the sayings. The first of the benedictions in this chapter relates to Israel as in his first possession of the land of Canaan, when the blessings of wealth and prosperity and victory are assigned to him. Balaam in his reply to Balak says, that he cannot go beyond the commandment of the Lord to do good or bad of his own mind. It was an external constraint which made him bless Israel, for his own mind was against it. In the second benediction of this chapter, he takes a further look into futurity; and the range of anticipation now before him gives a sublimity to the whole of this last utterance—more especially when he speaks of the Star out of Jacob and the Sceptre out of Israel. O may Christ the Star give light and guidance to my soul; and may He also the Sceptre have the entire rule over me. We deem the latter part of this prophecy to be yet unfulfilled, and that it will at length be cleared up by events connected with the second restoration of Israel to their own land. The ships that come from the coast of Shittim savour strongly of Europe, which Chittim is; and it does hold out the anticipation of a general break-up in our quarter of the globe, by which all the pride and power of mighty Europe shall be brought to an end. Then will the image of Nebuchadnezzar—the ten toes of which shadow forth the present kingdoms of Europe—give way before the little stone which is to become a great mountain, and to fill the whole earth. When this happens and the Jews become paramount in Syria, it is not unlikely that these predictions of Balaam relative to the various peoples in that country will be made intelligible by their accomplishment. When Thy judgments come, O Lord, may we learn righteousness. May we even now look for the coming of Christ. May we watch and be in readiness—prepared for the whole of Thy will. May our Church prove faithful in that day. May she be a powerful instrument in Thy hand for gathering in the elect of God; and meanwhile, Almighty Father, do Thou bless the measures which are now devised or devising for the Christianization of our own people. O strengthen and direct me. Be my counsellor, O God. Encourage and fortify and guide me; and O come forth with Thy Holy Spirit on the families through which we move, that a way may be opened up for us, and that the gospel of Jesus Christ may be admitted willingly into their houses and their hearts; and thus might many be led to embrace the truth, and to escape the day of Thine awful visitation.

NUMBERS XXV.

How closely allied in the practice of ancient nations were the two vices of licentiousness and idolatry; and they are often spoken of convertibly in Scripture—insomuch that the one is frequently set forth by imagery taken from the other. The lust of the flesh is opposite to the love of the Father; and there cannot be imagined a passion which more concentrates one's thoughts and regards upon the creature to the exclusion of the Creator—setting our affection on that which is beneath, and so in proportion to its intensity and force withdrawing it from the things which are above.—My God, not only do Thou rebuke all incipient tendencies towards this evil and accursed sin, but give me a juster and quicker moral sense of its enormity. My mind is not sufficiently cast in the mould of the Celestial Ethics, and like men of the world I have a far more indignant feeling of the odiousness of deceit than of impurity. This is a department of duty in which my sentiments need to be reformed. To be like unto God, which I must be if created anew after His image in righteousness and true holiness—then I must hate that which He hateth, must recoil even in the antipathies of the inner man from that which His soul abhorreth. Repair then, O God, this defect, this mutilation, far yet from being fully accomplished; and give me that purity of heart without which I cannot see God. Let these instances of the Divine anger, of hot displeasure from the upper sanctuary, help to rectify the sad deformities and distempers of my ethical constitution.

What I want Phinehas had in an uncommon degree; and I may learn what to me is a most necessary lesson from the recital of his doing. His zeal against the libertinism of the people was zeal for the Lord of Hosts; and let me hence gather how much it is that the abhorrence of this evil thing is identified with true godliness. What a high testimony it drew forth from Him in whose light I desire clearly to see light—and more especially that light which might enable me to see things as they are, or to see them as God seeth them; and then should I have a just moral estimate, a right knowledge both of the good and the evil. This forbidden and unlawful indulgence inflicted a sore deterioration on the children of Israel. The wiles of the Midianites vexed and vilified them; and let me be aware and on the watch against those lusts which war against the soul. They have a most beguiling influence—and to these perhaps more than to any other would we look for the exemplification of that property which is spoken of in Scripture under the expression of the *deceitfulness* of sin. Save me, O Lord, from the wiles of the adversary—for we war not only against flesh and blood, but against spiritual wickedness in high places.

NUMBERS XXVI.

The surveys with the view of ascertaining the numbers and strength whether of a nation or of a Church, are useful for the regulation and government of both. Let me study to do aright by such general computations as these, and this without passing unnoticed the most striking or important peculiarities that may happen to come under observation—as in the remark here made of Dathan, and the judgment which he and others incurred by their rebellion against Moses. They are held forth as a sign—and thus it is that even in otherwise the dullest catalogues there are often intermingled very interesting and instructive notices. It is well too that we have the sanction and example of Scripture for their way of methodizing and dividing the subject of management—as in the classifying the children of Israel according to their tribes and families. There is another judicial infliction referred to here in the death of Er and Onan.

We find that an equal respect is—speaking generally or in most things—held throughout Scripture to both sexes. In Christ Jesus there is neither male nor female; and it is a noble and high achievement when all the inferior distinctions of our common humanity are merged in the absorbing consideration that every son and daughter of Adam is possessed of an imperishable soul, and that all are one in Christ Jesus.

The Lord is the disposer of all things. There is no mere chance or contingency in the world. Though the lot was the proximate determiner, yet did God really and absolutely determine for the tribes of Israel as for all men the boundaries of their habitations. And what they got at the first, though it might seem in the chapter of accidents, yet if occupied for a certain time, becomes theirs by a possessory right, the legitimacy of which is felt and acknowledged by all men.

The judicial infliction of Nadab and Abihu is also recurred to in this place. O God, may we offer Thee not what is ours but what is Thine own. May our prayers and our praises, and all our affections towards Thee, be the genuine products of Thy Spirit in our hearts, called forth by fire from the sanctuary, and not by the mere ardour of our own natural temperaments.

The chapter concludes with a still more general judgment than any which had been noticed in it before. God will surely execute His threatenings on the children of iniquity. Let us stand in awe and sin not—and count it a fearful thing to fall into the hands of the living God. Out of Christ He is a consuming fire; and let us have a care lest by our unbelief we fall short of the heavenly Canaan which awaits those only who flee to Him for refuge and for salvation.

NUMBERS XXVII.

Zelophehad died in his own sin: he shared in the general sinfulness, and so shared in the general mortality. Sin brought death into the world—and Christ came to destroy death by making an end of sin. When the time of my departure comes, let me not die in sin but sleep in Jesus—that mine may be the inheritance in heaven which fadeth not away, because an heir of God and joint-heir with Christ. Give me, O God, to set my affections on the things which are above, so that I might sit loose to all the pleasures and possessions of this world.

Surely it is high time that I now look onward to the coming eternity, and take a steadfast view of the heavenly Canaan, that my conversation might be there, and my treasure there, and my heart there. Soon now shall I be gathered unto my people, even as many of my brothers and sisters have been before me. Yet where is the intent prospect or busy and earnest preparation for that which awaits me! Give me, O Lord, to be more familiarized with death, to dwell upon it more in thought, to consider well my latter end—that I might take a firm hold of everlasting life, even in the act of fleeing from the coming wrath, and fleeing for refuge to the hope set before me in the gospel. And let me not only take but keep this hold—holding fast my confidence and the rejoicing of my hope firm unto the end. But he who hath this hope in him purifieth himself even as Christ is pure. O may the God of the spirits of all flesh fit and prepare my spirit for this high destination. That I might be qualified for dwelling in the place of unspotted holiness, may I give all diligence to be found of God without spot and blameless in the day of reckoning—that so I might make my calling and election sure, and have an entrance ministered unto me abundantly into the everlasting kingdom of my Lord and Saviour Jesus Christ. O that it could be said of me as of Joshua—a man in whom is the Spirit; and that under the instigation of this Spirit I might be ever asking counsel of the Lord after the judgment and direction of His holy word. Then under the guidance of this light unto my feet and this lamp unto my path, I shall be led in the way that I should go, that narrow way which leadeth unto life. And I pray not for myself alone being made wise unto salvation; but O may the Free Church of Scotland ever have the benefit of counsel and direction from on high. May this large and increasing Congregation never stand in want of competent and qualified leaders to guide her through all her difficulties; and not by carnal but spiritual weapons to prevail over all the might and all the machinations of them who are opposed to her. Let them not be as sheep having no shepherd; but may they who bear the rule over her be abundantly endowed both with affection and intelligence for their high charge.

NUMBERS XXVIII.

Burntisland, July, 1844.

This daily presentation of the typical should surely suggest to us the duty of a daily remembrance on our part of the real sacrifice. The sacrifices of the law were offered year by year and day by day continually; but now that the Mosaic economy has passed away and these sacrifices are no longer repeated, there ought at least to be a constant repetition of those mental acts in which we recognise the Saviour and do homage to the sufficiency of His atonement, by placing at all times our full and confident reliance thereupon. O may a believing sense of Him be ever present both at morning and evening prayers —nay, may it enlighten my path and give a tenor of cheerfulness to my thoughts all the day long. Thus let me joy in the Lord alway, and let this joy be my strength, and enhanced every Sabbath morn, as I think of the resurrection of my once crucified but now exalted High-Priest.

And there are seasons more peculiarly set apart to sacredness, even by the practice of our own Church, and which are signalized above an ordinary Sabbath. There are communion Sabbaths on which the utterances of a believing heart should ascend to God with all the acceptance of a sweet-smelling savour.—O for a closer and more constant fellowship with Him through Jesus Christ, with the mention of whose name He is at all times well-pleased. O that I knew more what it was to joy in God through Him by whom I have received the atonement, and that through Him my God would rejoice over me to bless me and to do me good.

And enable me, O Lord, to present my body as a living sacrifice. May all that is sinful be so crucified that the body of sin might be as effectually destroyed as is the body of a slain animal when offered up as a burnt-offering. For let me not forget that beside the objective sacrifice by Christ to which I must look as the ground of my reconciliation with God, there is a subjective sacrifice in myself by which I must deny all worldly lusts; and with the self-mortification of the Israelites when they ate unleavened bread, I must purge out the leaven of all malice and wickedness and carnality from this my corrupt and tainted nature, and learn to live soberly and righteously and godly in this present evil world. And O that I could possess my soul not in patience only, but in positive and high enjoyment, when separated by circumstances from the busy interest of any servile and outward work; or when, without aught of express and formal occupation, I could be solaced abundantly by meditation upon God, by direct spiritual converse with my Father who is in heaven. O be not to me a weariness, or as a wilderness, or as a land that is not inhabited. May I know what it is to delight myself in God—and that whether in solitude, or amid the social exercises of the family, or the public convocation. May I so delight myself in God that He may give me the desires of my heart; and let those desires be ever towards the advancement of His kingdom, both in my own soul and in the world at large—the good of the immortal souls of my fellow-men.

May I learn to honour the Lord by my substance, and from the first-fruits of all my increase. Save me from sinful parsimony; give me to devise liberal things; teach me with free-heartedness and free-handedness to cast my bread upon the waters. Prepare me for such sacrifices as might be required for the localization of the West Port of Edinburgh; and O fulfil all that is right and holy in my wishes concerning it. Pour down such a blessing on the enterprise that there might be no room to receive it. Bring forth my judgment as the noon-day; and O may the power of Christianity be rendered manifest by many being led to find the kingdom of God, and all other things, whether pertaining to life or to godliness, being added thereunto.

NUMBERS XXIX.

Though we should not see the reason or the principle of every mandate that cometh from above when viewed merely in itself, and apart from the authority which enjoins it, yet there is enough of reason and of principle to secure the observance of it in the sacred consideration that—Thus saith the Lord. And even in this chapter there do occur expressions full of meaning and application, and which are altogether savoury to the evangelical taste, such as—"a sin-offering to make an atonement," "a sweet savour, a sacrifice unto the Lord," "a holy convocation"—all imparting a relish even to the records of that older economy which has now gone, because of its prefigurations and analogies to that gracious economy under which we now sit, and under which the method of reconciliation is more clearly pointed out, and the way of acceptable worship to the God whom we had offended. O let us not forget that to the faith of the gospel we must add the repentance of the gospel, and afflict our souls by the mortification of the evil desires of an evil and accursed nature. Let us remember that to the great sacrifice offered once for all by our risen High-Priest we must add these spiritual sacrifices which are acceptable to God by Jesus Christ our Lord. To the burnt-offering of self-denial we must add the peace-offerings and meat-offerings of Christian liberality—mindful to do good and to communicate, for with such services God is well-pleased. And neither let us forsake the assembling of ourselves together. Bless, O God, our religious convocations; and O may the fruit of them be strict conformity to Thy will in all things. May the members of our Free Church be signalized by their adherence to the duties both of the first and second table of the Law, so as both to be acceptable to God and approved of men.

NUMBERS XXX.

A vow is to a promise what an oath is to an assertion: it is a promise made to God, and not to be broken, save with the qualifications made in this chapter. It binds his soul with a bond, and he must do according to all that proceedeth out of his mouth. O my God, wash away the enormous and—save by the blood of Thy Son—the otherwise inexpiable guilt of violated vows. I would wash out all my sins in the blood of the Lamb. Increase my faith in the great propitiation; and as the unfailing consequent of this, strengthen me for the fulfilment of all my vows. And let the faith extend to my acts as well as to my person; or in other words, let me believe of my doings that they are acceptable, as well as that I myself am acceptable to God. O that I had the comfort of knowing that my labour in the Lord is well-pleasing and not in vain; and then indeed mine would be a new obedience. Deliver me, O God, from all the freezing imaginations both of legalism and of the orthodoxy that has become morbid and ultra-sensitive. Give me to proceed confidently and cheerfully and fruitfully in Thy service. I seek not to be released from the bonds of any rightful or moral obligation, but from those bonds, whether of conscious guilt or strong natural corruption, which fetter me down to the inaction of a cold and leaden despair. In this sense, O God, do Thou loose my bonds, that henceforth I may say with the Psalmist —" Truly I am Thy servant; I am Thy servant: I will offer to Thee the sacrifice of thanksgiving, and call upon the name of the Lord. I will pay my vows unto the Lord now in the presence of all His people." (Psalm cxvi. 16-18.) O my God, do prepare me for entering with Thee into a solemn and ever-binding covenant. Let me strike a league of reconciliation; and forbid that I should count the blood of this covenant an unholy thing. Do Thou, O God, make this covenant with me. Put Thy law into my heart, and write it in my mind; and henceforth may I walk before Thee as my God, myself being one of Thy people, and so abounding in all those fruits of righteousness which are by Jesus Christ to the praise and the glory of God. But O let me never lose sight of this precious article in

Thy covenant, with my eye constantly upon which there would be a perpetual sunshine in my soul—even that my sins and iniquities Thou wilt remember no more. Let me hold fast this confidence and the rejoicing of my hope even unto the end.

NUMBERS XXXI.

The objects of the enjoined vengeance were the seducers of Israel; and hence the unrelenting order from heaven that the women should not be saved alive.—O that I felt the indignation and took the revenge I ought on all those affections which war against the soul. Let me crucify and resolutely kill those enemies of that holiness without which I cannot see God. On this matter let there be no tampering and no vacillation. Give me to reflect on what Balaam suffered because he thus tampered, under the temptations of ambition and avarice, and what I too shall suffer if I tamper under the temptations of licentiousness. Let me not be deceived, then, or hearken to the sophistry of my own evil desires, and fall because walking in the counsel of my own heart. Let mine be a war of extermination both against lust and against the deceitfulness of lust. Enable me to make clear and conclusive work of it; and rather than enter on the path of destruction, let me be in readiness to cut off a right hand or pluck out a right eye.

May I know what it is to honour the Lord with my substance, and with the first-fruits of all my increase; and let a larger portion go to sacred uses, because of the abundance and the peace that hitherto He has permitted me to enjoy. And O God, lead me to manage aright the obstacles and difficulties which lie in the way of my devising liberal things and carrying them into effect; and give me the wisdom to devise rightly as well as the will to dispense liberally. Let me never forget that the labourer, and more especially the ecclesiastical labourer, is worthy of his hire.

And O that I had the heart to give voluntarily and overflowingly, as well as the conscientious principle which would lead me to give up to the point of strict obligation. Let me think of the sad deficiencies that obtain in our day, and how much is to be done ere the requisite apparatus can be raised, or the requisite means be provided, for the Christianizing and the educating of our wofully neglected population. Let me dispense with all that is superfluous and might be spared for the advancement of so great and good a cause. O pour forth the spirit of generosity on my coadjutors and their friends in the work of cultivating the West Port of Edinburgh; and let such a memorial of Christian philanthropy be set up in that place as to be a praise and an example both in the city of our habitation and in the other cities of our land.

NUMBERS XXXII.
August, 1844.

True religion denounces the selfishness that would look only to its own things and not on the things of others also. The Reubenites and Gadites were happily free from this in the instance before us; but the apprehension of Moses regarding the character of their proposal has drawn forth a valuable lesson which needs to be strongly urged on the professing friends of the Church, or those who hold themselves to be the members of the spiritual Israel in our present day. Verily the support and full settlement of the Free Church in Scotland calls for the united generosities and efforts of all her friends ; yet how many are there, alas ! who would leave others to do for them what they ought to do for themselves—who would draw at large, and without the least restraint of shame or conscience, on the wealth that is offered from other sections of country than their own—who would leave the whole burden of sustaining and extending our Church on other associations, while theirs would contribute little or nothing to the cause—satisfied if they but get a secure maintenance for themselves, and this, too, at the expense of parties on whom they would leave the whole weight of their sordid and beggarly dependence. O that they had more of the spirit of the Reubenites and Gadites and Manassites as depicted in this chapter, and then would they whose churches are already up and whose congregations are already formed come forth with far larger and more liberal aid in behalf of those who have not yet attained to such a state of sufficiency and full equipment as themselves. O God, rebuke the narrow and contracted spirit which is so prevalent in the midst of us. Liberalize and enlarge the minds of men in all classes of society. Make them willing in the day of Thy power. Let not our hearts be discouraged by the shortcomings of the people's generosity in so many quarters of the land. O unite them as one man in the support of that great and glorious cause which has for its object the gathering together of thine own elect by a universal gospel proclamation which might be heard throughout all our families. Put the means into our hands by which we might be enabled to knock at every door—to build churches, to build and endow schools for all. Thus our Church, instead of being confined within the limits of its present acquisitions, will, under Thy fostering care, break forth and overspread and obtain the occupation of our whole territory. With the help of those congregations which have already made good their settlement and sustenance, we shall be enabled to settle and sustain those congregations which are yet unprovided, and now look for aid to the precursors in this great undertaking.

NUMBERS XXXIII.

Moses wrote this record at the express commandment of God—and all Scripture is profitable. Let us not, therefore, slight any part of it, but as far as we can seek a benefit to our souls from all and every passage in the oracles of Divine truth; which things, says the apostle, may be allegorized. God brought the Israelites with a high hand out of Egypt. Interpose with Thy might, O Father in heaven, and bring me forth out of spiritual Egypt, so that I may be delivered from the sore bondage of sin and of the world. Set my feet on the sure pathway to the Jerusalem above, along which I may look straight forward, turning neither to the right hand nor to the left; and least of all, not looking back with regret or hankering to the objects of those evil and earthly affections which war against the soul. O let not the influences of sense and time—these powers of the god of this world—suffer them not any more to lord it over me, but destroy the work of the devil in my heart, and execute Thine own righteous judgments on all the enemies of my salvation.

Carry me in safety over all the obstacles which nature may have interposed on my journey to the Canaan which is above. Doubtless it is a wilderness which I traverse—yet here and there are there comforts and refreshments upon the way—palm-trees and fountains of water; yet by these I may not linger, but proceed onward by successive stages, under the guidance, let me pray, of a Providence and grace from on high—working specially, and if need be, miraculously in my favour. For what are the saving operations of Thy Spirit, O God, but real, though it may be hidden and not ostensible miracles? O may this Spirit put me even now into a state of preparation for going hence—so that when at the going forth of Thy commandment my breath departs from me, I may be found meet for that glorious inheritance which Thou hast destined for those who are Thine own.

Let me hold no compromise with evil. Save me, O God, from being so tempted that I should fall upon the way. Find out a way of escape from every temptation that I may be able to bear it. Thou knowest, O God, both my exposures and my susceptibilities, and though they be of such a nature that the destruction of the objects were not a duty but a crime—yet though I may not destroy, let me at least, so far as it is right and possible, keep at a resolute distance from these; let me at least keep the inner man with all diligence, so as that all pictures of vanity, the deceitful imagery of sin and Satan, may be so expunged and put forth as never to be present to my thoughts. Thus may I be rid of all those snares and annoyances which might so entangle and enchain me, that my latter end shall be worse than my beginning.

NUMBERS XXXIV.

Such are the prescribed boundaries of the children of Israel, and which have not yet been fully occupied because of their sins. The original grant from Egypt to the Euphrates eastward, or from the river of Egypt unto the entrance of Hamath, if this be indeed the mouth of the Orontes, has never yet been overtaken, save, it may be, for some brief period during the reigns of David and Solomon. For this fuller and at the same time permanent occupation, we look onward to the accomplishments of prophecy, which may God hasten in His good time and way. We would pray for the restoration of the Jews, we would pray for the peace of Jerusalem. Things look portentous, though we are too well aware of the disposition to magnify present events, and to found some great prophetic evolution thereupon, for us to speak confidently on even the immediate issues of what is now going on. If it be Thy blessed will, O God, do Thou so overrule the general commotions of the world, as that at least some quiet and secure place may be left where special manifestation might be given of the power of Thy taught word, the power of Christian instruction or of gospel calls, when brought home to every family, to reclaim an aggregate population. I pray, O God, for an object very near my heart—the success of the mission at the West Port; and forbid that the people's minds should be so engrossed by the events of a war, or the apprehensions of danger from without, as to be diverted from the great home-interest of having a well-taught and well-conditioned commonalty.

There is a wisdom which presides over all the arrangements of the Divine polity, and I pray for a portion and supply of that wisdom from above. Give me to distribute aright over the face of that little territory which I have undertaken, and where nothing will succeed unless Thou, Lord, wilt deign to bless and to guide the endeavour. But it is not human skill, or even that skill directed by Scripture, if it be confined to the outward things of the house of God—it is not this which will be of any avail, unless the Spirit of God work mightily in the hearts of the people. Blessed Father, let me have the countenance of Thy grace from on high shed forth on many hearts, so as that the preaching of Thy word may prove mighty to the pulling down of the strongholds and habits of sin and of Satan. Enable us to prevail over the inveterate corruptions which we shall be called to make head against; and may the coadjutors in this great work strive mightily, through Thy grace working in them mightily.

NUMBERS XXXV.

These cities and glebe lands given to the Levites serve to exemplify, and we think to vindicate, this species of a national provision for ministers. But when the national bounty cannot be enjoyed without sin, let us endeavour to make up for it; and may God, who here ordered dwelling-places for the Levites, may He cause to prosper the enterprise now on foot for dwelling-places or Manses to our Free Church ministers. In thine own good time, O Lord, let them have lands also. But however poor Thou mayest suffer them to remain in this world's goods, make them the honoured instruments of saving many souls—souls made rich unto God by the prayers and the instruction and the labours of an efficient and fruitful gospel ministry in the midst of us.

We clearly see that the man who killed another by accident or mishap, as by the throwing of a stone for example, when he did not see the sufferer and had no enmity against him—that in this he was reckoned not a murderer but only a man-slayer, and had the benefit of a city of refuge. But if when he thrust him suddenly on the impulse of sudden passion without previous enmity or *malice prepense*, was he in this case to be dealt with as a murderer? Perhaps not; and at all events there are degrees of culpability in the shedding of blood, and lesser degrees which do not infer the irremediable sentence of death. But there was also a guilt of higher or highest degree for which no satisfaction was taken, and for which the perpetrator was surely put to death.—My God, save me, save me from that foul and fatal delinquency, that guilt of sinning wilfully for which there remaineth no more sacrifice for sins, but a certain fearful looking for of judgment. Debar me not from a place of refuge; but may I seek unto Him and abide in Him who is a refuge from the tempest and a hiding-place from the storm. Let me never quit my confidence in Christ, but ever keep within the secure and ample fold of His mediatorship. O keep me from presumptuous sin—for often, times and ways without number, have I been surprised into sin, hurried sometimes away by sudden impulses, but sometimes also I fear not without a mixture of guilty premeditation, and most certainly a most culpable failure of the requisite and incumbent precautions by which I should have done all to stand against the wiles and assaults of the adversary.—My God, let not sin have the dominion over me. Let the law of the

Spirit of life in Christ Jesus have mastery within me over the law of sin and of death. Emancipate me from the degrading bondage of those base and carnal affections which war against the soul, and usher me into the glorious liberty of Thine own children.

NUMBERS XXXVI.
September, 1844.

What respect is evinced throughout Scripture for the feelings and the rights of property, and also for the order and the methods of good government—the one standing related to the natural instincts of the mind, and the other to its natural wisdom as well as to human experience. The miraculous did not supersede the natural; and many things are provided for by the establishment of an ordinary course, instead of being left to the interposals and the immediate rectifications of the Divine government. A sense of property and of the equities which are involved therein stands directly opposed to utilitarianism, or to that very laxity of principle which undervalues and would resist the precious doctrine of our atonement. It implies the recognition of justice as having a character and claims of its own distinct from those of benevolence; and every expression or example of our homage to the virtue of justice between man and man, goes to strengthen our reverence for that still more sacred justice between God and man which challenges our obedience as His due, or which on the obedience being fallen from calls for an expiation. And then as to the good government of this chapter, it was well that the integrity of the possessions belonging to each tribe should thus be provided for—lest either the value of them should be lessened, or the territory of each should be broken down into distant and isolated fragments. There occurs here a conflict between two principles—yet is it so decided as to convey the expression of a deference for both. It is said to be good that the daughters of Zelophehad should marry whom they thought best; and thus are we informed of the privileges of female affection, of its right to feel and act upon its own preferences. And yet too do we behold a restriction here laid—insomuch that, confined within a certain and a prescribed range, it had to give way when the higher objects of a good civil or a good economical polity demanded the sacrifice. Let us in everything defer to the authority and the examples of Scripture; and more especially bear in our remembrance that God is the author not of confusion but of order in the Churches, even as He is the author not of confusion but of order in the world.

DEUTERONOMY.

DEUTERONOMY I.—May the sublime and holy lessons of this Book both elevate and sanctify my soul; and forbid, Lord, that the impression of them should be at all deafened or intercepted or in any way obscured by the frigid influences of a misunderstood or misapplied orthodoxy. Let me not forget that though righteousness—the righteousness of man—is no longer available for the establishment of our right to the heavenly inheritance, yet that it abideth all in all for an infinitely higher object than a mere right of entry, even the establishment of heaven or of the kingdom of God in our hearts—so that we may recover His likeness, and stand perfect and complete in His will, which is our sanctification. The teaching of narrative or information are here intermingled with the teaching of a high preceptive morality, and it is our part to make the improvement of both. And first let me learn to do much by deputation, and to devolve much of what I am not personally able for upon others. And guide me aright, O Lord, in the selection of right instruments. I am most unfavourably circumstanced for this; and O may Thy providence supply the defect, whether of my own opportunities or my own skill. And when acting in the service or for the glory of God let me not fear the face of man, but let me be strong in the Lord and in the power of His might—ever resisting the dread and the false delicacy which would restrain me either from saying all or doing all which I judge to be for the good of the Church. Neither let me be discouraged by the hostile influences which are arrayed against me in the territory on which I have now placed my footstep; but moving fearlessly onward, may I at length obtain such possession of the West Port as that the gospel of Jesus Christ shall have the moral ascendency over a goodly number of its families. And let me not forget the conquests of Thine all-subduing grace, and the preservations of Thy faithful servants in the history of the missions of other days. And O in this as well as in other work let it be my care to follow the Lord fully; neither let me go up thither unless Thy presence and favour go along with me. Thou surely hast not forbidden this enterprise; and therefore will we ever pray that Thou mayest prosper and extend it. We would give Thee no rest, O Lord, till Thou hast opened the window of heaven and caused righteousness to run down that street like a mighty river. Endow, O Lord, the agents with the requisite gifts for their respective ministries, and make the people willing in the day of Thy power. We deeply feel that in ourselves there is no strength. We are but earthen vessels, which do Thou fill, O Lord, with the treasures of Thy grace, even that they may be dispensed abundantly for the healing and the enrichment of many souls.

DEUTERONOMY II.

The Lord hath been bountiful to me, and this is an argument (suggested to me by the text) why I should meddle not with others—thus connecting the duty which I owe to God with the justice which I owe to man—a respect for the sacred rights of property with a full recognition of the sentiment that all property is of God. Between man and man the distinction of mine and thine is indelible. Between man and God there is nothing mine but all is Thine. I am but the steward of what He hath entrusted unto me; and not only therefore must I refrain from touching what He hath placed in the hands of others, but teach me, O God, how amid the claims of family I should consecrate all which Thou hast placed in my hands, to Thy service and glory. The claims of family I behold deferred to in this passage. What was Esau's was not to be meddled with because he was the brother of Israel. The same principle is to be observed in their prescribed dealings with the Moabites and Ammonites, who were the descendants of Lot the nephew of Abraham, and so in common with the Israelites all the children of Terah. Not so with the Amorites, yet even they, although they had no special family claim, yet they too had the general proprietary claim against all invasion and encroachment by others. But when God interposes,—He who is the origin and the fountain-head of all property, He in reference to whom all property is but a temporary trust, to be revoked and disposed of by Him at pleasure—it is with Him to modify and transfer and make all such arrangements, as seem unto Him good. Without His sanction the inroad of the Israelites on the Amorites would have been robbery, but not when the territory became theirs by gift from heaven—not after God had said unto them, which He does in the text— "Behold, I have given into thy hand Sihon the Amorite, king of Heshbon and his land: begin to possess it." This forms the great vindication or case of the Israelites, whether in their dispossession or their extermination of the heathen, whose lands and whose lives God had bestowed upon them—their part being obedience to do what God commanded, to abstain from what God forbade them. And let me not fear the face of man when doing God's work and God's will. The dread which I ought to shake off from myself He can transfer to the hearts of my enemies, if they be the enemies of righteousness and truth. In support of these let me quit myself like a man and be strong.—My God, bear me in safety through the remaining warfare of this life, and plant me and mine in that heavenly Canaan, among the eternal abodes of peace, and love, and holiness.

DEUTERONOMY III.

Let me ever be enabled by faith to say that God is my helper, and I will not fear what man can do unto me.

But O may I ever be found in the way of duty; and to this end let me ever have the understanding to know what the will of the Lord is, for it is only when doing His will that I have a warrant for saying—who shall harm me if I be the follower of that which is good? And let this reflection sustain me against all the oppositions of an evil world, whether I am engaged in the prosecution of my own soul's good, or stand in the fore-front of a righteous cause, as did the Reubenites and Gadites of old, for the good of others. But above all, arm me, O Heavenly Father, with a sacred boldness against the instigations of him who is the God of this world—whether he act as the accuser of the brethren, or as the great tempter and adversary of human souls. In either case let me not be afraid, but only believe—resting in the first place on the declaration, "Who is he that condemneth? it is God who justifieth;" and acting in the second on the precept of— "Resist the devil and he will flee from you."

Even in our own day the Lord hath done great things for us, whereof we are glad; but greater things must still be done ere that the word of promise and prophecy be wholly realized, or that Christianity shall have taken full and quiet possession of the earth. It is yet but the day of small things with us; and I in all likelihood shall be taken off ere that much greater progress is made in the advancement of the blessed gospel throughout our land. But give me the foretaste and the confident foresight of this great Christian and moral triumph ere I die. Let me at least, if it be Thy blessed will, see—though it should be only in one or in a small number of specimens—a people living in some district of aliens—as the West Port, reclaimed at least into willing and obedient hearers, afterwards in Thine own good time to become the doers of Thy word. Give me, O Lord, a token for the larger accomplishment of this good ere I die. Go forth conquering and to conquer—so that the strongholds of the present wide-spread corruption might all be overthrown. O that we had possession even of one of these strongholds—a presage of the final overthrow of the prince of darkness who now rules and holds the ascendant over so wide a territory, and throughout such a length and breadth of our country's population. Continue to fight for us, O Lord. Perfect what Thou hast begun. On Thee and on the power of Thy might do we devolve this cause. There is no other strength than Thine that is adequate to so great an achievement, and to Thee would we look as all our desire and all our dependence. And, O Lord, in my present helplessness and imbecility, teach me how to direct and encourage others, and cause many to arise who might do both wisely and valiantly in the battles of the faith.

DEUTERONOMY IV.

How frequent the calls in Scripture to hearken, and to hearken diligently—" Hear, and your soul shall live." Let me read heedfully and diligently. Rebuke, O Lord, my lightness and listlessness over the page of inspiration. Teach me that first and foremost of wisdom which is to fear Thee and keep Thy commandments—then shall my light shine before men; and O that it shone more effectually before my own children, whom it is my duty to teach and to train in the nurture and admonition of the Lord. I am sadly deficient here.—My God, help me; give me the requisite courage and wisdom for lifting up at all times a faithful and profitable testimony on the side of God and goodness. God's covenant with Israel was the ten commandments; it is His covenant with us still. Put these laws in my heart, O God, and write them in my mind, that I may observe them diligently; and should I be true to my part of the covenant, Thou wilt not be wanting in Thine. Thou wilt cause me ever to remember and obey Thy holy commandment; yea, and for the sake of Thy Son, who hath shed for us the blood of an everlasting covenant, our sins and our iniquities Thou wilt remember no more. Let me worship not the god of my own fancy, but the God of Scripture; for if in these days there was the idolatry of images, there is still the idolatry of vain imaginations. Let me ascend from the great and the beautiful of that materialism which is before my eyes, to the contemplation of Him who sits behind the elements that He formed, and who both made and upholds all things; but let me cast a regardful eye not only on the present exhibitions of this mysterious Being in nature, but also on the past evolutions of Him as recorded in sacred history. And what a wondrous descent was that which He made on Sinai, when the heavens broke silence, and the unseen God manifested Himself to the thousands of Israel, both by a voice and by the visible symbols of His presence. Neither should the annals of that eventful period, big with miracles and most stupendous manifestations of the Deity from Egypt to Canaan, be thrown away upon us—written as they were for our admonition too, on whom the latter ends of the world have come. Let us thence learn to magnify the Lord—to stand in awe and sin not; and arousing ourselves from the slumbers of our past ungodliness, let us now seek unto the

Lord with all our heart, and all our soul, even till we find Him.

And blessed be Thy name, O God of our redemption, for that place of refuge which Thou hast opened up in Thy Son's mediatorship. This is the door of entry through which we seek for access to, and acceptance with God.

I pray for grace, O Lord, to keep all these statutes and testimonies. Let me not fall short by unbelief of the everlasting Canaan, which is reserved for the faithful and the obedient; but in Thy Spirit within me may I have at once the earnest and preparation for this glorious inheritance.

DEUTERONOMY V.
October, 1844.

Give me, O Lord, an interest in that Prophet who is like unto Moses, and who stands between us and God—out of whom Thou art a consuming fire, but in and through whom we might draw so nigh as both to see and hear Thee and yet live. Enter with me, O God, into that better covenant which is established on better promises. It is still our part to keep Thy holy commandments, but it is graciously Thine to put these commandments into our hearts and to write them in our minds, nay Thyself to walk in us and dwell in us—not only enjoining but enabling and disposing us to do Thy will, and crowning all with this blessed declaration—that our sins and our iniquities Thou wilt remember no more. What Thou didst at one time grave on tables of stone, and hast graven on the tablets of an outward revelation, do Thou now grave on the fleshly tablets of my heart—then will Thy statutes become my songs, as they were those of the Psalmist, in the days of my pilgrimage. Give me, O

Lord, the experience of this as my present salvation—salvation from the love of all sin, and conversion to the love of all righteousness; and these as the pledges, nay the preparatives for my future and everlasting salvation. Be Thou throned in supremacy over all my affections; and let not other gods, the idols of an earthly affection, lord it over me. Spiritualize the whole of my obedience; and to instance no more, give me to love Thy Sabbaths and to rejoice in all the opportunities and appropriate exercises of this blessed day. O may it be a day of sacred rest from all the disquietudes and cares of an evil world—a day on which I might realize and have the foretaste of my coming heaven. My God, Thou hast said, O that there were such an heart in them that they would fear me and keep my commandments always: I bring my heart, I submit it, I make it over to Thee. Take it such as it is, make it such as it should be. Surely if I am willing to be sanctified, and Thou art willing to sanctify, there can be no let or obstacle in the way of my reunion with God. Make me willing in the day of Thy power. Put truth into my inward parts; turn me and I shall be turned. Thou must begin the work as well as carry it onward. But surely I do feel a desirousness to be and do as I ought. Fulfil, O Lord, this desire of my heart; perfect that which concerns me. Despise not the day of small things, for small and miserably small they still are. Incline me to walk not in one way or in some ways only, but in all the ways which the Lord my God hath commanded. Let mine be an unreserved and unexcepted obedience. Christ apprehends His own to make them perfect in holiness and in all virtue; may I labour with Paul to apprehend that for which I am apprehended;

may I aspire to and make progress in all righteousness—looking all the while unto Jesus, having respect unto Him as my mediator, who has disarmed my contemplation Godward and heavenward of all its terrors, by whose atonement I am shielded from wrath, by whose power resting on me I am helped over all the infirmities of my corrupt nature.

DEUTERONOMY VI.

Give me, O Lord, rightly to understand, as also strongly and practically to feel how it is well, and how well it is to obey God—and deliver me from all the imaginations of legality. Canaan was a grant from on high to the children of Israel. They neither built its houses nor planted its vineyards, nor was it theirs by right, but by gift from that God who both told them how they were to enter on its possession, and what their incumbent love and loyalty to Himself, both before and after their establishment therein. Deliver me, O Lord, wholly and conclusively in this contemplation from the stumbling-block of my own right and my own righteousness. Let me take hold of eternal life on the evangelical tenure of its being a gift and not wages; and open my heart to the alone principle of a right and acceptable service in all ages—even the love of the Lord my God with all my heart and might and soul. But not only should these words be in my heart, I should teach them diligently to my children; and where is my diligence in this, O God? I should talk of them daily and hourly, in season and out of season; and what room I would ask, have God and the things of godliness in my speech and conversation? Mine should be a life of perennial sacredness, and both the memorials and the occasions of sacredness should meet me everywhere, so as to overrule and to keep in perpetual check the earth-born secularity of my nature. Give me to feel, O God, the burden of my past deficiencies, and teach me how to repair them. Loosen my bonds, and clear away the sore impediments to a high-toned, consistent, and unflinching Christianity. My desire, O God, is for this—O put me on the way of its accomplishment. Release me from all my false delicacies; and let mine, while a walk of wisdom, be also a walk of decided and devoted piety. Open my mouth, O God, and so increase my faith, that I might amply share in the experience of those who because they have believed therefore have they spoken.—And let me, further, have the evangelical fear of God—not that fear which perfect love casteth out, but that godly fear and reverence wherewith we are enabled, by grace, to serve God acceptably. Let me henceforth dismiss all the idolatries which have lorded over me; and abjuring the fleshly wisdom which seeks after fame or ease or the objects of selfishness, let my single aim, and with all simplicity and godly sincerity, be to please God. Thus let there be an increase of my personal and an increase of my family religion, so that I may be gladdened with the melody which there is in the habitations of the righteous, and fully experience that in the keeping of Thy commandments there is a very great reward.

DEUTERONOMY VII.

To me also belongs the lesson of this chapter. It is woful to reflect not on the ease and readiness only, but on the congeniality of feeling wherewith I can associate with the ungodly, and feel their ungodliness to be no burden, no drawback on the enjoyment. How can this be without the infection of a worldly spirit, and without the obliteration of all those characteristics which serve to distinguish God's own special people? I earnestly pray for a deep radical thorough revolution of my tastes and spirit and whole man from the carnal to the spiritual.—And let me begin at the beginning—let me set out with the principle, not that I loved God but that God loved me. O work in me this faith, and along with it all the accompanying fruits of gratitude and devotedness and new obedience. Shed abroad, O Lord, the love of Thyself by the Holy Ghost. Because God first loved me let me love Him back again. Let His faithfulness and mercy be the antecedent *because;* let my studious and busy observation of all His commandments be the consequent *therefore*. I can get at the new habits of the new creature in no other way; and henceforth is it my desire, and O let it be my honest endeavour, not to go out of the world, but to shun the evil of it even in its best and most alluring forms, to make no voluntary movement towards its unsanctified elegance or rank or literature, but to let my delight be with God's own people—even with the excellent ones of the earth. And here let me make mention of God's providential goodness in that the connexions hitherto of my family (verse 3) have been with those whose heart's desire is on the side of God and goodness. Let me be resolute and unsparing in parting with all which is adverse to the life of God in my soul. O let me not misunderstand the covenant so as to think that there is salvation on the one side, and but a bare and barren faith on the other. If I enter not on a life of sanctification, and aspire not with practical aim and effect to all its virtues, I have neither part nor lot in that covenant. Let me rid myself of all the present hostile influences wherewith I am beset and exercised, and God will enable me to dispose aright of all future ones: He will get me over the oppositions and difficulties of my remaining journey, and not suffer me to be tempted beyond what I am able to bear, but with the temptation will provide a way to escape, that I may be able to bear it. Let my house be the seat of pure spiritual undefiled religion, nor bring aught into it which is adverse thereunto.

DEUTERONOMY VIII.

I can speak of my Lord's dealings with me, and for more than forty years back I can testify both for His undeserved good and for my own sad and wayward ungodliness. I could make mention of many and most grievous specific delinquencies, over and above which my predominant habit has been that of a carnal earthly spirit. Truly I have been proved, and that most abundantly, and have been found altogether wanting. In me—that is in my flesh—there dwelleth no good thing. There is nought by nature in me but what is corrupt: this is the great lesson of my past experience. O that I may be thoroughly taught and humbled thereby, so as that henceforth walking no more in the counsel of my own heart or in the sight of my own eyes, I may submit to the grace and guidance of Him who alone can stablish my feet in the way of His commandments, and who alone can give me strength to fulfil them. This is the day of our holy sacrament; and I feel as if now on the confines of a sure and wealthy place, where encircled by all spiritual blessings my soul may delight itself in fatness. O may this be a day of refreshing to my soul; and not only so, but may it be such a day of grace and unction from on high as to prove the " anointing which remaineth," (1 John ii. 27,) so that, as if by a passage over Jordan, I shall be ushered into a new state, where all the exercises and the enjoyments of my life here shall be the preparations and the foretastes of my eternal blessedness hereafter. But let me grow in humility as I grow in holiness. If made fruitful in righteousness by the Spirit, let the sentiment be ever present of—" Nevertheless not me, but the grace of God that is in me." Let me forget not the rock out of which I am hewn, and be ever humbled in the retrospect of all that leanness and barrenness—nay, of positive crimes and rebellions, which so deform and disgrace the years that are past. Let me not be high-minded but fear, for it is not in my own righteousness but by faith that I stand. Let me therefore be fearful of grieving and alienating that Spirit in whom alone my strength and sufficiency lie. Let me obey the Holy Ghost, and then will He be more and more abundantly given to me. Thus must I have respect unto my doings, for as much hinges upon these as upon the doings of the Israelites of old, who, by their misdeed, forfeited Canaan and all its blessings—even as I will should I quench the Holy Spirit by my resistance to the lessons of that Scripture to which He, and He alone, imparts all its energy. My God, save me from the defection and the backslidings of those who draw back to the perdition of their souls, who fall short of that glorious inheritance which Thou hast destined for Thine own people.

DEUTERONOMY IX.
November, 1844.

I am now near to that Jordan which separates this world from the next—the land of my pilgrimage from the heavenly Canaan. Let me cherish the hope of an inheritance there—incorruptible, undefiled, unfading in the heavens. Let Christ be found in me the hope of glory. Let me proceed on the honesty of the invitation—Whosoever will let him come and drink the waters of life freely. Thus may I lay hold of eternal life by faith; but let me never forget that in so doing I must so relinquish my hold on the mere interests of time as to sit loose—only using the world so as not to abuse it. Having the hope of heaven in me, let me purify myself even as Christ is pure. Yet having done all, let me both feel and confess myself an unprofitable servant. The song of the redeemed in heaven is not that their own righteousness had won for them that place of immortal bliss, but it is— Glory to the Lamb who was slain, and who hath redeemed us from our sins by His blood. There nothing that defileth or that maketh a lie can ever enter; and so the vain and arrogant pretensions of self-righteousness will never be made in heaven. But let me utterly abjure them now. If I judge myself I shall not be judged; and I desire to confess and repent anew of my multiplied transgressions—a habit of disloyalty and rebellion against God, with the frequent eruptions of many a specific delinquency. Verily I have no ground on which to rest the sole of my foot but the righteousness of Christ as mine by faith. Sad and oft-repeated have been not the corruptions only but the crimes of my bygone life; and if it was a sore aggravation of Aaron's offence that he was a priest, and whose wicked example therefore was all the more ruinous to others—this is the very aggravation which confers a like enormity on many passages of a history known in all its deformity to God and my own conscience. Forgive and forget, O Lord; and let me walk humbly and holily throughout the brief remainder of my fleeting days. My sins have gone over my head—let them not overwhelm me: blot them out, O God, from the book of Thy remembrance; and blot not my name out of Thy book of life. Impute not unto me my trespasses; and even now may I believing hear the call of—" Come now let us reason together, though your sins were as scarlet they shall be as white as snow, though they be red like crimson they shall be as wool."

DEUTERONOMY X.

Moses continues his recital, and opens this chapter with what may be quoted as a remarkable instance of the condescension and long-suffering of God—His making two tables of the law a second time after that the first had been broken. But how surpassingly marvellous is the forbearance of God, in that He hath passed by those sins wherewith we have times and ways without number broken the law that was engraved on these tables; and entering anew upon a covenant with His rebellious creatures, graves this broken law upon their hearts, and puts it in their minds—so as that henceforth they should serve Him not in the oldness of the letter, but in the newness of the Spirit. Incline our hearts, O God, to keep Thy law; and may the law of the Spirit of life in Christ Jesus keep us free from the law of sin and of death. Let it be the great security for our not sinning that we are not under the law but under grace—for then sin shall not have the dominion over us. Give us ever to recollect that we are not without law to God but under the law to Christ; and may that law be our meditation and our delightful exercise all the day long.—And let me henceforth be one of that separate and peculiar people whom Christ shall purify unto Himself—having rescued me out of a world lying in condemnation; and let me therefore, if I share not in its destruction, let me share not in its wickedness and ungodliness. But O may we in all time coming persevere in that course which is here so persuasively set forth. Now that the Lord hath showed us that which is good, let us walk in the way and do the commandments that He requireth of us—let me love and serve Him with all my heart and soul. It is good to have had my guilt washed out in the blood of the Lamb, and good also to keep the commandments and the statutes which Christ has laid on all His disciples. In the keeping of these verily there is a great reward. Circumcise my heart, O God, and prepare it for the delights of this new obedience. From the place of glory where Thou sittest do Thou send forth the abundant showers of Thy grace upon earth; and let them more especially fertilize and bless the hearts of Thy chosen. Inspire me with the reverence and the godly fear which are due unto Thy great and holy name. Verily, He has done great things for us, whereof we are glad. Verily, He hath shewn thee, O man, what is good; and what doth He require of thee but to do justly, and to love mercy, and to walk humbly with thy God? I pray for grace, O Lord, to serve Thee acceptably, with reverence and godly fear.

DEUTERONOMY XI.

Even in the earlier, the rudimental dispensation of the Jews, the love of God had the precedency of all other duty. It was then too the first and greatest of the commandments. Shed abroad, O Lord, this love in my heart by the Holy Ghost, and then shall I keep Thy charge, and Thy statutes, and Thy judgments, and all Thy other commandments alway. Hitherto, O Lord, Thou hast preserved me; and while others younger than myself (Dr. Abercrombie) have been suddenly snatched away, I am still in the land, and amidst the calls and opportunities of living men. Let me acknowledge the hand of Thy providence and care in all the way by which I have been led; and now that I stand on the margin of eternity, O let me redouble my vigilance and my efforts to prepare for the occupations and joys of that glorious inheritance which is destined for all who have taken up with Christ as their leader and the Captain of their salvation. O let me be diligent in every good work and way, and more especially in the keeping of my heart, that showers of grace may descend upon me from heaven, and this soul of mine may become like a well-watered garden, abounding in all the fair and pleasant fruits of righteousness. Keep me, O Lord, from idols. Let me cleave no longer to an earth from which I am fast hastening. Let me sit loose to its interests and pleasures; and O that I not only cultivated for myself all the graces of the upper sanctuary, but that my conversation in heaven spread itself beyond my own individual hopes and exercises, and leavened the whole of my converse with others, and more especially with those of my own household. Surely he who provideth not for his own in things spiritual deserves the severe reprobation of the Apostle, and may well be said to deny the faith. Let me therefore be more at home in the matters of faith and eternity.—Let these be familiar as household words.—Let them be the things of daily and hourly talk with me. Give me intrepidity and readiness for this, O Lord; and then will a thousand obstacles that now seem so formidable vanish away like so many bugbears. Even the enemies of truth and righteousness will either be at peace or be taken out of my way; and I making choice of the good and the wise alternative will inherit the blessing, and have God for the strength of my heart and my portion for evermore.

DEUTERONOMY XII.

Let me know how to combine joy in God with a strict observation of all His precepts, whether positive or moral. Let there be a joy in His service, though with a surrender of that wilfulness which would incline me to walk in the sight of mine own eyes. And let it be a direct and immediate joy in Himself, apart from creature enjoyment—when I go up to His house, and so resign for the period of my confinement there all that is gladdening in the loveliness of external nature—the freedom of luxuriating, whether abroad among the green fields, or within the domestic enclosure of my own home walk, and my own cultivated garden. We doubt not that there was much of beauty associated with the idolatry of ancient times; and that to be restrained from the indulgence of its hills and consecrated groves and other tempting fascinations, was painful to nature. And we doubt not, too, that when the independence of the wilderness gave way to the regulated ceremonial of the Mosaic worship in the land of Canaan, this would be felt by many as an abridgment of the likings and liberty of their own spirits. And yet in the midst of all their restrictions and peremptory observances they were called upon to rejoice; and so would I, while deferring to the obligations both of the Sabbath and of the sanctuary, know what it is to rejoice with supreme delight—the delight of communion with God, in the midst of their holy services. And what a help to such spiritual joy is a generous and free-going liberality?—The good among the children of Israel not only joyed when it was said to them, Go up unto the house of God, but we read of them rejoicing, even all the people, *because* they offered willingly. Pour out this spirit, O God, upon our land. Let not the Levites be forsaken. O that the professing friends of religion were more alive to the duty of sustaining an adequate number of ministers who might go forth among the families of our land and reclaim its thousands and tens of thousands who are now wandering like sheep without a shepherd. Teach them to rejoice more in this than in the abundance of their luxuries or of the corn and wine upon their tables. And yet how exuberant in goodness is our Heavenly Father! He bids us eat and be satisfied, and frowns not on our convivial gratifications. Let us be understanding and wise in the whole of Thy will. Let us know how to maintain a scrupulous observation of all Thy sayings, and yet to serve Thee in the spirit of the law of liberty—using not liberty as an occasion for the flesh but in love serving each other. With but love for it every service is freedom; and so delighting ourselves greatly in all Thy commandments, may we be free even from the wish of adding thereto or diminishing therefrom.

DEUTERONOMY XIII.
December, 1844.

A diviner, a prophet, even a doer of miracles, though the feat he pretended to should be made good, was not to be listened to, if he enticed the people to idolatry. This argues that there was an evidence on the side of the true God which should have countervailed against every demonstration that the righteous Governor of men would suffer to be held forth on the side of heathen worship, nor is it difficult to understand what the influences were which should have operated in these days, and would operate with effect on every upright Jewish mind, so as to keep it in steadfast adherence to the good old way of his fathers—the overwhelming records and traditions of a past, as well as the visible and immediate signs of a present theocracy. And in like manner is there an evidence still for the pure doctrine and morality of the Bible that should carry it over all the likelihoods and plausibilities whether of infidelity on the one hand, or of worldliness and worldly wisdom upon the other. Protect me, O God, from all those adverse influences that would seduce me from truth and godliness. Save me from the sophistry of my own evil affections, and from the conformities of a world that is wide asunder from its God. Nor let me be deceived by the seemliness of my own favourite enterprises—ostensibly on the side of the people's Christianity—nay really so, and yet prosecuted it may be under the impulse of motives taken from lower places in the moral scale than the supreme love of God, and so having in them a certain mixture of earth and earthliness. O that I were more jealous over myself and with a godly jealousy. The scholarship, the civilisation, the recalment to habits of decency and industry and self-respect of our present miserable and degraded families—these are objects dear to every heart of strong general philanthropy, yet short, very far short of that high and heavenly affection which called forth the apostolic utterance of—" Brethren, my heart's desire and prayer to God for Israel is, that they might be saved." Give me, O Lord, an affection for human souls; save me from the deceitful and refined idolatry of our modern day; and teach me that none of its disguises can shield it from that unsparing vengeance which in former ages was denounced against its more literal and ruder forms.

DEUTERONOMY XIV.

Let our peculiarity consist in holiness and zeal for good works—not in any of the Shibboleths, whether of a puerile or pernicious sectarianism.

And under our glorious law of liberty we are freed from even those peculiarities by which in outward observances and things the children of Israel were required to distinguish themselves from the surrounding heathen. Still in both dispensations the great distinction from others lies in holiness. The Jews were at one time bidden to refrain from the external observance of not cutting themselves, because they were a holy people unto the Lord, (verse 2); and at another to keep the external observance of not eating certain animals, because they were a holy people unto the Lord. (verse 21.) The Lord hath not so commanded us; but still with them and with us alike, the grand distinction which we are required to maintain is holiness—for holiness lies neither in circumcision nor uncircumcision, neither in eating nor in not eating, but in keeping the commandments of God.

Give to us, O Lord, give to the people at large, and more especially to the friends of the Free Church, a spirit of greater bounteousness and generosity in support of the gospel throughout the land. Teach the people to honour the Lord with their substance and with the firstfruits of all their increase. Enlarge their heart, O God, that they may run in the way of this commandment. And do Thou, O Lord, give me to be wise and unprejudiced, and withal scriptural in the matter of general as well as religious charities. In this passage Thou hast spoken for a legal provision in behalf of widows, and fatherless, and strangers, and Levites. Let me cast down all imaginations of mine own, and bring every thought of my heart into captivity to the obedience of Thy word. And O bestow grace upon us to tithe *truly*, and so be able to give a faithful account of our stewardship. Let my fear of God extend to the distributions I make of the wealth wherewith He has entrusted me; and let me taste how joyful a thing it is to offer unto God the sacrifices of thanksgiving. Let me especially feel the preferable claim of the Levites, transformed in our day to the officer whether of common or Christian education. May schools and schoolmasters, churches and ministers, the moral and religious objects of liberality, come in for a large share both of my own liberalities and those of the Free Church public at large—but not to the exclusion of the other objects so distinctly specified in the closing verse of this chapter.

DEUTERONOMY XV.

Enable me, O Lord, to carry fully out Thy second great law. Thou hast imprest on the heart of man strong proprietary feelings, but Thine authority is often interposed to overrule these; and do Thou strengthen me, O God, for the consequent and the incumbent spiritual sacrifice. Let me at Thy bidding freely and cheerfully surrender my own dues, or what, but for Thy bidding, would have been my dues; and lift me above the anxieties of a sordid and selfish calculation. O give me the full sense of my stewardship, that I may feel my property, my powers, and my all, to be only Thine, and so at Thine absolute disposal.—And I furthermore pray that no science, no speculation, no favourite doctrine of political economy, shall either bedim the light, or shut my heart against the lessons of obvious Scripture. More particularly give me an eye for pity, and a hand that opens wide to the necessities of those around me; and whether in the forgiveness of debts, or in the relief of poverty, let me approve myself in all things the genuine disciple of Him who though rich yet emptied Himself, and for our sakes became poor. And, O Lord, enlighten me on the question now to be agitated—of slavery. Give me grace to comport myself with meekness in the face of adversaries, and guidance that I may walk in wisdom towards them. May I be enabled to acquit myself rightly of the argument. Enable me to find my way through the difficulties and complexities of a casuistry that is all the more unmanageable because both the moral and the political, the personal and the public, are therein blended together. Nevertheless may I be so conducted through all the intricacies of the question that by walking in the light of Scripture and of Thine own Spirit, I may realize the saying of wisdom being justified in her children.

Let me honour Thee with my substance, O God. Let me not fail in thank-offerings to the Giver of all my benefits, and at the same time let my service be a joyful service—a joy both felt by myself and shared with others. O that our festivals were more enlivened by the felt and acknowledged presence of God; and that we knew more of what it was to rejoice before Him. Give us to offer willingly and with largeness of heart, and this will serve as an ingredient of joy. May there be no paltry or deceitful reservation in my free-will offerings.—And do Thou enable me to discriminate aright between Thy temporary and Thy permanent requirements, so as to do Thy whole will, and without infringement on the glorious law of liberty.

DEUTERONOMY XVI.

Let me keep the passover alway. Let me be ever looking unto Jesus—even unto Him, our Passover, who has been sacrificed for us. And let me not be unobservant of that solemn rite which Himself hath instituted, and by which we show forth His death till He come again. And O that His precious and atoning blood were sprinkled upon my evil conscience, that it may remain an evil conscience no longer, or that I may have no more conscience of sin— no more be in terror lest the destroying angel should lift the avenging stroke against me. May he pass over without touching me. May I pass over from sin unto righteousness. May I evermore eat the unleavened bread of sincerity and truth.—My God, I would die unto the

Egypt of this world, I would live by the powers of the world to come; I would die unto Satan, I would live unto God. O let not the great adversary of human souls have the advantage over me, but may the power within me be broken of him whose works Christ came to destroy; for he does practise in my heart, he does enter into my household and stir up the provocatives of brooding and resentful imagination. Give me, O Lord, notwithstanding his devices, to love those whom I ought to cherish as my own, and not to be in bitterness against them.

And released from the sore bondage of guilt may I break forth into the free-will offerings of thankfulness and charity. May I rejoice in God myself, and cause others richly to partake of that joy—not forgetting that readiness to communicate and willingness to distribute are sacrifices wherewith God is well-pleased. Let me, in remembrance of the rock whence I was hewn, do with all cheerfulness the statutes of the new obedience of the gospel.

How gladness of heart and liberality of heart go together—let me verify the union of these in my own character.—My God, help and encourage me in the midst of all my difficulties; and pour down a spirit of free and diffusive generosity among the friends of the Free Church, that each may give according to his ability, and that the blessed fruits of an extended Christian ministration may appear in the midst of us.

Purify, O Lord, the justice of our land. Spiritualize its religion. Save us from the idolatries which the Puseyism of the age threatens to revive; and at the same time may we maintain a seemly respect for the places where the worship of God is celebrated.

DEUTERONOMY XVII.

Let the offerings of my liberality for the good of Thy Church be not of such things as I care not to possess—like the odd or mutilated volumes of a book made over to a parish library—but let them have an entireness in themselves, and be given ungrudgingly and freely.

Next follows a lesson not devoid of application to my own professional concerns. A student preparing for the Free Church ministry is reported to me as of irregular conduct. Let me do in it what is right, and under the direction of two moral forces—first, that of regard for the honour and purity of a religious institute; and second, of equity to the accused, so as not to proceed against him but on the full measure of testimony. Let me not shrink from my sacred duty, O God, but let me have the guidance of Thy wisdom and rectitude in the prosecution of it.

And Thou hast not left me without a palpable direction in this matter. There are Courts of various description in our land, each having its own assigned province, its own appropriate functions. Let me in this matter have respect to the local Presbytery where the alleged offences have been committed, and to whom, in the first instance, the alleged offender is responsible. But if it be Thy blessed will, O God, may Thy Spirit convince him of sin, and effectually reclaim him from the error of his ways. Otherwise, let us do uprightly and as public men all that is incumbent on us, that others in his situation, and with his purposes of future life, may stand in awe and sin not.

We pray for the influences of Thine all-subduing grace on the rulers of our country. May our great men be good men. O God, do Thou Christianize the spirit and the counsels of our Government. May the Bible be their directory, that the law of the land might rest upon and fully harmonize with the law of God. Give them well to understand that it is righteousness alone which exalteth a nation, and that sin is the reproach of any people. May their earnest regards be so directed to the moral state of the commonalty in our realm, as that they might be led to adopt the right and necessary measures for a universal Christian education. Thus may the throne be established in righteousness; and thus may our Queen be abundantly blest in length of days, and in the lasting prosperity both of her subjects and of her children.

DEUTERONOMY XVIII.
January, 1845.

Let all worthy and devoted ministers in the exercise of faith give up their anxieties for a provision in this world, and cast them upon that God who specially careth for them, and is the sure inheritance of all who serve Him aright, and more particularly in holy things. On the other hand, let all private Christians who are not teachers but taught, in the exercise of liberality acquit themselves of their obligations, and generously communicate of their carnal things in return for the spiritual things which they receive at the hands of those who labour amongst them in word and doctrine. May such, O God, be the mutual and respective graces and exercises both of ministers and people in the Free Church of Scotland. I would commit this cause to Thy holy keeping; and I desire henceforth to give up all the painful feelings, all the morbid apprehensions, and most of any, all the hasty effusions of impatience in which I have hitherto indulged on this subject.

There is here a clear and explicit direction in regard to what the Israelites were to feel and do in reference to the abominations of other lands. The injunction is a very plain one—even that they were to take no part themselves in these abominations. Give me, O Lord, Thy direction and guidance in a matter that is not so plain—even how we should comport ourselves either to a country in the aggregate, or to its inhabitants in particular, where an institution adverse to the rights and the character of men has prevailed for centuries, and been handed down from generation to generation. Give me, O Lord, to adopt the right view, and to pronounce it clearly and convincingly, on the subject of American slavery.

What a blessed transition from a matter that is ambiguous to what is lucid and palpable as day—even the duty of doing all things whatsoever which Christ hath commanded. Let me hearken unto Him in whom are all the treasures of wisdom and knowledge, and who stands to His people as an intercepting screen between them and the fire of the wrath of Almighty God. Teach me the distinction between His words of wisdom and the words of those presumptuous men who would conjure up their own articles of Church communion, and propound their own factitious additions to the morality of the gospel. But give me to be faithful and even-handed on this question, dealing fairly and equally with both sides of it, and sparing the cruelty of the oppressors as little as giving way to the undigested crudities of those who would palm their own arbitrary imaginations on the acceptance of all, and denounce their refusal, or even their hesitation, as the highest possible enormity.

DEUTERONOMY XIX.

Save me, O God, from presumptuous sin. Let me not fall into the great transgression, or into that wilfulness of wickedness for which there remaineth no sacrifice. Let not the place of refuge be shut against me; but may I ever share in the benefit and use of the precious declaration, that if any man sin we have an Advocate with the Father, Jesus Christ the righteous. But O let me not forget that these things are written in order that I sin not. In the very act of providing the cities of refuge do we find the charge laid upon the Israelites, that they should keep all the commandments to do them—that they should love the Lord their God and ever walk in His ways. How much more does it lie upon us both to love and to obey; and of how much sorer punishment shall we be judged worthy, if the great gospel provision shall embolden us not to draw nigh that we may receive grace, but to turn grace into licentiousness, to make Christ the minister of sin, and count the blood of that covenant which was shed for the sanctification of men an unholy thing.

Make me scrupulously observant of a neighbour's rights There is a property not in wealth or goods alone, but in reputation. Let me not trespass upon this, or amid the jealousies of literary competition withhold honour from those to whom honour is due. The very term of such being *due* leads me to the conception of a land-mark in this too which it were unjust to violate.

And, O my God, direct me to what is right in the matter of testimony. The coincidence is singular, that to-morrow, the day after my meditations in this chapter, I for the first time in my life shall have to give evidence in a court of law on a question affecting one who lies under a serious criminal charge—that of having forged the subscription of my name. Save me from sinful anxiety, grounded on the fear of man, which is a snare. Let no man despise me. Enable me to give a clear and upright and impartial witness—yet free from all morbid scrupulosity, and such as to subserve the ends of substantial justice. Give me to have and to show a becoming respect for the constituted authorities of our land—for judges and governors and all in high places. O let me ever acquit myself before men as a consistent professor of the truth that is in Jesus; and may such be my deportment and walk at all times, that on me the saying might be realized—of wisdom being justified in her children.

DEUTERONOMY XX.

Let me not be afraid of men. Save me, O God, from this snare; and seeing that besides the military there are other kinds of warfare with our fellow-men, be my stay and my confidence, O Lord, when called to embark in needful or righteous controversy. Let me seek not mine own ease, and sustain my faint or nervously agitated spirit amid the strife of human tongues; yet let me not be anxious. I would commit my cause to Thee, and trust in Thine own promise of the Holy Spirit, who can put the right words into my mouth, and the well-timed suggestion into my heart. The preparations of the heart and the answer of the mouth are alike from God. I pray, and more especially in the matter of an internal question which affects the character of our Free Church, I pray for grace and guidance from on high.

And as much as lieth in me, and as far as it is possible, let me live peaceably with all men; let me seek peace and ensue it. I breathe with the utmost discomfort in the stormy element of debate, and now long to the uttermost for peace and retirement. I would still wait Thy time, O God; but O, if pleased to lengthen out my season upon earth, do let me depart in peace from the arena of public business ere I take my final departure from the world—that I may have a precious season of repose and pious contemplation ere that I go hence and am no more. Meanwhile let me, if compelled to fight, fight in the spirit of peace, and under the check and control of this authoritative saying—that the man of God shall not strive but be gentle with all men.

But even in our controversies there are certain deadly practices or errors to which we must give no quarter, but carry on with them a war of utter extermination—contending earnestly for all the essentials of our faith, and distinguishing rightly between these and such flaws of sentiment or expression into which even a Christian brother might be betrayed, although he should have the root of the matter in him. When such as he is thus overtaken, let him be restored in the spirit of meekness; and let care be taken, even in the necessarily unsparing warfare, let the utmost care be taken lest in pulling up the tares we should pull up the wheat along with them; or lest in putting extinctions upon the heresy, we should extinguish or destroy some of that sound and scriptural aliment which lies near or almost upon its borders. Churches have often done this with their precise and pointed deliverances—as in defining particular redemption so, and laying such limitations on the extent of the atonement, that obscuration is cast on the freeness and universality of the gospel call, and ministers are shackled in making their honest tenders of salvation to all and to every.

DEUTERONOMY XXI.

But beside the overt sins of which my memory might tell that I have not committed them, how many such, and of a very gross and grievous description too, into which I have fallen—and how many, over and above, are my secret faults as well as presumptuous transgressions! Give me, O Lord, and especially on this the morning of a Communion Sabbath, to have an unshaken faith, and if it be Thy blessed will, a lively sense too of the virtue of that blood which cleanseth from all sin. O manifest Christ in all the fulness of His grace and truth to my soul. I have much to confess, O Lord, this day, and little or nothing to disclaim. My deeds in time past have been full of sin. O let my desire now, my real and honest desire be against all sin; and give me a part and interest in that redemption which is through the blood of Christ—even a full and free forgiveness. Be merciful to me, O God; and in the blood of Christ may my own blood-guiltiness be washed away; and as the alliance between faith and repentance is indissoluble, let me henceforth and for ever do that which is right in the sight of the Lord.

God winked at many things and suffered them in the ruder and earlier stages of His great and progressive moral administration, because of the hardness of men's hearts. O purify my heart by faith; and bring me altogether under the influence of this our higher and more spiritual dispensation, that henceforth I may ever glorify the Lord with my soul and spirit as well as body, which are the Lord's.

Let me not only love my children so as to deal with them equally, but let me love them so as to deal with one and all of them spiritually. Animate and guide me, O Lord, in this high department of Christian duty; and let me not be ashamed of the testimony of Christ, either in the face of general society or in the midst of my own family.

I have here to record my gratitude for the blessing of dutiful and obedient children. I have much to be forgiven for my impatience with the infirmities of my own parents. O impute not to me my heinous and manifold trespasses; and assist me, O God, in converting the docility of my children to their spiritual and everlasting welfare.

In the name of Christ who became a curse for us, and so bare upon His own body the burden of our offences—in His name do I supplicate for pardon and acceptance, and that my sins may be washed out in the blood of the Lamb; and not only so, but that cleansed from all pollution, I may be made meet for heaven, into which nothing that is defiled can enter.

DEUTERONOMY XXII.

February, 1845.

There are beautiful touches of humanity in the Jewish law—the openings as it were to our own dispensation of love and mercy, the occasional glimpses of a something better and higher that was coming. In this passage there is inculcated a faithful and tender regard to the property of others; and the remarkable dissuasive from not hiding ourselves, generalized elsewhere into the precept of not hiding ourselves from our own flesh. We must not shun the observation of a lost thing belonging to a brother, or make ourselves off from the trouble of securing it for him, and far less secrete it for our own use. I pray for the increase of this principle in my soul—this scrupulous, and honourable, and unselfish regard for the property of my fellow-men. It is a very serious defect when there is a want of the equitable and the social.

Then follow certain finer traits both of benevolence and decorum—an injunction against what is unseemly, and which might lead to still grosser violations—a law that respects the right of inferior animals, as being the proper objects of our sympathy and care—and certain other ordinances which, whether we discern their principle and rationale or not, are at least fitted to exercise our obedience to God, and to bring out in its naked and proper force the principle of godliness.

Let me abhor the evil thing for which God hath so signally testified his abhorrence.

Let me give no quarter to that which is evil in myself at least, while I observe the utmost equity towards others, and cherish the utmost compassion for their infirmities, considering that I also might be tempted.

DEUTERONOMY XXIII.

We discern in this passage traces of the same jurisprudence which, through Adam, extends to the whole human species. Children suffer because their ancestors have sinned; and without attempting to scan the rationale of such a constitution, let us take refuge in the counterpart and analogous economy, alike mysterious, however, in respect of principle with the other—that they who will receive Christ, and so become the children of God by faith in Him, shall enjoy the reward which Christ hath earned. My God, accept me in the Beloved, and teach me how to walk in His footsteps, that I may be one of His adopted family; and thus instead of being dealt with according to the transgression of the first Adam, I shall be dealt with according to the righteousness of the second Adam —washed in His blood, sanctified by His Spirit, justified by His obedience even unto the death for me.

There is a purpose and a principle in the physical disgusts and antipathies wherewith God hath endowed us. Let us bear respect to these ultimate and instinctive tendencies of that constitution which His own hand hath impressed on us, and be the scrupulous observers of all the decorum and all the delicacies to which they lead.

Then follows a testimony that might prove available on the humane side of the question in regard to American slavery. O that I could combine all the excellencies of the Scriptural code, and with its tender and expansive benevolence were equally alive to the abhorrence of impurity—and so as along with the charity of the gospel to have its unpolluted sacredness.

Liberalize me, O God, and give me a larger and freer spirit than heretofore. Let me cease my alarm for the advances or proposals of my needy acquaintances—avoiding suretiship, yet lying open to all the representations of distress; and never hiding myself from my own flesh.

Give me strength, O Lord, to keep my vows. May I never in particular forget my sacramental obligations. Impress on me the sense and feeling of my stewardship—and that mine is not a property but a trust. Let me honour the Lord with my substance, and let the first-fruits of all my increase be His. And whatever is done in this way let it be done as unto the Lord.

There may be an excessive, even a superstitious scrupulosity in regard to a neighbour's rights, and certain freedoms which in the spirit of a frank and honourable confidence on both sides, a well conditioned neighbour would thank us for taking. But along with this let us cultivate a supreme regard for substantial justice—providing for things honest both in the sight of God and of men.

DEUTERONOMY XXIV.

Thou knowest, O Lord, how much I ought to be humbled and ashamed for. Thou seest further than man; and canst find even in the state of the heart that which to Thee is abomination—even when all is seemly and right in the eye of the world. Create, O Lord, a clean heart within me. May a sense of Thy presence and Thy holiness restrain the wandering of my thoughts and desires. Give me, O Lord, to maintain such a love only as Thou hast prescribed and sanctioned. Let mine be the affection which the Apostle enjoins when he bids us love one another with pure hearts fervently.

Let me study so to walk in a perfect way at home as to be at once the light and the happiness of my domestic circle.

Let my humanity be ever alive to the tender consideration of others' needs and others' sufferings.

And while I cleave to that which is good let me abhor that which is evil. Let the denunciation and sentence passed here upon man-stealing fortify my abhorrence of oppression in all its modes and varieties. I pray for guidance on the question of American slavery, and that I might be conducted to a right and wise deliverance thereupon.

And while I aspire after moral righteousness in all its branches, let me be strictly observant of all the positive precepts which God hath issued for our government; and wherever my natural sense of morality is deficient, let Bible morality supply its place.

Let these beautiful delicacies of Scripture toward the dependent and the poor be loved and cultivated to the uttermost. And O may the repeated testimonies of the great God of heaven and earth on behalf of the lowly, dispose me not only to succour the destitute but to honour all men.

Let me ever render unto servants that which is just and equitable, and maintain the most sensitive respect for their feelings of what is due to them.

While I feel the obvious equity of the rule as to fathers and children for an earthly government, let me acquiesce in the Divine jurisprudence by which Adam was constituted the representative of his posterity—aye and until the day cometh, when the mystery of God shall be finished.

Let all political economy give way before the claims as stated in the Bible of the widow and the stranger and the fatherless.

Neither let me forget that not only are they spoken of as having special claims, but they are singled out as the objects also of our special compassion.

DEUTERONOMY XXV.

There is severity tempered with mercy in this law.

Thou knowest, O God, the peculiar interest I at present have in an alleged case of delinquency. Let me have both the principle and the wisdom to temper these aright—so as neither to extenuate the evil of sin, nor to bear with undue hardness on the transgressor. How I need to abide in Christ that He may abide in me, and be my guide and guardian amid all the difficulties and all the exigencies of my history.

Pour forth on the people of our Free Church the care and consideration for their ministers which the Apostle hath evolved from verse 4, as a lesson for the observance of all Christian congregations.

The next passage is the occasion of a still more illustrious reference in the New Testament; and the noble lessons have been founded on it both of an immortality beyond the present life, and that there is no marriage there.

Let all my habits and acts be characterized by a strict and high-toned delicacy, and this not that my days may be lengthened in an earthly Canaan, but—higher sanction now—that I may be qualified for admittance into that land into which nothing can enter that maketh or loveth a lie, and which the Psalmist seems to have had in his eye when he speaks of the land of uprightness.

Here is another example of God dealing corporately with nations, and on the principle that a corporation never dies with the change and succession of the individuals who compose it. It is interesting to mark the traces and example in detail of such a procedure throughout the sacred history; and they remind us of that more general jurisprudence in virtue of which all men have been made to suffer, because Adam the head of his posterity has sinned. It is not for us to question the ways of God; but let us all the more rejoice that by an analogous constitution in the gospel, the way to connexion with another Head has been opened for us. Let us seek to be grafted in the second Adam; let us hold by Him as our Head; and our participation in Adam's sin will be nobly compensated by our participation in Christ's righteousness—when, because the children of God through the faith that is in Jesus, we shall share in all the immunities and all the privileges of children.

DEUTERONOMY XXVI.

March, 1845.

Give me, O Lord, to know the rock whence I was hewn. I brought nothing into the world—or brought into it an inheritance of guilt and a nature tainted with corruption. Give me to feel aright the nonentity of the state from which I sprung, and the misery of the state in which I was born—so as to stand in need not of a creation only but of a redemption also. Thou, O God, art my all in all—my Proprietor, both in having made and having purchased me, so that I am not my own, neither have I aught which is my own. Make me, O Lord, to be habitually sensible of my stewardship, and that all I am, and all I have, and all I hope for are Thine. Let me honour, then, the Lord with my substance and with the first-fruits of all mine increase—rejoicing in the gifts of Providence, yet with a grateful heart to the Giver; and ever experience that joy in God which stands allied with kindness and generosity to my fellow-men.

May mine alms ascend with my prayers in memorial before God. We do not live under the same sort of strictly numerical or of tale and measure regimen with the Israelites of old; yet let that not restrain, O God, the exuberance of my charity. Let me keep a good conscience in this matter—such a conscience as I might bear with me to God in prayer. Let my heart condemn me not, that I may have confidence towards God. May I know how to avoid the legality of the Jew, while I maintain the fruitful and life-originated and willing obedience of the Christian; and give me the comfort of knowing that my labour in the Lord is not in vain.

Let me enter into covenant with God; let me take up with Him as my God—avouching my appropriation of Him; and O may He be the strength of my heart and mine everlasting portion. May I view Him as holding out to me the right hand of reconciliation; and let me ever from this moment regard Him as my reconciled Father in Jesus Christ. And let me not say that I *would*, but that I *do* enter into this relationship of peace with Him—for the gospel has made all ready for this latter step, and I so long as I stop at the former am just holding the gospel in abeyance; therefore, O God, take me from this time forward such as I am, and make me such as I should be. I hear Thy voice telling me to do all Thy commandments; and I rely on Thy promise that I should keep all Thy commandments. Take me then as one of Thy peculiar people, and form me to Thyself that I may show forth Thy praise. Make me holy even as Thyself art holy; and give me a heart and a soul to delight in Thy law, and in the doing of all its requirements. Henceforth I would walk in Thy ways; and as on Thy part of the covenant Thou hast promised not to withhold Thy grace, so on my part do I promise not to withhold my service. So help me, God; enable me to fulfil my vow. Give me all needful supplies in Christ Jesus. Out of that blessed Fountain would I draw all my sufficiency for a life of godliness; and let me never falter or fall back on the good way which I have chosen.

DEUTERONOMY XXVII.

Incline and enable me to keep all Thy commandments, O God, and give me to be instrumental, in the hands of Thy Spirit, in graving them on the hearts and the memory of those who come after me, specially those of my own household. Do Thou, O God, who providest monuments and memorials for the admonition and the guidance of successive generations, do Thou write Thy law in the minds of those who are near and dear to me. Keep alive O Lord, a remnant, a goodly, yea an increasing remnant of grace and godliness in our land—that not only there might be a family altar in many a house, but that there might be a public testimony, visible to the nation and to the world, for the pure faith and doctrine of Him who poured out His soul as a propitiation for the world's sins. Give us, O Lord, to rejoice in Thee through Him by whom we have received the atonement; and may His will and the way of our new obedience be made so plain to our eyes, that even though fools we shall not err therein.

If we are the Lord's people the conclusion is that therefore we must obey His voice. Let us understand and proceed upon this as the tenure of our connexion with God as His reconciled children. We shall else inherit the curse and forfeit the blessing. Put love into our hearts, O God, and then shall we work no ill—observing all the negations of a threatening and prohibitory law. But from these prohibitions let us gather all the more distinctly and feel all the more forcibly what the will of the Lord is. Let me beware of worshipping a God of my own imagination, who may differ from the true God, and thus lead me astray, even as those idolaters who fell down before images the work of their own hands. Let a strict and sacred integrity preside over all my dealings with men. Let me be careful not to mislead those who have been committed to my guidance and instruction. Let no economical dogmas have the effect of shutting my heart against the special claims so often and so earnestly repeated in Scripture, of the stranger and widow and fatherless. Let me refrain from the low arts of calumny by which a neighbour might be injured, or still more the character of an innocent or deserving person might be blasted and overthrown. And along with all these observations give me, O Lord, to feel the burden of my grievous and innumerable deficiencies. Convince me of sin. Cursed is he that confirmeth not all the words of the law. Have I confirmed all, have I kept all? May a sense of my manifold delinquencies shut me up unto the faith, even unto that faith which availeth, because working by love; and so enabling me henceforward to serve God not in the oldness of the letter but in the newness of the Spirit.

DEUTERONOMY XXVIII.

O my God, let ours be the righteousness which exalteth a nation. Let our example make it palpable that the religious and economic wellbeing of a people go hand in hand. These temporal blessings by which Thou signalizedst Thine ancient people when they kept in the way of Thy commandments may still be realized. O that Britain were thus distinguished among the nations of the earth; and that a reverence both for the doctrine and the will of God, as set forth in Scripture, presided over both the counsels of our rulers and the habits of our families. Then indeed should we be a holy people unto God; and ours would be the wealth and the victory and the honour. But, alas! it is not so with us. Even now may it be said that we go after other gods and serve them. We are giving in to the idolatry of other nations and powers, even as the Israelites of old gave in to the idolatry which surrounded them. We well-nigh inherit the character of the rebellious and stiff-necked Jews; and shall we not inherit also these fearful curses? Unless a remnant save us, a purifying and preserving salt in the midst of us, how can we escape those dread denunciations of which in the history of a nation peeled and scattered we behold so dread a fulfilment? Truly it is a fearful thing either for nations or individuals to fall into the hands of an incensed God, who rains down wrath upon His enemies. O let the chosen few of our day, even in this day of our sore degeneracy, avail for the salvation of the kingdom. Save me in particular, O Lord, from the cursing and vexation and rebuke in all that I set my hand unto for to do; and more especially let me neither be vexed nor triumphed over in the matter of the West Port enterprise. Command a blessing, O God, upon that undertaking; and let the power of Thy Son's gospel be magnified by the success of it. Send abroad, O Lord, a spirit of reformation in this our day; and let it take a missionary direction toward the families of our own land—that the people thereof may be reclaimed to the faith and the following of Jesus, and be saved from the plagues and the judgments which come upon those who fear not the glorious and the fearful name of the Lord our God. What a graphic delineation have we here of the actual history of the Jews for nearly two thousand years. Their plagues have indeed been wonderful—so as to make them an astonishment and a byword to others, and a weariness and burden of despair and terror to themselves all the day long. What a demonstration of God's truth is given forth by this history, both in the Book of His prophecies and in the Book of His providence. Do Thou speed, O Lord, the enlargement and restoration of this wonderful people.—Do Thou recall the dispersed of Israel, that they may be under one Shepherd, and be in one and the same sheep-fold with all who love the Lord Jesus Christ. We would not keep silence, O God, but give Thee no rest till Thou hast established and made Jerusalem a praise in the earth. They shall prosper that love her.

DEUTERONOMY XXIX.

The covenant here spoken of is distinct and different from the covenant made in Horeb—which is a covenant of simple and absolute law, the counterpart terms of which are a commandment or commandments upon the one side, and the required obedience upon the other.

The covenant of this and the following chapter again presupposes an infraction of the former one. The object of it is to make provision for the sinfulness and rebellion of Israel. The blessing and the curse had already been fully set forth in the hearing of the people; and the reiteration of the latter particularly is to be found in some of the following sentences; yet are we told now what had not been told in Sinai—that the curse is not irrevocable. Intimation is here given of forgiveness upon repentance; and not only so, but of regeneration also, as will afterwards be seen, so as to present us with a more advanced development of the evangelical than we had previously met with. The Lord had not yet given them a heart to perceive or eyes to see or ears to hear. And in historical accordance with this how dire were the perversities and impenitence of the Israelites, and this, too, in the face of all the mercies which they had experienced and all the miracles which had passed before them. On the strength of these does Moses renew his solemn charge on the people for their obedience, and his threatenings against them should they transgress the covenant of their God—a covenant not confined to those who heard him, but extending to posterity, and so to those who were not with him on that day. Their obstinate inclination to the idolatries of the heathen was the root of bitterness, a poison both of deceit and destruction, which first beguiled and led away the nation, and then ruined them. Against this he holds out both his menaces and his warnings, with the full knowledge at the same time that they would prove ineffectual, for God had not yet given them a heart to perceive or be susceptible to an effectual sense either of their duties or of their danger; and so God rooted them out in anger and great indignation. Mysterious indeed are His ways who withholds grace, and punishes those who sin under the want of it. But in the way prescribed to man there is no mystery—a way of plain, and if man will of practicable obedience. Let us regard with lowliest reverence and respect the secret things which belong unto God, let us proceed on the revealed things which belong to us and to our children—things on which the children of Israel from generation to generation had but to act that they might remain the favourites of heaven, a happy and holy people unto God. Ever blessed be Thy name that ours too is the pathway of a plain commandment —which is, to believe on the name of the Lord Jesus Christ, and to love one another, even as God has given us commandment.

DEUTERONOMY XXX.

The evangelical character of the covenant in hand comes more fully out in this chapter. There is in the first instance a clear declaration of forgiveness upon repentance, of a returning compassion on the part of God to His strayed children if they will but return unto Him. O my God, recall me from the dreary alienation of a life spent without God, and of a heart uncheered by the light of Thy gracious countenance. Gather me and mine from a world of deep ungodliness, and rejoice over us to do us good and to cause us to abound more and more in all the fruits of righteousness; and not only so, but circumcise my heart and the hearts of my children. Shed abroad in them the love of Thyself by the Holy Ghost. Make us willing and obedient in the day of Thy great power, that we may do all Thy commandments, turning unto Thee with our whole heart and our whole soul. Turn us, and we shall be turned; draw us, and we shall run after Thee. Let us not take shelter under the plea that religion is a thing so remote and inaccessible as to be beyond our comprehension, or that to understand the part we have in it we must go in quest of ingenuities from afar—that we have either to scale the transcendentalism of the heavens above, or to search into the profundities of the earth below. Verily there is a plain word and a plain way—a lamp unto our feet, a light unto our paths. O make Thy word at all times very nigh unto me. May I ever keep it in memory, may it dwell *richly* in my heart in all wisdom. May it be in my heart as well as in my mouth—not in word only but in power. Surely there is no want both of plain sayings and of plain sanctions. The alternative of life or death is set evidently before us. There is an importunity and a desirousness for our wellbeing and well-doing in the gospel of Jesus Christ, as well as in these vehement—affectionately and desirously vehement protestations of Moses. O may we at length give way. May we no longer withstand the voice of a beseeching God. May we choose life—entering now on its pleasant pathway, and travelling onward now to its glorious landing-place. Let me not be drawn away by the love of aught that is earthly or created, but cherish it as the supreme felicity of my nature—the love of God. O give me not only to say but to think, and not only to think but to experience, that the true and only habit of the soul for obedience is that of cleaving unto the Lord.—I would do so with full purpose of heart. I desire to make the wise and the good choice for eternity, to take up with heaven as my home—the Canaan that is above, and on which I would henceforth set all my affections. I would lay up my treasure there that my heart may be there also. I would keep by this better part, and labour not for the meat that perisheth, but for the meat that endureth unto life everlasting.

DEUTERONOMY XXXI.

April, 1845.

Moses was denied the personal gratification of entering the land of Canaan. He sowed and another man reaped; he laboured, and another entered upon his labours. Let me not be impatient, O God, though I should never see in the flesh that which I have for many years longed after. Let me bear more resignedly and more Christianly the delay, and disappointments, and oppositions by which I am sometimes tempted to feel that I have been sorely thwarted. What are my sufferings from this cause when they are compared with those of other men!—Let me renounce all vanity and self-seeking; let me acquiesce in God's providential dispensation; and withal let me cherish the confidence, that sooner or later He will bring to pass all that shall make most for His own glory, and for the greatest good of His creation. I stand much in need both of a higher philosophy and a stronger faith than have hitherto actuated or sustained me.

What a firm pathway was constructed for the descent of an historical evidence, by these public and periodical readings. We bless Thy name, O God, for such a light upon these earlier records, that if we believe not Moses and the prophets, neither should we believe though one were to rise from the dead.

But God foreknew the defections of the future generations of Israelites, and proceeded against them in the way that seemed to Him best. He lifted a testimony against them—such a testimony and such a warning as if they did not reclaim these stiff-necked children would at last seal their condemnation. There is an overhanging mystery here—but only on God's ways, not on ours. We have testimonies enough for our guidance, and our business and duty are simply to proceed upon them. Let Thy statutes, O God, be my songs in the land of my pilgrimage.

What thankfulness we owe for the careful transmission of the sacred ancient books to modern times. What was then written was written for our admonition too on whom the latter ends of the world have come. It was unavailing with the Israelites; and it is strange that the very predictions told so little on them. Let us take heed too lest we fall after the same example of unbelief. Stay Thy judgments, O God, and let a standard be lifted up in the midst of us against the floods of ungodly men—lest our candlestick also be removed out of its place, and some fearful catastrophe befall both our Church and our nation.

DEUTERONOMY XXXII.

This sublime song, the product of a lofty inspiration, speaks to our adoring piety as well as to our susceptibilities of poetical impression. How it sets God before us in the majesty of His power, and the sacredness of His high moral attributes—the perfect righteousness of His judgments and ways, and withal the perfect reliance with which all who have not forfeited His protection may resort to Him as their refuge and the rock of their confidence. But, alas! what a contrast, verified as well as predicted, between a righteous God and a rebellious people. Lord, I have many spots—but may they be those of Thy children, and may I give all diligence to be found without them and blameless in the great day of reckoning. But the great reference is to Israel, for whom this noble composition was made, and to whom it served all the purposes of a warning and commemorative song. In what stately succession and pace does it move onward along the footsteps of the history of Israel, to whose state and fortunes as a nation all other history was made subservient. How touchingly beautiful is the description of His care over them; and what grandeur withal in the outlines of this whole representation. But what a requital for all this high distinction and special goodness of the Most High towards them! At first they had no strange gods, but soon did they provoke the jealousy of Him who had singled them out among the nations, and who is the only living and true God. They forgat the God that formed them, and were unmindful of the God of their salvation. And how fearful are the judgments here denounced upon them, and how fearfully have they been realized—yet were the judgments limited towards Israel and at length transferred from them to their adversaries, lest, vain and godless, they should bear it haughtily, and disown Him who sitteth above, and whose purposes regarding His own people shall not be finally thwarted and overthrown, but all be fulfilled in the latter day. O that the now captive and scattered people were wise, and would but consider their own high destination, and there will be a recovery. God will not abandon them for ever. He will turn and have pity upon His own heritage; and when their power is clean gone, then as if man's extremity were God's opportunity, will He interpose and have all the glory of their restoration. There is more of prophecy in this singularly precious and preserved document than appears on the first cursory reading of it; and the discovery of this as the result of a deeper insight and attention enhances our sense and feeling of its inspiration. What a magnificent view is here given of the day of vengeance and of victory over the enemies of Israel and Israel's God, when not only His own peculiar people will be made to rejoice, but the nations of the then Christianized earth will rejoice along with them. Altogether does this song sustain its character as a standing memorial of God and of His administration upon the earth, to become soon we trust the study of the Jews, and helpful to their conversion on that day when Jews and Gentiles shall unite in singing the song of Moses and of the Lamb. I desire to bless God for the confirmation I have felt in this morning's study of it.

Whether I shall be spared or not to witness in the flesh these great accomplishments, do Thou prepare me, O God, for mine own latter end. Do Thou guide me by Thy counsel and enrich me with the treasures of Thy grace while I live, and afterwards take me up unto glory.

DEUTERONOMY XXXIII.
No. 8, Bruntsfield Links, Mrs. Coutts'.

Thou lovedst the people, yet issuedst a fiery law for them; and they sat at Thy feet, and heard Thy words. And give us, O Lord, to reciprocate aright to these Thy varied aspects of our Father and our Sovereign—standing in awe of Thy majesty and Thy sacredness, and yet with all the confidence and affection of reconciled as well as with the docility of obedient children. May we know what it is to mix trembling with our mirth, to serve Thee without the fear of torment and terror, and yet to serve Thee with reverence and godly fear.

And give me, O Lord, a part and an inheritance in these blessings of Jacob. Quicken me that I may have the life of God in my soul and abound in the fruits of righteousness. Strengthen me by Thine all-sufficient grace, so that I might overcome all my spiritual adversaries. Give me an understanding to know Thy will that I may both observe it and keep it and be able to instruct others also—and ever recognising the sacrifice of Christ and the incense of His merits. O through Him may my services be accepted, and may I have comfort in the work of my hands.—And grant, Lord, that I may dwell in safety under the covert of Emanuel's love and with the good-will of Him who dwelt in the bush, enriched with all blessings from above, and the glory of the Lord shining upon my ways. And O that we knew what it was to rejoice in the Lord, and under Him to rejoice in all the works and the ways of righteousness—not only enriched but enlarged by Him, and so as to attain the glorious liberty of His children, receiving both the wisdom to discern and the power to execute all His pleasure. O to be satisfied with His favour, to be filled with the fruits of His Spirit, to grow in acceptance both with God and man, and to experience amid the ills and the vicissitudes of life that as my day is so my strength shall be.

O may the images both of security and glory wherewith this benediction so magnificently closes, may they in me be abundantly realized. Let me not be afraid of the Holy One because of His greatness, but let my confidence be this—that the strength and greatness of the Most High are all upon my side. May my help be in Him who rideth upon the heavens, may the eternal God be my refuge, and underneath be the everlasting arms, and let the good-will which was sounded forth from the skies on the shepherds of Bethlehem be over me and round about me. Let me be one of the people saved by the Lord; and then will all be safe and glorious—safe from the storm of the Almighty's wrath—safe from without and from within—safe from a malignant world lying in wickedness—and safe from the evil affections of my own heart, those tyrant appetites which are the cruellest and worst of enemies, for they war against the soul.

DEUTERONOMY XXXIV.

Moses laboured and Joshua entered upon his labours. The great prophet and legislator was not permitted to enter that land to the borders of which he had conducted the children of Israel. The glory of settling them there was reserved for his successor. Such was the disposal of the rightful and righteous Sovereign—and Moses acquiesced in it.

My God, give me this property or characteristic of a true faith—"He who believeth shall not make haste." I have been a projector in my day, and much as I have been employed with the economics of society my conviction is more and more strengthened in the utter vanity of all expedients short of faith in the gospel of Jesus Christ, whose disciples are the salt of the earth, and through whose spirituality and religion alone we can look for the permanent civilisation and comfort of the species, or even for earthly blessings, which come after and not before the kingdom of God and His righteousness. I have made little progress, but let me wait Thy time; and now that I am hastening onward to the end of my days, let me cherish the confidence of a great and coming enlargement—

even notwithstanding the dark and menacing appearances of a gathering hostility to the cause of truth and righteousness.

Let there not be wanting, O Lord, men in whom resides the spirit of wisdom, and who will guide both with a right spiritual and a right secular discernment the affairs of Thy Church upon earth—men who will act according to Thy commandment and will, and who will command the attention so as to wield a legitimate influence over the people and ministers. Give Thy Spirit, O Lord, to the friends and followers of the Free Church of Scotland; and now that the prospects of Protestantism are reversed—now that, instead of setting forth to possess the land, the power of Antichrist threatens the dispossession of a pure and Scriptural faith—now that our attitude is like to be changed from that of invaders on the territory of darkness to that of defenders against the might and machinations of the enemy—do Thou rally around Thine own cause men who will have the wisdom to guide and the courage to withstand in the hour of trial. Let there never be wanting pastors and leaders according to Thine own heart, who might carry forward the gracious purposes of Him who sitteth above, and whose instruments they are. And O do Thou prepare me for an abundant entrance upon the heavenly Canaan, that when death comes its gates may be open to receive me; and after passing the Jordan which separates from the land of promise, I may find myself placed among the joys of that bright and smiling region. It is with no small interest, and somewhat the sensation of farewell regret and melancholy that I now in the progress of these lucubrations take my second and final leave of the great lawgiver of Israel.

JOSHUA.

May, 1845.

JOSHUA I.—How large and how encouraging the promises of God to Joshua—not to supersede, however, but to stimulate and direct his activity, and to put into him that inspiring faith which actuated and directly led him to all obedience. O Lord, in Thy good time do Thou restore the outcasts of Israel, and fulfil upon them all Thine original purposes, and grant them a speedy and secure settlement over the whole extent of that territory which reaches from the Mediterranean even unto Euphrates. But there are commandments as well as promises, and so Joshua had to do as well as trust. He had to be observant of the whole law of Moses, and to make it his constant and earnest meditation, in order that it might be his diligent practice, and that he might execute fully and faithfully all which was written therein. The promises were suspended on the obedience—for it was when he did according to what had been thus prescribed to him, it was then that his way should be made prosperous, and then that he should have good success. And so, O God, may we address ourselves with all fidelity and determination to the fulfilment of Thy precepts, with a comfort and a courage grounded on our confidence in Thy promises. Let us not be afraid of our spiritual adversaries, because of Thee our strength; and let us experience that in the keeping of Thy commandments Thou art with us to help us, and to ensure the conquest over all our temptations.

Joshua, thus divinely warranted, went forth on the instant execution of his task; and they to whom he delivered his commission as instantly obeyed him. And it is remarkable that he does not plead the authority of the message which God had imparted to himself directly and personally, but bids them remember the word which Moses the servant of the Lord had commanded them— thus acting as Moses' minister even after his death, and content to set himself as subordinate to him who was his master when alive. Let us in like manner, when dealing with the people, plead the authority of Moses and the prophets, for he who despiseth them despiseth Him who sent them. And O that our people were as obedient to the words of these inspired men as the children of Israel professed themselves to Joshua when quoting the injunctions and the charges of the holy man who had gone before him. Verily, if they believe not Moses and the prophets, neither will they believe though one should rise from the dead. Work this faith with power, O God, in the hearts of many; and O that the unregenerate in the West Port were effectually quickened and raised from their state of death in trespasses and sins.

JOSHUA II.

This is a chapter not of historical only but of great evangelical importance, as we gather from the use made of it by the Apostle in his Epistle to the Hebrews. Hers was not a faith which superseded the use of means: Rahab believed that it would redound to her advantage could she secure the flight of the spies, and this set her upon her busy expedients for their concealment and safety—among which we can observe that sort of untruthful policy which was current at that time even among those who are recorded as the righteous and the believing; and which seems to have been not only tolerated among men, but in these days of the world's yet rudimental morality to have been permitted by God—the days of ignorance which God winked at, and when concessions were made of a less strict and elevated morality, even to His own people, because of the hardness of their hearts.

It should be observed that the faith of Rahab was a religious faith: it had God for its object; it was the assurance of things not seen. The terror of the Lord had fallen upon her in common with all the people; and she knew that He had given to Israel their land. She believed the report of those great things which had been done for the invaders now upon the borders of their territory; and this historical faith, which seems to have been universal throughout the land, was ripened with her into a theological faith—even that the God of Israel was God in heaven above and on the earth beneath. Accordingly she perished not: she was saved at least in the limited sense of having been rescued from the destruction brought on the families of Jericho—a salvation this which was extended to her kinsfolk; and we have no reason to believe otherwise than that she was made the heir and the partaker of a higher salvation in virtue of a faith which worked repentance here, and invested her with a right of entry into that heaven whereof she acknowledged the God of Israel to be the Sovereign and the Proprietor. Wean me, Almighty Father, from the evils which still lurk in my heart, and which deformed my past history. I stand in need of a salvation for the chief of sinners; and ever blessed be Thy name, that commensurately with this, the blood of Christ cleanseth from all sin, and that where sin abounded grace doth much more abound.

The spies too had their faith, but theirs was not the faith of hearing as Rahab's was. They saw and believed. They grounded their confidence on their observation of the state of the country and its people. O for the blessedness of those who see not and yet believe!

JOSHUA III.

We have here the passage over Jordan, and cannot fail to observe how thoroughly religion had to do with it.

The direction was that the eyes of the people should be kept steadfastly upon the ark—even the ark of the covenant. In passing over to the heavenly Canaan through the dark valley and shadow of death, may I look fixedly on Him who is the Mediator of the new covenant, and the ark of safety to all who take refuge therein. He is our Forerunner, in that not only He is now in heaven, but in that He entered it by the very road which we have to travel—by the steps of a death and a resurrection.

Let me sanctify myself to follow Jesus. Without holiness no man can see the Lord.—O that this consideration came to me not in word only but in power. I pray for this great miracle being worked upon me; for what a godless, what an earthly creature I naturally am. In the act of looking unto Jesus may I be made like unto Him—that when landed on the other side of death, and on the shore of eternity, I may find that I shall be ever with the Lord.

How God carries His own people over all difficulties! O that we could trust Him more, and then would His strength be manifested in our deliverance from the evils that seem to block up our way.—My God, take pity on my lamentable weakness and want of confidence in Thy Son. Let me against hope believe in hope; and if not called upon to trust for a miracle of nature, let me never abandon my reliance on the promises of grace, and more especially may I through Thy Spirit be enabled to wait for the hope of righteousness by faith.

The prescribed order for the passage of Jordan was given, and it was found to be sure and effectual. And the passage from earth to heaven is equally well ordered, equally and altogether sure. Let us obey the commandment which lays it down, and we shall succeed in the great object of a safe and glorious transition from time to eternity. And this is the commandment—that we believe in the name of the Lord Jesus Christ, and love one another, even as He has given us commandment. Let our eye be steadfastly fixed on the great High-Priest, on His work, and on His will, and He will conduct us entire over the dark and narrow way which leadeth to life everlasting.

JOSHUA IV.

I would not forget Leslie's argument as founded on the history of this chapter—even the monumental evidence furnished by the stones of Gilgal for the truth of the miraculous passage over Jordan. They were set up there expressly for a sign; and let us not undervalue the force or the importance of it. But give me, O Lord, more especially to discern Thy hand and the signatures of Thy wisdom in the work itself. May the lessons given forth there evince their own divinity to my understanding, through Thy Holy Spirit bringing them home with power and with much assurance. Let the entrance of Thy words give me light ; and may the Scriptures make me wise unto salvation through the faith which is in Christ Jesus. Yet the miracles are not to be overlooked as proofs whether of a special agency or of a special revelation from heaven. Let us recollect the stress which our Saviour laid upon them when He appealed to the mighty works which the Father had given Him to do. And their importance was not limited to the age in which they were performed. Here, in particular, do we observe a method devised—and that by the setting up of visible memorials, for the express purpose of making known the miraculous passage of Jordan to the men of future and distant ages—and not only of making them known, but of making them credible also for the conviction of posterity, as well as for their information. And no doubt the miracle was truly a stupendous one, and made all the more impressive by the sacredness of its visible accompaniments. These the subsequent generations of Israel had not the advantage of, and the prodigy itself was far distant from the eye of their observation. Yet these stones of Gilgal though but the inarticulate records of its truth, were designed by God Himself to supply the want of ocular or sensible demonstration ; and the same purpose is served by the narratives which have been handed down, or the articulate records both of the Jewish and Christian revelations. These too are helpful to the great moral intention which God had in ordaining the vestiges of the first entry which the Israelites made on the land of Canaan, viz., that all the people of the earth might know the hand of the Lord that it is mighty, and that they might fear the Lord their God for ever. With such a sanction—and for such an object—to the monumental evidence, let us not underrate the historical evidence for the truth of the Old and New Testament. Still it holds true that the internal evidence is that which germinates a saving faith. But let the external constrain our attention to the Bible, the word of God's prophecy; and let us give earnest heed thereunto till the day dawn and the day-star arise in our hearts.

JOSHUA V.

June, 1845.

We cannot wonder at the terror of the Canaanites when the judgments of God were made so manifest, and brought so near to them. Let such terrors persuade us now, lest they should overwhelm us afterwards. If not won by the compassion and long-suffering and forbearance of the Lord hitherto, let us be saved by fear; and if His goodness lead us not to repentance, let us behold His severity, and flee from the wrath that is to come. After the miracle of their passage over Jordan, Joshua addressed himself to the work of obedience. Cause me, O Lord, to pass out of darkness into the marvellous light of the gospel, after which may it ever be my honest inquiry at all times—Lord, what willest Thou me to do? O circumcise my heart, Almighty Father—cut off all its idolatries and carnal affections. Long have I abidden in an uncircumcised state, immersed in earthliness, and with my aims, and purposes, and desires, set on the vanities of this passing world. Henceforth may I live by the powers of a world to come. May my conversation be in heaven, and my heart be there: and on my way thitherward may

I be refreshed and satisfied from time to time, by the ordinances of the gospel, and more especially by that blessed sacrament in the taking of which, if I do it worthily, I take Jesus Christ for my propitiation. Let me lay confident hold on Him, and then will all old things be passed away—all things will become new with me. Give me the new tastes of the new creature in Jesus Christ, and then shall I relish and feed upon the new objects which are adapted to them—with my affections now withdrawn from the things which are beneath, and set on the things which are above. Give me the meat which the world knoweth not of—not the meat and the drink wherewith the men of the world are satisfied, but righteousness, and peace, and joy in the Holy Ghost.

There is here the record of a most remarkable manifestation—I doubt not of the Angel of the covenant, the same who appeared unto Moses, and bade him also take off his shoes, for that the place he stood upon was holy ground. This is a language we hold that no created angel would have used, an order that no such angel, the fellow-servant of Joshua, would have given. The angel who appeared to John in the Apocalypse forbade the homage which the angel who appeared to Joshua enjoined, and Joshua obeyed him. This Captain of the Lord of Hosts is identical with the Captain of our salvation, with Him whose coming we look for—when He shall appear without sin unto salvation. These evolutions from time to time of this mysterious personage are fitted deeply to interest and to solemnize. They connect the two dispensations, and give us to perceive the same overruling agency in both.

JOSHUA VI.

The falling down of the walls of Jericho was a signal miracle—yet not done by an instant fiat, but at the termination of a process. So God willed it; and the will was duteously complied with by Joshua, and those who were under him. The effect certainly of the preceding steps in this series must have been to enhance the reverence of the people both for their commander and their priesthood—both for the civil and ecclesiastical authorities which God had placed over them. But irrespectively of this, it was the incumbent duty of the parties in this operation to do as God had prescribed; and still it would be very clear to them that the resulting miracle, though preceded by their instrumentality, was the effect of God's power, and not of their own. In like manner it is our part to observe the processes of nature and experience, which though not laid down to us by the word of God, are palpably set before us as the work of God. And after all we should ascribe the final or resulting event to the will and power of Him who chooses to institute an order of means, sometimes for the achievement of what is supernatural, and always for the bringing about of what is ordinary or natural. The city being accursed *to God* reminds us of the savour of death unto death—and this a sweet savour too. Rahab, however, was exempted from the curse, and this exemption is represented by the Apostle as the effect or reward of her faith. She believed in the report of the spies. She resisted not the impression of those signatures which they bore of God being with them, and hence a faith that was pleasing to God. We cannot but remark on the unsparing execution of that mandate which God had given forth. It was a mandate of extermination—revolting it may be to nature, but this overborne by the high authority of Him who is the rightful Judge and Sovereign of all below. The curse which Joshua pronounced on Jericho was fulfilled many ages afterwards—the one standing to the other in the relation of a prediction to a history, and so evincing at one and the same time the omniscience and the government of the Almighty. There seems to have been an unfailing adherence to God's decree of a total destruction in this first achievement of the Israelites against the people of Canaan—though in the next, temptation prevailed over the unfortunate father of one of the families, in consequence of which he and his household were consigned to destruction. No wonder that the report of those doings should have spread terror upon all around.

JOSHUA VII.

There is much to be gathered from this narrative of the accursed thing. We have read of God's intolerance of evil, and how bitter a thing it is to sin against Him; and if the solitary transgression of Achan brought judgment upon a whole army otherwise innocent thereof, let us no longer wonder that even one act of disobedience, though it stood alone in the history of a life—free with but this exception of all blame—should bring guilt and judgment unescapable on the head of the individual who had committed it. If a multitude were made to suffer because of the single deed of a single person, how much more clearly might that person be made to suffer for the single offence into which he might have fallen? Let us not then deceive ourselves; surely it is not for us to build up a deceitful security on the imagination either of few sins or small sins. Let us but think of our habitual ungodliness, nay, and the many grievous and palpable delinquencies which might be charged against us; and let us think, moreover, of that holy and heart-searching, as well as life-searching God with whom we have to do, and let us betake ourselves to that city of refuge where alone we are safe. In this passage we are presented with the deep and mysterious, as well as with those other characteristics in the method of the Divine procedure which our understanding can go more easily along with. We are told of *Achan* having sinned, and of the anger of the Lord being kindled in consequence against the *children of Israel.* There is even the imputation of his guilt extended to the whole community; for it is said that "*the children of Israel* committed a trespass in the accursed thing." The whole of Israel is charged, and in the defeat at Ai the whole of Israel was punished for the crime of one of their own number. "Israel hath sinned" is the utterance of God Himself, and Israel in consequence fled before their enemies. The guilt of one man was reckoned to other men—because of the same nation, yet along with this we read here of to us the more obvious equity whereby Achan was made in his own person to bear his own burden. He was singled out for a tremendous act of vengeance; yet with this proceeding, too, there is mixed up the deep and the unsearchable of God. The household of Achan was involved in his awful punishment. Others than the actual perpetrator shared both in the sentence and in the dread execution of it, because they were of the same family. The theological doctrine of our guilt in Adam is here brought to view in this historical exemplification of it. O God, how unsearchable are Thy judgments, and Thy ways past finding out!

JOSHUA VIII.

God having now turned from the fierceness of His anger proceeds to encourage Joshua. If God be for us who can be against us? And He was pleased to grant an indulgence at Ai which He prohibited at Jericho: they were permitted to take possession of the spoil. In everything let us do according to Thy commandment. It is worthy of remark that even the immediate direction of God Himself did not supersede the adoption of tactics or the methods of ordinary generalship—and this too was the will of God. His strength does not supersede our performances—He gives us strength, and so makes us strong for action. His wisdom does not supersede our plans—He gives us wisdom, and so makes us wise in counsel. Reveal to me, O God, the right tactics, the right way and method of proceeding in the management of the affairs of the West Port. O that I were enabled to pull down the strongholds of sin and of Satan which are there; and O save me, save me from the difficulties to which I am exposed should hollowness of heart or principle be found to obtain with any of the agency. O how incompetent I feel myself to be for acting the part of a cautious and wise general in the midst of them. Be my help and my adviser, O God, and tell me by Thy word and Spirit what I ought to do. Surely there is such a thing as asking counsel of God and receiving from Him an answer. O may Thy light so shine upon Thy word that the entrance thereof may give light to me who am simple. Save me from the fear and the flattery of man, and keep me firm and unfaltering in the path of integrity.

Joshua obeyed God on the field of battle against the enemies of Israel, and He obeyed Him in those sacred services which he was called on to perform in midst of the solemn assembly. There was much committed to writing in his day; and we may here see how close and consecutive that testimony is which has handed down to our day the early revelations of God to the world. Let neither the blessings nor the curses of the law be lost upon me. Let not the formularies of a human orthodoxy disturb the impression of them. I am under the law to Christ. His beatitudes hold true, and take effect on all who realize the graces to which they are annexed. And so far from curses being done away, we read of the how much sorer condemnation that is incurred by those who sin wilfully and do despite unto the Spirit of grace, and count the blood of the covenant an unholy thing—and all this under the gospel dispensation. Let me stand in awe and sin not, O God.

JOSHUA IX.

Monzie.

We here see that Joshua was imposed upon. Let us not think then that any strange thing has happened to us should we also be deceived. We sympathize with the Gibeonites, and think them excusable in the deceit which they practised. Let us not be carried away by our indignation against those who have less reason than they had to abuse our confidence. Thou knowest, O God, the nature of the trial by which I am exercised, and that through one in whom I trusted. But let me not give way to provocation; let this tribulation work patience. Give me wisdom and the meekness of wisdom in the management of this affair. And have not I done the reverse of Joshua? He had no wish for a league with the Gibeonites; but have not I been far too ready to league with the ungodly in my enterprise in the West Port—at least to league with them because of qualifications which often might obtain apart from godliness? There is all the difference in the world between him who sought such a league, and Joshua who would cordially and with his whole soul have shunned such a league. I completely shared of the error of Joshua in that he asked not counsel of the Lord respecting this thing. O how little have I been in the habit of consulting or of holding conference with Him who is above in any of my matters!—My God, teach me to look up unto Thee, and do Thou establish every thought of my heart.—My God, teach me how to combine all fidelity with all meekness and gentleness: Thou knowest my infirmities and what my incapacity is. Guide me in this matter, O God; and I pray for a gracious operation in the heart of him who has so disappointed me and filled me with such anxiety. Enable me to assign for him the rightful service, in which may he prove really and usefully serviceable. Above all, be Thou very strong in him by the power of conviction. Put truth in his inward parts. Forgive wherein I have said or done amiss in regard to him. Make himself thoroughly Christian; and may he be helpful in the great work of Christianizing others also.

JOSHUA X.

July, 1845.

There was a composition of the miraculous with the

natural in this discomfiture of the allied kings. Joshua had to do his part; and God encouraged and strengthened him so that he fought valiantly and slew many by the sword; but more still were slain by the hailstones sent down direct from heaven upon them. If in that age of direct and ostensible miracles human co-operation was not superseded, how much less now!—but let me remember, that though we cannot look for the directly miraculous, yet God might encourage and strengthen us for the work and warfare of Christianity, even as He strengthened the hands of Joshua for his war against the Canaanites. Give me, O Lord, to war successfully against the powers of the flesh and of the world. O may He that is in me be greater than he that is in the world. Save me from the influences that are without, and save me also from the deeply-seated corruption that is within. Thou knowest my frame: Thou knowest how much it is that Nature hitherto has lorded over me. O give me to be temperate in all things that I might overcome.—What a stupendous miracle is recorded in this chapter! I accept of it with the docility of a little child; and think, moreover, that there is the wisdom of the philosopher, as well as the piety of the Christian, in this unqualified surrender of myself to the testimony that is here put forth. These are harsh doings in which Joshua was engaged—but the authority of God was concerned; and all His works, whether by men as the instruments of His power, or by the direct inflictions of it, are done in truth and equity and judgment. It is our part to obey where He commands; and let us learn the lesson from this history of His relentless and unsparing hostility to sin. A decree of extermination had gone forth, and Joshua was appointed the executioner thereof.

God had said it, and shall He not do it? Let us stand in awe and tremble.—Let us fear lest we also should be cut off, for most assuredly the face of God is set against all the children of rebellion and impenitency.—Let us flee therefore from the wrath that might come upon us also, and flee for refuge to Jesus, the Captain of salvation; for God will most assuredly make an end of His enemies, and every saying and sentence of His will without fail be accomplished.—Let us make our peace then with this terrible and irresistible God; and O what an immunity is held out to us in the gospel—the day of reconciliation still lasts.—Let us no longer persist in that ungodliness or unrighteousness against which the wrath of God will arise in its might upon every soul of man that doeth evil. —Let us flee for refuge in this the day of our mercy and peace to the Mediator between God and man, lest the day of reckoning shall come, when we shall seek, but seek in vain, to hide ourselves from the wrath of the Lamb, when sitting in the throne of judgment, He will say, Depart from me all ye children of iniquity.

JOSHUA XI.

Joshua had yet far from fulfilled his task. The direct and miraculous power of God did not put itself forth to such an extent as not to leave him very much to do in the way of natural and ordinary warfare. The line of demarcation between these we cannot trace, but it is good that it should be adverted to; it proves that what God judges to be the best result may at times be brought about by the composition of both: and thus too would we argue the question of the plenary inspiration of the

Bible—contending for the optimism of the Bible, in that as to the result or product it is immaculate and perfect; while we admit, that along with the superhuman influence there is much of their own natural peculiarities discernible in the respective writers of that volume, all of which was given by the inspiration of God. It does not appear that there was any miraculous intervention in the recorded battles of this chapter. Joshua seems to have overcome his enemies by his own prowess and generalship; and yet it was the Lord who delivered them into the hand of Israel. Give us to recognise Thee, O God, in all the departments of business or of action on which we might be called to enter. Be Thou ever done homage to as being all in all. The " leaving nothing to breathe " is a strong expression; but he did according as Moses—or as God by Moses—had commanded. He was but the executioner of that fell decree which had gone forth against the people in the land of Canaan. The war was lengthened out by a gradual process; and God had a purpose in it which is announced to us in this chapter. The people who yet remained ought to have discerned the hand of God in the previous victories of Joshua; but they persisted in their moral hardihood notwithstanding; and this brought on them, in the form of a judicial award, the destruction which at last came over them. They thereby awakened all the more the resentment of Israel, so that they could get no favour from their human enemies; and they became more rightfully amenable than before to the retributions which came upon them from on high, and at the hand of their righteous and avenging Judge. It was so that He hardened the heart of Pharaoh, even as we read of His hardening the hearts of the Canaanites. O give me to discern aright the signs of Thine administration; and make my heart soft and tender, under the sense of my own iniquities and of Thy sacredness, in that evil cannot dwell in Thy presence. At length Joshua fulfilled his task, though it appears afterwards, that the whole of the land promised for an inheritance was not conquered by him.

JOSHUA XII.

Aberfeldy.

Out of the very enumerations of this chapter a vein of sentiment may be struck which it were profitable to follow after. With the exception of the kings Sihon and Og, whose territories are specified, we have nothing more of the other kings than mere nomenclature. Yet could we but realize their history—the busy play of their interests—the families under them—the fulness and amount of that living consciousness which is now extinguished or at least swept off from the earth, embracing tens of thousands whose very names are unknown, saving only a bare and barren catalogue of kings whose names are all which remain to us—such a contemplation might well bring home the lesson of our own insignificance—sharing alike with the men of past generations in the brief and ephemeral character of our own little day; and hastening onward, like as they did, to the deep oblivion of death, and leaving room for a posterity who shall forget us and all our doings. O that we could contrast aright our own subordination and vanity with the greatness of Him who liveth for ever—who standeth at the head, and is the originator of this mighty series of changes—whose counsels embrace not only all nations but all worlds; and whose grand design in Creation reaches forward from everlasting to everlasting.

There is a wisdom, a profound and at the same time a practical wisdom, to be gathered from this retrospect of the antiquity that is now rolled by. We think it should loosen our hold upon time. It should teach us a wider and a nobler survey than is taken by those whose views reach no further than to the evanescent objects of an evanescent world. It should inspire a wisdom as much higher than that of this world as eternity is greater than time—as the life that is to come is greater than the life that now is. Give me, O Lord, experimentally to realize of Scripture that all of it is profitable. Let me not think lightly of any of its informations. Teach me a supreme veneration for Thine own perfect and immaculate word; and when I read therein of nation succeeding nation, and add thereto the instruction that might be gathered from the book of experience—with what speed and certainty old families give place to new ones; and when I am led to refer all to the power and providence of God, who in judgment and according to His own pleasure roots out one and builds up another—when thus looking to myself as the tenant of a short-lived existence, and to the living God who presides over all the changes and movements of a universe, whereof Himself is both the parent and the upholder—let me thus be borne aloft to that transcendental and more ethereal region in which *he* breathes who hath set his affections on the things which are above, and lives by the powers of a coming eternity.

JOSHUA XIII.

I am fast approaching to the state of being old and stricken in years. My ambition has been to possess the land, to occupy it with good and right institutions from one end to the other of it. How partial, how short has been the success of my endeavours; and I cannot dare to claim even the humblest fraction of any part in the saying—that ye have laboured and other men have entered into your labours. The truth is that more land remains to be possessed than at the outset of my efforts to reclaim it—a vastly larger population to be provided with churches and schools than I encountered at the commencement of my attempts to overtake them. This might well humble me, but there is another, and to me personally, a far heavier consideration than this, which should prostrate me to the ground that is under my feet, and make me lie down in dust and ashes—and a consideration, too, suggested by the state in which Joshua left Canaan, with its subjugation incomplete, and a multitude of Canaanites and idolaters still within its borders. O my God, how much within me remains to be subdued of those vile affections and idolatries which war against the soul! If the Canaanites, whom they ought to have extirpated, were a thorn in the side of the children of Israel, does there not remain a thorn in my flesh to exercise and to humble—nay, so to convict and to mortify that I might well sink into despondency, if not to the lowest depths of despair? Thou knowest, O God, the sad infirmities of a constitution overrun with all that is noxious and corrupt; and against which the new creature in Christ Jesus—if Christ indeed be formed in me—ought by this time to have gained the prevalency and the power, if not to have utterly exterminated. Indwelling sin must, I fear, ever abide in me on this side of death; but worse than this, greatly worse than this, has not indwelling sin still the mastery over me? Have not I this very day given way to unbridled anger? Enable me, O God, to rally and to recover myself from the snares of the devil. Give me repentance unto the acknowledging of the truth; and not only so, may I walk as do the children of the truth, so that though I should feel the motions of the flesh I may not walk after the flesh. What we feel we may not follow. But O that I were thoroughly cleansed from all filthiness of the flesh as well as of the spirit, and then should I neither feel nor follow. Give me, O Lord, to keep my heart with all diligence. Turn not my sight and eyes only, but my very thoughts from dwelling upon vanity. Wash me from all my pollutions; cleanse Thou me and I shall be whiter than the snow. There seems to have been a more thorough extermination on the east than on the west side of Jordan. And one territory of the moral constitution may have been more cleared of its defilements than another. But he who sinneth in one point hath broken the law; and let mine be an unsparing and universal warfare against all that is evil. There seems to have been something good about Balaam, but he tampered with temptation—and let me gather instruction from his latter end. See how God destroyeth one nation and setteth up another; and in the contemplation of this mighty power let me stand in awe when I read this saying—That if any man defile the temple of God, him will God destroy. No inheritance was given to the tribe of Levi—the Lord God of Israel was their inheritance. My God, be Thou the inheritance of the Free Church ministers. The silver and the gold are Thine—open the hearts and the hands of her worshippers, so that they who are taught may communicate to their teachers in all good things.

JOSHUA XIV.

August, 1845.

The greater part of the land of Israel was disposed of by lot, but not all; for the country to the east of Jordan was given to the two tribes and a half, not because it cast up to them by lot, but in consideration of its peculiar suitableness to the habits and circumstances of these tribes. But in regard to the nine tribes and a half—the distribution of the land to them was that which the wisdom and authority of man had nothing to do with. It was divided by the lot, or rather by the direct will and appointment of Him who has the ordering of the lot, and is Lord of all things. And is not this an argument for acquiescence in the existing order of things, and more especially in the existing distribution of property throughout the land—ordered as it has been in the course of history, and so by the providence of God? The strength of the possessory feeling has long struck myself as one of the most conspicuous evidences of design in Him who gave us our nature, and made thorough adaptation of it to the nature and properties of external things. It is He who ordained the laws and regulates the whole mechanism of human society. Let us not rashly attempt to supersede them—as if by the skill of man a better system of distribution could be arrived at than that which actually obtains and has the sanction for it of use and wont through the various countries of Europe.

Give me, O Lord, like Caleb, to follow Thee fully; and if it be Thy blessed will let there be a portion even of the good things of this life for me and for my children. But however Thou mayest see meet in this, be Thou at all times their and my portion, and the strength of our hearts. May the Lord be the inheritance of me and of my family. O let mine be a Christian household—wise for eternity, and rich towards God. But let me not expect blessings upon them for my sake, unless there be in me a full purpose of heart and endeavour after the new obedience of the gospel. Thou knowest, O God, my besetting sin; enable me to set it aside, and to run with perseverance in the race that is set before me. Save me, O God, from all those affections which war against the soul; and if it be Thy blessed will do Thou even in the present life give me rest from this warfare. But if not rest, let me at least have the final victory. Let me have the blessedness of them which overcome, and the rest which remaineth for the people of God.

JOSHUA XV.

There is a whole chapter devoted to the description of the lot of Judah, it being far the most distinguished and most populous of the tribes of Israel—Judea, in fact, with the comparatively small accessions of the territories of Simeon and Benjamin, being able to cope with all the rest of Israel, and to maintain their ground against them. There is a charm in the geography of the Holy Land when comparing the accounts of modern travellers with the names and the narrations that occur in Scripture history, and there seems a warrant, too, for cherishing those sacred asociations with places of sacredness which serve to augment and to strengthen the religious principle. If I forget thee, O Jerusalem, let my right hand forget her cunning, if I do not remember Jerusalem above my chief joy. Good and faithful Caleb obtained the portion which he earned as the reward of his faithfulness. He drove out the former occupiers of the land that had been assigned to him. He was strengthened in the day of battle by that God whom he had served; and was so fully instated in his inheritance that he took quiet possession thereof, and had the power of disposing it as he would to his children. He granted the request of his daughters, as we are told in a plain narrative that partakes of all the simplicity of primitive times. The allegorists of Scripture have laid hold of one expression, and spiritualized the upper and the nether springs into the influences of the Spirit from above, and the refreshments that are furnished both by the Bible and at the pool of ordinances below. Without consenting to this as a legitimate application, still let us acknowledge in full the undoubted truth and importance of doctrines which do not need the far-fetched demonstrations of those who see a mystery in every clause and sentence of the word of God. Give me neither to quench the Spirit nor to despise the word. Give me, O Lord, of the living water that comes direct from the sanctuary above; and give me to wait also upon the prescribed ordinances below, to give earnest heed unto the word of Thy prophecy till the day dawn and the day-star arise in my heart, and to experience, moreover, the good of Thy Sabbaths and of Thy sacraments. May I be blest with spiritual blessings in high places; and in passing through the valley of this world may I find wells of consolation. Even in a catalogue of names instruction is to be found; and to them who are well read in Scripture those narratives of Scripture history which relate to this one or that other name will be called to remembrance in the perusal of these verses. The hill country of Judea is prolific of great interest.—The Jebusites were not driven out at the time that this book was written.—My God, expel from me the lurking enemies of my soul. Let it be my shame that sin should dwell in me. May its hateful presence lead me to watchfulness and alarm. Keep me from the great transgression, and let not sin have dominion over me.

JOSHUA XVI.

There is first laid down the inheritance in the general of both tribes—that is of Ephraim and that half-tribe of Manasseh, whose lot was on this side of Jordan. It is good to verify as far as we can the geography of Scripture—identifying it with the geography of the present day. There is great delight in the study; and let me here testify the enjoyment which I have had in the *relievo* map of Palestine. We shall not be able however to assign their place to every city or even every boundary that is here laid down—though in regard to the eastern and western extremities of all those tribes which reach from the Mediterranean to the river Jordan, there can be no mistake. After that the inheritance of the two is laid down in the general the special inheritance of each is set forth—and first that of Ephraim, which occupies the remainder of this chapter. There is an instance given here of some of the cities assigned to one tribe from the territory of another. The Ephraimites, famous though they were in war, and great in power and numbers, were not able to drive out all the Canaanites from their portion. They could not dispossess them, but they subdued them. There were some of the native idolaters who still dwelt in the land, though the Israelites had dominion over the land. The Canaanites became subject to them, and served under tribute. And so it is with every Christian so long as he remains in the body : his sinful propensities are not extirpated but kept under check. They do not rule but serve, and serve under tribute too—for they do not get all they desire after, and all they would have had but for the mastery of the principle of grace within that soul in which they still reside, and vex—nay, endanger by their presence. O my God, give me to be ever aware of this near and besetting enemy, to keep him under, to rule over him, and finally to destroy him. In *me*, that is in the old man or flesh, there dwelleth no good thing ; but still let *me*, that is the new creature in Jesus Christ, so prevail as to walk not after the flesh but after the spirit.

JOSHUA XVII.

Before defining the limits of Manasseh on this side of Jordan, there is reference made to the inheritance which part of the tribe had obtained on the other side of it, even to Gilead and Bashan, the lands of which were rich for the pasture of cattle. The Manasseh west of Jordan was conterminous with Ephraim, and on the north side of it ; and agreeably with the preceding chapter, we here read that while the city of Tappuah was Ephraim's, the land of Tappuah belonged to Manasseh. In like manner as Ephraim had towns in Manasseh, Manasseh had towns in Issachar and Asher. Neither could Manasseh utterly drive out the Canaanites who would dwell or chose to dwell in the land, and made good their point. But though they had their dwelling there, they had not always the dominion there. For when the children of Israel were waxen strong, they put the Canaanites to tribute. Give me, O Lord, to be strong in the faith, and strong in the grace that is in the Lord Jesus—that though I may not be able to exterminate the evil passions which war against my soul, I may at least obtain and furthermore keep the victory over them—holding them as my subjects and tributaries, and wielding the entire sovereignty and dominion over enemies whom I cannot dispossess, and of whose presence I shall never be wholly freed till I have reached that heavenly Canaan where I might serve God without frailty and without a flaw. There is instruction to be gathered from the application of the sons of Joseph (including both tribes) to Joshua, and from his reply to them. They sought additional land as a gift, but Joshua bade them go forth and win it by working or warring for it. They called themselves a great people; but this instead of being sustained as a plea for their receiving gratuitously what they asked was made to react upon them as an argument for putting forth all the greater strenuousness to seize and take possession of the country for themselves. And let me in like manner feel that the more I have in the way of endowments or talents from above, the more responsible I am for the use of them. Let me not only pray for more grace, but let me work for it. It is thus that the saying is fulfilled—To him who hath more shall be given; and larger spiritual gifts are bestowed when smaller spiritual gifts are put to their right use and exercise.

JOSHUA XVIII.

The setting up of the tabernacle at Shiloh has attached a sacredness to the place, and given an enduring celebrity to the name. But by this time the land for three tribes had only been portioned out on this side of Jordan. There had probably been very much land subdued beyond what was yet possessed—seeing that the surveyors who were sent forth could go over what was intended for the immediate occupation of the seven tribes with so great security. This land they were to divide into seven parts, five tribes having already been provided for. After the description and division were given in, the distribution of the seven parts among the remaining tribes was submitted to the lot; or in other words, to Him who has the disposal of the lot. And accordingly Joshua said that he would cast the lots for them, after they had returned, before the Lord their God. Heavenly Father, may I recognise Thee as the sovereign Disposer of all things; and when events do occur which thwart or vex or annoy me, O may I receive grace to meet them as so many messages from Thyself: they could not have happened without Thine appointment: they are the consequents of Thy providential will; and let me meet them with a resolute purpose that in my conduct under them I shall be altogether regulated by Thy revealed and not by my own natural will. Such an event has befallen me at this time; and I most earnestly pray that in my treatment of it I may altogether acquit myself as Thou wouldst have me, and be enabled to lay the right control on my own waywardness. When the report was given in the lots were cast; and first the portion of Benjamin was determined contiguous to Judah, and between it on the south, and Ephraim on the north. It seems to have touched upon the Mediterranean, (verse 14); and the description of its boundaries would give the impression of a very ample territory—whereas my idea of it is a small inheritance, and somewhat of a pendicle to Judea. It seems exceedingly well defined in regard to its east and south-east border, after which we have an enumeration of its cities, the names of several of which are conspicuous and of frequent recurrence in Scripture history—as Jericho, and Gibeon, and Ramah, and Mizpeh, and above all Jebus, which is Jerusalem. The description indeed in verse 16 presents us with the limit as passing along the south side of Jerusalem, and thence descending to En-rogel—a place also famous in the history of the Israelites.

JOSHUA XIX.
September, 1845.

This chapter completes the account of the division of the land. The tribe of Simeon is the least distinguished in Israel; and the assignation to it, not of any distinct territory but only of part of that of Judah, is connected by many expositors with the prophetic malediction of Jacob on his death-bed, pronounced by him both on Simeon and Levi—" I will divide them in Jacob, I will scatter them in Israel." Another instance this out of many in which God, not historically or naturally merely, but judicially or in the form of a retributive sentence, deals with men according to the deeds of their progenitors. Thy judgments, O God, are unsearchable—Thy ways past finding out. And in the lot which cast up for Zebulun, too, might we recognise the Divine continuousness of Scripture history. What was prophesied by Jacob —that he should dwell at the haven of the sea, and be a haven for ships—took place in the days of Joshua. The prescience which foretells all was verified and fulfilled by the Providence which directs all. We cannot trace the same connexion of prophecy with accomplishment throughout the remaining inheritances which are recorded in this chapter; but this arises from the absence of geography in the blessing pronounced upon them by the dying patriarch. There are other things adverted to, however, in these benedictions—such as the characteristics or conditions of the various tribes, of which we can discern the fulfilments in other parts of the Bible. The part assigned to Joshua was according to the word of the Lord, and might well be justified on the principle that the labourer was worthy of his hire. The evening of his days reminds us of other generals and patriots who were alike rewarded and ended their days in the same manner. He was the General Washington of Palestine, and was well entitled to a choice portion in the land that he had subdued. What a deal of most deeply interesting history has vanished from the world. One should have liked to know the diary of his remaining life, his habits and enjoyments, of the grateful veneration in which he was held, and whether the Timnath-Serah of Mount Ephraim was not eyed and resorted to with the same feelings of affectionate patriotism which still glow in the bosoms of the Americans when they visit Mount Vernon. On the principle of the identity of human nature in all ages, we should imagine or rather believe that it must have been so. Joshua was a good man, and occupies a high place among the worthies of Israel.

JOSHUA XX.

The cities of refuge are regarded as a type of the Saviour; and many are the substantial and savoury things which have been said of the analogy between them. This analogy does not fail even in the provision being only for those who slew their neighbour unawares and unwittingly, insomuch, that if done deliberately and with *malice prepense*, there was no admittance to any of the asylums that are spoken of in this chapter. For there is a counterpart to this in the declaration and doctrine, that if any man sin wilfully after having come to the knowledge of the truth, there remaineth unto him no more sacrifice for sin. It was held punishment for an accidental manslayer that he was confined within the limits of one city till the death of the high-priest; and it is by the death of our High-Priest that the prisoners of hope are set free. The whole subject presents us with a complex imagery; but in each of its aspects the contemplation is a very delightful one. Under one aspect we are called upon to turn into the stronghold, and flee for refuge from the coming wrath to the hope set before us in the gospel, and take up with Christ as our hiding-place from the storm and the tempest. In the other aspect we are said to be delivered from captivity, and to be released into the glorious liberty of the children of God, where we can walk at large, and the avenger of blood, the accuser of the brethren, shall have no more power over us.—My God, accomplish upon me the whole of this glorious liberation, that I may not only be released from all obligation to the penalty of sin, but be released from my servitude to its hateful tyranny.—May it no longer have the dominion over me.—Set my feet in a large place, and thereon do Thou also enlarge my heart that I may run in the way of Thy commandments. Mark here that the provision was not confined to the children of Israel, but was extended also to the stranger who was amongst them. Even in the very ordinances of the Hebrew code do we meet with the promises and the openings towards a more expanded dispensation—as if Judaism were but the germ, and Christianity the full-blown tree; or the one in full the development of the other in embryo. Make known to me, O Lord, all of Christ and His gospel that is to be found in the Old Testament; and then shall I better comprehend of Him as of the Lamb slain before the foundation of the world.

JOSHUA XXI.

There was ample provision made, and that by express Divine commandment, for the Levites who composed the ecclesiastics of Israel. And so it should, and so it will be we apprehend under the Christian economy, when the kingdoms of the earth shall have become the kingdoms of our Lord and Saviour Jesus Christ, or when the governments of the world shall have become Christian governments. Hasten that blessed fulfilment, O Lord—and meanwhile pour forth a spirit of liberality on the hearers of every true Church, that he who is taught might communicate to him who teacheth in all good things. More particularly do Thou open the hearts of all the friends and adherents of the Free Church of Scotland; and as the Levites had cities to dwell in, do Thou prosper the enterprise that is now on hand for the provision of dwellings for her ministers—that our Church may become a fixture in the land and a perpetual blessing to its people. And as the Levites were the educationists as well as the ecclesiastics of Israel, do Thou cause that our Free Church schoolmasters and our colleges be in like manner provided for. The tribe of Levi seems to have been put in charge and occupation of all the cities of refuge. Grant, Lord, that our ministers might declare effectually the blessed gospel of Jesus Christ, and effectually hold out the refuge which is propounded there to all who are seeking to flee from the wrath that is to come. May the open door of Christ's mediatorship be clearly pointed out to the view of all inquirers, that the terrors of the law might shut them up unto the faith, and that sinners might know whither to repair for a refuge from the tempest and a hiding-place from the storm.

Thou art a promise-keeping God. Thou wert mindful in the days of old of Thine oath in behalf of Israel. There failed not aught of any good thing which God had spoken to them; and the promises in Christ Jesus are also yea and amen. Let us cast our confidence on the faithfulness of God.—Let us in virtue of these lay hold of eternal life and cherish the immovable hope of it—grounded and settled in the faith, and not moved away from the hope of the gospel.—Let us look onward to the Canaan that is above, the place of our everlasting habitation; and henceforth let our heart and our conversation be in heaven.

JOSHUA XXII.

What an amount of spirituality after all there is under the Jewish economy, even at its earlier stages. Let us take the lesson of Joshua to ourselves—not only to walk in the ways of an outward commandment, but to love the Lord and cleave unto Him and serve Him—and this not with the hand only, but with all our heart and all our soul. But there broke out a misunderstanding between the two portions of Israel, which was speedily however cleared up and done away—the fruit of a faithful and vigorous challenge on the one hand, and of a satisfactory explanation on the other. The two tribes and a-half had done what awakened the apprehensions of the rest of Israel lest they should lapse into idolatry. It is well to be fearful of the first approaches and appearances of evil. Give me to be jealous of these, and jealous of myself, O Lord. In particular, let me be careful to keep my heart from idols, and to keep it in the love of God. This precept laid upon the Israelites, even in that rudimental period of the world, is not only laid with fresh and powerful motives upon us, but the very method of upholding this affection within us is clearly propounded. We must build ourselves up in our most holy faith—we must pray in the Holy Ghost—we must look for the mercy of our Lord Jesus Christ unto eternal life. Thus shall we be enabled to sit loose unto a world the love of which is idolatry and opposite to the love of the Father. One likes to see the tenderness of the Israelites at this period, and more particularly the happy result of the conference which took place between the accusers and the accused. If I have any charges to make against such as I conceive to have erred, let me do it with frankness and firmness; but, O my God, save me from being hurried into any wrathful or intemperate effusions. I desiderate and pray for wisdom, and stand especially in need of the meekness of wisdom. And perhaps I may exaggerate, even as the nine tribes and a-half did in the imaginations which they had of their brethren. Such an account may be given as shall quiet my fears. I may find that there is every wish on the part of my colleagues to give in to the most enlightened and disinterested patriotism in regard to the various institutes and doings of the Free Church. At all events, let me not be so disturbed or cast down as I have often been hitherto, but be still and know that Thou art God.

JOSHUA XXIII.
October, 1845.

There is something venerable and touching in the last appearances of good old Joshua. His exit from the public stage was a most graceful and impressive one. But he had spent a good many years in peace and retirement—at least from the dangers and fatigues of war, for it was a long time after the Lord had given rest to Israel that Joshua in his extreme old age delivered the address of this chapter—the counsels and exhortations of wisdom and deep piety, of piety in one of its finest aspects, as it fell from the lips of a veteran soldier who had had manifold experience of the guidance and care of Providence, and now did homage to the God of battles as the author of all his victories. How he speaks of the many nations that occupied what we should regard as but a small territory even for one kingdom. But let not the small material extent of the territory occupied by the children of Israel deduct from our sense of the importance of their history, or of the high lessons given forth by it. There is a parallel to this in secular history, for what a space do the Athenians fill in our retrospect of the past, although their Attica had neither the size nor the population of one of our counties? There is an absolute prophecy of a full and much-enlarged possession delivered here by Joshua, which had a temporary fulfilment in the days of David and Solomon. But it was a fulfilment sadly mutilated and impaired because of their sins, for the prophecy, though absolute at the first, was soon modified, and that expressly into the conditional before the address was ended. The prophecy did not supersede, but presupposed the continued loyalty and obedience of the nation to the King of heaven. They were to abstain from idolatry and to exterminate all its temptations. They were to cleave unto the true God, and to take good heed lest they should fall away from the love of Him. They were more especially to shun all contaminating intercourse with idolaters, which if they failed to do, then so far from a naked and unqualified prediction in their favour they were bidden know for a certainty that God would abandon them to the power and oppression of the nations whom they had not driven out. How affecting the announcement of this great captain that he was "going the way of all the earth," and what a noble testimony is here given by him to the faithfulness of God. Not one thing had failed of all the good things which he had promised. And such, O Lord, will be the experience of us all if we depart not from Thee and from Thy ways. Save me, O God, from a declension so melancholy. Save me from the fellowships of a world lying in wickedness. Save me from the secularizing influences of sense and of time, and from the idolatry of my own inordinate affections. Turn, O God, my thoughts and mine eyes from vanity.

JOSHUA XXIV.

This seems a second convocation and address by Joshua before his death. It is ushered in by a prefatory recital of bygone history, and in this respect is of a piece with

Stephen's address before the Sanhedrim, and with Paul's in Antioch of Pisidia. (Acts xiii.) Such an introduction is well fitted to propitiate the attention of a Hebrew audience; and the present has in it a certain venerable and antique air from the remoteness of the outset which it makes, beginning with Terah, the father of Abraham. Altogether, though general, it presents us with a remarkably clear and compendious view of their previous fortunes; and after cementing the past with the present, effloresces into sentiments and lessons of imperishable value for all ages. Enable me, O God, to make a right choice between God and the world, the love of which is idolatry. O may I henceforth serve Thee with sincerity and truth, and put away every evil affection, and more especially the sin which doth most easily beset me. O may I carry into effect the holy purpose of good old Joshua when he said—As for me and my house we will serve the Lord. Such too was the profession of the people as well as of their leader; but they did not keep by it. How miserably soon they fell away; and so, too, shall I if I have nought but my own strength to uphold me—so prone am I to defection from God, so powerful are my own corrupt inclinations. Save me, O God, from this provocation of Thy jealousy, lest I find Thee to be a consuming fire. O incline my heart so that with full and steadfast purpose from this time forward I may cleave to Thee in all faithfulness and loyalty. Put truth into my inward parts that now I may with a good conscience and without faltering call on Thee to witness my integrity. Purge me, O God, from all regard to iniquity, and then wilt Thou hear the prayer which I now lift for the requisite aid from on high, that my infirmities might be helped and I enabled to pay the vow which I now make of fulfilling, in the strength of Thine almighty grace, the new obedience of the gospel. If it be Thy blessed will give me a peaceful, but withal a pious old age. Prolong my usefulness up to the measure of my opportunities and strength. Endow me with an affection for human souls, and let me never cease to pray and as far as in me to labour for the Christian good of my Church and neighbourhood. I would not live alway; but prepare me, O God, for my coming change: and grant that ere the grave closes over me I shall have served my day and generation and made my peace with God.

JUDGES.

Judges i.—Give me, O Lord, to ask counsel of Thee in all my doings. May I know what it is to commit my way unto God, and ever stand in awe that I sin not—seeing that Thou art a God of justice who will not let evil pass without a chastisement or without a reckoning.

We would not take undue liberties with Thy holy word; and we doubt that the upper and the nether springs which Caleb bestowed upon his daughter have been unwarrantably spiritualized, and yet we would pray, and with all earnestness, for the blessings which these have been made to represent. Grant me, O Lord, a plenteous supply of living water from above; and grant, too, that I may inhale and be refreshed from the pool of ordinances below. May Thy Spirit be shed on me abundantly, and Thy Bible, with its truths and its statutes, be my song in the days of my pilgrimage. Grant too that I may find the fellowships of the faithful to be wells yielding strength and consolation to me in this vale of tears.

Lord, be Thou with me as with Judah of old, and then greater will He be that is in me than he that is in the world. Yet I cannot look for a thorough and total extermination of the sin that so cleaves and lingers with me on this side of death. May I at least subjugate the evil which I cannot wholly drive out or expel, so that the sin which dwelleth with me—indwelling sin, may not have the dominion over me.

There are traits and incidents which temper the ferocity of war. There are also stern duties which we may be called on to perform; but let me rejoice in mercy, that darling attribute of Him who sitteth on high. Save me, O God, from the extremes whether of weakness or severity in my dealings with my fellow-men.

Teach me, O God, how to comport myself aright among the companies of the ungodly. Let not my growth in grace be impeded by the growing up of tares on every side of me. They may not be rooted out; may they be made subservient to my spiritual discipline and contribute so to the vigour and maturity of my principles, that I may shine forth as a light and an example in the midst of a crooked and perverse generation.

There is a contest going on between the principles of nature and grace. Nature keeps possession, but let grace maintain the prevalence and the power. Let even the sins which do most easily beset me be kept effectually in check. Save me, O God, from the enemy within, whom if I cannot extirpate, let me at least subordinate and control.

JUDGES II.

The people made a solemn covenant with Joshua that the Lord only they would serve; yet how soon did they fall away. On this very day, O my God, do I purpose sitting down at the Lord's table, and there renewing my engagement to be Thine and Thine only. O may I be enabled to make a great spiritual sacrifice, and to renounce conclusively and for ever the sins which do most easily beset me. Let me make no league with the tempters so as to fall again into the temptations of a world of which all the lusts are opposite to the love of the Father. Let not the evil affections of an evil and accursed nature be any longer a snare unto me; but on this day of renewed dedication may I make an entire surrender of all those sins which have so seduced and lorded over me. Let me think of what little avail is a mere weeping repentance, even though accompanied with the rites of sacrifice. Let mine, O God, be the sacrifice of a broken heart penetrated with godly sorrow, and having its fruit in that repentance which is unto salvation.

Let me beware of those sad declensions which occupy so large a place in the history of backsliding Israel. Give me strength, O Lord, for the fulfilment of this day's vow—a day of special calling on Thee, and in which of all other days throughout the year I say Lord, Lord. O let my profession be founded on a rock and not on the deceitful sand, that I may not be of the number of those who call Thee Lord, Lord, while I do not the things which Thou sayest. Save me from the evil heart of unbelief that would cause me to depart from the living God. Thou knowest what the fascinations are which most lead me astray and cause me to forsake Thee and to follow after other objects of desire, and to cast all sense of Thy law and Thy holiness away from me. When I think of Thine anger with sinners every day may I stand in awe and sin not. Rescue me from the hands of the great adversary that I may not be taken captive by him at his pleasure; and let me not forget his tactics, that I may conduct aright my spiritual warfare with his policy and power. Let me be aware that every wayward indulgence strengthens the tendency to evil, and that incipient freedoms or tamperings with any object of temptation invests that object with a greater power over me in all time coming.—My God, let the judgments and testimonies of Thy holy word be my defence against the evil influences of an evil world. Or if these are not to be withdrawn, let me stand my ground against them; if left to prove me, give me the victory, O Lord, and the blessedness of those who endure and who overcome.

JUDGES III.

November, 1845.

There is here what does not resolve the question, but suggests some plausibilities regarding the origin of evil, or at least one of the purposes to which it may be subservient. It subserves the object of moral discipline and trial—as when the Canaanites were left to prove the Israelites—the tares are suffered to grow up with the wheat, and the wicked to continue mixed with the good to the end of the world. Let me note that not culture merely but *manifestation* is often stated to be one great design of God's method of administration, as in this instance to know whether God's people would hearken to His commandments.

And practically the experiment, if we might venture thus to call it, offered in its results a melancholy exhibition of that human nature which was the subject of it. The children of Israel gave in to the example both of the nations wherewith they were mingled and of the nations which surrounded them. Their whole history presents us with a series of alternations between the good and the evil, in which the evil greatly predominates. The moral history of Judea is an epitome of the moral history of the world.

This rude and primitive history has many charms for me.—And beside presenting us with pictures of the olden time which regale the imagination, there are lessons of great weight to be drawn from it, and from which we might learn both the goodness and severity of God. The provocations of rebellious and stiff-necked Israel and the forbearance of God are alike marvellous.—My God, give me to feel how long Thou hast borne with me, and enable me henceforward to renounce all the passions and all the perversities of a sadly distempered nature. I should not like to spiritualize the literalities of the Bible beyond what is warrantable, and certain it is that the lessons drawn from Ehud's address to Eglon—" I have a message unto *thee*," are grounded on a text of mere accommodation, yet how precious the lesson, though not resting in this instance on a right substratum. Give me, O Lord, ever to entertain Thy gospel as a message to myself, and ever to expound it before others with a special application to every one of them—bidding each take the comfort of its promises, if along with this he takes the direction of its commands and its warnings. One cannot appropriate too closely, if he look at the Bible comprehensively, dealing with it fairly and equally throughout, and while cherishing its offers as his own, not shrinking from the application to himself of its precepts and its threatenings.

JUDGES IV.

We have again another repetition of the usual steps constituting a brief series that was so often realized in the history of rebellious Israel. We have their lapse into wickedness and idolatry when left to themselves. We have the chastisement that was inflicted upon them in the oppression of their victorious enemies. We have the repentance of the subjugated people, not the mere cry of suffering or distress, for we read that it was a cry unto the Lord. Lastly, we have the return of the Divine compassion towards them, and a glorious deliverance at the hand and by the help of Him who is the God of battles. We have here an exhibition both of man and of God—of man who in the day of prosperity forgets, and only in the day of adversity considers; and of God whose patience so exceeds the measure of our provocations, and who is plenteous in mercy notwithstanding our selfish and ungenerous abuse of the same, as if the riches of His goodness and forbearance and long-suffering were wholly inexhaustible. Keep me, O Lord, from the extremes both of presumption and despair. How frequent or rather how habitual are my relapses into ungodliness. O do Thou, Almighty Father, who hast promised to turn away ungodliness from Jacob—do Thou remove this plague from my heart, and raise me to spirituality and faith against the earthly bias of a soul cleaving unto the dust—so that Thy goodness might lead me, not as it did Thy perverse and stiff-necked children of old away from God, but might lead me to and confirm me in repentance. We confess ourselves revolted by some of the instrumentality here put forth for the execution of God's purposes. There is everything to propitiate and charm the imagination in the aspect of the venerable prophetess, Deborah; but how much there is to horrify in the proceeding of Jael. There is an overhanging mystery in these things which will at length be finished; but in which we in the meantime acquiesce, by force of the consideration that what we know not now we shall know hereafter. We are in the midst of a progression, which at that time was still in the rudeness of its comparative infancy, but which will at length terminate in the everlasting reign of love and righteousness. Nevertheless, it would seem that it is through the medium of a great and general destruction that this era of blessedness is to be ushered in. The atrocities of war are not yet ended, and there still lies before us the slaughter of a great and coming sacrifice. (Rev. xix. 17.)

JUDGES V.

This is a truly sublime ode, and its effect is greatly enhanced by the rude and distant antiquity whence its utterance is poured forth upon us. It is interesting to mark the primitive tendencies to song in the different ages of the world—proving how poetry and music are bound up as it were with the first elements of the human constitution. The instance before us is one of the most powerful and picturesque that has come down to us from any of the older periods of the world. The invocation to

God is truly magnificent; and the representation of the state of Israel, one of the most graphical that can well be imagined, when the Philistines lorded it over the country, and the people had to take shelter in hiding-places. "The mother in Israel" sets before us a most venerable and impressive figure. The blessing ascribed to God because of the people's willingness is an homage to His ascendency over the hearts of men. He made them willing in the day of His power. O God, make me willing for every service Thou mightest be pleased in Thy providence to assign for me. It marks the simplicity of these ages, when the dignitaries of the land rode on white asses; and how exquisite are the descriptive touches, as that of the archers taking aim at the people when congregated at the wells. The rapid sketch of Israel by its tribes is highly poetical, and the pen of the ready writer has descended to us from one of the notabilia of this song; and so has the utterance that characterizes them who came not to the help of the Lord against the mighty. On the other hand we are revolted by it, as a trace of the barbarism of these earlier times, when in the recital of what took place, highly poetical though it be, we read the eulogy of Jael. But there is nothing in Ossian to equal the description of Sisera's mother looking forth with her ladies through the lattice, and waiting the return of their victorious lord. We may here note the licentiousness of war.—"Why are thy chariot wheels so long in coming?" ranks also among the notabilia of Scripture. And what a mighty imagination is that of the stars in their courses fighting against Sisera. We may pass two reflexions on this chapter—first, how much of the memorable and great, both as acted in reality and set forth in history, may take place on a theatre of small material extent.—Both Judea and Greece, and I should say Rome, when limited and surrounded by little states, give examples of this. Second, what attractions of eloquence, and beauty, and grandeur are mixed up with religion, as exhibited in that Book which is the record of its doctrines, and also of the doings that took place in the world, viewed in the peculiar light of its being God's world.

JUDGES VI.

Another of those moral cycles so frequently described by the children of Israel, and one of the most memorable on record. Gideon stands forth like Barak among the worthies of his nation in the catalogue of Paul. (Heb. xi.) In a few brief sentences we are here told of the rebellion, and the judgment, and the penitential prayer, and the remonstrance by a prophet, and lastly, the visit of mercy by an angel.—My God, I pray for the grace of a genuine and enduring repentance ere the day of grace and forbearance shall have come to an end. Turn me and I shall be turned.

What an impressive description have we here of the interview between Gideon and the messenger. From the very terms of the dialogue we learn that He was the Lord Jesus Christ, the Angel of the Covenant—not understood to be such by Gideon himself, but so named by the sacred historian, who interchanges with the merely angelic title awarded to Him by Gideon the appropriate and peculiar designation of Jehovah, reserved exclusively for the only living and supreme God. This is one of the most signal manifestations made in the Old Testament by our Lord and Saviour.

Save me from idolatry, O God. Be they images of pleasure, or profit, or fame, on which I have placed my affections, let me bring them all forth and slay them before Thee. Thou knowest, O God, the various ways in which I am tempted and exercised; but O keep me singly intent upon what is right—seeking not my own glory but Thine, seeking not my own pleasure but Thine. Let me ever acquiesce in Thy providential will, and ever observe and obey Thy declared will. Give me courage and resolution for every sacrifice which Thou requirest at my hands—even for all such sacrifices as are acceptable to God through Jesus Christ my Lord. Shed abroad in my heart the love of Thyself; and let this supplant every forbidden, and subordinate every lawful or allowed love.

I pray for the visitation of Thy Spirit, both to point the way I should go, and prevail on me to take it. I count not on the manifestations by miracle of other days; but do Thou shine, O Lord, on Thy Scriptures—that these may prove a light unto my feet, and a lamp unto my paths. And may the evolutions too of history, whereof Thou art the sovereign controller, open up a way for me. And not only may Thy wisdom ever direct, but may the dew of Thy grace ever descend upon me to the refreshment and the strengthening of my soul. Let me shine forth as a light in the midst of a perverse and crooked generation; or rather, instead of partial droppings from above, let Thy living water come down in a universal shower on a world now lying in wickedness.

JUDGES VII.

Thou, O God, canst save by many or by few. I do

fear that there are exceedingly few in our Free Church who are purely and singly devoted to the great object of a gospel ministry—the Christian good of the people. Many, very many I fear, if not all, seek their own things rather than the things of the Lord Jesus. These will not effectually fight the battle against the forces of a world lying in wickedness. Grant a remnant of the good and the true, O Lord, and such a remnant as might suffice through the aids of Thy Divine grace, to vindicate Thy cause, and keep alive the faith and righteousness of the gospel among the people of Scotland. There can be no effectual co-operation for the prosperity or extension of our Church among those who, fearful of their incomes, refuse what is best for the furtherance of our cause, lest these should be encroached upon. And there can be as little effectual co-operation from those who perhaps might not be counting on the diminution of their allowances, but who would draw all from the central reservoir which they could, and not be satisfied with the proportions which each might earn by their own efforts for the support of the Church in their own respective localities.—My God, how many or how few are there who will abide by the high and holy objects of a pure missionary or apostolic enterprise after that these are bidden away! However few, Thou canst save our country and our Church by their instrumentality alone; and it is my earnest prayer that Thou, O Lord, wouldst hasten in Thine own good time this blessed consummation, and make bare Thine own right arm, and speed the establishment of Thine own righteous cause. And, O my God, shew me a token for good; raise me above this despondency—for I am indeed in great heaviness. Teach me what I should do. Give me simplicity, and at the same time decision of purpose. Cause the light to shine out of darkness; and though small should be the body of my adherents, let me cast my care and confidence on Thee, O God, and do Thou both shine upon the path of wisdom and duty, and therein uphold my goings. And speaking of the likelihoods of futurity, it does seem the more probable opening for victory on the side of what is right and the defeat of adversaries, that they should fall out among themselves. But I am yet in perplexity: I would wait the farther evolutions of Thy providence; I would be still and know that Thou art God. At present it may be so, that my strength and wisdom both are to be still—meanwhile, I would commit my way unto the Lord. I pray that by Him every thought may be established. I would trust in God, and lean not to my own understanding. Thou wilt bring it to pass, and therefore let me neither fret nor be impatient. Let me fret not myself in anywise to do evil. What a blessed Psalm is the thirty-seventh to one in my circumstances! Let me drink in its spirit under the present trial, nor think that any strange thing has happened to me.

JUDGES VIII.

December, 1845.

A soft answer turneth away wrath. What a promptitude in me to return indignancy of feeling for the charges of injustice. Let me take an example from Gideon, and cultivate the charity which endureth all things. And there has been an application made of this narrative to the Christian life which I would do well to act upon—faint, yet pursuing.—My God, let me not be weary, but endure unto the end.—or though weary, let me not give up my Christian perseverance, but continue working and waiting upon Thee till Thou renewest my strength, when I shall walk and not be weary, when I shall run and not faint. And yet this Gideon could discriminate and be severe at one time, while, whether from policy or duty, soft and yielding at another. He pacified those of the tribe of Judah who had aided him, while he punished the men of Succoth and Penuel who refused him aid.—And though not perhaps cruel beyond the usages of war, yet war at the best, and in the hands even of those who stand highest as the recorded worthies of Scripture, is a very coarse and revolting affair.

Perhaps his severest trial was the usage that he afterwards received from the ungrateful Israelites, but meanwhile he himself proved a snare unto them. It was hazardous to tamper with their idolatrous propensity, or to supply the least fuel for its gratification—far better that he had not meddled with the fabrication of that ephod. They evinced enough of compliance with the wishes of Gideon in giving up their ear-rings and golden ornaments. But how transient is human affection!—They would have enthroned him and his posterity; but how miserably soon did they fall away—first to idolatry, and then to disloyalty. They renounced their heavenly, and let us not wonder that they should forget their human benefactors. It was thus that Gideon and his house suffered by the ephod which tempted the people, and perhaps even tempted themselves from a pure and single-hearted allegiance to the true God. Though Gideon was free from ambition his conduct in the matter of the ephod seems not to have been altogether blameless.

Let this history—first, of Israel's defection from God to

idols, and secondly, of their unkindness to the house of him who had been their great earthly deliverer—let these impress on me the two lessons of neither trusting in man nor being seduced by the world—or rather, the one lesson of not suffering the creature to usurp either the confidence or the affection which is due to the Creator. Be Thou, O God, the supreme object both of my trust and of my regard, and let everything else be prized only in subordination to Thee. May I enjoy the good things of life in the spirit of thankful acknowledgment to Thee as the giver. May I love my brethren and all men in the spirit of the second law, and as being like unto the first.

JUDGES IX.

In these rude and unsettled times humanity gives forth its most revolting exhibitions, yet proceeding from the same evil affections which are exemplified and are still in full force, though perhaps in a different style and complexion, even at the present day. Let us not think, for instance, that any strange thing has happened to us though both communities and individuals should be unmindful of former services, and a treatment both unkind and ungenerous should be all that we receive in consequence at the hands of men. Let my trust and refuge be in God. Be Thou the habitation to which I may resort continually; and though in the world I should have tribulations, may I ever experience that in Christ I have peace. The narrative here given bears testimony to the righteousness of an ever-watchful Providence which, it is true, permitted the violence which is here recorded, but which, at the same time, avenged it, and which made ample demonstration of itself both in the final catastrophe and in the prophecy which foretold it. Let me therefore, while I beware of men, cast all my care and confidence on God.

The part which God directly took in this remarkable passage of the Israelitish history is abundantly manifest in that He sent an evil spirit between Abimelech and the men of Shechem. There may have been a demoniacal agency employed for this fulfilment, or the evil spirit may have been merely a spirit of dissension raised up between the parties, and which terminated in their mutual destruction. On either supposition we cannot fail to recognise God as the universal Sovereign, having all the elements both of the moral and the material world at His disposal. This should reconcile us to all the crosses and annoyances and mortifications which come to us from the perversities and the evil passions of our fellow-men. Let me regard these as so many inflictions, and that for the purposes of a salutary discipline at the hand of Him who is the great spiritual husbandman. Let me count it all joy, therefore, when I fall into these various tribulations. What a lesson does this chapter hold forth of a Divine superintendence in the affairs of men, which, to the minutest particular, are under the absolute control of Him who reigneth over all—giving, for example, that impulse to the woman's heart which led her to throw the stone, and that direction of it to the person of Abimelech, which resulted in his death—and all, we are told, for the object of a just retribution on both the parties in the atrocity that was perpetrated on the family of Gideon—rendering their wickedness upon the heads both of Abimelech and the men of Shechem, and so accomplishing the curse which by the mouth of Jotham He had Himself pronounced upon them.

JUDGES X.

There seems to have been nearly half a century of prosperity and peace for Israel under the administration of the two next judges—a long period for so brief a notice, and where the chief feature in the record is the simple yet picturesque dignity of one of the ruler's establishments. Let me feel the insignificance of my own ephemeral day, and no longer make a resting-place of that world whose fleeting generations pass so rapidly from the stage of time, and from the remembrance of those who come after them.

In this sad narrative of Israel's perversities and rebellions, there is some alleviation in the thought that a so much larger space is given to the history of their transgressions, and their misfortunes, and their wars, than to that of their quiet and undisturbed periods, when each family lived and flourished under their own vine and their own fig-tree. The expression that they did evil *again* in the sight of the Lord, (that sight which was constantly upon them and upon their ways,) implies an interval of comparative goodness, or at least inoffensiveness throughout the nation, who relapsed however into another of their frequent idolatries, and called down upon themselves the anger of a jealous and sin-hating God, who gave them up for a series of years to the power of their enemies. Thus were they sorely beset on both sides of Jordan, till in the extremity of their oppression they cried unto the Lord—confessing their sins with the mouth, though there is every appearance of its being the cry not of penitence but of distress. In the remonstrance that follows on the part of God we see Him to be a God of judgment: He reasons the matter with them and is clear when He speaketh. So, doubtless, will it be found in the great day of reckoning—even that just and true are all the ways of Him who is the king of saints. The sequel exhibits Him who is a God of judgment to be also a God of mercy. The Israelites did set up an external reformation, and mixed performances with their prayers ; and it is truly affecting, yea encouraging to read that the soul of the Lord was grieved for the misery of Israel. Truly judgment is His strange work, while mercy is His darling attribute.—My God, save me from presumption on the one hand, and from despair upon the other. Let my views be concentrated on the great work of redemption, and then all is harmonized. Truth and mercy meet together ; peace and righteousness enter into an enduring fellowship, a covenant well-ordered and sure.

JUDGES XI.

It is God who assigns to all the people on earth the bounds of their respective habitations. In the argument of Jephthah there is an obvious recognition of the directing and controlling power that is above, and an appeal to His judgment withal. And the Spirit of God seems to have dictated his words, at least it actuated and gave him might and courage for the war. Jephthah was an instrument in the hand of Providence for the deliverance of Israel, and for the fulfilment of a mercy not yet extinguished by the multiplied provocations of the stiff-necked and rebellious people. This chapter forms one of the most memorable passages in the history of these rude and primitive times ; nor should we overlook that Jephthah who seems to have lived the life of a marauding captain at the head of a company of banditti, before he was called to the command of the national army—that he is named by the Apostle as one of that glorious band who lived and died in the faith, and are set forth as examples thereof to us of succeeding ages. Indeed, his reference to the God of Israel throughout the pleading that he held with Ammon, and the descent of the Spirit upon him, and even the vow wherewith he entered upon his undertaking, prove him to be of a religiously disposed mind, and are so far in keeping with the Apostolic testimony regarding him. As to the controversy respecting his daughter—whether he acquitted himself of his vow by dedicating her to a life of virginity, or by a literal burnt-offering—we abstain from it in this place, and would only ground upon it here a fervent supplication to God, that He would strengthen us for all such spiritual sacrifices as are acceptable to Himself through Jesus Christ our Lord. O for an entire dedication of all I have and am to the glory of Him who made me. Draw me to Thyself, O Father in Heaven, and prepare me for the entire surrender of soul, and spirit, and body, unto Thy service and glory. Conform me to Christ both in His death and resurrection, and then shall the world be crucified unto me, and I unto the world. May I be enabled for every necessary act of self-denial however arduous—giving myself as an entire offering unto God—putting my soul into His hand as a devoted thing set apart altogether for sacred uses—living no longer to my own will, but to the will of Him who died for me and rose again.

JUDGES XII.

January, 1846.

Save me, O God, from the heart-burnings of party

warfare. Let me seek not my own glory or my own will but in so far as it accords with Thy will and the good of Thy cause upon earth. Save our Church from division. On this day, being the commencement of the week set apart for prayer, would I supplicate the descent upon us of that wisdom which is from above, and which, though first pure, is then peaceable. Do Thou supersede by the all-powerful operation of the Spirit of love all those selfish and angry passions whence come wars and fightings amongst us. Give to myself in particular, O Lord, such methods of propounding what I hold best for the prosperity of our Zion as may not exasperate the brethren, but conciliate as well as convince them. Let me abjure with all earnestness that spirit of the Ephraimites which led them to attempt the overthrow and destruction of a great public benefactor because themselves were not sufficiently signalized. In honour may I prefer others, and never may self but always the Church be the object of my solicitude and care. May those Shibboleths of distinction which have given rise to so many fierce internal wars be lessening every day in number, and finally done away, yet all with a steadfast adherence to the faith once delivered to the saints, and for which we are required to contend earnestly. Let the great stamp of peculiarity be upon the Church at large in contradistinction to the world. In reference to them who are without may hers be always a peculiar people. May this be her Shibboleth—" Behold these Christians how they love each other."

The brief notices regarding that succession of judges who followed Jephthah in Israel, beside the one picturesque evolution of verse 14, give forth the impression of a peaceful and prosperous age in Israel—when, secure from enemies, they sat each under his own vine and his own fig-tree. We cannot figure that then there was a sinless generation, yet a generation so free of all that was flagrantly and generally enormous as to have been let alone for a time, so that the scourge of war and the other instruments of God's displeasure were for a season kept back. Altogether it presents us with a delightful vision, and one cannot help the pleasing persuasion that in these days there were many pious families of Israelites indeed. But let the rapid succession of years here described by a few touches, and which in very deed pass so rapidly away—let this consideration solemnize and warn me on the first Sabbath of a new year, that I may prepare with renewed earnestness and vigour for my latter end.

JUDGES XIII.

Israel fell again into another of its many defections. We may well wonder at such glaring perversity and waywardness in the face of such manifestations as were time after time vouchsafed to them. But are we sure that we would not have done the like in like circumstances? Is theirs a rare and monstrous peculiarity; and instead of this, ought we not on the perusal of their history to be humbled for ourselves, to be humbled for our common nature? There follows one of those remarkable appearances from heaven which serves to connect the old with the new dispensation, and strikingly to prove of these two economies that they were under the same identical guidance—nay, that it was the same identical personage in whose hands was placed the direct and immediate superintendence of both—He being the Angel of the

Covenant, the Lord Jesus Christ. He who is the great deliverer of our race appeared at various intervals as the deliverer of Israel: He appeared as an angel and came in the likeness of a man though His countenance was very terrible, and did not tell His name even though asked, because it was secret—as if His were indeed the incommunicable name. It is true that He was sent by God, but so was Christ sent by God into the world. Gabriel told his name, but this angel did not and would not tell his; and are we not on all these considerations to join in the conclusion of Manoah that he had indeed seen God? This angel who it is said did wondrously, is not this He whose name should be called Wonderful and the mighty God?—We think so, and hold this to be one of those deeply interesting evolutions from the upper regions of which there are several like examples in the Old Testament. O Lord Jesus, be enthroned in my heart. Be no longer lightly esteemed by me. He who hath seen Christ hath seen God. Believing in God may I also believe in Him.—These were truly august accompaniments wherewith Samson was ushered into the world. Nor are we to overlook in the warrior—and a warrior, too, according to the rude and boisterous character of the times—the man of God whom the Lord did bless, and whom He moved by His Spirit. Heavenly Father, grant me this precious boon, and arm me with strength for the contest against the enemies of the Lord and of His Church.

JUDGES XIV.

There is a strange mixture here of the native and the rough-hewn with that finer element which comes from heaven—for let us not forget that Samson was visited by the Spirit of God, and that he is included by Paul in his enumeration of the Old Testament worthies who were signalized, nay even, I should think, who were saved by faith. It is true that they are said not to have obtained the promise—that they lived in those ages of the yet unfulfilled prophecy regarding Christ, whereas we live in the light of His finished revelation. But some, most assuredly, and perhaps all will " obtain a better resurrection."—At all events let us not be deterred by any measure of barbarism, or even of profligacy, from attempting the evangelisation, whether of those immersed in the darkness of heathenism, or of those immersed in the worst and most revolting depravities of our own land. In the first ages of Christianity they had very coarse materials to work upon—insomuch that Paul had to lay it upon the bishops that they should be no strikers. Grant us, O Lord, the requisite courage and prudence for our enterprise in the West Port, and above all the wisdom of winning souls. The Spirit of the Lord came mightily upon Samson to strengthen him for his various feats and achievements, and let us hope too for the salvation of his soul. He was obviously however a warrior of the ruder stamp, and of strong untamed passions— the picturesque exemplification of such virtues, whether bodily or mental, as were most esteemed in a primitive and barbarous age. It may well be said that without the humanity and purity and other refinements of character which have sprung from Christianity, they were not " made perfect." And save us, O God, from being deceived when we peruse the recital of these infirmities and faults which characterized Thy servants under a grosser and darker dispensation—from being deceived into connivance, or into the extenuation of what is vicious and wrong. The picture here given of these earlier times is fitted to engage the fancy; but let it not bring a soil either on the sentiment or the sacredness which belongs to a spiritual disciple in the school of Christ. In contemplating the impetuous, but withal the susceptible mind of Samson—the fierce anger on the one hand, the uxorious softness and sensibility on the other—let us pray to be delivered from the tyranny of those evil affections which war against the soul.

JUDGES XV.

Samson continues to pursue what to us appears a wild and wayward course—a man of strong passions and keen sense of justice withal, and thoroughly patriotic, notwithstanding the alliance that he made with the Philistines; and yet this matrimonial connexion with one of their families is said to have been of the Lord—and certainly it did furnish the occasion to Samson for signal triumphs over these enemies of Israel. In this instance he visited the injury done to him by his father-in-law on the whole nation, or on others at least, and because of that nation. His were the bold and irregular doings of a guerilla man —we can scarcely say of a guerilla chief; for we read not of any band of followers—his being solitary exploits performed by the strength and prowess of his own single arm, and prompted by the desire of vengeance for his own personal wrongs, though done with a greater *con amore*, because done against the tyrants and oppressors of his own land. There is something graphic and picturesque in his situation on the rock Etam, reposing from his toils, and breathing further deeds of valour and gigantic force against the Philistines. It is said that in the marvellous other achievements of this chapter—the breaking of the cords that bound him, and the slaying of a thousand men with the jaw-bone of an ass—that the Spirit of the Lord was upon him mightily, and further, that God provided him with water by miracle to relieve him of his thirst. To what different and higher ends does the Spirit of God now work upon men—to strengthen inwardly with all might in the inner man for victory over the devil and the world and the flesh. I pray for such victories, O God. May I work mightily according to Thy grace working in me mightily. Give me to do all things through Christ strengthening me—strong through the grace that is from Him, and enabled both to act and to endure as a good soldier under the Captain of my salvation. And do Thou sustain my fainting spirit under all my fatigues and in every discouragement. But where, alas! is my Christian warfare—where my overcomings of the world by faith—where my efforts, or my sacrifices, or my self-denial? Forgive my love of ease, my self-indulgence, my self-seeking; and help me to prevail over these by the aids of that grace which Thou bestowest on those who are humbly sensible of their manifold defects and infirmities.

JUDGES XVI.

Burntisland, February, 1846.

Samson is included in the list of Paul's Old Testament worthies who signalized themselves and obtained a good report by faith. There seems here then another evidence of progression in the moral government of God, even that God who winked at times of ignorance, and who, for the hardness of their hearts, permitted to the Israelites what Christ forbade to His disciples. Whatever justice, on the contrary, there might be in this hypothesis, let me not be deceived or led astray by the example of those who have a good reputation. And purify my heart as well as my practice, O God. But let me still in every good work consult my own soul.—Let me not give way to the urgency of others on matters of principle; and I pray for the wisdom that can discern the right path, and the firmness which in the midst of every distracting influence can enter upon and persevere in it. O save me from every fascination that would bring me under the power of others, "lest I give my honour to others, and my years to the cruel." Such was the end of poor Samson; and yet his prayer was heard for strength to avenge himself on his enemies. In like manner, though times and ways without number I have sinned against Thee, O Lord, cast me not off utterly.—Give me to repent in time—henceforward may all old things be done away and all things become new with me.—Let mine be a high work of soul and heart-holiness—a holiness of thought and desire as well as of outward demeanour. O God, I know not what trials and afflictions may be in reserve for me during the remainder of my days on earth. If it be Thy blessed will, let mine be an old age of peace and of piety; but let me not forget the precedency of principle over privilege—first pure, then peaceable. Prepare me for the whole of Thy will. Tempt me not beyond what I am able to bear. Provide me, O God, a way of escape. May I profit by Thy wise and salutary discipline; and let the effect of Thy spiritual husbandry be that I shall bear more fruit, that I shall abound more and more in all the fruits of righteousness. Thou knowest, O God, the history of my past as well as my prospects and plans and fears for the future. Preside over every footstep of my way. I pray with all earnestness for grace and guidance from on high. I would commit all the thoughts of my heart unto Thee—stablish them, O God.—I would trust in the Lord, and lean not to mine own understanding.

JUDGES XVII.

Samson was the last of the Judges of whom we read in this Book, which is closed with passages of episodical and miscellaneous history. The tale or narrative of this chapter affords a curious glimpse of the spirit and manners of that early and semi-barbarous period, and proves how deeply the Israelites were infected by the example of the surrounding idolaters, or rather of the idolaters with whom they were intermingled, and who had been left for their punishment and trial to continue in the midst of them. The religion of the Israelites in these days seems to have been of a very mongrel character—a compound of Judaism and Paganism—image worship strangely mixed with the recognition of the true God, and a reverence for the national institutions which He had appointed; for the graven and molten images which the mother of Micah had intended to frame were for the purpose of being dedicated to the Lord Jehovah; and after they were framed they formed part of an apparatus that was completed by the admission of other things into it of Hebrew origin and ordination, as an ephod and teraphim, and finally a priest consecrated from among the sons of Micah—who at the same time felt that he had made a great advance and acquisition when he got instead a Levite for a priest, and because of it comforted himself with the thought that now the Lord Jehovah would do him good. We have here an instructive and memorable verse, from which we may gather of what vast importance it is to society to be placed under the control of a strong ruling authority; and this not only to check civil offences, but which if righteous as well as strong would have operated as a restraint on such waywardness of religious practice and observation as we read of in this chapter, and which would not have taken place under the government of a pious and enlightened king armed with principle enough to have laid his discountenance on idolatry, and with power enough to have enforced his decrees against it. There are traces here of as lax a morality in that age as of a corrupt theology—as instanced in the son's theft of his mother's property, and in the mother's joy at the restoration of it without any seeming rebuke, but the contrary, on her son's misconduct. The lesson should not be lost on us—the avoidance of all composition in things of religion—a lesson mightily wanted by the conformists and the borderers of our day, who vitiate their Christian profession by the spirit and usages of a world lying in wickedness. Deliver me, O God, from this fatal snare.

JUDGES XVIII.

There was a general commission under the authority of which it was probably a legitimate thing for the Israelites to drive out the original inhabitants when they could, and that for ages after their first settlement in Canaan. Certain it is that these Danites valued a Divine sanction, as is obvious from their application to Micah's priest to ask counsel of God—though it is a very ambiguous question whether there could be aught of real intercourse between heaven and earth in this way, amid the strange corruption and composition of their midway state at that time between the true worship and idolatry. There was at all events respect had to the Levite as an ecclesiastical man, and for which there was a better foundation than for our modern Puseyism. But the religion in both instances stops short at men; and we pray to be delivered from the influence of all such earthly respects as tend to exalt the creature above the Creator, the sensible above the spiritual, the human above the divine—whether in the form of a superstitious veneration for human office or human authorship. The Danite invasion recorded in this chapter is sufficiently revolting, made as it was on a quiet and unsuspecting people. It bears on it all the characters of a marauding and murderous expedition—though an express ordination from God would afford even to such an act its most ample justification. But not only did they proceed against Canaanites, they perpetrated a deed of robbery on one of their own nation; and we behold here another strange mixture of violence and theft on the one hand, with a value for Divine things upon the other—sadly vitiated no doubt, and composing altogether a motley assemblage of objects—such as images with ephod and teraphim, and a Levite to sanction and in their estimation to sanctify the whole concern. It marks after all the strength of the religious element in a man's breast, of which we have many examples in all ages—

an element not stifled even by the grossest enormities. Idolatry is far more congenial to the human spirit than atheism; but let us not wonder at the jealousy of the true God far more expressed throughout Scripture against the one than the other—as if the most entire oblivion of Him were less offensive than the usurpation of His throne by false and evil and imaginary powers. There is much to revolt in the treatment of these careless and secure people at Laish; and a very extraordinary worship set up among the Danites, who had a service and a priesthood in this remote and sequestered place on the far north of the land of Israel—inaccessible for ages to their brethren, seeing that their peculiar and most corrupt religion lasted till the days of the Captivity—nor did even the tabernacle at Shiloh withdraw them from their own ritual. Short distances sufficed to keep asunder in these days.

JUDGES XIX.
Newliston.

Another passage in the history of these unsettled times still more revolting than the former. The information by which it is ushered in, of there being no king in Israel, is another remarkable testimony to the importance of a strong as well as a righteous government for the well-being of society. One might infer from the alleged open concubinage of the Levite that there was a general relaxation of morality throughout the land, but it admits of question whether this concubine was not his wife, and certain it is that her father is named his father-in-law, and the woman is spoken of as if she had committed adultery against him by her unfaithfulness. However this is decided we certainly are presented here with the narrative of a very foul enormity perpetrated in one of the towns of Israel, and with the cognizance, it would appear, of a multitude in the place. The history of the Levite's reception by one individual does not alleviate the charge of a general inhospitality in the place; for, like the exception which confirmeth a rule, it came in the train of a vain expectancy for a time on the part of the Levite, who complained—" there is no man that receiveth me to house." But even with this host there is something of a very loose and disjointed character. The compromise here offered to these sons of Belial looks very strange to us, as also that of the Levite in putting forth to them his wife or concubine; yet we are not able to compute in how far this was due to the violence of terror, or to the lightness of moral feeling in regard to these awful misdoings. The whole transaction came to a most tragical consequence at the first, and to a still more tragical end afterwards in the course of this revolting history. It is certainly well that there was such a reclamation of conscience and of the moral sense against this dire perpetration on the part of the collective mind of Israel. No doubt the aggrieved man took a most effectual method of creating a general and wide-spread sensation on the subject of his wrongs. One likes to observe their own peculiar national history to be so fresh in the remembrance and so currently in the mouths of the children of Israel; and the prompt reference which they make to what might well be reckoned their commencement as a nation—even the day when they came up out of the land of Egypt. The disgrace felt to be inflicted on national honour by this proceeding marks a not altogether extinct national morality. And let us not imagine of such recitals that they are inapplicable to present times, or unfruitful of lessons to an earnest reader of that Book —all of which is profitable. When one contemplates the atrocity of these final outgoings to the desires of licentiousness it surely carries in it the admonition of vigilance and self-restraint and self-denial as to the very first beginnings of them.—My God, do Thou send a purifying influence into the very fountain-head of my moral state and being—even that heart which should be kept with all diligence, seeing that out of it are the issues of life. O my God, deepen my sense and conviction more and more that in me—that is in my flesh—dwelleth no good thing.

JUDGES XX.

March, 1846.

This was a great outburst of national feeling and the manifestation of it on the largest possible scale. And they seem to have proceeded righteously in the matter, not wishing to inflict a wholesale vengeance on the tribe, or even on the city where this great wickedness was done, but proposing that the retribution should be laid on the personal transgressors, and requiring that they should be given up. It is marvellous that Benjamin should have had the hardihood to refuse, but there is no answering either for the wisdom or the principle of democracies, for such each tribe in these days may be regarded when there was no king or no other dominant power over them. One might have thought that the comparative numbers would have deterred them; but there is a delusion by which bodies of men are carried away, and in which they encourage each other, and a popular assembly are not arithmetical in their views. It is very remarkable, nor can we guess the reason of it, that God should have counselled

Israel to go up unto the battle at two different times, and yet each time should have suffered them to be defeated. The third time His bidding was accompanied with a promise that they should prevail over Benjamin. It is a dreadful expression that in the pursuit they *gleaned* of them five thousand men—reminding us of some of Oliver Cromwell's despatches, when he writes that in pursuit of the flying enemy they had good execution of them. It shows what a barbarous thing war is and how uncontrollable the murderous spirit is when once it is awakened— seeing that the men, who under the hurrying impulse of the fight scattered death around them, after a short period wept over the desolation that had been made by their own hands. They were not appeased short of killing all whom they could reach, and burning up every city they came to with fire. Let us pray for the cessation of war from the earth. Let us hope that Christianity may become universal, and that the universal reign of truth and righteousness may banish this master evil from the habitations of men. But not we fear will this blessed consummation be realized till the present economy be taken down and replaced by the new heavens and the new earth. Teach me meanwhile, O God, the peace and the charity which will qualify me for these scenes of perfection that are yet coming.

JUDGES XXI.

Here we have another most striking fluctuation of popular feeling—yet not an unnatural one. They who had been so full of vengeance and fury before, mourned over their own sad handiwork, and wept sore. What a savage and unrelenting spirit gets up amid the fierceness and cries of the latter. The poor women of Benjamin then it would appear were all sacrificed in this affair of wholesale murder; and it would appear the children of an entire tribe also—else they would have had another security for the perpetuation of the tribe than merely the six hundred men. They had no other method than to provide these with wives, but before this was done another most barbarous interlude had to be acted on the men of Jabesh-gilead—and this too on the plea of an oath, or on a religious plea. But how came women and children to be included in the execution of this oath?—Should they have been counted among the defaulters who had not come up to the battle; and what possible vindication can be alleged for their slaughter? These truly were coarse times; but let us not count on human nature as if essentially different now from what it was then. Should anarchy let slip the dogs of war upon us, there might the same atrocities be acted over again—and how dismal to think of the unquelled spirit for war that still tumultuates in the hearts of many people, and even in some of this world's governments. Let not horrid war, O Lord, which seems now to hang over us break forth among the nations. We deserve judgments at Thy hand. Our long peace has been shamefully abused; and we have become in the course of it a far more Sabbath-breaking, antiscriptural, and infidel community than before. Avert this awful visitation if it be Thy blessed will, O God. May there be peace and truth and righteousness in our day.—And yet who can discern prophecy and the signs of the times without the apprehension that ere the kingdom of Christ shall be established, there must be an awful midway process of force and violence, by which all the kingdoms of the earth are to be overthrown? The murder of almost a whole tribe and then of nearly all the inhabitants of a city, was followed up by another outrage for the purpose of making out the complement of wives for the remnant of Benjamin. Surely this was a rudimental period in the history of God's administration, for religion seems to have been strangely mixed up with doings which, contemplated in themselves, we should regard as most hideous and revolting atrocities. It was because they had so sworn—that they would not give their own daughters in marriage to the Benjamites, that they exterminated the inhabitants of Jabesh-gilead. It is fitly said at the conclusion of this verse—for it goes far to explain the enormities of that turbulent period—that there was no king in those days, but every man did that which was right in his own eyes.

RUTH.

RUTH I.—What an exquisite and pleasing interlude between the larger histories of the two eras in Israel—the era of the judges, and that of the kings. Let us remember that our Saviour was descended of Ruth according to the flesh, for that the blood of the Gentiles flowed in that royal line, of which Christ came, who is over all, God blessed for ever. The Moabites were by the Jewish economy excluded from the congregations of Israel for ever; but they enter into the earthly parentage of Him who is the author and the finisher of our faith—a faith which, like Him from whom it sprung, is no respecter of persons, but extends its privileges to him of every nation who feareth God and worketh righteousness; and so making grace co-extensive with nature, or in keeping with the large and comprehensive designs of Him who made of one blood all the nations that be on the face of the earth. But there is something more than a diffusive liberality to be learned from this narrative: have we ever read of aught so intensely domestic, or of an affection so special and so linked by the strongest ties of affinity and kindred, as are set forth in this primitive tale of utmost beauty and utmost tenderness? Let me cherish these home feelings more habitually and practically than ever; and, O my God, if it be Thy blessed will, do Thou so order events by Thy providence, as that at rest from all controversy without, I may henceforth spend in the bosom of my family, and in the midst of family affections, an old age of piety and peace. But whatever may be Thy will as to my future history in this world, let me so labour as that I shall enter into that rest which remaineth for the people of God—looking to a heavenly and not an earthly paradise, and meanwhile acquiescing in the whole of that discipline which a gracious God might see meet for nurturing within me the graces of faith, and patience, and charity. I am fast tending to the grave; and indeed my thoughts often wander onward to the day and place of my burial. But while deferring to the strong natural preference so touchingly exhibited both by Joseph and Ruth for being laid beside those who were dear to them on earth, let me seek above all things to realize a part and interest in the resurrection of the just. Grant, grant, O Lord, the descent of a strong converting influence upon my household; may we from henceforth be a family of devoted and aspiring Christians; may all false delicacy, all sinful and cowardly shame from this time forward give way; and may such be the result of my prayers, and example, and conversation in the midst of them, that when we rise again, I may say of them all—Behold, Lord, here am I, and the children whom Thou hast given me.

RUTH II.

What benevolence and often what piety is expressed in our common salutations! If they be not the indications of what is actually felt, they are at least of what ought to be felt between man and man.—" The Lord be with you," and "the Lord bless thee," which passed between Boaz and his reapers, are charged both with the recognition of God as the fountain of all good, and with the utmost good-will to our fellows. O that these were not in word only but in power, and that the Spirit of God would animate the letter of our courteous and kindly expressions, and cause the dead bones to live.—This history of Ruth may, like that of Esther, be regarded as one of the most striking of the records of Providence in the world, and should carry the lesson of a Divine superintendence and direction in the affairs of men. The humanity of Boaz towards the helpless stranger is a highly creditable exhibition of him; while the cautions he lays upon Ruth, and his guardianship of her that she might be safe from the annoyances or seductions of evil company, mark a respect for strict morality as well as a disposition to compassionate those who are in distress. It is well, too, that having heard of her good report he should offer so full a tribute of admiration to her filial piety and good conduct.

Let me imitate her in my attentions to the desolate, and perhaps the needy, among those with whom I am connected; and give me, O Lord, in this walk of duty to acquit myself rightly and well. Another affecting exhibition here given is the simplicity of these ancient times, and on what easy terms they were satisfied if but the calls of hunger and the most urgent of their physical wants were appeased. Weaken more and more in me every day all factitious desires for anything beyond these; having food and raiment, may I be therewith content. O may I know what it is to consecrate what I have and what I am to Thy service. Remove, O Lord—and in a way that is consistent with the best and highest interests of those who are near and dear to me—every obstacle in the way of indulging such liberalities as may conduce to Thy glory and the wellbeing or extension of Thy Son's Church. Let me see how things worked together for the good of the aged Elimelech. Shed abroad the love of Thee in my heart, that all things may work together both for my own good and that of all my relatives and friends.

RUTH III.

In this record of ancient manners there occur such incidents and traits as we are not fully in circumstances to appreciate. The simplicity and severe labour of those times might have ensured the safety of exposures which could not be weathered or withstood now but by dint of severest virtue. The uniform lesson of the gospel is, that when at liberty from the calls of duty or necessity to choose either to flee temptation or to brave it, we should take to the former alternative—Enter not into temptation—Be not led into temptation—Turn away our sight and our eyes from viewing vanity—Flee youthful lusts—cherish the humility that is distrustful of our own powers, and then shall we receive the grace to overcome which is given to the humble—be not carried away by the vain imagination of our own sufficiency, else might we be left to a humiliating overthrow by that God who resisteth the proud. Our Saviour bids us pray against temptation, that we might not be led into it—that we might not enter it; and what is most material to the work of practical Christianity, He also bids us watch as well as pray. Let me ever be vigilant and on my guard—shun the first approaches and appearances of evil—resist the first intrusion or presentation of evil thoughts. What I greatly stand in need of is an observant and sustained discipline of the inner man, so as that my Christianity might become a business—a thing of deed and not of word only. It would supply me with that paramount and engrossing object which should ward off or at least subordinate all others, and so in fact as that a whole host of petty cares and cogitations would give way before the power of a ruling, and this a righteous ambition. Then should I realize an experimental religion, and by actual finding, come at length to know the life and the peace of those who are spiritually-minded—the great peace of those who love God's law—the promise that the peace of God which passeth all understanding should keep my heart and my mind in Christ Jesus my Lord—the well of water springing up unto everlasting life—the secret of the Lord which is with them that fear Him—the manifestations given to those who keep His sayings.

RUTH IV.
April, 1846.

Let me bear respect to the arbitrary and complex forms for the conveyance of property which seem to have prevailed in all ages; and give me direction, O God, for the right and wise conveyance of that wherewith Thou hast entrusted me; and let a sense of stewardship have a guiding influence upon my own heart and descend in full force to my children. The person who declined connexion with Ruth has not had the honour or distinction put upon him of having his name recorded in Scripture. He comes down to posterity only as "such-a-one." Had he been the brother-in-law of Ruth a widow, a positive stigma would have been affixed upon him for this refusal. The blessing pronounced upon Boaz at the marriage is very interesting. Pharez is singled out and not Judah, as the head of a house so flourishing and prosperous, to form the model after which it was prayed that the house of Boaz should prosper likewise. Pharez the son of Judah was the ancestor of Boaz, and his descendants would form a distinct section of the tribe of Judah, of which tribe the Lord came; and of which house, also, the house of Pharez, and farther down the house of Boaz, and farther down and most illustrious of all, the house of David, did our Lord come, made of the seed of David according to the flesh. I confess a special sympathy with the affection of Naomi for Obed. It is like my own for dear little Tommy.—My God, do Thou bless him abundantly; may he grow in grace as he grows in stature; may he grow in the knowledge of the Lord Jesus Christ. If it be Thy blessed will, do Thou improve his health and eyesight; but above all, may his soul prosper, and in Thy light may he clearly see light—gifted with spiritual discernment, and having that precious acquaintance with God, the fruit of which is peace. Save him from the evil communications which corrupt good manners; and when sinners offer to entice him may he not consent. Conduct him to a manhood of usefulness and honour, and admit him at length into the rewards of an immortal inheritance. I pray, O God, for Thy distinguished favour to me and mine—to each member of my family. May my children be the children of God; may ours be a Christian household, from us at the head to all the branches of it. Give to each of us a part and an interest in the atonement and righteousness of Christ, that we may all share in the song of eternity to Him who hath redeemed us and washed us from our sins in His blood.—Altogether this Book of Ruth is a most precious little record.

I. SAMUEL.

Sundhope, April 12, 1846.

1 Samuel i.—I have a great value for those incidental notices which let us into any of the habits and peculiarities of other times. We there see what the practice was of well-conditioned families in these days, who went up to Jerusalem with their yearly homage of worship and offerings. We also see the perfect toleration that there was then for a plurality of wives, which might be put down to the theory of a progressive moral education carried forward through successive economies from the less to the more refined—a progression this that, for aught we know, may continue through the endless stages of our future

immortality. The portions given to the family of Elkanah are portions, we presume, of the free-will offerings. We see the jealousy of wives in a state of polygamy. It was cruel in Peninnah to triumph as she did over the barrenness of poor Hannah—a matter, it would appear, of great disgrace and humiliation in these days. The tears of Hannah and the gentle remonstrances of Elkanah are very simply and naturally told.—One likes the piety of that time, and the expressions of it as adapted to the dispensation then in force. The vows of mothers and the consecration of their sons to the public and peculiar service of God were not unusual. Then Eli's suspicions of Hannah mark too plainly that the spectacle which he now conceived of Hannah was not unusual—a woman in a state of intoxication, even in the act of going through the forms and solemnities of worship at the door of the tabernacle. It is to be apprehended that the drunkenness even of females was not an infrequent phenomenon, though, as is obvious both from the accusation of Eli and the vindication of Hannah, there was a stigma attached to it. The blessing of Eli seems to have acted on the mind of Hannah with all the comfort of a prophecy, which she confided in from the lips of the high-priest. Hannah was true to her vow, and Elkanah was compliant—saying, "Do what seemeth thee good." Altogether it is a simple and pleasing narrative. There is no such express and formal dedication of children now to the Lord; but ought they not to be dedicated in fact?—ought they not to be consecrated to His service? What a lamentable deficiency if this be not made an express object. May God forgive—but this is not enough—may God rectify and reform. Direct me, Almighty Father, to the right methods for savingly influencing my children. O may they be brought up in Thy nurture and Thine admonition. Hear my prayers, Almighty Father, in their behalf. Thou willest intercessions to be made for all men: I now intercede in behalf of my family, even that my wife and children might be saved, and come to the knowledge of the truth. But let me watch and work as well as pray.

I. SAMUEL II.

How like to each other are these devotional effusions of Hannah and Mary the mother of our Lord—confirmatory of the notion that Samuel was a type of Christ. Her great enemy seems to have been Peninnah, from whose reproaches she was now set free. She had been proudly and injuriously treated by her adversary; but she obtained redress from Him by whom actions are weighed, and who judged righteously between them. Give me to feel the control over my actions of the Omniscience that is above, and which estimates aright all our works and all our ways. There is a largeness of view and sentiment in this utterance of Hannah which gives it a prophetical character, and forces the impression upon us of a greater than Samuel being here.—Keep my feet, O God; uphold my goings in Thy paths; and humble me under a sense of my own nothingness, so that I may cast all my sufficiency upon God—for by his own strength shall no man prevail.

Samuel was dedicated to the public service of the Lord from his youth, or rather from his infancy up. Let me watch over the souls of my descendants.

This avarice of the sons of Eli was a great scandal to

Israel. Give me, O Lord, to abhor all taint of secularity and selfishness in the conduct of things sacred; and in providing for the things of the Lord, let me provide things honest in the sight of all men.

Hannah lost nothing by what she had given to the Lord. She parted with her child Samuel and resigned the domestic enjoyment of her first-born; but it was all made up to her, for she was blest with a family of sons and daughters. And there are other gifts beside those of children wherewith we should honour the Lord—even with the first-fruits of our increase in this world's goods; and most sure it is that we shall not suffer by it.

The monstrous iniquity of the sons of Eli met with far too gentle a remonstrance from their mild and amiable but withal too indulgent father. The necessities of the case, and the demands of principle, required a far more stern and authoritative discipline at his hands. What a contrast to these young men was Samuel; and how like what is here said of him to what is said of his great Antitype in Luke ii. 52—that " He increased in favour with God and man." But how appalling the message from God to Eli, and what a fearful menace is it the bearer of to all who suffer their natural affection to overbear their duty to God and their regard for His honour. O Lord, be Thou enthroned in my heart, that I may render the glory which is due unto Thy name.—May godliness have the paramount ascendency over me; and let it be my earnest prayer and study that this should form the reigning characteristic of my family: thus and thus alone can I look for mine being a sure house. But is there not a reference in these words to the everlasting government of Him who is the Priest upon the throne?—and when

God speaks of mine Anointed or my Christ, does He not speak of the Messiah our Saviour?

I. SAMUEL III.

The word of God coming in the way of special revelation, and coming rarely to a select individual, was all the more precious because of its scarcity. And in our present day, though the word, the literal word, the Bible, is frequent and to be found everywhere, the vision or spiritual discernment of that word is not so. Do Thou open mine eyes—do Thou shine in my heart, O Lord, that I may behold the wondrous things contained in Thy law, and that I may also behold Thy glory in the face of Thy Son. I desire that in Thy light I may clearly see light: this is what I hunger and thirst after; let me pray for it—yes, and let me work for it, that I may obtain the promised manifestations. This is the morning of a sacramental Sabbath.—Meet me, O Lord Jesus, at Thine own table; enable me to discern Thy body; let me not confide in the flesh which profiteth nothing; may the symbols of my atonement be so used as that they may prove spirit and life unto me; may I rejoice in Thee through Him by whom I receive this atonement; and do Thou through Him rejoice over me to bless me and to do me good. How simply yet impressively is the narration given of this revelation to Samuel; and what an emphatic, yea awful, message is it to Eli—full of warning and most weighty application to us all. My God, let me not reckon it enough that my children are free of all visible delinquencies; give me to watch over their souls, and to make a real business of their Christianity. There does not readily occur anything they do from which I should restrain them, but many things in which I ought to urge them forward and direct them. Give me, O Lord, both the will and the way to be their spiritual adviser; and let my speech henceforth be seasoned with salt, and minister more abundantly to the use of edifying. Let this be my aim in all time coming; and let me draw nigh to the communion service this day with full integrity of purpose not in this alone, but with full purpose of heart and endeavour after the whole obedience of the gospel.

Poor Eli was a man of pious sensibilities, but of great facility—worked upon by his natural affection, and leading him to the culpable indulgence of his children. There is something touching in the resignation wherewith he submitted himself to the message from the Lord. Let not, O God, my disposition to be happy with my children, or to make them happy, lead me to keep back those grave instructions which benefit the soul. Let my chief earnestness be for their blessedness in heaven; and O prepare me and them for an eternal abode in the mansions which Christ hath gone to prepare for His followers.

We have noticed an analogy to our Saviour in ch. ii. 26, as compared with Luke ii. 52; and there occurs here another analogy both with Christ and his forerunner in verse 19, as compared with Luke i. 80 and ii. 40. Certainly Samuel did grow into a star of the first magnitude.

I. SAMUEL IV.

May, 1846.

Here we have the dread accomplishment of what had been foretold against Eli and his house. God hath said it, and shall He not do it? He is not to be mocked; and O that I could carry this solemn and alarming consideration to all his other threats and averments against the children of disobedience. Let me not be deceived—they who sow unto the flesh shall of the flesh reap corruption. Tribulation and anguish and wrath are revealed from heaven against every man who doeth evil. My God, Thou knowest my temptations and frailties.—Keep back Thy servant from presumptuous sin.—Break off from me the yoke of every tyrant appetite.—Purge me also from secret faults; and whatever way of wickedness be in me, O turn me therefrom into the way everlasting. Surely that fear which seized even upon the rude and idolatrous Philistines, when they heard that the symbol of God's presence was brought nigh unto them, might well take possession of my heart in the thought that God is at all times in the midst of us, and that His presence is universal. Give me, O Lord, a constant sense of this presence; and may it come with seasonable force upon me, with a prevailing moral energy, when like to be overset by the urgency and the power of any temptation. Save me from the superstition of those who tremble before the mere symbol or visible representation of a present Deity, while all practical sense of the living and true God has no place or operation in a heart insensible to the power of Divine things. Quicken within me, O God, the principle and power of godliness, and more especially that restraining power under which I might stand in awe and sin not— visited in the hour of need with the consideration, Shall I do this evil thing and sin against God? Let not I-chabod be inscribed, O Lord, either upon our Church or our country. Give me the patriotism which Eli had, but not the dispensation which caused him in the agonies of wounded affection for the now departed glory of Israel to fall back and expire. We are surrounded with Philistines on all hands; and many there are who would lift up their shout of exultation and triumph on the disgrace or overthrow of the Free Church of Scotland. And there are disorders and disagreements among ourselves; O for wisdom to clear my way among such unmanageable elements, and, what I greatly need, for temper to keep me calm and collected while resolute in the conflicts of argument. There is a facility which should not be given way to, as well as a firmness which should not be carried to the length of obstinacy.

I. SAMUEL V.

Craigholm.

These manifestations of the true God struck terror into the heart of the Philistines. They at least stood in awe of His judgments if they did not learn righteousness therefrom. They learned something however. They put the dreaded thing away from them not from a movement of duty but of pure fear, the most selfish and degrading of all the passions. Still it was a selfishness which led them to do the right thing; nor is the operation of this selfishness superseded so as to lose its place and its usefulness even at this day—even in the way and on the business of that great transition by which men are led out of darkness to the marvellous light of the gospel. "Knowing the terrors of the Lord," says Paul, "we persuade men." "Some save with fire," says Jude, "while others with compassion, making a difference." Give me, O Lord, a right practical sense of Thy power and Thy fearfulness.

Give me to fear not man, who can only kill the body, but let me fear Him who, after that the body is killed, can cast both soul and body into hell—yes, let me fear Him; let me never forget how fearful a thing it is to fall into the hands of the living God. The principle of God's dealings with other than Jews and Christians is to us a great mystery—or what the treatment and final destination of the heathen is to be in the judgment and under the righteous government of God. We find that He left not Himself without a witness in the land of the Philistines; and from verse 5 we learn that the remembrance of the testimony thus given was kept up till at least the writing of the First Book of Samuel, and may have lasted for generations afterwards. The purpose, however, of such lessons, and by which the men of religions that are false are made to know something at least of the God who is true—the purpose or effect of such partial lessons as they may be called, we cannot fully scan. This belongs, however, to God's part in the dealings He has with men, not to our part; and therefore does not enter into any present or practical concern of ours. Yet such histories of the manifestations which God made of Himself in past ages should not be without their influence on us of the present day—they are the manifestations of the unchangeable God; what He was then He still is; and we increase in the knowledge of Him from the discoveries He makes of Himself at whatever time. He is still a God not to be mocked, still a consuming fire, jealous as before of His honour; and none of whose ordinances, be they positive or moral, can be profaned with impunity. His throne of righteousness, it is true, has become a throne of grace, and we are invited to approach with all boldness. But there is nothing in this latter economy to encourage an unholy boldness. There is now a free and plenteous ministration of grace, but it is of a grace which enables to deny ungodliness, to serve God acceptably with reverence and godly fear.

I. SAMUEL VI.

These Philistines had a conscience and a fear of which the true God, though unknown to them, was the object. Their regards were strangely mingled between the true God and their own diviners. He who leaveth not Himself without a witness had made such manifestations of Himself to these heathen that they were forced to recognise Him; nor had the miracles and manifestations of other times yet spent their efficacy, for we find the traditions of the plagues of Egypt still kept up among them, and an argument founded on their comparison between these and the plagues wherewith themselves had been visited.—And so they came to the conclusion that they must harden not their hearts. My God, what a lesson to us in these days of clearer light and a clearer revelation. Let me harden not my heart: the night is approaching, the day is far spent with me. O that I had more of real, practical, operative earnestness, more of prayer, that I were more given to sanctification as a work and a business. Open up my way, O God; remove all the obstructions which an artificial theology has laid upon it; bring me into direct contact and communication with Thy Bible; and throwing aside the arguments and the articles of a controversial divinity, let me from this time forward take my guidance and obtain all my supplies both of encouragement and wisdom afresh from the fountain-head of Thine own word. And not only may I learn from Thy Bible the way wherein I should go, may I study aright the indications of Thy providence; may I put a true interpretation on the events whether of public or personal history; may I own the hand of God in them all, and know how to educe from them the lessons of sound and intelligent piety. There is much to gladden the heart in the ordinances of religion. "I joyed," says the Psalmist, "when they said, Go up with me to the house of God." And the Beth-shemites rejoiced when the ark of the Lord came up to them and made entry within their borders. But they mixed not trembling with their mirth; they stood not in awe, and so God made dread indication of His majesty and His sacredness in the midst of them. Let no goodness, let no condescension, let no assurance of faith displace from our hearts the reverence that is due to God. There is forgiveness with Him, but it is a forgiveness that He may be feared. Let us be solemnized as well as give thanks at the remembrance of His holiness. We have a warrant for coming boldly to the throne of grace, but to obtain what? —to obtain grace, which grace will dispose and enable us to serve God acceptably with reverence and godly fear. My God, let me deviate not either to the right hand or to the left. Let me keep fast the confidence of the gospel which hath great recompense of reward, but let me not cast its sanctities away from me.

I. SAMUEL VII.

Let the priests of the Lord be holy. Let the ministers set apart to declare the gospel of salvation be themselves a peculiar people, that they may be the instruments of forming to the Lord a peculiar people purified from all iniquity, and made zealous of good works. And O that under them a spirit of repentance were to go abroad over the land, that the men of our country and our day would turn to Him whom they have pierced, and with that godly sorrow which worketh repentance to salvation never to be repented of. May the inhabitants of these realms lament after the Lord.

But something more than lamentation is required of us —there must be reformation also. There must be a putting away of the idolatries which have heretofore enslaved us. All old things must be done away; all things must become new. Prepare my heart, O Lord, to serve Thee only; enable me to renounce the world, the devil, and the flesh. May I give up all my vanities, and henceforth be dead to pride, and anger, and sensuality, and every lust that is opposed to the love of God and to His entire supremacy over my affections and my doings. O that I became a passive and a consecrated thing in His hand. Let me put away my Baalim and Ashtaroth, and cleave with full and single purpose of heart unto the Lord. Hear the prayers which I know to be lifted up on my behalf, and give me also the spirit of intercession for others; and O may they and I, confessing our sins and washing them out by faith in the blood of the Lamb, take to the following of Christ—and to the advancement of His cause, both in our own hearts and throughout our respective spheres of influence and operation. Save me, O God, from mine enemies. Discomfit their evil machinations. Let them not triumph over me. Enable me to walk in wisdom throughout the matters of controversy wherewith I at present have to do. Let equity preside over all the measures which I take, and let my moderation be known unto all men. O loose my bonds, and deliver me out of the hands of those who would entangle and enslave me. Thou hast helped me hitherto: Thou hast rescued me out of many dangers. Well may I set up my Eben-ezer, and live henceforth a monument of the forbearance, and the tender mercies, and the preserving care of Him whom I have so often offended by my perversities and grievous sins. My God, forgive and reform, so that henceforth I may please Thee in all my ways, and my enemies become at peace with me. O for an old age of peace and piety for the retirement of the domestic altar; and at the same time such a life of usefulness as my experience and my testimonies might enable me to devote for the service of the present and rising generation. Let there henceforth be peace between the Church and her enemies; and without arrogance or self-seekings or self-aspirings of any sort, do Thou enable me to promote the Christian good of the people in these lands.

I. SAMUEL VIII.

Every record of age should now come home to me; and the case of Samuel's family should lead me to bethink myself on the character and habits of my own children. His public cares may, as in many other instances, have so far undomesticated him that his duties as a parent were left undone. Let me admit of no such apology for myself; but let me pray, and admonish, and lift up my Christian testimonies with a special view to the souls of those who are near and dear to me, and that my household may become a household of faith. What a display of nature—

nay, of popular and plebeian nature, this demand of the Israelites for a king—urged on by a comparison of themselves with other nations, and by the obvious imagination that such an appointment would contribute both to their safety and their grandeur as a people. The impiety of the demand lay in their preference of a human to a divine government, in their wish to interpose a power created by themselves between their nation and the direct theocracy, under which in the form of divinely commissioned judges and leaders they had heretofore been placed. Let us not confound a monarchy raised in such circumstances with those monarchies under which the various nations of the world now find themselves to be placed by Providence, in the course of a history over which they had no more control than over the power and the purposes of Heaven. There is much to be gathered from the contrast here laid before us between an earthly, and we shall not say a heaven-appointed but a heaven-directed king. The manner of the former in reigning over his people is altogether distinct from the manner of the latter; and we look forward to the time, not when monarchy shall be abolished, but when the kings and kingdoms of the earth shall become the kings and kingdoms of our Lord and Saviour Jesus Christ. But meanwhile, and before the universal reign of truth and righteousness is ushered in—let us forget not that the powers which be are ordained of God; and that it is ours to lead a quiet and peaceable life in all godliness and honesty, to honour the king in the fear of God, and to meddle not with those who are given to change. May the throne in our realms be established in righteousness. Do Thou surround our Queen by the wise and faithful of the land.

Defeat the policy of ungodly statesmen; and O purify and direct our Parliament. Save us, O Lord, from all oppression, from the violence of a headstrong multitude, as well as from arbitary power. Keep, O Lord, the battle from our gates. Do Thou save us from the war that has been so loudly threatened, and that is still hanging over us. Thou hast crowned us with victory in India; but we would rather be in peace than conquer in war. And do Thou, who art not only the God of battles but ruler over the hearts of men, rebuke the hostile policy of the ambitious and the proud.

I. SAMUEL IX.

June, 1846.

There is the remarkable exhibition here of God's providence. What apparently more wayward and contingent than the movements of stray animals at large from the guidance and restraint of their keepers? yet even these are subject to the oversight and are in fact overruled by Him who ruleth all in all. And so also Saul in pursuit of them was conducted through his wanderings from one neighbourhood to another to the very place whither God had said to Samuel a day before that He would send him. Nothing lies beyond the power and prescience of God; nothing falls out at random; and we would recognise all events from the most minute to the most momentous as but the evolutions of His will and essential parts of his administration. God's eyes are in every place, and He hath both the knowledge and the foreknowledge of all things. In virtue of the latter He could tell His prophet that Saul would cast up on the morrow; and in virtue of the former he could tell Saul through Samuel that the asses he had been in quest of were found.—Restore, O Lord, to the people of our land the habit of liberality to the ministers of religion, which prevailed in the olden time, now that they depend on the free-will offerings of those among whom they labour. May they receive more plentifully of carnal things in return for the spiritual things whereof they are the dispensers and the channels of conveyance through the word and ordinances of the blessed gospel. How pleasing and picturesque are the simplicities of the earlier and ruder periods of the world—how the maidens went out to draw water—how the people assembled on their days of religious service; and the very name they gave to their prophet and judge is not without its interest. There is something venerable, perhaps, from its having the mould of antiquity, in the title of seer. Give me, O Lord, to see if not into things future, at least into the things of Thy written revelation—that I may behold the wondrous things contained in the book of Thy law. What an affecting representation is here given of God, as moved with compassion because the cry of His people had come unto Him. On this compassion would I throw myself, O God. Have pity on my weaknesses, and pardon my nameless and numberless iniquities, O God.—What a fine subject for the genius of a painter would be Samuel and Saul upon the house-top.

I. SAMUEL X.

The powers that be are ordained of God; and though He sometimes in judgment visits a nation with a wicked king, that does not necessarily absolve us from our loyalty, or from the respect that we owe to the providence and the appointment of God. David felt this strongly in reference to Saul; and so ought we, even when perverse and infidel rulers have been set over us.—O God, save us from the anarchy that now threatens in high places. Give faithful counsellors to our Queen. Still the tumults whether of the multitude or the competitors for power, and let ours be the comfort of a Government at once strong and righteous. Guide me aright should I be called upon to exercise my right as a voter; and so overrule the passions and politics of men that Thy cause may be represented in Parliament.—Samuel evinces his prophetic endowments to Saul in such a way as must have confirmed him in the faith that he had indeed been anointed of the Lord. What particularity and detail in the statement of those whom Saul should fall in with—two men, and three men, and what each of these three were carrying—all set in picture before the mind of the prophet; and afterwards the whole company he should meet, with their musical instruments, and along with whom, visited by inspiration as they were, he should prophesy. The fulfilment of these things would surely be evidence enough for Saul that God was with him; and accordingly God gave him another heart, and also brought all these predictions to pass. Yet it does not appear that the heart given to Saul was that of a new creature, or that the Spirit imparted to him anything higher than gifts, or if graces, anything so high as the grace that is unto salvation. He seems, however, at the commencement of his reign to have demeaned himself cautiously and wisely.—Let me not alienate from me the Spirit of God, but may I be conducted by Him from one degree of spiritual advancement to another till I appear perfect before God in Zion.

Samuel assembled the people, and with all the intrepidity and faithfulness of an old prophet, remonstrated against them—for what? their preference of an earthly king over a theocracy. They had virtually rejected God who *Himself* saved them—that is, either without instrumentality, or by such instrumentality as He raised up for the occasion. But He overruleth all, whether by His friends or against His enemies. He who has the sovereign disposal of the lot and of all things did fix upon their king, and held forth one of His own selection to the view of all the people.—And still it is at Thy hands, O God, that we receive either the blessing of good or the infliction and the curse of evil rulers. O that we had a religious senate, or some men in it who would fearlessly appeal to the Book of God as the alone rightful directory of government, as well as private individuals and families.

I. SAMUEL XI.

How awful the barbarity of man against his fellow-men; and the mere surface-dressing of our modern civilisation forms no security that such may not recur both in foreign and domestic warfare. The emotion wherewith the intelligence from Jabesh was received in Israel is quite what would have been felt in like circumstances in all ages; and even the impulse of the Spirit on the mind of Saul is in striking harmony with the impulse of nature. But this is also true of many other of his impulses; and give me, O Lord, to experience the benefit of His continued presence and operation—that at every time and on every occasion I may be and do and feel as I ought. The conveyance of his will by action, and by such cruel action, too, throughout the coasts and among the children of Israel, one cannot so readily sympathize with, yet it may have been the cause instrumentally of that fear which fell upon the minds of the people, though here denominated the fear of the Lord. It called forth a very large and unanimous gathering from all parts of the land, and an interposal for the relief of Jabesh-gilead, which is in curious and striking counterpart with the national movement recorded in the last chapter of Judges, for the very opposite purpose of destroying the same place. We regard the enumeration here given of the assemblage of all Israel's fighting men though large in itself, yet when compared with other enumerations as so small that it seems to carry proof of a great depopulation in Israel through the period of the rule over it by the Philistines. One can readily enter into the grateful loyalty of the people towards their monarch after the successful result of the expedition against the Ammonites. Saul never appears to such advantage again during the whole of his ill-conducted and ill-fated history.—Lord, do Thou speedily work another and higher salvation not only in Israel but for Israel—that we may speedily witness the glorious development of the revelations and prophecies of ancient days. The proposal made by Saul is strikingly of a piece with similar ones made by him afterwards—rash and wayward, yet demonstrative of a certain impetuous—though often with him forward—zeal for the God of Israel. The present instance, however, does not appear to have called forth the rebuke or remonstrance of the great prophet who was still amongst them.

I. SAMUEL XII.

Good old Samuel in this address to the people could appeal to them with all intrepidity and confidence regarding his own integrity, but not so regarding that of his sons, whom he mentions notwithstanding, and this, perhaps, to conciliate towards them the goodwill of the community, in whose hands they were. O that I bore a kindlier, but withal a more Christian and moral regard to my own children. Direct me, O Lord, how to labour for their souls till Christ be formed in them—counting it not enough that they acquit themselves with honour and respect in society, but watching over them as one who is responsible for their immortal part and for the good of their souls. There is something very interesting in this remonstrance which the judge and father of his people holds with the multitude before him, and to observe how he rests and fortifies his argument—and places their religion and religious obligation—on the foundation of their old history, urging the service and the gratitude which were due to that God who, in bringing the people out of Egypt, may be said to have visited and redeemed His people. Let the history of a greater redemption tell a like lesson to my heart and conscience, O God. But O what defections I have to record from the humility and the holiness and the charity of the gospel. Thou hast long borne with me, even as Thou didst with Thy stiff-necked children of old, and here I am at this day, the subject of many warnings but without the inflictions that I have deserved, even though they had been such as would have cast me into destruction and utter despair; but I have been spared hitherto, having been often made to hear the voice of God's thunder and to stand in awe of his menacing demonstrations, yet without the lightning stroke that would have destroyed me—in like manner as he here solemnized these assembled Hebrews, yet allowed them space and opportunity for repentance. I have done wickedly as they did, and as themselves confess they had done—yet with that richness of forbearance which in my own person I have so signally experienced, did He say once more to rebellious Israel, Fear not, for His own name's sake the Lord will not forsake His people. I too am as the fig-tree let alone; let me continue therefore to follow the Lord my God; let me turn not aside nor again to vanity; let me not lapse into sinful despair nor cease to hope and pray. Teach me, O Lord, the right and the good way. Put truth into my inward parts, that I may serve Thee, not with eye-service, but from the heart. Let mine be a life of entire dedication to Him who by His many preservations hath done such great things for me. Let me now bethink myself in good earnest—for should I lapse again into wickedness what might not the end be? If any man sin wilfully after having received the knowledge of the truth there remaineth to him no more sacrifice for sin.

I. SAMUEL XIII.

July, 1846.

We have here the first exhibition of Saul's waywardness and audacity in things ecclesiastical—and indeed his whole history presents us with a series of such exhibitions, which may be viewed as so many evils or penalties which Israel had incurred by their own natural and voluntary act in having renounced the pure theocracy under which they had been aforetime governed, and, in insisting for a king, had vitiated their system by the importation of a secular element. Saul's offering of the burnt-offering was a clear invasion of the civil upon the ecclesiastical—a corruption from which we shall never be conclusively freed till the kingdoms of the earth become the kingdoms of our Lord and Saviour Jesus Christ. Saul's was a case of unauthorized will-worship, and by which he laid himself open to the rebuke of the old prophet. The application to a great public and general question is obvious; but let me not miss the personal lesson conveyed by it—the paramount authority of Divine ordinances, and that I should obey God rather than man. There was a certain zeal for things sacred in these aberrations of Saul—a zeal Godward, and yet what a fearful doom he incurred by giving way to it.—Let all my religious services be such as are warranted by Scripture, unmixed with human authority or with any gratuitous fancy of my own. Saul did foolishly in not keeping the commandment of the Lord; he violated the prescribed methods of sacrifice and worship, and forfeited the kingdom both for himself and his family.— My God, save our country from the evils which our rulers threaten to bring upon it—and this, too, from their intromission with things ecclesiastical. They meddled beyond their sphere with the Scottish Church; and a fatality seems to have overhung all Church proceedings of theirs ever since. They seem careering onward to Popery—at least to the bestowment upon it of such a national countenance as will infer both a guilt and a judgment alike national. Deep and difficult questions are before us. The Free Church may perhaps be put on the trial both of its principles and its wisdom. Should it accept the proffers of a demi-infidel Government, and in so doing participate it may be in the sins of an Administration to which truth and error are alike indifferent—equally supporting and patronizing all? I pray for a special direction from on high upon this question.

I. SAMUEL XIV.

Jedburgh.

Thou savest, O Lord, by many or by few. We pray for the spiritual salvation of our land—we fear that Thy people in it form but a very little flock.—O may they prove a preserving and purifying salt in the midst of us. Save us from the tyrannic rule whether of infidelity or of high-churchism—having the spirit, at least, if not the name or all the forms of Popery. Send such a terror or sensation of it into the hearts of our enemies that their opposition might be effectually neutralized. Let there be trembling in the host—not, however, to issue, if it be Thy blessed will, in their destruction, but in their conversion to the cause of truth and righteousness. Divide their counsels, so that they might neutralize each other, and leave the victory of principle to the faithful disciples of Thine own Son. We have many adversaries, but they agree not among themselves, save in their hatred and hostility to our Free Church. Cause us to please Thee in all our ways, that these may be at peace with us. They differ among themselves in many things: turn them so against each other that we may look on in safety, and the whole may issue in a triumph—not to our denomination, not to us as a party or a sect, but to the followers of the Lamb whithersoever He goeth. Let them who are Israelites indeed prevail over the Philistines of our day; and bring about the speedy consummation of our present disorders, to issue in that period when the kingdoms of our world shall become the kingdoms of our Lord and Saviour Jesus Christ.

But preserve us meanwhile, O God, from all that is wayward or injudicious or rash. Save us from the influence of such factitious obligations or principles as might be compared in their absurdity or temerity to foolish vows. Let us not trouble the consciences of our adherents with aught that is not clearly warranted by the word of God. Saul gave way to his own fanciful conception; but many are the fanciful conceptions, too, of a popular assembly— against which, O Lord, we pray that the counsels of truth and soberness may ever defend us. Let us not enter into any rash covenants or resolutions. May we be guarded from all that is obviously and unquestionably sinful; but may we not be encumbered with aught that is arbitrary and gratuitous, or which has not the clear light of reason and principle to rest upon it.

Give us the victory, O Lord, over all our enemies on every side of us. May we be enabled to deliver our own people from the hands of their persecutors, and also from the guilesome fascinations of an evil world. But though we should prevail successively over this one and that other opposition, it may be long and very long before we are at rest: for many days yet may there be sore war between us and our antagonists. Do Thou rear up a valiant generation of warriors; may we not suffer from the want of able counsellors and leaders; may the Church be wise in the selection of those to whom it shall give its confidence, or shall prefer to a station of danger or honour or command. May the Church-militant become, in Thy good time, the Church-triumphant even upon earth, when the brilliant days of the Apocalypse shall at length be realized.

I. SAMUEL XV.

We have here an historical verification of what looks to us as so mysterious in theology—a distant posterity suffering for the misdeeds or favoured because of the good conduct of their ancestors. Let me meanwhile acquiesce in the mystery, and rejoice in the support which it gives to the blessed doctrine of the imputation of Christ's all-perfect righteousness, in which and in which alone I desire to stand before God—assured of my acceptance in the Beloved, and through Him of all spiritual blessings.

Saul was constantly running into his own wayward deviations.—But what a view is here given of the steadfastness of God's administration, and of its immovable adherence to its own principles? There seems to have been a notion of sacrifice, and so of religious duty in his mind, when he reserved of the cattle of the Amalekites; but this did not save him from the doom consequent upon his disobedience, in sparing what he had positive orders to destroy; nor could the cries and prayers of Samuel avail for the remission of his great offence—the breach he had made upon that obedience which is better than sacrifice. He forfeited his birthright, and like Esau there was no place found for repentance, though he seems to have sought it carefully. Let me beware of rebellion so denounced and characterized in this passage—which like witchcraft may have its fascinations, and which not only from the deceitfulness of sin against God, but even against earthly powers, may deserve the same appellation when disaffected men are carried away by the imagination of there being a high patriotism and principle in their cause. Stubbornness is well pronounced upon as idolatry. Let me have a care lest my adhesiveness to my own conceptions do not incur this condemnation—even that I walk after the counsel of my own heart and in the sight of my own eyes.

There is another mystery in this chapter—the repentance ascribed in it to God, allied with the question whether the Divinity is susceptible of emotion, but involving a still deeper enigma than this—for it seems to ascribe to Him a defect of foreknowledge. It gives a clear sanction to the practice of modifying one scripture by another, that in the same chapter where we read of God having repented, (verses 11, 35,) we also read that He is not a man that He should repent, (verse 29 ;) and so He kept by His fixed and resolute determination of changing the dynasty, and removing the family of Saul from the throne of Israel.

I. SAMUEL XVI.

Let me not persist too long in mourning over a loss or even a sin that is now irrevocably past. But O accompany with this resolution the resolute purpose of forsaking all sin, and more especially of bringing forth and slaying before God that sin which doth most easily beset me. Whatever men judge of my appearance, what would even they think did they but look into my heart? And O who can bear the inspection of Him whose eyes are as a flame of fire!—I may well tremble at this consideration. My God, I pray for Thy grace, and that it might lead me to work out my salvation with fear and trembling. I would flee to the great sacrifice—that I may be anointed with the blood of Christ, and so henceforward the Spirit may come on me, and not only teach but enable me to deny ungodliness and worldly lusts, and be in all time coming a king and a priest unto God.

My God, teach me what the expedient is by which the unclean spirit might be put out of me, that I may ever and anon recur thereto as did Saul to the harp of the son of Jesse. My God, let not Thy Spirit depart from me, and leave this weak heart of mine to be taken possession of by fouler and stronger spirits than before—a cage for every unclean and hateful bird. Is there no heavenly spell by which to charm away these hurtful imaginations? O may Thy Spirit interpose, Thy grace help in every time of need. May He who can take of the things of Christ and show them unto me, bring such thoughts into my heart as will rebuke and overrule all the instigations of evil. O that I breathed freely and freshly in the pure element of holiness. Give me to watch as well as pray; and let not Thy gospel be only to me as a very pleasant song, charming the ear but not subduing the heart. O may it search into my inward parts, and make full entry and establishment there of all its lessons. Give me to hear gladly; but let not the sound only, the mere cadence of evangelic doctrine, be enough to please and to satisfy—falling away from the ear and forgotten by the urgencies of the god of this world. Let me resist the devil that he may flee from me. Let me give him no place and no advantage over me. Let me overcome the world by the Word—calling it in upon every occasion of exposure to the wiles of the adversary, the power of the prince of darkness. Thus may I be enabled to repress and to calm the turbulence of all unholy affections.

I. SAMUEL XVII.
August, 1846.

The great lesson in this chapter is confidence in God for the final triumph of a righteous cause, and that confidence in the face of all adverse appearances, whether arising from hostile men or hostile circumstances. But be it my care, O God, that every cause in which I am enlisted be a righteous one, and then may we say boldly, The Lord is my helper, and I will not fear what man shall do unto me. Grant me this holy boldness, O God, both in behalf of my Church and of myself personally. Saul and the people of Israel were greatly afraid, nor had they reason to be otherwise, for they had forsaken the Lord, and displeasing Him had lost every legitimate ground of courage in the day of calamity and danger.

Not so David, who was strong in the favour of God and strong in the consciousness thereof: and let me, O God, ever have reason to be alike strong. When adverse combinations threaten to prevail over the cause of truth and righteousness, let me feel with David that it is the case of the Philistine bidding defiance to the armies of Israel. And let me resemble David in another thing where I am wofully deficient: he persevered in his confidence notwithstanding the opposition of Eliab. Let me in like manner take up my ground; and if taken up aright let me keep firmly and impregnably thereupon. It is true that like Eliab I might well pass for an old man; but better late than never, and therefore, O God, enable me whether in the government of the Church or government of my family to consult my own soul, and save me from the lamentable weakness which has adhered to so many of my proceedings hitherto. It is right to be easily entreated, but not right to carry my facility so far as to surrender my clearest convictions both of duty and Christian expediency. But to return to David—what nobler than his fearlessness amidst the general consternation of those around him. Thou, O God, hast vouchsafed to me many great and signal deliverances—from the paw of the lion and from the paw of the bear—aye, and from the hand of the Philistine. Give me to be just, and Thou wilt free me at length out of all my troubles. And in the present lofty aspect of an advancing Popery, with a pusillanimous and ungodly Parliament as well as people giving way to it, let me not be afraid. Let us meet them in the name of Him who is the great Head of the Church, the Captain of their salvation to all who trust in Him. The battle is the Lord's. And let there be no sword in our hands but the sword of the Spirit—even the word of God.

For an explanation of the difficulty which lies enveloped in verses 55-58, see our " Horæ Biblicæ Quotidianæ."

I. SAMUEL XVIII.
Strathleven.

It is said that we have no precepts in Scripture for the grace or virtue of friendship. But we have examples: we have our Saviour's special friendship for John; we have the most beauteous exhibition of it in the case of David and Jonathan. I feel a void in my own heart from the want of an object on whom I might concentrate this affection in full—loving him both in the flesh and in the Lord. (Philemon, 16.) There is a shyness or coldness or want of full and free congeniality about me, in virtue of which I feel that my capacity for the enjoyment of social intimacy has not been met by aught that is adequate for my entire satisfaction in this way. Let me take refuge in God, whom I pray that I might love supremely, and that He would put both the first and the second great law into my heart. We read more of Jonathan's affection and of David's wisdom. Let me combine both; and let my desire of being acceptable to men be that I may have an influence over them for good. Save me from the envy which so ate inwardly on the dark and distempered mind of Saul. Let me ever recur to that grace which is in the hand of Him who is at once the root and the offspring of David, that I may be saved from the jealousies and malignities of self, and from that wrath of man which worketh evil and worketh not the righteousness of God. What a precious text were verse 16 on the household visitations of a minister.—Save me from the evil affections by which the gloomy breast of Saul was actuated, and let them never work out into the vile and unworthy artifices which he plied for the destruction of him who was the object of his hatred. O God, enable me like David to clear out a safe and honourable way for myself in the midst of all difficulties and all dangers. I pray for the wisdom that might guide me aright in the matter of the Queen's chaplaincy. Let me know when it is my wisdom to act and when it is my strength to sit still. Elevate my soul above all that is sordid and selfish, that I may do the things which are honest in the sight of man as well as of God. Perhaps I have many adversaries: I know not. Give me to ply the right counsel and maintain the right conduct at all times; and should my name be set by, let me seek through it not the furtherance of my own glory but of God's glory and the interests of the Redeemer's kingdom.

I. SAMUEL XIX.

How beautiful the tenacity and perseverance of Jonathan's affection for David, and how beautifully it is told. And there was great faithfulness as well as great feeling in this friendship of his—a truly serviceable and not a merely sentimental friendship to him whom he loved. He too had a difficult part to perform between his father and his friend, though he could not be said to labour under the lack of powerful, and what ought to have been all-persuasive arguments. The guilt and ingratitude of such a design as Saul meditated against David are forcibly set before him by his son, yet all was ineffectual at the last, though it made its impression at the time. The evil spirit again came upon him and prevailed. The very services of David exasperated the monarch all the more; and the wretched envy of his bosom, stirred up it may have been by fear as well as jealousy, impelled him to the worst and most atrocious designs against the life of his most loyal subject and truest benefactor, so that, but for the timely flight of the destined victim and the venial falsehood of his wife, he might have fallen a sacrifice to the fury of his master. There is something mysterious to us in those visitations of the Spirit which came upon Saul and his messengers; but our most certain inference from them is, that a man might in some way become the subject of an influence from the Spirit and yet remain an unconverted man. This seems obvious regarding Saul in the Old Testament; and in the New Testament we read of gifts of the Holy Ghost unaccompanied with the graces which are unto salvation. There may even be an enlightenment given, and a taste or relish for divine things impressed by the Spirit of God on men who afterwards fall away—so that notwithstanding the doctrine of the saints' perseverance, there remains as great a call for watchfulness and care and busy endeavour as if we were still under the old economy of the law and could have been the authors of our own salvation. Lord, let me not be highminded but fear, and take heed lest I fall. Let me watch for the Spirit with all perseverance,* and do nothing to repel this heavenly visitant, to vex or to grieve or finally to quench Him, and lead Him to abandon me for ever to the counsels of my own heart and the sight of my own eyes. Let me not think that I have yet attained, or am already perfect. My God, give me to feel my own nothingness, to have no confidence in myself, but to rejoice in the Lord Jesus; and grant that as the effect of this I may serve Thee in the Spirit—remembering that there are fruits of His which avail us more for the preparations of eternity than the understanding of all mysteries and all knowledge. Charity or love is better than the gift of prophecy.

I. SAMUEL XX.

Morriston.

The remonstrance of David in his circumstances of danger, and smarting under a sense of the injustice and the ingratitude he had met with, was a very natural one. The policy was in those days deemed venial which was found necessary, even though it required some falsehood to carry it out. This is due to what I have designated as that scheme of progressive morality in virtue of which every succeeding regimen or economy is farther advanced towards the ultimate perfection than was that which preceded it. There were times of ignorance and immature principle as well as knowledge which God winked at. Nothing can be more touching and beautiful than the fidelity of Jonathan—one of the most loveable characters in Holy Writ. David seems his superior in mental sagacity and strength —yet Jonathan seems to be fully his equal in sensibility, although at the parting scene of tears and emotions it is said that David exceeded. The love which he bore to David, equal to that wherewith he loved his own soul, gives a truly endearing view of his character and heart. He, as if inspired, knew what was awaiting David in the way of preferment, and that he would be at length seated in the throne of Israel. It is strange that he should have covenanted with David not to be killed by him when he obtained the power; but there are rough doings in high places, and when the contest is for power and the safe possession of it, there is no calculating on the length to which combatants on the high field of politics and arms will be carried. And it was not only kindness to himself, but kindness to his house, that he attempted to provide for in this agreement with David—who in his after reign did shew kindness to a certain degree, if not so fully, to all the members of the house of Saul, as would have made him appear more amiable in some passages of his subsequent history. The dark malignant passions of Saul broke out on this occasion into fierce ebullition; but nothing can be more affecting than the fidelity of dear and devoted Jonathan; and yet the exhibition of David at the time when they separated entitles him, too, to much of our tenderness and sympathy.—Altogether this chapter forms a perfect drama; and I pray, my God, that I may learn from it a more deep and tender regard for the good of my fellows.

I. SAMUEL XXI.

Poor David, like a hunted partridge, is driven he knows not whither; and in the extremity of his danger and suffering makes free both with the moral and ceremonial law—with the former by the deception which he practised on Abimelech, with the latter by eating of the hallowed bread, which was not lawful but by priests only. This part of the history is referred to by our Saviour, who speaks indulgently of the one violation, while the history makes it evident that God winked at both; and that the plea of necessity and mercy was sustained for the one transgression as well as for the other.—Let not such instances ever tempt me to swerve from the obligations of that rectitude which is immutable and everlasting, but remember that on the scheme of a progressive morality and worship some better thing has been provided for us under a dispensation at least nearer to perfection than the former, if not yet made perfect. (Heb. xi. 40.) And let us not think that any strange thing has happened to us, whatever the cruelty or injustice might be which we meet with in the world. Let us take a lesson from the sore trials and adversities of David; and let the spirit breathed forth by him in the Psalms guide and actuate us, save when he indulges in the vindictive strain. The theory of progression serves to explain this phenomenon also, and it needs explanation; for nothing can be more adverse than is the spirit which often seems at least to break forth in the Psalms to the spirit of our own Christianity. It is in a high degree confirmatory of the Bible, when we observe the symphonies which obtain between these compositions of David and his own direct history, and the illustration thereby cast, by a sort of mutual reflection, upon both. What a monster of inhumanity and wickedness Doeg must have been! and let us not think that the human nature of our own day is without its full share of such specimens. How innocently Abimelech was led into those proceedings which terminated in the sacrilegious murder of so many priests at the merciless bidding of Saul and by the unfaltering hand of bloody Doeg! And what shifts poor David was reduced to in the policy—a truly venial policy—to which he resorted for the safety of his own life—preserved instrumentally by his own devices, but efficiently by the providence and the power which watched over him.—Give me, O Lord, the wisdom and the piety of David, that I may be alike protected from all hostile machinations.

I. SAMUEL XXII.
September, 1846.

What a picturesque account of these loose and warlike adventurers; and what an impression it gives of the power which essentially and inherently lies in a government from the mere circumstance of its being the actual and established one. Saul, with all his worthlessness and tyranny, was the king *de facto*, and also *de jure*. David with his whole weight of character, and who when in favour was hailed with far louder hosannahs than his master, when an outcast was abandoned by the nation at large, and was repaired to chiefly by those who were themselves the mere stragglers and outcasts of society. This is a great lesson to us—inasmuch as it evinces the strength of those securities which God hath provided on the side of the powers that be, and serves to enhance our sense and feeling of the deference that is due to them. They are ordained of God.—David did not suffer his anxieties and fears for himself to overbear his affection for his parents, likewise in danger because of their connexion with him. But David was not long permitted to remain in this concealment at the head of his guerillas, for at the bidding of the prophet he took his departure from the hold, and came forth to more public observation.

We have here the dark suspicions of the dark and distempered mind of Saul, who imaged of himself, not only that he was plotted and conspired against by David, but that even his very servants withheld their sympathy, and were perhaps in league with him. Do I cherish no undue imaginations of this sort? Is there no morbid tendency in myself to be apprehensive of hostile and mischievous designs towards me? Do I never tumultuate in the thought of injustice and hostility against myself on the part of other men? Restore this agitated bosom, O God, to peace and charity and confidence; and let my closing days be lighted up by the love of all whom I meet with, and by fervent wishes and designs of usefulness for all mankind. Fear is the parent of cruelty, as in the case of Saul—an explanation, though not an excuse for him, which we cannot make in favour of the bloody and bloodthirsty Doeg, whose deeds of blood in the slaughter of the priests inflamed his desire after more blood in the destruction of their city.

One can enter into the natural and pungent grief of David on the occasion of this dreadful tragedy.

I. SAMUEL XXIII.

What a support to David, in the midst of his perplexities

and fears, that he had the presence and counsels of the Most High. The arrival of Abiathar with an ephod in his hand is brought in as explanatory of the method by which David made inquiry of God.

The next inquiry is deemed to be of great theological importance, as evincing God's foreknowledge, not of the absolute only, but of the conditional, and in virtue of which he told David what would take place, but which did not take place, because suspended on the condition of David remaining in Keilah. This, as exhibiting another phase and perfection of the Divine foreknowledge, does not impair, but the contrary, either the power or the prescience of God, nor relax in the least the doctrine of an absolute predestination. And yet it reveals to us the importance of conditions, the necessary place which these hold in the scheme and system of the divine government. Lord, let me neither derogate from Thy sovereignty, nor slacken my own obedience to Thy will. It reduces not but enhances the necessity of these conditions, that they too are overruled by God, whose ordination extends to the means as well as to the end. Thou knowest, O God, but not I, whether my name be in the book of life, or heaven be my destined inheritance; but I know, for Thou hast told me in the book of revelation, that without holiness I shall never make entrance into heaven. Let me therefore, with all prayer and endeavour, make good the holiness, else heaven will never be made good by me, will never be my eternal dwelling-place. Thou who predestinatest unto life predestinatest all the heirs of life to be conformed to the image of Thy Son.

Jonathan comes again upon the stage; and how beautifully does he sustain the character of fidelity and perfect amiableness which shone forth in all his previous history. There is no Scriptural personage to whom my regards are so irresistibly drawn.

David had need of all these encouragements human and divine, for his troubles were not yet ended; yet Saul, too, with his honest—though wholly groundless and morbid dread of him—was an object of compassion. And so David was hunted like a partridge in the mountains—had many hairbreadth escapes, and much to exercise his faith in the providence of God; and it was a providence which forsook him not, but found out for him ways and methods of extrication. Suffer me not, O Lord, to be tried beyond what I am able for; but provide a way of escape, that I may be able to bear every adversity and trial Thou mayest be pleased to lay upon me.

I. SAMUEL XXIV.

Saul, diverted for a time from the pursuit of David, returns to it with fresh preparation and energy. And Providence so ordered it as to give David the opportunity of making a signal demonstration by which he vindicated himself, and should have utterly shamed the monarch out of his dark and unworthy suspicions. He might have killed Saul if he would, but he would not. It is quite beautiful to observe how much of religion there was in the loyalty of David. His men would fain have had him to deal out the fatal blow of destruction upon his persecutor; but in diametrical contrast with them, he felt compunction—his heart smote him even because of the small liberty which he had taken with the anointed of the Lord. But it was well that he had done so. The exhibition of the skirt which he had cut off carried in it a complete justification of himself, and ought also to have carried conviction into the mind of Saul. And it did so for a time, so as to secure for David, at least, a respite from the cruel attempts to destroy him, which had cost him so much of suffering and anxiety for a long period. It was a noble remonstrance which David lifted in the hearing of Saul—the remonstrance of an injured man—and which told at the time upon his adversary, who was struck with contrition and wept aloud. He was a person of strong sensibilities, yet sadly selfish and distempered withal, and was not unsusceptible of strong emotional feelings on the side of what was just and good. Yet what a moral wreck withal: he was even for the moment full of gratitude to his preserver, and visited with a strong sense thereof made ample acknowledgments both of David's innocence and generosity, and also of his own unworthy treatment in having rewarded him evil for good. What a contrast between the two characters; nor can we forbear admiring the conduct of that Providence which brought about such a conjunction of circumstances as served to evolve the manifestation of both. But more than this, it exercised as well as exhibited the good principles of David—while, though it drew out a flood of sensibilities from the impetuous Saul, it in the upshot greatly aggravated his condemnation; for while it made quite palpable to him the fidelity of David, and though he knew—for he himself tells us so—of his destination to the throne of Israel, yet did he, in the face of his own virtual promise to David, and of the proofs which he had given of his loyalty, as well as in contravention to the will of God, did he resume the guilty attempt of taking away his life. Lord, save me from the dark and envious spirit of Saul, and let me not think that I am altogether free of it—because I like him experience the impulses of penitential feeling, and it may be, of certain amiable susceptibilities which have the semblance but—destitute of the property of endurance—have not the reality of virtue—the unction that remaineth.

I. SAMUEL XXV.

One cannot help a sigh in parting with good old Samuel—one of the highest and most venerable of our Scripture worthies. But what diversity in the characters of men; what a contrast between Samuel and Nabal. Such as he abound in all ages; and when we do meet with those who, bent on selfish accumulation, are dead to all the claims both of gratitude and equity, let us not think that any strange thing hath happened to us. Yet even in this accursed world how is the evil mitigated with good, and how beautifully tempered is human society. We do occasionally meet too with such as Abigail; and how it calms the agitations of a spirit ruffled by passion or a sense of injustice, to hold converse with one of her bland and benignant disposition, and having a predominant intelligence and real force of principle withal, such as directed her to the transactions of this chapter, and by which she laid timely arrest on David's course of purposed vengeance. He had both the power and the opportunity of obtaining redress and inflicting retaliation for his wrongs. And in that age of ruder morality, in that earlier stage of the progressive advancement towards a better and purer system, David seems to have felt no scruple in thus taking his own cause into his own hand. Yet even here may we remark the tendencies towards the character and spirit of our own dispensation. Abigail felicitates David on his being stayed from the shedding of blood and the avenging of himself with his own hand; and afterwards David joins in this felicitation; and when Nabal was struck dead he blessed God that he had been kept from evil. There is here in fact a striking historical illustration of St. Paul's injunction on his dearly beloved that they should avenge not themselves—for it is written, Vengeance is mine, I will repay, saith the Lord. My God, let me act in this spirit towards all who have injured me; let me never forget that the Judge is at the door. Meanwhile, let me maintain a resolute forbearance; and O may patience work in me experience, and experience a hope that maketh not ashamed. Thus may I count it all joy when I fall into divers tribulations—rejoicing in hope of the glory of God, and having my soul bound in the bundle of life with the Lord my God— Christ in me and God in Christ—that I may be one with the Father and with the Son.

I. SAMUEL XXVI.

The exhibition which David makes of himself in this chapter is more unexceptionable than in the last. He had been deeply injured by Saul, and this fresh attempt upon him, after having so generously spared the life of his adversary, aggravated the provocation; yet he overcame the evil with good, and on the right principle too— The Lord may smite him, but not I; I will not be my own avenger, but I will leave him to the disposal and providence of an all-righteous God. What a contrast between this wandering outcast and his relentless persecutor—who, insensible to all the professions of his last interview with David, and to the obligations under which he lay for sparing him, set forth on the notice of his informers with a renewed attempt against the life of his faithful servant. We see in the hostile conduct of the Ziphites towards David, as well as in the ingratitude and hatred of Saul, ample matter for those psalms in which he complains of his enemies, and of the many straits and perplexities into which they had brought him. But he looked upwards to his God; and this was a dependence which did not fail him. The deep sleep into which his enemies had fallen, we are told, was from the Lord; and it gave him a noble opportunity for a second display of his innocence and high principle—not altogether the principle of forbearance—this would not have sufficed him in the case of Nabal—but along with it the principle of a chivalric as well as religious loyalty; and both together sufficed and brought him off gloriously in the case of Saul. He could not stretch forth his hand against the Lord's anointed. The *éclaircissement* seems to have had a more powerful and practical effect on Saul than he experienced on the former and similar occasion. He does not manifest the same degree of sensibility, but this is no measure of the effect; and certain it is that this was his last attempt against the life of David. We read of no promise by Saul to David at the last interview; but here a distinct promise is made, and it was adhered to. Saul shows himself fully aware on both occasions of the future fortunes of David—that he would surely be king of Israel, and he would do great things and still prevail.

The character of Saul is quite a study, with his instant sensibility to good impressions, and yet having no groundwork of right or solid principle. David was right both in conduct and sentiment: he acted wisely and well in all his dealings with the king, and committed himself in prayer and faith to Him who knoweth how to deliver the godly out of all tribulation; and God so delivered him.—Set me free of my troubles, O God.

I. SAMUEL XXVII.
October, 1846.

Notwithstanding these promises and professions of Saul, David had still great reason, from his former experience, to distrust him, and therefore resolved to make escape from his dominions—offering himself to the service and protection of the king of Gath. Saul, however, whether from regard to his promise, or from the hopelessness of success, sought no more for him. There was felt then a looser hold upon property than now, as when Achish with so much facility gave—made over as a present—Ziklag to David. It is true he engaged to render service to the donor in return; but one should have expected that it would merely have been occupation for service while the engagement lasted; but this engagement was soon broken up, and yet Ziklag continued to be David's. The right of contracts or of law was not nearly so strong in those days as to overbear the right of possession, and so Ziklag became a permanent accession to the Jewish territory.

Next follows a sad exhibition—not felt to be so sad or wrong at that early stage in the scheme of progressive morality, or in the then rude and primitive state of the practical code set up for the regulation and restraint even of God's own people. Looking and judging absolutely on David's proceedings as narrated in this passage, there were first robbery, and then falsehood, and last of all—to disguise the falsehood—there was wholesale murder, even to the extermination of young and old. We are aware of a commission in the general against the Amalekites more especially, though we do not read of any specific order from heaven for the expeditions which are here recorded. And indeed it is not easy, notwithstanding what we read of the sanction given by God Himself for the policy of the Israelites towards the Egyptians when they departed from their land—it is difficult to conceive an express warrant from God, either for the violence perpetrated on these cities of the south, or for the deceit practised upon Achish. It is true the lawgiver might dispense with his own laws; and this does alleviate the mystery, and more particularly when, instead of a general dispensation so as to substitute one rule or one principle for another, there is but a specified direction issued by God to meet the exigencies of some given occasion.—Yet let not this abate my horror either of cruelty or falsehood. O my soul, come not thou into their secret; unto their assembly, mine honour, be not thou united.

I. SAMUEL XXVIII.

Achish had unlimited confidence in David in striking contrast with David's skilful policy towards him.

Here follows one of the most remarkable passages in Scripture history, and told with all the power and effect of sublime drama. Let me not dispute the reality of those possessions and supernatural powers that were claimed in these days by many of our own species—deceitfully it may be in most instances, but warrantably and truly in some. Poor Saul had put away all such; but after the death of Samuel, and when there was no authorized vision in the land, he himself had recourse to them. The Lord kept back all answers—the legitimate channels of communication between Him and the people of Israel being now closed up. It was a marvellous permission that the woman whom he consulted should by her word raise Samuel, whom when she saw, she was visited with the instant discovery that Saul was her visitor. The ascent and appearance of Samuel are very powerfully given; and the question put by him, the complaint he made of being disquieted, casts a glimpse of revelation—though dark and uncertain—on the intermediate Hades occupied by human souls. Saul was in sad extremity, and had not strength to withstand the reckoning of the old prophet. The charge which is singled out against Saul is that he executed not the fierce wrath of the Lord upon Amalek. This might be carried back to the last chapter, and if applied to David, might serve to mitigate our estimation of his conduct. The denunciation that "To-morrow thou and thy sons shall be with me" carries a certain solemn terror along with it—directing us anew to that unknown region whence Samuel had just come, and whither Saul and Jonathan, with others of the family, were so soon to go. No wonder at the sore trouble, at the utter prostration of all his powers, whether bodily or mental, into which Saul was thrown.—To put one's life into one's hand is a frequent Scripture expression, and seems to signify that

I have exposed it to the facility of its being taken from me, ready to be snatched away as any loose and patent thing in the view of my enemy, and which he might at once seize upon.

My God, solemnize me by a sense of the awful realities of the invisible world. May I become familiar with the thoughts of death and of the futurity beyond it. Give me that firm texture of soul which the faith of immortality is calculated to impart, when it is the hope of everlasting bliss resting on the sure ground of the promises of the gospel.

I. SAMUEL XXIX.

We cannot but admire that chain of providence by which David was extricated from a position that might eventually have proved one of the greatest difficulty and embarrassment, and from which he could not have been freed but by joining in the war against his own countrymen, or by an act of foul treachery against Achish. But by his previous expulsion from the army of the Philistines through the dread and envy of their lords, he was delivered from the necessity of committing either of these enormities, and at the same time poor Saul was removed from the field of politics, and a way to the throne of Israel was opened to him.—My God, I would roll the whole of my perplexities and fears over upon Thyself: Thou hast all power and all wisdom: Thine empire is supreme over the human heart as it is over the universe at large: Thou canst make even enemies to be at peace with me; or if they should persist in their hostility and malice, Thou canst cause their very wrath to redound both to my deliverance and Thine own glory, whilst the remainder of that wrath Thou canst restrain. In all my ways then let me acknowledge Thee, and do Thou direct my paths. But David seems not to have been perfectly single-minded in these transactions.—Did he purpose to join in the battle against Saul as he professes in his speech to Achish? Was it quite a pure and honourable appeal that he made to this hospitable king when he protested his innocence and fidelity up to the day of parting with him? Did he not bring in an untrue account of his proceedings, when at the head of his marauders he carried a war of extermination into other countries than those where Achish would have sent him and had him to serve? There may have been many things which God winked at in these earlier ages of the world; but we live in a different moral era; and I pray that God would enable me to unite with the wisdom of the serpent the harmlessness of the dove. Let me ever observe the simplicity and godly sincerity which become the followers of Him who was separate from sinners, and neither was any guile found in His mouth. Let mine be the magnanimous policy of—" Fiat veritas, fiat justitia, ruat cœlum."

I. SAMUEL XXX.

In the episode of this chapter we obviously recognise, and that apart from David's inquiry of God and the answer which he received from Him, that invisible power which watched over and directed the future monarch of Israel throughout all his ways. We have elsewhere remarked on the advantageous contrast in which the Amalekites stand to David—in that they committed no slaughter, but spared both great and small when they smote

Ziklag and burnt it with fire, whereas David had carried on a war of extermination against them, leaving nothing that breathed. And yet these Amalekites were accursed of God and outcasts from His favour and family—an historical proof that the greater amiableness and less atrocity of one's doings might consist with utter alienation from the condition and characteristics of God's own children. My God, let me not be deceived into a false estimate of my own state because of any generous movements that I might experience whether of admiration at what is naturally good or of indignancy at what is naturally and revoltingly evil. Be Thou ever uppermost in my regards, and let me at all times look up to the place where Thine honour dwelleth, asking counsel and obtaining it from the Being with whom I have to do. And when beset with hostility and in the very midst of perplexities let me, in imitation of Him who was after Thine own heart, encourage myself in Thee as the Lord *my* God. Be Thou *my* God, Almighty Father. Let me appropriate the offered reconciliation of the gospel. Let me not be afraid, but only believe; and accepting the overtures of Thy friendship, let me henceforth rejoice in Thee as indeed my friend. And from this precious, because appropriating faith, let there flow as from a spontaneous and exuberant fountain all the social virtues of human life, all the equities and the kindnesses which man should observe to his fellows. The law which David ordained in Israel was a law both of justice and humanity—these virtues of our own terrestrial platform, and which at least among his own people he superadded to his piety towards God.

But in the closing verses there is also the manifestation of another social virtue on the part of David—that of gratitude towards the people of his old haunting-places, from whom, we have no doubt, he experienced protection and favour in the days of his wandering exile, with much of the rough hospitality of that period.

I. SAMUEL XXXI.

We have here the sad and final catastrophe of the history of Saul, whose distempered life was correspondingly followed up by the most fearful of deaths—the death of a suicide. The only other scriptural instances of this which occur to us are those of Ahithophel and Judas, whose ends also were in keeping with the crimes of which they had been guilty—bringing each into the desperado state, whether of agonizing disappointment or agonizing remorse, under which they made away with themselves. Dear Jonathan also fell, but not by his own hand, yet in circumstances and by a way sufficiently tragical to read in it the natural argument for the soul's immortality, grounded on the sufferings of the good in this world, on the inequality here between their character and their fortunes, to be repaired by the distributions of a new and everlasting economy. My God, let this spectacle of Jonathan prostrate on the field of battle, lying side by side with his wicked father, and the ungodly Philistines rejoicing victoriously over both—let this reconcile me to the evils of our present state, so that I may endure hardness as a good soldier of Jesus Christ, and count not when preyed upon by others that any strange thing hath happened to me. These Philistines for a time had it all to themselves. It was a dark and distressful period for the children of Israel; yet Providence was at work and upon their side, nor can we sufficiently admire the preparation that even then was going on for their deliverance, hidden at the time from themselves, but unfolded to us by the pen of history. What a light it casts on the wanderings and the fortunes of David which looked at the time so mysterious; and with what profound skill was the crisis of his separation from the Philistines and the overthrow of God's people made subservient to their future enlargement. And still the Lord reigneth—let the earth, even in the midst of all that is adverse and menacing, let the earth rejoice. O my God, enable me to look on present appearances with the eye of him who is spiritual and who judgeth all things. Bring good in Thine own way out of all that looks now so disastrous and foreboding—the impending famine, the ungodly administration, the advances of some of our Churches towards Popery, the obvious affinity to this idolatrous system on the part of the upper classes of society, and along with this the countenance of Government upon it; and last of all, the sluggish indifference even of our evangelical bodies to the objects and the work of a vigorous and effectual home missionary enterprise.—My God, bring order out of confusion; and in thine own good time and way work out for us a purer and better economy, under which our rulers may Christianize their legislation and philosophers their systems, and society at large, renouncing all the perversities and practices of a world lying in wickedness, may enter on that walk now only trodden by a few peculiar people, but then so widened and expanded that what at present is the strait and narrow path shall become a broad way leading to everlasting life.

II. SAMUEL.

2 Samuel i.—The *dénouement* proceeds—for so we should call it looking at it historically; but looking to it spiritually, we should say that the design of Providence is now advancing towards a further manifestation. Like prophecy, what is dark in the perspective becomes plain in the fulfilment and the event; and the purposes of the invisible God who is above nature are yet carried into effect by the laws and according to the processes of nature. We feel ourselves among the common likelihoods of history and human life as we read of the poor Amalekite seduced into a falsehood by the imagination of his bearing joyful intelligence to David, and claiming to himself the part which he professed to have had in it. We cannot but commiserate him, while in this instance we would ascribe the stern severity of David's award not to cruel policy, but to the urgencies of an honest and deeply felt principle, and in virtue of which he held it as sacrilege to lift up the hand against the anointed of the Lord. Let this not be without its practical efficacy on myself in tempering and restraining my expressions of indignancy against the powers that be, seeing that they, too, if not anointed, are yet ordained of God. It is on this occasion that our warrior poet came forth with one of his most beautiful effusions—one of the finest, indeed, and most pathetic to be found within the whole compass of literature. How softened—nay, how complimentary now to the monarch who had persecuted him through life, but whom, as if disarmed by the view of his mangled corpse, he now mourns over—not, we feel assured, with factitious and

pretended, but with honest genuine and heart-stirred emotion. "Death," says one of the heroines in a novel, "death clears all scores." But indeed David required the excitement of no such appliance; for what could be more generous, what more magnanimous and noble than the whole of his conduct towards his king—even when chasing him like a partridge upon the mountains, intent on the destruction of his own most faithful and devoted servant? And now let me take the last leave of my beloved Jonathan—the most engaging character, and perhaps the most perfectly drawn of all the merely human personages whom either profane or sacred history has recorded. The specific moral property by which he is most signalized was the entire devotedness of his love to David, passing the love of women—not our love to them, but their love, the love of a constant and pure-hearted and affectionate female to him on whom she has fixed the preference of her most intense and unalterable regards.

II. SAMUEL II.

O that I knew what it was to inquire and ask counsel of God on all the occasions of my history, instead of acting, as I too often do, on the impulses of my own waywardness. And it is particularly wrong to abandon myself to a sense of utter helplessness and despondency when obstructions and adversities are thrown across my path—this did happen on a very recent occurrence, from the effects of which we have still obtained no extrication. But have I not a God to look up to? Should not He be the habitation to whom I should resort continually? Should not I when beset by the urgencies of that evil world, whereof my Saviour hath told me that therein I shall have tribulation—should not I be able even at the worst to say of God—My soul, return into Thy rest, and so experience the fulfilment of the promise, that in me ye shall have peace? O let me cast my present care and all other cares upon Thee, and let me experience this result—that the peace of God which passeth all understanding shall keep my heart and mind in Christ Jesus my Lord. And, O my God, while I thus pray for peace inwardly, do help me in the outward concerns of the West Port.

David had many obstructions and trials on his way to the predicted monarchy over all Israel. Let me take a lesson from his deportment under them, and more especially from those psalms which give forth the exercises of a mind disciplined by adversity. Like him may I be enabled to say—What time I am overwhelmed and in perplexity, I shall flee to the Rock that is higher than I.

What a coarse instrumentality is here in operation for the advancement of the Divine purposes, and in connexion with that throne which is the prototype and the precursor of Christ's everlasting kingdom. He who can make the wrath of man to praise Him, and when it offers to go beyond this end can restrain the remainder thereof, He can make wars and hatreds and the rivalry of hostile peoples all subservient to the furtherance of His designs. Do Thou overrule, O God, for the prosperity both of Thy Church and of our country, the emulations and antipathies which obtain amongst the various sects and sections of our empire. Do Thou give a better direction than heretofore to the proceedings of the Evangelical Alliance; and O that wise and Christian measures could be taken and made effectual for the pacification of Ireland—so that there might be peace among our Churches and peace throughout the nation.

II. SAMUEL III.

How legible are the characters written by the finger of Providence throughout the whole history of David, both as regarding his transition to the throne of Judah, and then his intermediate transition to the throne of all Israel. In the case of David we see that his political engrossments did not displace his personal and family affections; and so these nearer interests had to be adjusted before he would entertain the public question between him and Abner. My God, enable me to rule my own household well—else how am I fit for taking part in the affairs of the house of God? and forbid that any more distant or general undertakings should supersede the attentions and the duties which I owe to my own kindred, and more especially to the children whom Thou hast given to me.

But David met with sad difficulties and trials on the way to the consummation both of his own desires and of God's designs concerning him; and like most of such trials, they arose from the perversities of men. Teach me, O God, to beware of men. Save me from the fear of man which is a snare; and save me also from the facility which inclines me to all confidence in their plausibilities and profession. Let me look upwardly; and withdrawing my trust from the arm of flesh, let me place all my reliance upon God. We observe that David most naturally gave way to his feelings, and poured forth his imprecations on the murderer of Abner; and perhaps we should add, most justifiably—whether we regard the malediction as a prophecy, or as right at that early period in itself, on our hypothesis of a progressive morality. But there can be no question as to the rightness, along with the extreme amiableness and beauty of the exhibition which he made at the grave of the slaughtered man—infamously slaughtered by the hands of a perfidious assassin. We know nothing more impressive than his whole lamentation, and particularly his eulogium on Abner—the prince and the great man who had fallen in Israel. The complaint too of his being so overborne by these sons of Zeruiah and of his helplessness in their hands, is true to all the human and historical probabilities of the case; and we believe is often, very often, verified not in courts only when the monarch has to succumb under the weight of the grandees and counsellors around him, but also in other spheres and corporations both of a civil and an ecclesiastical character, when the man of greatest wisdom in the management of affairs is forced to resile from his own propositions, because of sons of Zeruiah who are too hard for him.

II. SAMUEL IV.

November, 1846.

We here see the hand of Providence in clearing and opening up a way for David to the monarchy of all Israel, though by the agency of wicked men—an order of events not uncommon in the divine administration of the world. He who maketh the wrath of man to praise Him makes also the wickedness of man to subserve the purposes of his all-wise and righteous government. Let us not fret then because of evil-doers; they are but instruments in the hand of God. The ill-usage and injury which provoke when we look to man the immediate author, when we look to God may be but the adversities by which He is pleased to discipline His children for their moral good—nay, too, by which He often prepares the way for the advancement of their interests in this world. This lesson is frequently and very finely brought out in the Psalms; and accordingly how usual it is for David, after complaining of the cruelty and injustice of his fellow, to turn him to God as his refuge and place of rest, the habitation to which he resorts continually. This whole lesson is beautifully expanded and set forth in that most precious composition the thirty-seventh Psalm. Let us give way then, neither to fear nor wrath, because of wrongs at the hand of our enemies. The wrath of man worketh not the righteousness of God; and God is our helper, therefore let us not fear what man can do unto us.—But not only may we learn from this chapter a lesson of patience under injustice in the usual and general sense of the term, we may also learn from it patience under injustice in the particular form of calumny. It may often be the pure effect of misunderstanding. Men of a lower standard are incapable of estimating the worth of those who are better and higher in the scale of character than themselves. They misconceive and so misrepresent the whole spirit and motives by which they are actuated. It is obvious both of the poor Amalekite whom David makes mention of, and of the wretched men whose atrocity is here recorded—that they formed a wrong judgment of David, and so forfeited their lives in virtue of their miscalculation. One cannot on the other hand but admire the lofty and righteous tone of sentiment manifested by David on this occasion, and his noble indignancy at the deed of horror—the monstrous perpetration of those who thought to do him service. He seizes aright on what that was in which the essential and aggravated guilt of these desperadoes in crime lay; and in following the impulse of his own righteous spirit he in fact acquitted himself of his best and truest policy—even as when he mourned at the grave of Abner, and sent his message of grateful acknowledgment to the men of Jabesh-gilead.

II. SAMUEL V.

We now reach the consummation of David's enthronement over all Israel—the people most naturally led thereto by their gratitude for his past services, and the well-earned confidence they had in him; and David most rightfully acceding to their proposal in that he knew of his appointment from on high, through Samuel the prophet. The league between him and his subjects presents us with the historical example of a national compact; but it was a league before the Lord. And here at least we have the Divine right and the people's choice fastened upon one and the same person. Even they themselves plead the will of God in argument for his assumption of the royal authority over them. After his ascension to the monarchy he prospered whithersoever he went. The first of these recorded successes is against the doomed inhabitants of the land, who were still in force and in strongholds; but we here read of his taking the chief of these in possessing himself of Mount Zion—first a citadel, but afterwards expanded into a city, the city of David. Then did he also prosper in the direction of his foreign alliances —receiving homage and civilities, for instance, from the king of Tyre. Yet in all this did David recognise a higher hand—that it was the Lord who had established him, the Lord who had exalted him. Yet did not his piety restrain him from those indulgences which now should be held as positively unlawful, but which were connived at, winked at, by God in these ruder and earlier stages of that progressive morality under which our species are carried forward, by successive tuitions, to greater and greater degrees of elevation, till they shall stand perfect before God, and shall be like Him, for they shall see Him as He is. The allowance of polygamy is one of the most telling evidences for that system of gradual advancement from a ruder to a riper and more refined ethics which we have often advocated.

And lastly, he prospered against his external enemies, and prevailed over them—yet visibly, and with the full consciousness of David himself, under the Lord, of whom David inquired, and from whom he received the answer both of a bidding and a promise. It was an appropriate celebration of the victory over the Philistines to make a bonfire of their images.

The second victory over the Philistines is signalized by this peculiarity—that not only the Lord commanded the battle, but prescribed its tactics; and on the observance of them did He suspend the promise of His own aid. His authority reaches to the means as well as the matter of every commandment that cometh out of His mouth; nor let us look for success but in the way that either Scripture or experience demonstrates to be the way of His appointment.

II. SAMUEL VI.

We have here both the goodness and the severity of

God—His goodness in the very ascription to Him, that He dwells between the cherubims, and His severity in taking vengeance on every unhallowed approach to the place where His honour dwelleth. Yet even in this latter manifestation is the gospel shadowed forth, that gospel which while it proclaims a welcome admittance to all through Christ, proclaims also that no man cometh unto the Father but by the Son. The people had the benefit of the mercy-seat, through their high-priest who entered within the vail once every year—when it would have been death for any other to have entered. But we have a High-Priest who has now entered within the vail of the upper sanctuary, and through whom one and all are invited to make their confident approaches unto God. My God, let mine be at all times a hallowed approach—or with a true heart while in full assurance of faith, and so not counting the blood of the covenant an unholy thing. Thus might we joy in God through Him by whom we receive the atonement—even through Him who is the minister of the true sanctuary, and the dispenser of far richer blessings than those of which the earthly ark was the harbinger to the family and house of Obed-edom. Did we do aright by the apparatus of our redemption there need be no fear at least of terror, for perfect love would cast out that element. Behold it is I, says Christ, be not afraid. And so the ark of the Mosaic ritual at which David trembled, when vengeance was inflicted on the worthless liberties that had been taken with it, was afterwards when rightly and warrantably dealt with, the object of unbounded confidence and joy to David and all his people. Thus let me rejoice in the Saviour, and thus in the face of every possible disparagement let me testify for the Saviour.

Let me exalt him, however vile it might make me in the sight of others—nay, let my own sense of my own exceeding vileness lead me to have no confidence in the flesh, but to rejoice in the Lord Jesus. Withal let me ever be offering to Him the sacrifices of thanksgiving—never forgetting that to do good and communicate are the special sacrifices wherewith God is well-pleased.

II. SAMUEL VII.

David in the exuberance of his gratitude would have done more for his high and heavenly Benefactor, but was restrained by a message through the prophet. Nevertheless it was well that it was in his heart; and though his proposal was not accepted, yet is it most graciously met, and this with exceeding great and precious promises—the complete fulfilment of which, however, is yet to come; and which fulfilment we look forward to as the sure mercies of David—an everlasting house, an everlasting throne, and everlasting security from all that can defile or disturb the subjects of that kingdom wherein dwelleth righteousness. Israel is still under chastisement for its dire iniquities—yet is not the mercy of the Lord finally and conclusively taken away; and though He should make a full end of other nations, yet will He not make a full end of Israel, but will at length establish it as the great metropolitan nation over all people and all countries in the world. My God, I have received chastening at Thy hand, but have not adequately profited thereby; and often even under the heaviest of Thine inflictions have iniquities prevailed over me. Henceforth, O Lord, may I acquit myself as a dutiful and obedient son under the fatherly corrections of the great spiritual Husbandman; and may the fruit of all Thy chastisements be righteousness and peace. I would join David in his prayer. With him would I humble myself in the thought of the great goodness which the Father hath bestowed on me, that I should be called a son of God. O redeem me to Thyself, and that I may be Thine for ever. Redeem me from a world lying in wickedness; and do Thou, O Lord, become my God. Do Thou love me, O God, with an everlasting love, and not after the manner of men—for Thy thoughts are not as our thoughts, neither are Thy ways as our ways. Cause me to hope in Thee, according to Thy word, for Thy word is true—the basis on which we would rest our confidence before Thee in all our supplications. Let it be enough for my faith that Thou, O Lord, hast spoken it. And what a foundation too for our trust and our encouragement in praying for the peace and prosperity of Zion, and in giving the Lord no rest till He hath made Jerusalem a praise upon the earth! Fulfil this great event, O God, in Thine own good time upon earth. May Thy prophecies tell what ought to be the subject of our prayers. Let not the former supersede the latter, but rather call them forth more trustfully, more importunately, more perseveringly—till the universal kingdom of truth and righteousness shall be established in our world.

II. SAMUEL VIII.

This chapter is a record of David's victories—telling us how the Lord, by enabling him to conquer, gave him rest from all his enemies round about. One recoils from the cruelties of war, and feels perplexed at the obvious sanction bestowed upon them from on high; but these mysteries will at length be all cleared away. What an aspect of barbarity to us has the measuring line that he cast over the poor Moabites, and by which every two for one were assigned for slaughter. Could not he have made them tributaries at a less expense of human blood? and seeing too that their affinity to the children of Israel placed them out of the curse which attached to the Amalekites and Canaanites. Yet David was a man after God's own heart; and save in the matter of certain great and recorded transgressions, did God smile upon his works and his ways. These conquests extended the influence, at least, if not the territorial sovereignty of Israel even to the Euphrates—so as for a time to realize that extent of territory, which seems to have been promised by God to His people, and which Dr. Keith contends is still in reserve for them, when theirs shall have become the metropolitan empire of the world. And amid the narrative of these doings we are told that the Lord preserved David whithersoever he went. Preserve, O God, the heralds and missionaries of the gospel in their perilous enterprises, that under Thy guidance and guardianship they may achieve their moral and spiritual conquests over the wilds of heathenism, and so that the whole earth shall be subdued unto the obedience of the faith.

David got him a name, and the fame of him went abroad over many lands. And one fruit of these victories was, that the kings of other lands sent their messages of peace and proffers of alliance, along with valuable gifts, wherewith David commenced the accumulation of those treasures which he dedicated to God, and which were afterwards expended on the temple of Jerusalem. And such was his wondrous combination of talent, that adding the civil to the military, he ruled over his own subjects with the same first-rate ability which he showed in war—and better than ability, his reign was one of justice and judgment. In the list of his official arrangements we read of Joab as commander-in-chief, who often gave him great trouble.

II. SAMUEL IX.

We have here a kindlier and more amiable exhibition of this great hero—and to which he was spontaneously prompted by his own grateful and friendly recollection of dear departed Jonathan—causing inquiry to be made after the state of his surviving family. It gives a sad picture of the bustle and confusion of war, that he should ever have lost sight of them. His proposed kindness to those of the house of Saul was for Jonathan's sake; and, as to him a new information, there was reported to him a son of Jonathan himself. Ziba was of Saul's household, and from him he got accounts of the state of the surviving relationship. And so Mephibosheth was brought to him and we behold a descendant of the last royal family prostrating himself before him who was the shepherd boy and a servant in the household of his grandfather. David had to bid Mephibosheth fear not, and his words of patronly encouragement were replied to by words of utmost humility and obeisance. The arrangements on his behalf were made in a style of princely munificence—being vested in the property of Saul's land and of all that belonged to him. He devolved the management of the estate upon Ziba, who discharged the office of factor; and in that capacity had his hand in, as it were, or directly intromitted with the tangible goods and substance of Mephibosheth—a place of great temptation, as is often exemplified in our day. Ziba made very great professions of fidelity at the outset of this connexion ; but we shall see. Meanwhile Mephibosheth had many privileges assigned to him—was made a daily guest at the king's table, and put on a level with the king's son. He would be a very considerable person in Jerusalem, and I confess a strange curiosity for a most unattainable object—the journal of his daily life, as made up of talk and social intercourse, and domestic occupations. Will these longings for the knowledge of the forgotten past be gratified in Heaven?

II. SAMUEL X.

Doubtless it was a great indignity which David sustained at the hand of the Ammonites, and all the more provoking that it was in return for a real and honestly intended kindness on the part of the king of Israel. It does not appear whether this affront was or was not the *proximate* cause of the war. Certain it is that the Ammonites, conscious of the irritation which their conduct must have excited, were apprehensive of an invasion, and sent for mercenary troops from the neighbouring powers; and it is only when David hears of this hostile demonstration that we read of his sending Joab, the generalissimo of his armies, against the combined forces of the enemy, and whose great military talents obtained for him the victory over them all. It had become now as much a war for the protection of the national safety as for the vindication of the national honour. It is interesting to observe the religious ingredient of Joab's speech to his soldiers—his committal of the cause in which they were engaged to the God of battles, and its consequent effect in leading on the men to a successful termination of the contest—yet not wholly terminated as far as the Ammonites were concerned. They were only as yet shut up in their capital city, to be afterwards besieged and taken, and then followed up by a dreadful vengeance for the insult done to the ambassadors of David. Meanwhile, as the fruit of these successes, he obtained an extension of service, if not of tribute, from the people whom he subdued. The cities of his God were rendered secure from the inroad of the enemies who had menaced them; and God in thus defending His own people did what seemed unto Him good. If the appeal made to the Lord of Hosts by Joab carry in it no evidence of personal religiousness on the part of this rude and regardless warrior—a coarse specimen of ancient heroism—it at least evinces the skill wherewith he could address himself to the deepest and most influential feelings of the host that were under his charge.

II. SAMUEL XI.

This is a sad chapter of David's history—a passage of his life that was fruitful of many results, the chastisement of great and multiform trials, the scandal of the serious, the exultation of the ungodly, this last a most bitter humiliation to poor David himself; and lastly, under the inspiration of that God who bringeth good out of evil, it originated those penitential psalms which have exercised and guided the devotions of the contrite and the sorrowful in all ages of the Church. It is a chapter which serves to illustrate the deep malignity of sin, even of sin in the deceitfulness of its fairest and most fascinating forms. Let us never look with indulgence upon transgression whence such fruits of bitterness grow, and grow too as if by a natural process which causes them not to be the rare but the frequent and customary effects of a most tempting indulgence. What dire perpetrations were those into which David was led under the delirium of a passion which so warred against his soul, and from the fear of a disgraceful exposure—the cunning, the falsehood, at length the deliberate murder, followed up by an adulterous marriage—and all the result of a surprise by which in a moment of unguardedness he was so miserably overcome. What a lesson for strictest vigilance that we might repel all unhallowed thoughts and turn our sight and eyes from viewing vanity. One recognises the hand of an overruling Providence in that train of events by which David after his great transgression was led onward from step to step till the consummation of his guilt and the infliction of its penalties—penalties which followed him through life, and caused him afterward to walk softly and humbly all his days. There was an obvious providence in the determination of Uriah to keep by the king's palace and not go to his house. How much would the guilty charge of David to Joab bring him under the power of this fierce and unruly warrior in all time coming.—Altogether, this grievous fall seems to have been the turning point from days of bright and joyful prosperity to the harassments and calamities and cares of a sadly chequered history afterward: and yet there were yielded at the last the peaceable fruits of righteousness. And what an evidence is here presented to us of that mercy in God which rejoices over all His works, and in the midst of all His attributes. David was sorely chastened, but not to death given over; nay, recovered both the state and the character of the man according to God's own heart.—My God, while I feel the encouragement of this reflection, let me never turn it into an encouragement for sin, and henceforth maintain the closest vigilance over all my thoughts and all my ways.

But God is not to be mocked, and followed up this enormity of David by the manifestations of His sore displeasure.

II. SAMUEL XII.

This is a chapter which should go home to the conscience. What a searching appeal is made in these words—Thou art the man! O my God, let me bear it closely and faithfully upon myself; and while convicted in my own conscience, even as the accusers of the woman were to the Saviour, of manifold infirmities, may I at the same time not faint when chastened of the Lord, but take both the encouragement and the warning which lie in the gracious utterance of—" Neither do I condemn thee; go and sin no more." It is here made quite palpable that this transgression of David proved the great turning point of his history, and that it distinctly gave birth to those innumerable trials of which we read both in the direct history and in those confessions and prayers of an humbled and penitential spirit which have been recorded in the Book of Psalms, as lessons and exercises for the Church in all ages. It was because of the great sin he had committed that the sword was not to depart from his house, and that both in his family and kingdom he was to be variously and sorely afflicted—and this by Him who afflicts not willingly; and yet he was taken into pardon and reconciliation—a forgiven man, and not to death given over. My God, pardon my heinous offences, and suffer me not to be tried beyond what I am able to bear. Provide a way of escape; and above all save me from giving occasion for the enemies of the Lord to blaspheme. I would fear alway, I would walk softly and in humbleness before Thee all the days of my life. O for the high-toned purity and principle that would recoil even in the solitude of a man's own thoughts from every wrong and unhallowed imagination.

The threatened death came upon his child; his agitation beforehand and tranquillity afterwards are true to nature. What a wondrous view of God—that after He had administered the medicine, after He had finished the act of discipline, His love for David—both for him and his, was still unquenched. He loved Solomon.—Let us behold in this narrative both the goodness and severity of God. O let me work out my salvation with fear and trembling.

We can sympathize with the temptations and the infirmities and the remorse of David, but we cannot sympathize with him in these horrid cruelties. There is a mystery in the Divine tolerance, perhaps in the Divine sanction and approval, of these dread proceedings. One might have hoped that the Ammonites, the children of Lot, the kinsfolk of Israel, would have been exempted from them.—How I should like a book of graphic travels through that land, the capital of which was Rabbah, the city of waters.

II. SAMUEL XIII.

The fulfilments proceed of the sentence passed on poor

David. The first was the death of his adulterous child, and now follow the outbreakings of incest and murder among the children of his own family: and one of the saddest among the penalties inflicted on him was his own moral powerlessness as the judge or the rebuker of these enormities—disarmed as he must have felt himself to be of authority and weight by his own sense, as well as knowledge on the part of others, of the enormity into which he himself had fallen. What an impressive remonstrance—What hast thou to do to take my judgments into thy mouth? And so it was after the prayer of—Restore unto me the joys of Thy salvation, and uphold me with Thy free Spirit, that David said—then will I teach transgressors the way, and sinners shall be converted unto Thee. Give me, O Lord, the confidence and the consciousness that might warrant my speaking with authority to others, and save me from all which might detract from my usefulness or bring dishonour on a sacred or righteous cause. It may have been that the hardness which Amnon felt in the way of obtaining his desire lay partly in the barrier of his own conscientious scruples; but let not an experience of these alleviate the criminality of an unlawful deed; the conscience being felt will not excuse us if conscience be disobeyed. It is said of poor David that he was very wroth upon this occasion; and we have no doubt that his sufferings were aggravated by the haunting sense of his own position—a position of great moral impotency, because of his own sad misconduct in the matter of Uriah. If Amnon went deliberately to work so did David, who must have felt himself restrained by the paralyzing recollection of his own guilt. Let me not overlook the aggravation of consanguinity in the case of the son. The sad sequel, the awful tragedy which ensued, tells what an evil and bitter thing it is to sin against God; and more especially that, under His moral administration, that vice which of all others puts on the fairest and most fascinating form, will not go unpunished, but sooner or later, though to the entire destruction of the sinner, will meet with its recompense. The plot of Amnon was succeeded by the plot of Absalom; and so another stroke of the chastening rod came down upon David, who wept very sore. And yet mark his unquenched love for Absalom; and let us not forget the lesson which our Saviour drew from the affection of earthly parents—" If ye then, being evil, know how to give good gifts unto your children, how much more shall your Heavenly Father give the Holy Spirit to them who ask Him?"

II. SAMUEL XIV.
December, 1846.

The good old king yearned with a father's heart towards Absalom, which was perceived by Joab who grafted his court policy thereon. How much it was the habit of these days to convey sentiment or even information not literally, but symbolically and allegorically. Nathan did so in his message of denunciation from the Lord to David. The widow of Tekoah does so in the present chapter; but the highest sanction of all for this style of communication is the parables of our Saviour. There is one expression in the speech of the wise woman when stating the hopelessness of death, from which recall is as impossible as to gather up the water which has been spilt upon the ground, that has become proverbial from its application to other things, and especially to the word of God when thrown away upon the soil of a hard and barren heart, and so yielding no fruit unto righteousness. Deliver me, O God, from this hopeless condition of being beyond recovery, and recall me to the ways of truth and holiness. Recall me from this state of spiritual exile; take Thy banished back again; bring me nigh through Him who died, the just for the unjust. And O what ground for encouragement in the thought, that if David—an earthly father—so longed for the return of murderous and disobedient Absalom, how much more will my Father welcome me back to His house from which I have so waywardly expatiated among the dreary outfields of alienation from God. Let me no longer in the face of such a consideration stand at a mistrustful distance from Him who is now holding forth the overtures of reconciliation. David perceived the drift of the woman's address, and consented to the return of Absalom—yet placing him under a certain measure of restraint and discipline. He made a most ungenerous return for this parental act of clemency, and I pray to be kept from the like ingratitude towards my reconciled God. But give me a full sense, O Lord, of this reconciliation; admit me into Thy presence; keep me not without the threshold of Thine own blessed fellowship, O Lord. O may I know what it is to have access with confidence, and to have a part in those gracious manifestations which Christ hath promised to him who hath His commandments and keepeth them.

II. SAMUEL XV.

The conduct of Absalom towards David is of a piece

with our own towards God; we turn his gifts into the means of a most rebellious idolatry against Him. It were well that we saw how monstrous and unnatural is that ungodliness by which we suffer the creatures of His bounty to seduce us away from the allegiance that we owe to our Creator—unnatural in respect to its utter incongruity with the fitness and propriety of things, though intensely natural in respect to our natures being obstinately perverse and corrupt—altogether turned from the right way, or way of original righteousness. Poor David is now in the very thick of those judgments which were denounced upon him as the penalties of his sore transgression; and let us fortify ourselves from this and similar narratives, as well as similar experiences, in the principle that sore and evil indeed are all the freedoms and transgressions of licentiousness. My God, save me from the power of all impulses to that which is wrong, and save me from all confidence or self-complacency because of the felt impulses within me to that which is good—as benevolence or honour. Let me recognise as paramount to, and supreme over all, the will of God, the absolute rectitude in itself both of acts and dispositions. The Gittite, like the good Samaritan of the gospels, proved himself better than the bulk of the Israelites were—for we can infer little from the manifestations of the popular grief on the eve of David's departure from Jerusalem. They were overset by the moving spectacle, but took to the rebellious hosts of their countrymen, who flocked to the standard of Absalom. How affecting the meek and patient resignation of David to the will of God under that parental chastisement which he felt he had so rightfully incurred. And while it seemed good unto God to inflict this salutary discipline on the spirit of David, it also seemed good unto Him by the arrangements of His providence to open a way for its prosperous termination. The return of Zadok and Abiathar, but more especially of Hushai, was the preparative in the order of events for the safe and happy return of David himself in triumph to that very city from which he was now taking flight as a mournful outcast. The same God who laid this trial upon him provided also the way of escape from it.

II. SAMUEL XVI.

The selfishness and treachery of Ziba now begin to be developed. Let us not think that any strange thing hath happened here. How much of iniquity alike gross is realized in our own day, either without law, or when the legal is present but the moral utterly wanting, under the semblance of its forms. O that I were so spiritualized as to be equally prompt in my recoil from the licentious or the intemperate as I am from the violations of gratitude and truth.

Poor David's trials are fast multiplying; and how obvious it is that he views them as coming from the Lord. With him this whole series of afflictions is obviously a process of discipline;—the Lord is chastening him sore, though not giving him over unto death. He takes it all as from the hand of God; he knows the meaning of these various and repeated visitations; and how meekly docile and submissive is his bearing under them. Spare me, O God, spare me the life of Mrs. C. Withhold, if it be Thy blessed will, Thy correcting hand. By Thy good spirit deepen my convictions of my own wretched infirmities;

let me profit by the warnings of Thy providence, that its lessons may be fixed in my heart and practice by the workings of Thy grace. Try me not, O God, beyond what I am able to bear; and let all Thy chastening redound to the good of my soul.

The last of the recorded chastisements in this chapter which David at the hand of God was made to undergo, was a peculiarly appropriate though most severe one— brought about by the infamous counsel of Ahithophel, so as to subject the now penitent and sorely suffering monarch to a penalty the precise counterpart of that grievous offence into which he himself had fallen. His unfaithfulness to the sacred rights of another man was repaid upon himself—not, however, to the full measure of taking from him his life as he had from Uriah, but as if to compensate for this, by the peculiar disgrace and enormity of the violation being perpetrated by his own son. What an ordeal he had to pass through!—Lord, Thou hatest iniquity. Lord, spare me, sanctify me. Give me the command over my strong affections; enable me to keep my heart with all diligence; may I keep it in the love of Thyself, which do Thou shed abroad, O Lord, by the Holy Spirit; and then shall I overcome all which is opposite to the love of the Father.

II. SAMUEL XVII.

The workings of Providence now turn in favour of David. He who turneth the hearts of men whithersoever He will inclined Absalom to listen to Hushai rather than to Ahithophel, and thence a change of affairs ruinous to the cause of this great rebellion. What men of reach and policy there were in these days—men profound in counsel as well as men skilful and heroic in war. But let us chiefly prize the lesson that God is pre-eminent and supreme in the moral as well as the material world, making men as subservient to His purposes as any of the elements of nature. It was the Lord who had appointed to defeat the counsel of Ahithophel, and this to the intent that He might bring evil upon Absalom. It was not only He who put the counter-advice into the heart of Hushai, but it was He who inclined Absalom and the men of Israel to follow it. After He had achieved this service he commissioned Zadok and Abiathar to convey the tidings to David of the state of affairs. All these three had left David and returned to Jerusalem for the express purpose of counterworking the policy of Absalom. The minute workings of the providence of God are very apparent in the journey of the two messengers, and let us remark how consistent these are with the busy working of all the human passions and interests—fear and cunning and contrivances for eluding the enemy under the strong impulse of the law of self-preservation. Hushai must have been still afraid lest the counsel of Ahithophel should prevail. Ahithophel saw in exercise of his shrewd discernment that all was now over with the cause; and what perhaps was sorer to him than this, there was the mortification of wounded vanity in that the counsel of Hushai was preferred before his own; and so in the extremity of his agonized feelings, he, like another traitor of still greater notoriety, went and hanged himself. He is the Judas of the Old Testament; and herein contemplating the like fate of these two men —the one who betrayed David his king, and the other who betrayed the Son of David his Lord—we may see the certain and ultimate prevalence of that course by which the sure mercies of David will at length be made good, and the spiritual kingdom of truth and righteousness be established to the utter defeat and overthrow of all enemies. In what beautiful contrast does the conduct of good old Barzillai and others stand out with that of Ziba and Shimei and Ahithophel!

II. SAMUEL XVIII.

Their care of David is a fine trait of the people; and it is always well when those in station and authority so conduct themselves as rightfully to have earned the favour of the multitude—such as the English bishops when imprisoned in the Tower, and among the rest Trelawny, who awoke such enthusiasm throughout the peasantry of Cornwall. One can sympathize too, though not in a way so unqualified, with the parental anxiety of the monarch's heart for his son Absalom; but O let me not fail to make the application and evermore to rejoice in it—that as our Father in Heaven is likened by our Saviour Himself to earthly fathers in that they give good gifts unto their children, so the affection manifested here in the face of such a monstrous and unnatural rebellion on the part of him who was the object of it, abundantly warrants the confidence that God will meet with His welcome and full acceptance even the worst of returning sinners who now seek after Him if haply they may find Him. But what a ferocious man of blood and moral hardihood this Joab must have been, whose life was signalized by a number of the most cruel and treacherous murders, and which at length brought him to his death by the hand of an avenger. The figure which this soul of iron presents to the reader of the Bible is one of the most graphic in the whole platform of Scripture history. The narrative, too, of David beside the watch-tower, and the two runners, is exceedingly picturesque, though I know not if the subject of it has ever come under the hands of any painter. Indeed, the traits of nature in this chapter are very strikingly given, insomuch that the brief descriptive touches in which it abounds carry the evidence of their own truthfulness along with them. Such are the impatience of Joab with the man who brought him tidings of Absalom, the very utterance he gave of it, his preference of Cushi over Ahimaaz as the messenger to David—seemingly because of the firmer nerve wherewith he could reply to the anxious interrogation of the monarch—the delicacy of Ahimaaz' answer, and finally, the overpowering effect of the intelligence upon the king's feelings when all was made known to him—all these are historical statements which bear upon them the strong impress of their own credibility. David sunk the patriot in the parent, yet we cannot but love the exhibition of his tenderness. There was perhaps a certain sturdy patriotism in the deed of Joab, yet we cannot help being revolted by the heart which prompted, by the hand which perpetrated so fell an execution, though inflicted on one of the worst of criminals.

II. SAMUEL XIX.

The same shining internal character of reality continues throughout all that remains of this narrative. There cannot be a stronger verisimilitude than is here set forth in the conduct of the army, who though flushed with victory, stole off like conscious malefactors on hearing of the king's grief at the death of Absalom. It marks the power of that great moral ascendency which the king had over their spirits; yet was he forced to succumb when their rough and resolute commander interposed and compelled the monarch to show himself. One wonders not at his growing repugnance to these sons of Zeruiah, and how he should have meditated to supersede Joab by making Amasa the general-in-chief of the forces. The effect of the victory over the tribes of Israel is perfectly in keeping too with human nature, and so is the preference of David for being invited first by the men of Judah, as well as the consequent jealousy that broke out in fierce invective between the two great divisions of the nation over which David ruled. We further read of the mighty hold which David had over the hearts of those of his own tribe. This return of the king was followed up by a speedy but withal most natural reaction on the part of those who had deserted or despitefully treated him in the day of his adversity—among these Shimei makes just the appearance that we should have expected, whilst the noble reply of David to the suggestion of Abishai carries in it the expression of his antipathy to these coarse and resolute and withal able and influential men, the sons of Zeruiah—now, we doubt not, his greatest eye-sores. We scarcely know how to account for the king's award in the case of Mephibosheth, of whom, we might think, he must have entertained some lurking suspicion that he divided his property with the servant who had reported against him. But all is genial and right and perfectly beautiful in the final settlement which took place between David and Barzillai, wherein the virtues of gratitude and devoted loyalty are so conspicuously blended.

How exquisitely in keeping with the most natural desires of the good old man's heart that he should die in his own city, and be buried beside the grave of his father and mother, while, by soliciting in behalf of Chimham, he gracefully softened his denial of the king's request by making a request in turn, and so putting himself in the condition of a dependent inferior seeking after the royal favour and patronage. Altogether there is a deal of what the painters would call truth in this chapter, both successive and contemporaneous, though we know not if any of the latter scenes has been attempted by the pencil of an artist.

II. SAMUEL XX.

The troubles of David are not yet ended—they "in number many be;" but yet, as he hath himself recorded,

> "But yet at length out of them all
> The Lord did set him free."

His next adversary was a man of Belial, just as we should have calculated, for rebellion against so good a prince of itself implies great wickedness. But he had a strong hold upon Israel, and doubtless their late outbreakings with Judah greatly favoured the enterprise of this new Catiline.

Then follows what may be termed the covering up, as far as might be, of the scandal which Absalom had perpetrated upon David's household in the sight of all; after which there succeeded another trial in the treacherous assassination of Amasa by the hands of the bloody Joab—moved thereto, in all likelihood, by David's known preference for Amasa, and his determination to place him in chief command over the army. Yet poor David had again to succumb—these sons of Zeruiah being still too many for him. The prowess of Joab, and above all, his popularity with the soldiers, made him very formidable in the eyes of the monarch; and a cruel use did he make of this power. We have no doubt that this Joab was often in the eye of the psalmist when he penned his complaints and maledictions against his enemies. Still he was of great practical service, and prosecuted with great energy this new war till he at length put an end to it. Such was his influence or the terror of his name, that though it was said of Sheba that every man of Israel went up and followed him, it is now said of Joab that all the tribes of Israel went also after him. It would appear from his speech before Abel that at this time the pacific, which was certainly the wise policy, was uppermost with Joab—the desirable thing being to consolidate and harmonize Israel. He had exemplified the same management before in the case of Abner; and altogether he appears to have been able in conduct and counsel as well as in war.—The wise woman has bequeathed a fine proverbial expression, now habitually applied to those of her sex who are signalized by their piety and Christian influence—" a mother in Israel," than which we know not a more venerable designation or more expressive one, when great worth and great wisdom are combined.—The chapter concludes with the formation of a new cabinet, in which David, like other limited monarchs after him, was constrained to acquiesce in appointments not altogether to his mind—and more especially in that of Joab, who, as master over all the host, would in those days have all the power of the prime minister.

II. SAMUEL XXI.

These must have been the grandchildren of Saul who were hanged before the Lord. Altogether it is a most mysterious story, though one of its difficulties is akin with that characteristic of the Divine policy which runs through the dealings of God with our race. We know what a tremendous wholesale suffering has been laid upon our whole race for the one transgression of our first ancestor; and this, if it do not reconcile us, might lead to silent acquiescence in the proceeding here recorded, and by which—with the Divine permission at least, if not by express appointment—seven of Saul's descendants were hanged for an offence of his, and this to avert a national judgment which it had brought upon the land. The conduct of Rizpah reported to David we hope interested and pleased him. The piety wherewith she guarded the bodies of her two sons and five nephews would commend, we trust, his approving sympathy, and indeed is of a piece with his own attention to the bones of Saul and Jonathan. The whole transaction must have been directly implicated with the counsels, perhaps the commands of Heaven—for we read that after that God was entreated for the land. There is a deep enigma in the matter which waits its full solution on the day of the revelation of hidden things. What we know not now we shall know hereafter; and meanwhile seeing that vicarious justice is a principle of the Divine economy, let these examples of imputed guilt endear to us all the more the precious doctrine of Christ's imputed righteousness, confident that as the principle is so sure to take effect when on the side of condemnation and punishment, it will not less surely take effect when on the side of justification under the government of that God whose darling attribute is the mercy that rejoices over all His works, and in the midst of all His perfections.

War was renewed with the Philistines—a trial too, though not of the same primitive character as the rebellion of subjects and children. David, however, was getting old and had a narrow escape; and it is beautiful to observe the anxiety and affection of his subjects. These sons of Zeruiah too, though sad thorns in his side, were very serviceable; yet by general consent David himself was held to be the light of Israel. David had had his day of fighting, and with formidable warriors too of the same nation, and also of the same household or family, with those who are here recorded.

II. SAMUEL XXII.
January, 1847.

This song is almost identical with the eighteenth Psalm. If placed here in right chronological order it looks back a far way—even to David's escapes from Saul, although only now did he achieve a full security from the party which Saul had in Israel. This song bursts forth at the outset in strong expression of gratitude to Him who had delivered him from all his troubles. It was by calling on God that he was saved from his enemies. In the description of his dangers and of God's interposal in might for his rescue, we feel as if it were typical of the Church's extremity, and at length its triumph by miracle from Heaven; such as when Christ shall appear to war against His enemies, and changes shall take place upon the earth, here described very much in the terms of a great geological revolution. O may I be enabled to preserve my integrity in the midst of all coming adversities and trials, for the Lord will deal with us according to our righteousness; and let me and mine be counted on that day worthy to stand before the Son of man. The latter half of the psalm seems more literally applicable to the personal history of David. Give me the confidence which he had, and more especially in the tried word of God. Let me try it by prayer, by dependence on Christ, by trusting to Him and His word at all times, and then see whether or not according to my faith so it is done unto me. What need have I for the enlargement of my steps. Give me ease and security and the freedom of a mind rightly made up, and strength to break through all obstructions which lie in the way of duty. I desire more especially at this time to testify for Christ, and urge the acceptance of Him on one of high genius whom I love, but who may be said to have lived without Christ in the world. Enable me, O God, to overcome the restraints of false and sinful delicacy, and generally to conquer all those spiritual enemies who ply against me the weapons of temptation. There are expressions here which mark out David as a type of Christ—a people which I knew not shall serve me. It is true that David's conquests reached to the Euphrates, and overlapped in other quarters the original possession in the land of Canaan; still we are carried to that greater extension of dominion and power by the Lord's anointed, when strangers to the uttermost ends of the earth submitted themselves to the doctrines of salvation, and became obedient to the gospel of Jesus Christ. The mercy of God is unto David and his seed, and pre-eminently to that seed through whom all the families of the earth are to be blessed. Hasten, O God, in Thine own good time this full and final enlargement. Speed onward the conquests of the faith. Grant that He who is head of the Church may anon become head of the heathen. As soon as they hear may they be obedient.

II. SAMUEL XXIII.

It is interesting to observe in the direct history of David that he is designed as the sweet psalmist of Israel—thus making one part of Scripture reflect evidence and confirmation upon another. What a fine and full expression of the inspiration by which he was actuated is the Spirit of the Lord speaking by Him—nay, of verbal inspiration, for it was the Spirit's word that was on David's tongue. O that our rulers were like him—just, and ruling in the fear of God. Does not the last clause associate with religion the direct business of government? whereas the sadly prevalent notion of the present day is that these two should be kept apart from each other. David's house and family were wofully irreligious, yet with himself had God made a sure and well-ordered covenant. O give me a part and an interest in this blessed covenant; give me of the sure mercies of David—this is all my salvation and all my desire. O make it to grow; and as my remaining life in this lapse of years dwindles into a brief space, may my moral and personal salvation grow apace; for, alas! how miserably short is my practical Christianity from the standard of the gospel.

This is followed by a record of David's mighty men, who were his defenders against the sons of Belial, and the destroyers of many of them; not but that David ascribed all his deliverances to God—although grateful commemoration is made at the same time of the human instruments to whom he owed so much. It was Eleazar who smote the Philistines till his hand was weary; yet it was the Lord who wrought the great victory of that day, as He did the next, and indeed all the victories which are here recorded. Indeed—humanly speaking—some of these victories were single-handed. Eleazar seems to have fought alone, after which the people had only to pillage. Shammah also fought by himself after the people had fled from the Philistines. We feel as if there was scrupulosity in David not drinking of the water which his captains had brought to him at the hazard of their lives—nevertheless it proves how much his conscience lorded it over him. These were coarse times, yet not worse we fear than those that are still coming, and when outrage and violence and blood will become as familiar as they ever were in the days of a ruder heroism. The enumeration is closed by a list of thirty—a sort of body-guard or legion of honour. They were gathered from all parts of Israel, nay, it would appear in some instances, from the regions beyond—as Zelek the Ammonite, and we should imagine poor Uriah the Hittite, whose name occurs last in the catalogue.

II. SAMUEL XXIV.

There might be things unrecorded, and which if known by us would render more palpable than now what the precise or the full delinquency was in David's act of taking a census of the nation. It appears from Joab's remonstrance that he had delight in this thing, that he had set his heart upon it; and perhaps the flagrancy of the sin—much the same as that of the people in the days of Samuel desiring a king—was that now of the king's glorying in the people. We have a similar instance in Nebuchadnezzar being struck with madness, because his heart lifted him up on account of the glories of his kingdom—a sin, it may be, more aggravated in the case of David, on whom it was still more incumbent in these days of a sensible theocracy, to place all his confidence and all his glorying in God. However we shall explain wherein it is that the sin lay, there still remains the enigma of its being a sin of which we read, (verse 1,) that God moved him to it, and this because of His anger against Israel—a remarkable case of what may be called a moral penalty, though here it is the sin of one party punished through the sin of another. Joab, amid all his roughnesses, was occasionally right, and especially so in the present instance. And David was made sensible of the enormity of what he had done immediately after that it was executed—though perhaps made awake to the full extent of it by Gad's previous utterance to him of God's message—a case then of the moral sensibility being called forth by a voice *ab extra*. He made the choice of punishment which most men would have made, from the shortness of its duration; but to which he was moved by a beautiful sentiment of piety.—My God, in judgment remember Thine attribute of mercy, for it is great. There is a sublimity in the angel stretching forth his hand upon Jerusalem,—was it ever made the subject of a picture? David's question—What have these sheep done? admits of an answer on the ground of what we are told in verse 1 Though David's sin was the proximate, yet the people's sin was the prior cause of this visitation—the last great though not the greatest trial of David's chequered history and life, for the rebellion of Absalom was both a national and a personal trial. The outbreaking of Adonijah, however, was a personal trial. In the converse between David and Araunah there occurs a sentiment which has become proverbial—that of serving the Lord with what costs us nothing. For the purpose of self-examination it might prove of eminent use as a touchstone. I should be serving God with what costs me nothing did my obedience lie exclusively in justice and humanity and activity in philanthropic schemes, for to these I am constitutionally inclined. Let me therefore study the acts and sacrifices of mortification and self-denial—give up all envy and bitterness and vanity—prefer at all times the good of others and glory of God to my own glory—cut off a right hand and pluck out a right eye—by the entire surrender of every evil affection which wars against the soul.

I. KINGS.

1 KINGS I.—There is something very affecting in the decline and infirmities of the good old king. How near I am to his extreme limit.—My God, give me to apply my heart unto wisdom. Let me realize the nearness of death and of the coming eternity beyond it; let me make myself over to God.

But age did not exempt David from family trials, which pursued him to the very end of his life. How singularly spared I have been in this respect—not yet a death in my dwelling-house, though a domestic man now since 1803; and what is more blessed still, no perversity or unmanageableness on the part of my children.—I pray for grace to their souls. It appears that Adonijah was full brother to the former great family rebel, Absalom; and that Joab now changed his politics in taking part against the king—a judicial infatuation perhaps for his many crimes, so as to prepare the way for a judicial death. There is something very picturesque and interesting in the interview between David and Bath-sheba. It is not unlikely that her continued presence would act as a remembrancer to David, leading him to see God's chastening hand in all his trials, and enabling him to say—My sin is ever before me. However, all was now forgiven, and David was again delivered from the hand of his enemies. This man of frequent and deep experience in the school of affliction looked up to God, and sware by Him who had redeemed his soul out of all distress—mixing at the same time with his confidence that he would still be blest and delivered, the most prompt and energetic measures; and by putting the words into the mouth of his servants—God save king Solomon, set him forth as the designed and the anointed from on high. Benaiah's prayer was that God might confirm what David had said; and the oil of consecration to the high office of monarchy was poured upon him by the hand of a priest. Tidings of this appointment and of its joyful celebration in Jerusalem were soon brought to the rebels, and to them it was a knell of despair. Solomon did well to forbear instant vengeance on Adonijah. He began rightly—in that prosperity and clemency went hand in hand. It does not appear that any immediate punishment was laid on the offenders.

There might have been an interval of some length between this event and the death; and not till after his death do we read of any such executions as those that followed after it. Solomon does make a reserve in the deed of pardon which he at that time granted in favour of Adonijah.

I. KINGS II.

Give me, O Lord, to realize my coming death—" the way of all the earth;" and in the contemplation of this great change may present interests and present cares sit light upon my heart. Meanwhile, let me be strong and show myself a man—be valiant for the truth, and walk with resolute and unfaltering step in the way of God's commandments. We have often recoiled from the maledictions of David's dying bed; nor do we remember what Bradley says to mitigate and justify them. Let me not forget, however, that both he and Solomon were, at least in certain of their acts and sayings, inspired men; and in this instance the one may have been the mere pronouncer and the other the executioner of God's righteous judgments on this man of blood—the nephew of David as well as chief captain of his forces. In contrast with this there rests a mild and beautiful light on all that relates to good old Barzillai—though again perplexed how to reconcile the charge against Shimei with the oath that he had sworn in his favour. What a memento to myself when I look back the whole length of David's reign and find that forty years ago I had been for some years a minister in the Church; and with what deep humiliation should I look back on those days. The first acts of Solomon had in them all the sternness which is often called for by state policy, and as often prompted by the fears of men in the occupancy of highest power. Yet we cannot and will not sympathize with the doom he gave forth on his brother Adonijah, and would shut our eyes against the execution of Joab; nor could we look with complacency on the treatment of Shimei. We now live under a more perfect regimen, and which denounces even hatred in the heart as having in it the guilt of murder by the hand. But we are not adequate judges in this matter: we find that the will of God and the designs of retributive justice are implicated with the transactions which are here recorded. There was the fulfilment of an old prophecy in the deposition of Abiathar from the priesthood; and in the death of Joab do we behold an act of righteous vengeance for the innocent blood which was so cruelly and deceitfully shed by him.

These long intervals between the crimes both of Joab and Shimei and their respective punishments, remind us of Butler's argument regarding a future judgment, in which sins long forgotten by ourselves, and for which conscience has now ceased to reproach us, may still be reckoned with, and if not repented of, may be turned to our everlasting condemnation. My God, remember not the sins of my youth against me; let them be blotted out of Thy book; let no more mention be made of them; and O realize upon me by the grace of Thy Spirit this most satisfactory test of their being forgiven—even that I have conclusively turned from and no longer indulge in them.

I. KINGS III.

The affinity with a heathen king is not here stated as

an exception against the religious integrity of Solomon, though the practice of sacrificing in high places seems to be regarded as such. In the face of this, however, there is a full testimony given to his character. The Lord seems to have sanctioned the irregularity in their mode of worship—appearing to Solomon on the occasion of a great sacred festival held at Gibeon, the chief of the high places. Let me imitate the desire and prayer of Solomon for wisdom; and what encouragement is held out by the promise that if we do ask for this He will give liberally! I pray for a deep sense of my own ignorance and dependence on light and information from on high. Give me, O Lord, to judge aright in the various questions which come before me, whether called to decide on the conduct of individuals or on matters of public concern. O let my prayers be ever according to Thy will that they may be well-pleasing unto Thee, and receive at Thy hand an answer of peace and graciousness. Verse 12 might be alleged in justification of the saying that Solomon was the wisest man in the world. Give me, O Lord, the wisdom to seek first Thy kingdom and righteousness, and then will all other things be added—even as Solomon in addition to that for which he prayed got that which he asked not for. Enable me therefore, O Lord, to get above those degrading anxieties about this world's interests which have hitherto so much engrossed and disquieted me; may I know what it is to cast all my care upon God. Thou hast lengthened my days beyond all which I could at one time have counted upon, O that the brief remainder were altogether consecrated to Thy service and glory! Grant me a more decided confidence in the simplicities of Thine own word; let me ever feel that it is a sure word; and let not this feeling be disturbed any longer by theological authorities or theological systems. Let me call no man master, but hang immediately upon Scripture both for the establishment of my creed and the guidance of my heart and history before Thee. Let no resolution, however, of mine, and no degree of success in the performance of it, exempt me from a felt dependence on the sacrifice of Christ—that great peace-offering for the sins of the world. It was well that Solomon earned so rightful an ascendency over the minds of his people. What I greatly want is more decision, more, perhaps, of confidence in myself, less of slavish deference to the judgment of others, and the habit enjoined in Scripture that in every good work we should consult our own souls.

I. KINGS IV.

This chapter describes the most brilliant period of Israel's outward prosperity, beginning first with the magnificent court and magnificent household establishment of the king.

But what than this was of far higher worth, we are told in one pregnant verse (20) of the happiness and prosperity of the kingdom. This verse I have a very old recollection of as the brightest spot in a history of which the general character is revoltingly dark; it forms the very palpable exhibition of a theocracy manifesting itself in a temporal dispensation of rewards and penalties, consisting either of good or evil in the present life. The representation here given of a nation eating and drinking and making merry under the complacent view of a God from whom all this directly emanated, derives its chief interest from the view which it affords of our benign and paternal Deity, who hath no pleasure in the affliction, but rejoices in the innocent pleasures of His children. We have exhibitions of the same sort under our present economy—as when the primitive Christians ate their meat with gladness; and Paul tells us that every creature of God is good, and nothing to be refused if it be received with thanksgiving. Let us know, however, how to use the world as without abusing it; nor let us forget the soberness and self-denial which are inculcated in the gospel. And we have here too an obvious connexion between all this fulness in the land and God's satisfaction with the righteousness of its government, or with the then dispositions and doings of Solomon. Neither let us imagine that the connexion between these two elements has now been done away, nor let us give in for a moment to the practical atheism which obtains so extensively in high places, and for which it is to be feared that the desolating judgments of the Lord have gone forth upon our country. What an awful contrast between the state of Ireland now and of Judea then; nor do we hold it superstitious or fanciful to connect this with the misdoings of a Government that would endow an idolatrous religion, and has disclaimed the Bible both as a text-book in schools and as a directory in public affairs. My God, look in pity upon our nation. Avert, if it be Thy blessed will, the horrors of famine; and let righteousness and piety again form the stability of our times. Give, O Lord, to our rulers wisdom and understanding and largeness of heart, but above all, the fear of the Lord. Save us also from the tumults of the people, and give them a sure prosperity, rejoicing on the basis of their own worth, and so that each in possession of a competency and comfort might dwell safely—every man under his own vine and his own fig-tree—from one end of the land to the other.

I. KINGS V.

But there was an outward as well as inward prosperity at this glorious period of Israelitish history, and we have the tokens of it in the homage and the attentions which Solomon received from abroad. And Solomon was yet in the way of obedience, what he did being well-pleasing unto God. He was intent on the accomplishment of that from which David was prevented—the building of a temple to God; a work more fitted for a reign of peace than of barbarous and bloody wars. And Solomon seems to have gone about it in the spirit of a genuine and devoted piety, and of gratitude to Him who had given him rest on every side. One sees in the correspondence between Solomon and Hiram the influence of the Jewish theocracy in keeping up the sense and recognition of the true God among the neighbouring people; and in this point of view it is interesting to read of the honest and heartfelt gratulations of the king of Tyre. Hiram took up the name of Jehovah, and made mention of Him as the giver of all this wealth and glory to the king of Israel. You see in the contract between these two parties the distinct places of the agricultural and the commercial, and the relation in which they stand to each other—the one party supplying food, and the other wood and work for the temple, as the Israelites had not the skill for working in timber that was possessed by the Sidonians. I pray, O Lord, for a beneficial and withal a peaceful intercourse among the nations of the earth. But we cannot expect a lasting tranquillity apart from the reign of truth and righteousness over men. In the instance before us there was a co-operation between two kings for a religious end. At present religion is as good as banished from all public negotiations; nor can we look for stable and universal peace till the kingdoms of the earth have become the kingdoms of our Lord and Saviour Jesus Christ. Hasten this blessed consummation in Thy good time, O Lord. Do Thou who turnest the hearts of men whithersoever Thou wilt reign in the hearts of our rulers, and dispose them for the support and advancement of Thine own cause. Lay, O God, the foundation of a secure and withal universal Christian economy in the world. May Thine own indestructible Church evince the strength and perpetuity which belong to it, surviving all the futilities and fluctuation of this world's restless and ever-changing politics.

I. KINGS VI.

We have here an account of the building of what may well be termed the most celebrated structure that was ever reared by human hands. It does not appear that there was the same particularity of direction from on high as to the architecture of this glorious fabric that there was in regard to the fashion of the tabernacle, even as God shewed to Moses when about to make the tabernacle, according to the pattern that he had seen before in the Mount. Yet the one might be termed an expansion of the other; and if not so formally an inspired production in all the fulness of its details, yet should these details have been left in any extent to the skill of men, it might not less be in all respects a Divine product than the Bible is a

Divine product, even though the Spirit of God left each writer to his own style and manner, and perhaps in many instances to his own peculiar phraseology. The complexity and minuteness and arbitrary character of these details no more dissociate the Supreme God from the fabrication of the temple than they did from the fabrication of the tabernacle, or than they do from the fabrication of our own bodies—of marvellous intricacy and complexity of parts, yet teeming with the evidences of Divine wisdom.

We do not read of any interposal on the part of God for giving directions as to the plan and parts of the temple—yet, conformably to that law of progression which seems to obtain throughout His successive economies, do we read here of His interposal for the higher purpose of inculcating that obedience which is better than sacrifices, and that keeping of the commandments which is better than the fat of rams. This perhaps was peculiarly called for—when on the eve of a more splendid and magnificent ritual service than had ever before been known in Israel. The favour of the Almighty, in this message to Solomon, was made to turn not on the punctuality of their temple services, but on the conformity of their lives to the law of God. In the oracle where the ark was deposited, and the distinction still between the holy place and the holy of holies, the tabernacle might be said to have been embosomed in the temple, which was so constructed as to adapt it for the fulfilment of the Levitical observances.

My God, condescend to make even this vile body of mine a fit habitation for Thee through the Spirit, that it might become a temple of the Holy Ghost, and that I might glorify the Lord with my body as well as with my soul and spirit, all of which are the Lord's.

I. KINGS VII.

After the building of the Lord's house we read of the building of houses for the king and queen, as also of the house of Lebanon. Let me ever give the precedency to the Church of the living God. Let me not incur the reproach of a magnificent dwelling for myself, while the accommodations for public worship and the extension of Christian instruction among men languish and are neglected. And yet how indulgent a Master is our Father in Heaven! He forebade not those erections which might subserve the temporal glories of the Jewish monarchy: and the like indulgence extends to private individuals, who will not suffer in their own temporal circumstances by their liberalities for the great cause of a Christian education among the people. Let us seek first then the kingdom of God and His righteousness, and all other things will be added unto us. It is not an indifferent matter when told that the foundation of one of the houses was made of costly stones, even of *great* stones. The present substructures in and about Jerusalem form a striking monumental evidence of its former greatness; the remains of these consist of very large and hewn stones, and more especially in the site which perhaps is one of the best authenticated as being the very ground on which the temple stood.

They had every facility for these stupendous works—the skill of a most accomplished artificer from Tyre, and half-blood a Jew—the accumulated store of David, gathered and laid up for the very purpose of building God a house—an indefinite command of labourers, both of skilled labourers from abroad, who were hired for the service, and of labourers whose strength was required for the coarser and more ponderous parts of this great operation, and who were raised in levies from among the children of Israel by Solomon, who had all the power of an absolute monarch. The works which are here more especially enumerated as having been done by Hiram were chiefly great and rich and elaborate articles of what may be termed furniture, placed either in or about the temple—as the brazen sea and lavers, beside the ornamented pillars on each side of the porch.

I. KINGS VIII.
February, 1847.

We have here the account of one of the greatest days in the annals of the children of Israel. When told that there was nothing in the ark save the tables of stone, we are put in doubt as to the tradition regarding the canonical books being placed there, though they may have been in a receptacle outside attached to the ark.

The miracle of a glory appearing from heaven in the form of a cloud had not yet ceased—though far more frequent in the days of the tabernacle than of the temple. The devotions of Solomon are highly impressive; but the prayer did not commence till he had delivered a previous narrative in the hearing of the people, who must have been greatly solemnized and affected in the presence and within hearing of their king—more especially when he spread forth his hands, and lifted before them his supplication to the God of Heaven. There are certain things in this prayer that might well be selected as notable.

The expression of God keeping covenant and mercy is one of these. Ours is a covenanted mercy; and in virtue of being so we place all the firmer confidence therein. The mercies to which we owe the favour of God are emphatically the sure mercies of David. The whole prayer is fitted to inspire the people with a special reverence for the temple —such reverence for a place as might by abuse degenerate into an idolatrous affection. To counteract this, there is the utterance here of a large and enlightened theology —that God's dwelling is in heaven, and that even the heaven of heavens cannot contain Him. Thus might we temper and restrain our reverence for mere locality, yet without the extinction of this feeling, and accordingly Solomon pleads for God having His eyes open towards this place, and of which He had said that His name should be there; and, moreover, he pleads for a special virtue not merely to his own but his people's prayers, when made in this place or towards this place. From the occasions and subjects of prayer here specified, this record of Solomon's prayer became we have no doubt a most useful directory of prayer to the children of Israel. What weight yet brevity in its two parentheses, expressive of God's universal omniscience and man's universal sinfulness.

And what a fine benediction does he pronounce on the people after his prayer had been ended. O God, incline my heart and make it perfect, that there may be in it the altogether upright and entire purpose of walking in the way of all Thy commandments.

And with prayer let me ever mix faith in the great sacrifice. May the sense of Christ my passover be a perpetual feast to me, so as at all times I may joy in God through Him by whom I have received the atonement.

I. KINGS IX.

What methods were taken, and what influences put into operation for securing the loyalty of Solomon to God! What condescension in this second visit; and how endearing in the great God of Heaven and earth to say that His eyes and His heart should be there, or on the house which Solomon had built perpetually! Nor are His eyes and heart withdrawn from the great objects typified in the elder dispensation, and shadowed forth by the services of the temple. He who now sitteth on the throne of Israel will fulfil all the purposes, and give their substance and verification to all the promises of the Father—even those promises which shall never fail, for they are yea and amen in Christ Jesus our Lord. But there was an alternative presented to Solomon, and he took himself to the worst term of it, and he fell into disobedience, and the glorious kingdom of Israel was rent in twain, and is now scattered to the four winds of heaven. But a time of restoration is coming; and He who is greater than Solomon will come and build up again what meanwhile has been destroyed, and the kingdoms of the earth will at length become the kingdoms of our Lord and Saviour.

Mark here how, even among people who profess a like reverence for the God of liberality and justice, there break out misunderstandings between man and man, on the ground that these virtues have not been kept up by the one towards the other. Could Solomon after such a profession and prayer take wilful advantage of Hiram? Lord, may I never forget that the second law is like unto the first; and give me that love to neighbours which worketh no ill. The instances of professing Christians giving in to avarice, and sacrificing the moral rights of others to their own selfishness, are scandalous and distressing in a very high degree. How interesting to read of Tadmor in the wilderness, the Palmyra of our modern day. Though Solomon did not make bondmen of the Israelites, yet the enormous levies which he raised from them we doubt not were very oppressive; and it is this which gave point and significancy to the remonstrance and petition that were presented to his son and successor Rehoboam. He did not levy a tribute of bond-service from them, but he drew largely upon the wealth of the people. It is interesting to read of his navy; and to observe how satisfactorily the site of Ezion-geber is fixed as being in the land of Edom, and a sea-port on the Red Sea. This also in so far fixes the situation of Ophir as being on the side of the Red Sea, and not of the Mediterranean. What verisimilitude, too, there is in the superior skill of Hiram's men both in maritime affairs and in manufactures.

I. KINGS X.

This famous story of Sheba is accredited by our Saviour in whom are hid all the treasures of wisdom and knowledge. These hard questions which Sheba put to Solomon, I should imagine, may have had more the character of riddle, such as that put by Samson to the Philistines, than the problems of a deep or substantial philosophy. They may, however, have been the deep things of God, and prompted by such a feeling of religiousness as contrasted with, and so were condemnatory of the indifference of the Jews to the claims of our Saviour on the sacred reverence and respect of His countrymen. It is interesting to connect this visit from the far south with the conclusion that even at great distances from Judea the true God was not altogether unknown. And she seems to have been as much astonished at the wealth and magnificence as at the wisdom of Solomon; and in her benedictions upon him proves her acquaintance with the one God, and with the fact that He had selected Israel for His people, and that His law was a law of righteousness, for that judgment and justice are the great ends of government; and government derives immediately from God—all the powers which are being ordained of Him, and rulers being designed as ministers for good. (Rom. xiii. 1-4.) The direct alliance here exhibited between God's favour to the king and the prosperity of his kingdom, should lead us to feel how dependent a nation is on the righteousness of its governors and of their administration. Reform our state, O God— Christianize the policy of our rulers; save them from the irreligion that would profane our Sabbaths, and uphold an idolatrous worship among our people. Let the judgments now abroad over our land tell upon them for good.

There is sanction given here to the splendour of a court. The ability for this, with all the commercial prosperity and abundance of these days, flowed direct from the same divine favour to which Solomon owed his mental endowments, and more particularly the wisdom which God had put into his heart. Both the riches and the wisdom in which he excelled all the kings of the earth were of God, and so also were the military strength and resources of his kingdom. His superiority to all other potentates of the earth in wisdom was put to a direct trial on the occasion of the visit from the queen of Sheba. It is interesting to note the value and respect felt for wisdom in these days, as evinced by all the earth seeking to Solomon to hear it, or by the general concourse from distances all round in quest of this object.

I. KINGS XI.

From this point the history of Israel gathers into darkness—that is, from the degeneracy of Solomon onward to the degeneracy of his successors, a degeneracy universal in the Samaritan branch, and prevailing by a great majority of reigns in the Jewish branch of the monarchy. Preserve me, O Lord, from the destructive fascination which turned away the heart of Solomon, and turned it too when he was old. What a train of evil consequences does this most deceitful of all sins draw after it; and how marvellous to think of Solomon's lapsing into idolatry after the special visits and palpable blessings which he had enjoyed direct from the great God of heaven and earth. Let me examine myself, and cast all the idols of fame, and pleasure, and the world, away from me. Let me never depart from the living God. Let me leave to my children the inheritance of a consistent and sustained piety—for the penalties of Solomon's transgression fell also on his posterity, and indeed the full recompense was deferred till after the lifetime of the transgressor. The indulgence thus given to him was because of his father's righteousness, (for David's sake,) as the calamity that befell Rehoboam was because of his father's delinquencies—marking a peculiarity in the Divine jurisprudence, of which our species at large forms a great and general exemplification.

Nevertheless Solomon did not escape the infliction of God's displeasure in his own person. For first we read in an interesting episode of an adversary from Egypt, of whom it is expressly said that God stirred him up; and so as an instrument in God's hand he became an adversary to Solomon.

And again did God raise up another adversary in the person of Rezon, who was the bitter enemy of Israel, and practised we should imagine a sort of guerilla warfare along its borders.

But worst of all, there arose in Jerusalem an adversary against him from amongst his own subjects, and who succeeded in the dismemberment of the kingdom, and his own preferment to the monarchy over the larger share of it. He was obviously a rod of vengeance of God—for by one of His prophets was he admonished of the destination that awaited him; and he framed his policy according to it. In the message of Ahijah we may read the long-suffering as well as righteousness of God—afflicting the house of David, "but not for ever"—an assurance this, the full verification of which is still in reserve.

Our reflection on the exit of poor Solomon is the danger of prosperity, and the frailty of man carried away by it into forgetfulness of Him who is the giver of all things richly to enjoy.

1. KINGS XII.

The people are here said to make the king—by which nothing more might be meant than to signify their consent and allegiance. They may have sent for Jeroboam to act as negotiator with the hereditary monarch. The yoke of Solomon was grievous probably in respect of his enormous levies both of men and money for the construction of his public works, and upholding the great state and splendour of the government. The youthful folly of Rehoboam and his advisers led to a very mischievous result. My God, clothe me with humility, and at the same time give me more both of the gravity and wisdom of age ; and enable me to be of service by those calm and temperate, and well-weighed deliverances which might command the respect and confidence of my fellows.

Mark how, though the proximate causes of the disruption which took place in Israel were human and secondary, yet the efficient cause of all was from the Lord. Let me ever look beyond and above the visible to the unseen, and refer all to the will, and providence, and presiding authority of Him who worketh all in all. He makes men and men's passions the instrument for fulfilling all His pleasure—as the wrath of man to punish His enemies, and redound to His own praise.

When Rehoboam prepared for war in order to recover the tribes that had cast him off, the purpose was arrested by a direct message from the Lord. And it is well that they hearkened to the voice of the messenger and obeyed it—the symptom of a still lingering loyalty in the tribe of Judah to the true God, which contrasts advantageously with the idolatrous defection which so instantly took place in Israel.

We can understand the powerful hold that Jerusalem was fitted to retain over the habits and affections of the whole nation far and near, and so the policy by which Jeroboam was actuated in dissevering the people from the great ecclesiastical metropolis of all true worshippers. But one marvels that a king whose elevation was so obviously of God—as announced to him beforehand by one of His prophets, should so soon have lapsed into idolatry. Save me, O God, save me from the devices of my own wayward and evil heart.

I. KINGS XIII.

There were here both a prophecy and a miracle—the evidence of the one guaranteed by the other. God did not forsake although they had forsaken God; for He continued to ply them throughout the whole of their history while a nation with messages and warnings innumerable: and we have here the first instance of this since their melancholy declension from the worship of the true God. The prophet who was sent to him withstood the invitation of the king, and on the ground that he could not accept of it without an act of disobedience to the God by whom he had been sent.

But though he withstood the lure of a kingly invitation he did not withstand the invitation of a prophet. His case seems a peculiarly hard one. The strength of his fidelity had been so far tested by his resistance to the bidding of a sovereign, but it gave way before the fabrication of one who had the character of a man of God, and whose story, as it would seem to us, it was quite natural for him to believe. To us who can see no deeper than the surface the whole case looks a mysterious one; but God, who does all things in truth and uprightness, sees into the heart, and weighing the secrets of the inner man might have, for aught we know, descried the principle as clearly as we can discern the act of disobedience. It aggravates the mystery all the more that the same prophet who had lied to the destruction of his fellow should have been after this honoured by a commission from God, or that he who had falsely alleged a communication from heaven should still have gotten a real communication thence. The poor prophet, who to all appearance did his duty well till misled by the man who deceived him to his ruin, was the great sufferer in this transaction; and the grief, as well as the seemingly real affection of the deceiver to him whom himself had been the instrument of bringing to an untimely end, seems altogether unaccountable. Yet the homage which he rendered at the grave on the score of the protest which had been lifted by him who was at once his victim and his dupe against the idolatry of Jeroboam, would bespeak him to be a man of piety and righteousness. This is one of the most noted of our Scripture stories simply and pathetically told.

But Jeroboam, in the face of demonstrations which should have humbled and reformed him, lapsed into the grossest profanation. The hitherto incorrigibly idolatrous tendencies of Israel seem to be as strong as ever. The time had not yet come for their being conclusively arrested by the judgments of God, as they seem to have been by the Babylonish captivity—insomuch that there was no national relapse into this sin after their return. The house of Jeroboam would not be reformed from it, and therefore was extirpated.

I. KINGS XIV.

Grange.

See how there is a certain remaining sense of the truth even in the minds of apostates. It breaks out on strongly urgent occasions, and proves after all that they have been sinning during the whole season of their defection against a light that their own consciences would hold forth, were these but stirred to their very depth. Jeroboam, in despair lest his son should be taken from him, draws upon his recollections of Ahijah, and as a last resource sends his wife to consult him; and a sorrowful message she heard from the lips of the old prophet, who, at the bidding of the Lord, observed the utmost plain dealing with her, though she was the queen of Israel. The authority of the prophet carries it over the pride and grandeur of royalty. He speaks to her in the style of a master and commander, and with all boldness—being the messenger of the High and Holy One, and charged with tidings of evil—even the death of her son and the ruin of her house. The "some good thing" that was found in him towards the house of Israel is an interesting circumstance. My God, I pray not only for some good thing but for the entire and sustained dedication of myself to Thee and to Thy cause. O how shamefully deficient, what a destitution of heart and zeal and thorough principle! My God, look on me with pity, and perfect Thy strength in my lamentable weakness. And as the prediction so was the fulfilment: God had said it, and shall He not do it? Heaven and earth shall pass away ere any of His words can pass away. The son died, and the prophecy respecting the ruin of the house had a commencing fulfilment in the death of Jeroboam.

There seems to have been a rivalship of evil between the two kingdoms of Judah and Israel. It is peculiarly lamentable to read of the defections of the former; God seems to have given them up to vile affection, and they to have fully entered on a career of headlong degeneracy. And yet for the sake of David He spared them, even after they had given in to the abominations for which He passed a decree of extermination against the old inhabitants of the land. For these iniquities did the Lord chastise without destroying them utterly. Rehoboam suffered damage and disgrace because of his idolatries; and after an unhappy and inglorious reign, under which the great disruption took place, and Israel ceased to be an entire monarchy, he is said to have slept with his fathers. His wars with Jeroboam may have widened the disruption still more, at all events they seem not to have tended in the least to the reunion of the parts which had been dissevered.

I. KINGS XV.

Abijam though a wicked prince was nevertheless during his reign that lamp which God had promised that He would give to David in Jerusalem, in that one of his own house and family should sit upon the throne. It is worthy of remark that the general testimony in favour of David is here also qualified by the exception of his conduct in the matter of Uriah.

During the next reign in Judah the lamp burned brighter. There are bright and sunny intervals in the Jewish branch of this history, nor did it flow down in that black and unmitigated tide of depravity which marked the history of the kings and people of Israel. Asa was a reforming prince; and the testimony given to his character is quite unqualified, for his toleration of high places is not brought in as an exception, but as that notwithstanding of which his heart was perfect with the Lord, and this too all his days—which could not be said of David, because of the dreary interval during which he perpetrated the worst of crimes. Yet David stands forth more illustriously as a righteous king than did Asa, though the one was guilty of a presumptuous sin whilst the other is only charged with an unconscious, and therefore to him a secret fault. O that my heart were perfect, even as that of Asa. Put truth in my inward parts, and then shall I not only pray to be kept from presumptuous sins but to be cleansed from secret faults. It is said of him that he cultivated an alliance with heathen princes and availed himself of services from that quarter, and said, too, without reproach. The disease in his feet was a personal, as his war with Baasha might be regarded in the light of a public or political trial.

The histories of the two kingdoms are intermingled; and in turning from the one to the other, if we leave a bright reign and a bright region in that of Judah, we are sure to find an unexcepted and unalleviated darkness in that of idolatrous Israel, and without any perpetuity or stableness in the dynasties. Bad men were raised up as the instruments of punishing and dethroning other bad men; and we have here a signal fulfilment of the curse denounced upon Jeroboam in the utter extinction of his family. There was not left to him any that breathed. He is spoken of repeatedly with this distinction of wickedness attached to him—in that he not only was a sinner himself, but in that he made Israel to sin by making idolatry the established religion.

I. KINGS XVI.
March, 1847.

The special delinquency charged upon Baasha is that he walked in the way of Jeroboam, and the peculiarity of this way lies in his having established idolatry, making it the national religion, and so making the people of Israel to sin. Baasha continued and countenanced the system of Jeroboam; and it is further remarkable, that though the prophet reproaches Baasha with rebellion against that God who had made him prince over His people, yet he further charges him with guilt in that he had killed or exterminated the house of Jeroboam. God turns the wickedness of man into an instrumentality for the accomplishment of His own purposes, yet punishes that wickedness notwithstanding—though it was a further aggravation of the iniquity that though he knew that Jeroboam was cut off, and by his own hand too, for having set up the worship of the calves, yet that very worship did he himself persist in making imperative upon his subjects.

Then follows such a succession of assassinations and dethronements as we read of in the worst periods of the Roman, and almost every period of oriental history, so rife in the dark and murderous intrigues of barbaric courts. Zimri was the rod of God's vengeance against the house of Baasha, just as Baasha was against the house of Jeroboam.

This wretched succession is kept up for several generations, and in the character of a continued warfare on the part of a jealous and avenging God against those idolatrous princes who imitated Jeroboam in making Israel to sin, and so provoking Him to anger with their vanities. If the tempter be a more heinous transgressor than he who is tempted, what a weight of guilt does the government incur which favours and patronizes an idolatrous superstition in the land. It was an awful termination for Zimri—that of suicide by fire. He, in verse 12, is represented as the perpetrator of a destruction which fell out according to the word of the Lord, and yet in verse 20 this perpetration is denounced as treason. He was another rod in God's hand.

Then succeeded Omri after a struggle for the monarchy, and who is chiefly remarkable as being the founder of the still subsisting Samaria, whose hill with its substructures and ruin can be recognised at this day. He is said to have done worse than all that were before him.

Yet his son Ahab outpeered even him in wickedness, for he did evil too above all that were before him, and his establishment of the worship of Baal is spoken of as a distinct aggravation of the sin of Jeroboam in setting up the worship of the calves. The reference to Joshua's curse on the rebuilder of Jericho forms a most valuable historical and bibliographical notice at the close of this chapter.

I. KINGS XVII.

The history otherwise so dreary and revolting is now enlivened into a delightful interest by the appearance and doings of Elijah, one of the undoubted magnates of Scripture. God did not even in these times of dismal degeneracy leave Himself without a witness; and his prophecy of a famine at the first of his recorded outset, with its dire fulfilment, was fitted to convince even the worst of men in his day, that verily there was a God who reigned upon the earth. The whole of this prophet's history is most graphically told, and many are the pictures which might be constructed on its various passages. Elijah fed by the ravens would form an admirable subject. The barrel of meal and the cruse of oil failing not during the whole of the famine form a most notable miracle. O that what befell the widow of Zarephath could now be experienced by the starving families both of our own Highlands and of Ireland—if not by miracle from heaven, at least by mercy coming down from heaven through the hearts of men below made willing to distribute and ready to communicate. What was effected then by an extraordinary gift conferred upon the prophet may it be effected now by the ordinary grace which descends on the souls of those who are made to abound in the fruits of the Spirit, and so to be fruitful in all good works. O my God, direct me how to treat this subject aright. Give me to deal evenly and equitably with all who are concerned in it. I pray for that wisdom from above which is without partiality, and which is peaceable after being first pure. Save, O God, save the people from the horrors of famine; and let each take the part that belongs to him for the mitigation of these horrors. Let us forget not that the supplies granted to the widow followed the act by which she gave to Elijah out of her deep poverty; and that if we give not out of our abundance these supplies might be withheld from us by that power which hath blasted the food of one part of the country, and can blast the staple food of our own neighbourhoods. The widow was touched in a part of still greater tenderness than her own subsistence when her son was attacked by a mortal disease and laid dead or insensible before her, and which event she interpreted into a chastisement for some sin not here specified. But the grace of God abounded to her more than did her sin. The child was restored by the miraculous answer given to the prayer of the prophet—his soul was recalled. Many are the Irish children who have died under the weight of their present visitation, for whose restoration we do not pray, because we cannot do so in faith; but we pray that God would stay His avenging hand, that He would put an end to this sore calamity, and cause that the liberalities of our rulers and our people should be commensurate thereto.

I. KINGS XVIII.

The story grows in interest. Elijah and his doings occupy one of the finest historic passages in Scripture; and Obadiah, the pious courtier, a servant of the king, yet who feared the Lord greatly, deserves a high place in that imperishable tablet—so that wherever the Bible is read the good thing which he did serves for a memorial of him. And to this fear of God he added faith—faith in the assurance of God's messenger that he should be safe from Ahab—a faith in God, therefore, which overcame his fear of man. That was a noble interview between Ahab and Elijah, in which one cannot but admire the intrepidity of the prophet when he rolled back upon the monarch the charge of being himself the real disturber of Israel, him who was the perpetrator of that wickedness which called down the judgments of Heaven, and not him who was the denouncer of it—a charge which is often alike made in the present day, and which may sometimes be alike disposed of; that is, be transferred from the agitator who stirs for the repeal of a grievance to the corrupt power by which the grievance was begun and is perpetuated. The address, too, of Elijah to the people who were concerned in the prosecution of the challenge which he held out to the priests of Baal is a very noble one; and the expression which he makes use of when he asks why they halt between two opinions is one that remains to the present day with all the weight and authority of a proverbial saying. Save me, O God, from the vacillations of an undecided mind. Guide me through all the ambiguities of such questions as present at the first an aspect of the dark and the doubtful. Let me be enabled to follow the example of Paul, who admitted of no middle ground between grace and works, (Rom. xi. 6,) and in that very passage too when Elijah is referred to; and yet, while clear and confident on every great, was most wisely accommodating on every small question, making no concession that could infringe by ever so little on the doctrine of grace, and yet could tolerate the opposite varieties of practice in regard to meats and days and ceremonies. The remainder of the chapter is crowded with interest. Let me but advert to the mockery of Baal's priests by Elijah—his noble confidence in the true God—the significancy of the twelve stones which he employed in building the altar, as marking out the peculiar relation in which God stood to the people before him as the God of Israel—the believing prayer which he uttered in the hearing of those around him, the decisive and miraculous answer to that—and finally, the consequent recognition by the people of the only true God. Then followed the slaughter of the priests; and what somehow I have ever regarded as the most picturesque of our Bible spectacles—Elijah on the top of Carmel. O may there be now such fervent and effectual prayer on the part of the righteous in our land as might avail much, and particularly for averting the horrors of a desolating famine.

I. KINGS XIX.

One can well imagine the deep hatred and burning

indignation which the slaughter of her prophets by Elijah would waken up against him in the heart of Jezebel—one of the most tremendous specimens in this world's history of female wickedness. The flight of the prophet affords some of those graphical representations in which the narrative of his life so abounds—at one time fed in the wilderness by ravens, at another by angels. But ravens and all creatures may be termed angels, for they are God's messengers, fulfilling His pleasure. Like our Saviour in the wilderness he seems to have fasted forty days and forty nights after the angel's second visit, unless he was thus sustained by repeated visits during that period. Then follows an illustrious passage quoted in the New Testament, and big with a most important and at the same time consolatory truth—even that God has His own, His hidden ones, and that too in times of greatest and to all appearance of universal degeneracy. He knoweth them though man should not. The answer to Elijah's complaint of there being none but himself who had not bowed the knee to Baal is that there were seven thousand souls; and let us therefore take courage, nor despair even now of the cause of truth and righteousness. Heavenly Father, we pray first for the safety and then for the prosperity of this great cause. Grant that Thy true disciples may not only have fellowship with Thyself, but may they find and have fellowship with each other. We cannot image a description of greater sublimity than we here have of these successive manifestations which ushered in the voice of Jehovah; and we believe it has often been remarked how much more pregnant with the sublime that voice is than all the force of the natural agencies which went before it. Let me be solemnized by the thought of Thy presence, O

God, for Thou art not far from any one of us; and may our attention to the still small voice of conscience mark our supreme reverence for Thee and for Thy law. O that I could ever exercise myself to have a conscience void of offence towards God and towards man. Forgive my recent delinquencies, O Lord, and in every question between me and my fellows let me know what it is to acquit myself with wisdom and with the meekness of wisdom. There seems a contrast between the transaction of Elijah with Elisha and what took place when our Saviour in the gospels bade a person to follow Him, and he asked leave to go and take farewell of his relatives at home. Elijah granted the request, while Jesus disallowed it: and from the saying which He then put forth that no man who looketh back is fit for the kingdom of God, I would pray for more singleness of heart and purpose, for freedom from the entanglements of life whatever resolution or sacrifice might be necessary to assert it, that my entire habit may be that of a pilgrim and stranger, living by the powers of a world to come.

I. KINGS XX.

The most noticeable part of this chapter is the facility wherewith Ahab let Ben-hadad go, in virtue of a sensibility which some would denominate an amiable weakness. One should have expected that the evident determination at the outset of Ben-hadad to seek his destruction would have aroused such an indignancy on the part of Ahab as might have lasted over the second victory which he gained, and led him to refuse all terms with the man who had been so intently set upon his ruin. But there seems to have been a softer part of his nature which made him give way

—probably the same which rendered him a dupe to the artifices and the influence of the wicked Jezebel. At all events duty must ever be regarded as paramount to feeling; and what causes me to fasten on this trait in the character of Ahab is that I do apprehend of myself an easiness to be practised on, a dread of hurting others, an over-disposition to relent when I see the least symptoms of humiliation in the party with whom I have to deal, which has led to a wrong and untimely surrender of my cause, and that not merely in questions where my own interest was concerned, but in the sacred contests of truth and principle. Forgive me, O Lord, that fear of man which is a snare, and in every good work enable me to consult my own soul. I am greatly too much influenced by the dislike of giving offence and by respect of persons —I do not mean of certain persons above others, but of that undue deference to my fellow-men in the general which leads me to forbear pressing my own opinion when it thwarts the views or the inclinations of those with whom I have to do. This whole chapter is a striking record of the divine power and providence, of the all-controlling agency of God in the affairs of men. He can save by many or by few; and let it ever be our confidence that the Lord is our helper, and we shall not fear what man can do unto us. And save the Church, O Lord, save her from ever coming to a deceitful or wrong compromise with the parties who are opposed to her. Save her now from this on the question of Government Education; but save her also from ultraism even in this direction. Save her altogether from the left, but save her also from going too far even on the right side of the question, for it is possible, nay likely, that she may on this hand too fall into a ridiculous extreme—the extreme of not touching the money, which might just be as bad on the question of education as on the question of slavery would have been the extreme of—sending back the money.

I. KINGS XXI.

The mental pathology of Ahab must have been a very susceptible one, but alive to all sorts of impressions—to a weak and untimely compassion in the case of Ben-hadad, to the mortification of wounded pride and selfishness in the case of Naboth. When the owner of the vineyard that he had set his heart upon refused his application for it he came into his house heavy and displeased, just as he did from the denunciation of the prophet at the end of the last chapter; and instead of himself devising any aggressive scheme of mischief against the man who had offended him, he sunk under the oppressive weight of his emotions, and took refuge in his bed. It was Jezebel who undertook the aggressive part of the wickedness recorded in this passage. That was her part; and Ahab's, again, was just that of a fit subject for being worked upon and giving way to the enormity of her daring proposal. He " was consenting unto the death"—and this from the utter want of right principle; whereas in Jezebel we seem to behold, in contradistinction to him, the active workings of a vicious and wrong principle. My own philosophy, however, inclines me to think that even she as well as he exemplified but the privative character of evil as it is termed by the schoolmen. She may have been more wanting in right principle, but the true explanation of the difference between them is that she altogether wanted his softness and timidity of nature, so that there did not exist in her heart that distaste either to the adoption or to the reckless and relentless prosecution of those measures which led to the destruction of poor Naboth. According to this view of the case Ahab sold himself to all wickedness; he sold himself to Jezebel; he made himself over to her to be disposed of according to her pleasure, and she made as free use of this as she would of any other of her property. Verse 25 marks this out in a striking way. Ahab sold himself to do wickedness in the sight of the Lord, and Jezebel stirred him up—he the passive instrument, and she the through-going agent in this monstrous piece of iniquity. The proclamation of a fast, along with the subornation of false witnesses and the perjury, was a most revolting aggravation. But the cry of this foul murder reached the ears of Him who sitteth on a throne of justice, and Elijah was commissioned as the messenger of coming vengeance to the guilty perpetrators. We do not read of Jezebel quailing before this denunciation from Heaven; but Ahab—and this is in perfect keeping with the explanation just given by us—did give way before its rebuke and its terrors. He humbled himself and fasted and went softly; and O what an exhibition of our great Sovereign as a God of mercy as well as justice that this deportment of the now contrite monarch led to a respite and mitigation of the punishment.

I. KINGS XXII.

This is an odd sort of conjunction between the wicked king Ahab and the good king Jehoshaphat, nor can we well comprehend how the latter could calmly look on during these consultations between the former and his idolatrous prophets. Save me from being unequally yoked, for what fellowship hath God with Belial? Except for its good, let me stand aloof from a world lying in wickedness. Yet did the king of Judah hold up his testimony for the living and true God, and called for one of his messengers, and overruled the objections of Ahab against him; and He who can prevail by few as well as by many gave vindication of and effect to the single testimony of him who was called in and confronted the whole ecclesiastical staff of Israel. Altogether there was upon this occasion a most picturesque and imposing array; and one cannot but admire the intrepidity of Micaiah in the delivery of his message—more especially as it carried a sore rebuke on the formidable host of false prophets who stood before him. What he tells of the lying spirit as sent forth by God himself to deceive them, brings us to the margin of all those difficulties which attach to the origin of evil—a margin that we shall make no attempt to cross, satisfied that what we know not now we shall know hereafter, and counting it enough to be wise not above but up to that which is written. The end of Zedekiah the prophet is not recorded, but from the closing words of Micaiah to him, we should conjecture that he was killed by his pursuer in the chamber whither he had flown to hide himself, and so he would be visited by a flash of manifestation before his death. There is no conjecture, but the most patent and prominent certainty in regard to the death of Ahab both as to prophecy and fulfilment; and his being killed by a bow at a venture, while Jehoshaphat—who was set upon—escaped, marks it all the more strikingly as the doing of the Lord.

There follows a very brief account of the reign of Jehoshaphat. He is characterized as a righteous king; and the only exception alleged against him is the common one of a toleration for the high places. His fellowship with Ahab is not mentioned to his discredit; and the result of it may have been that he was all the more confirmed by the issues of that unprosperous alliance in his attachment to the worship of his fathers.

There follows a still briefer notice of Ahaziah, whose reign was of the same dark hue with that of all the kings of Israel, characterized by all the wickedness of Jeroboam, and the still deeper wickedness of Ahab and Jezebel.

II. KINGS.

2 KINGS I.—How one welcomes the re-entry of Elijah upon the stage of this history, even though he comes now as a minister of wrath and vengeance; according to the economy of that period when wickedness was more patently and directly visited by temporal judgments. Ahaziah met with an accident which laid him on what turned out to be his death-bed—and he sent messengers to inquire of Baalzebub respecting the issues of this illness. He had far gone in alienation from the true God; yet God's eye was still upon Israel, and as if to recall it to the acknowledgment of Himself, again sent forth His prophet Elijah with fresh manifestations of His sovereignty and power. There are no writings of his left, and yet from his wondrous doings—and more especially from his translation into heaven without death, and his reappearance along with

Moses upon earth at the transfiguration of our Saviour—he ranks in our estimation as the most illustrious of the old prophets. In verse 8 we may remark the likeness of his costume to that of John the Baptist, whom he either prefigured, or perhaps even personified—though the actual death of John by the hands of an executioner makes against the latter supposition, more especially in the case of one who was caught up into heaven, and had undergone by another process than that of dying the change which qualifies an inhabitant of earth for being an inhabitant of these upper regions. However this may be, we witness in Elijah the same faithful and intrepid testimony as a Divine messenger by which the old prophets were generally signalized. At the bidding of the angel he went forth at once on what to the eye of nature must have appeared a hazardous mission, and encountered singlehanded not only the first messengers of Ahaziah, but the successive fifties who were sent forth to apprehend him. The captain of the first of these fifties seems to have delivered his message in the style of a peremptory order—while the second, warned by the fate of those who went before him, seems to have been softened into the manner of an obeisant entreaty. The third was still more prostrate and supplicatory, and prays that his life and that of his followers might be spared. There is no saying what effect such demonstrations may have had not only in confirming the faith of God's hidden ones who had not bowed the knee to Baal, but in multiplying the converts from idolatry. The contrast between Baal-zebub and the true God was thus made strikingly apparent, not only to the Jewish public but to the king himself on his dying bed. Altogether this is a memorable passage in the life of

Elijah, whose doings along with those of Elisha his successor, serve greatly to brighten the pages of an otherwise dark and revolting history. Ahaziah was succeeded by his brother Jehoram, being himself childless.

II. KINGS II.

April, 1847.

This is one of the most illustrious chapters of our older sacred history. Apart from the interest and magnitude of the chief event here recorded, there is much of the pleasing and picturesque in the devotedness of Elisha to Elijah, and in the sensation awakened along their progress to Jordan where the great consummation took place. It is remarkable the knowledge which all these prophets, as well as Elijah's own immediate attendant, had beforehand of what was coming; but these are what may be termed the mere earthly phenomena or accompaniments of the transaction when compared with the heavenly, the transcendental character of the stupendous transaction itself—a man taken up bodily and alive from the ground we tread upon to some mysterious place of occupancy beyond the sky which is over our heads. Yet we desire not to indulge in speculation; and the only use we should make of this wondrous fact, the only lesson we should draw from it, is thereby to strengthen our faith in another state of immortality—that state which Elijah has been transferred to by an ascension above, and which we too shall at length realize—and in the body, through a process of three great steps—a death, and a resurrection, and finally, an ascension. Lord, give me to live by the powers of a world to come. Lord, translate me from the walk of sight to the walk of faith. As Elijah was translated bodily from earth to heaven, so may I be translated mentally from affection for the things that are beneath to affection for the things which are above, that henceforward I may cease to mind earthly things, and have my conversation in heaven, whence I look for the Saviour, the επιφανεια when every eye shall see Him, and believers shall rejoice because of the coming of their Lord.—Elisha may be said to have had a double portion of Elijah's spirit, in that he displayed to a far more marvellous extent the power of working miracles—of which power he gave an immediate specimen by performing the identical miracle which Elijah had just done before him, and in the same way, too, by smiting the waters with the mantle which had fallen from the ascended prophet. We have further exhibitions of the same power in the course of this chapter. He had now fully entered upon his miraculous course, and gave demonstration to all that the spirit of Elijah rested upon Elisha. We cannot but again advert to the translation of Elijah, and to the mysterious secrecy in which the death of Moses is recorded, so that buried by the Lord no man ever found his body or his sepulchre. We cannot help associating these two events with the appearance of the two personages concerned in them at the transfiguration of our Saviour.

II. KINGS III.

We have here a clear distinction made between the lesser wickedness of the house of Jeroboam, and the more aggravated wickedness of the house of Ahab. It consisted chiefly in the idolatrous homage that was rendered to Baal, probably more enormous than the worship of Baal, from the more cruel and abominable rites wherewith it was associated.

It is remarkable the facility wherewith Jehoshaphat entered into leagues with idolatrous kings of Israel—though perhaps they had a common interest in warding off the encroachments both of Syria and Moab. He evinced, however, on both occasions, his faith in the prophets of the true God, and there was no such competition now as on the former occasion between the priests or prophets of the two religions. Elisha on this occasion stood alone; and with the grandeur of an office superior to that of king, he came forth with a noble intrepidity, and cast the rebuke of a heaven-inspired messenger on the monarch of Israel. And he strikingly accredited his mission before the eyes of both the kings, and of all the people who were with them, by a most stupendous miracle—what may be called a miracle on a large scale, and implying not only a command over, but an independence of all the elements of nature. Instead of acting by these elements, he acted without them; and independently of wind or rain, or of any contribution from the atmosphere, water was brought in abundance to fill the country and save the armies that would have perished by thirst. Elijah prayed for rain and prevailed. The miracle was performed by the operation of a second cause: the thirsty ground was refreshed in the usual way, so that all the languishing fields received from heaven above the moisture which satisfied and restored them; but through Elisha the ditches were filled with water from the earth beneath, or by a lateral movement from Edom—so that this prophet who received a double portion of his predecessor's spirit, made a doubly greater invasion than he on the constancy of nature.

Was the indignation against Israel awakened by the dire extremity to which they had reduced the king of Moab? And did they retire from the spectacle of an eldest son made a burnt-offering by the hands of his own father—horror-stricken at a deed so unnatural, and unable to withstand it? We should hope that this influence did mingle upon this occasion, and so give evidence that even amid the fiercest of war's excesses, there still survived some human sensibilities not wholly extinguished. We should be glad to think that even in these barbarous times there was a law of nature and nations the authority of which was felt though not formally recognised in any code or treatise of jurisprudence.

II. KINGS IV.

The history of Elisha is full of miracles, more than that of any other prophet in the Old Testament, and indeed not surpassed in the records of the New. There is a resemblance here between the multiplication of the widow's oil and the turning of the water into wine at the marriage feast of Cana—with this difference, that the wine was produced by a transformation effected on previous matter, quantity for quantity, whereas the miraculous oil instead of being palpably so, seems more like the product of a new creation. In this respect it is more like to the miracle of the loaves.

The prophet's chamber has now become proverbial. The great woman who dwelt among her own people was probably the wife of a chieftain who bore influence over them. The choice to remain at home rather than that she and her husband should have preferment and place among the splendour of a court, has been often quoted, and with the entire sympathy and approval of the best constituted spirits. She speaks more like a woman who is great in her own right than one who derived her greatness from marriage with her husband. The announcement made to her by the human messenger, Elisha, of a child, was made to Abraham by messengers from heaven.

And then there follows the stupendous miracle of restoring life to the dead. In the account of it there is finely exhibited the strength of the maternal affection; and while the failure of Gehazi as followed up by the achievement of Elisha, justified the resolution of the Shunammite to have him along with her, served also greatly more to accredit and exalt the prophet in her eyes, and she accordingly fell at his feet, and bowed herself to the ground before him.

Then follows another miracle, the narrative of which has also given birth to a proverbial expression—of "death in the pot." It was performed, as many others in Scripture were, through an instrumentality, although the very notion of miraculous power suggests that it might have been as well performed without one. But miracles are not always so ordered; and as the spittle or clay was applied to the eyes of the blind for the restoration of sight—so here meal was cast into the pot to discharge it of its poison. Then follows a miracle which ranks among the most signal, analogous to the feeding in the gospel of a multitude with a few loaves—who ate of them and left.

II. KINGS V.

We are now among the most memorable of Scripture

stories, each charged with moral as well as with incident. The story of Naaman has been a rich theme for the spiritualizers of the Word, but not more so than is clearly warrantable, and the lessons educed from it are above all others precious. And first, the quarrel which Naaman had with the prescription of Elisha has been likened to the offence of the cross, or the offence which sinners take at the great gospel remedy of washing out their sins in the blood of the Lamb. My God, reconcile, and not only this, but positively attach me more and more to this way of salvation. Let my recourse at all times be to the blood of sprinkling, and let me ever hold fast my confidence therein even unto the end. Save me from those operose methods of establishing a righteousness for myself which are dictated by the spirit of legality. I pray for the simple entrance of Thy word into my soul, that I may be ushered at once out of darkness into the marvellous light of the gospel. I believe, O God, help Thou mine unbelief; and give me that faith which standeth not in the wisdom of man but in the power of God. It is well that Naaman got the better of his pride and resentment, and better still, that after having tried the cure and found it effectual he should, under a movement of gratitude, have presented himself humbly at the gate of Elisha, and entreated the acceptance of an offering at his hand.—My God, fill my mouth with thanksgivings and my heart with devotedness to Thy will, that henceforth I may, with all the joy of one whose bonds have been loosed, run with alacrity and delight in the way of new obedience. Cleanse me thoroughly, O God, that the foul leprosy of guilt and pollution may depart from me—that henceforth purged from dead works I may serve the living and the true God. It is altogether worthy of being noted that the indulgence which Naaman sought for was so readily granted by Elisha. There is perhaps something more to be deduced from this than the facile accommodation of these earlier times. There may be instruction in it to us on whom the latter ends of the world have come; and I should feel inclined to see in this history a rebuke of those sticklers for small things who scruple not at great things, who strain at gnats while they swallow camels. The still streaming gratitude of Naaman led him to an exuberance of kindness towards Gehazi, with whose low sneaking selfishness the noble disinterestedness of the prophet stands very finely contrasted. Under the economy of the gospel there is a cure for the leprosy of nature to all who obey it as Naaman did Elisha; but no cure for such wilful sinners as Gehazi. Let us not deceive ourselves, O God.

II. KINGS VI.

Though we have often said that instrumentality is frequently put into requisition for the performance of a miracle, so as that it is not worked at a simple bidding or upon the mere utterance of a voice, yet this does not deduct from its miraculous character, from the obvious inadequacy of the means employed. And besides, the effect might be all the more distinctly to exhibit the person in whom the gift of miracles was vested—as Elisha in the instance before us, who himself and not another cast the wood into the water; and our Saviour, who Himself and not another anointed the clay with spittle and applied it to the eyes of the blind man whom He miraculously cured.

In the next passage we have not only a stupendous

display of the miraculous power but a noble sentiment that should ever be enshrined in the memory and have a sustaining power in the midst of all adversities and dangers. "They that be with us are more than they that be with them." Let me trust in God, and not be afraid of what man can do unto me. Let me hold up my face like a flint in the cause of truth and righteousness. Enable me, O God, at all times to give an intrepid testimony, whatever be the strength or the multitude of gainsayers. But let my utterances ever be respectful and in good taste; and let me not be anxiously careful when called before men, remembering that both the preparations of the heart and the answer of the mouth are from God. Open the eyes of my faith, O God, that I may behold the cloud of witnesses who encompass me, and let a sense of their vigilant observation over me uphold me against the fear of man which is a snare, and keep me calm and self-possessed should I be brought before the councils and governors of this world. Elisha virtually brought the messengers from Syria who had been struck with blindness to the man whom they were seeking, though he took them in the first instance to Jehoram, for he restrained the king of Israel from smiting, and they were suffered to go to their master in peace.

What an appalling account we have here of the horrors of famine. Save us, O God, from a repetition of these horrors in our day.—Certain portions of our territory have been so visited.—May we learn righteousness therefrom. Meanwhile, open the hearts of the benevolent to the sufferings which are not ended, nay, which may be fearfully enhanced between this and the coming harvest. Interpose, O God, in our behalf; and let me here offer a prayer for the Divine blessing on the publication of my views. Overrule this dispensation, O God, to the good of Thy Church and the furtherance of Thy glory in the world, and keep our beloved country in the hollow of Thy hand.

II. KINGS VII.

This prophecy of Elisha was in itself of very unlikely fulfilment, and was accordingly met by an expression of incredulity on the part of a Samaritan lord. It is well to mark how often such unbelief is rebuked or punished, which implies that it was morally culpable, and in this instance resolves itself into the heedlessness of the nobleman to all the tokens which the prophet had given of a mission from God. He has the whole of the complex instrumentality of nature at command, by a touch on one of whose springs he can give movement and direction to whatever may be designed by him. And accordingly by a movement on the part of four lepers he made known to the people of the city on the morrow that unbounded plenty was within their reach. But the miraculous was superadded to the natural, for by the former it was that He caused the flight of the Syrians from their encampment. Let us not therefore, even in the most adverse and unpromising circumstances, cease from depending prayer upon God; and we supplicate now, O Lord, for Thy effectual interposition in behalf of thousands of our famishing countrymen. May deliverance come to us speedily; and O may it be accompanied with showers of grace and of spiritual blessings from on high. Man's extremity it is said is God's opportunity; and certain it is that these sadly reduced Israelites were brought down to the lowest point of want and helplessness. Yet the resources of infinity were equal to the occasion, and they are equal still. Fill up, O God, the deficiencies of the present, and avert the famine of another year. Cause Thy sun to shine and Thy showers to descend upon us, sending us rain and fruitful seasons so as to fill our hearts with food and gladness; and may gratitude accompany the gladness. Thou hast caused many to consider in this the day of their adversity. Follow it up, O God, by such a prosperity as shall not lead them to forget; but may this signal chastisement yield unto them who have been exercised thereby the peaceable fruits of righteousness. How graphically the whole of this narrative is told—a vivid description of things visible, yet as vivid and powerful a recognition of the invisible God who overruled all. Even the death of the unbelieving lord, though supernaturally foretold, was naturally brought about so that it could have been naturally accounted for. Thou, O unseen Sovereign, art the cause of causes, the great efficient power which guides and governs the world—and this by a Providence as special as if there were no general laws, while by processes so regular and unvarying that man can gather wisdom and foresight from experience, and yet be an absolute dependent upon Him who worketh all in all.

II. KINGS VIII.

We read of none who had done greater things in the way of miracle than Elisha; and it is interesting to have Gehazi again brought upon the stage, and the king talking with him, and with that curiosity which was most natural—as evinced not only in this place, but by Herod in the case of our Saviour. How sublimely does the power of a prophet culminate over that of a king. The Shunammite's connexion with Elisha was indeed a most beneficial one for her. But, O God, save us, save us from such an infliction of famine as was laid at this time upon Israel; and do Thou prosper my views now in print upon this subject.

The prophecy regarding Ben-hadad has respect to the disease. It was not a mortal one. As far as it is concerned, " Thou *mayest* certainly recover;" but yet for all that thou shalt certainly die, and without rising from the bed on which thou art now laid. The prophecy of Elisha to Hazael respecting himself seems to have awakened no other feelings or purposes in his mind than those of ambition. He spoke of the unlikelihood, not that he should do this atrocious or cruel thing, but that he should do this great thing. It set him, in fact, on the prosecution of his methods by which to realize this greatness, and he began his guilty career by an act of foul assassination; nor was he moved by the tears of the venerable prophet from the after perpetration of those awful enormities which are here foretold of him, absorbed by the lust of power and of dominion.

It looks as if it had been one fruit of the over intimacy of Jehoshaphat with Ahab that his son Joram married Ahab's daughter—a most unpropitious alliance, and it sped accordingly. He walked in the way of the wicked family with which he had joined himself—that is, worse than the house of Jeroboam, in the way of the house of Ahab, and he experienced in consequence not destruction but severe chastisement. As was the manner of the old economy his wickedness brought temporal penalties in its train. He incurred the loss of dominion, for both Edom and Libnah revolted from him. In the short-lived reign of his son there was a further affinity established with the house of Ahab—that Ahaziah married the daughter of Omri the father of Ahab. If the immediate daughter, then she behoved to be the aunt of Joram's wife, or his own mother's aunt—a strange connexion, to marry his own grandaunt. However this be, never were two such queen-mothers as those of Judah and Israel at this time, though of the two I regard Athaliah as more the Lady Macbeth of Scripture. At the conclusion of the chapter we have a glimpse of the Syrian war with Israel, with the usurper Hazael at its head. Ahaziah would meet with Jezebel in Jezreel.

II. KINGS IX.

Jehu was a king of divine right, and yet far from perfect in his personal qualities, however fit as an instrument in the hand of God, who selected him for a particular service, and of which he acquitted himself with great zeal and energy; yet it was not a pure zeal for the Lord of Hosts, though he arrogated this credit. There were ambition and great cruelty, and defection withal from the true God, yet he served the purpose for which he was chosen—as the rod of God's vengeance against the house of Ahab. There is much of the graphic both in the representation of the prophet's interview with Jehu and in that of Jehu's approach to Jezreel. The driving of Jehu is proverbial even in our day. The kings were not long of inferring that he was coming as an enemy. When Joram and Jehu met, the latter assumed the character that was laid upon him by the prophet as an avenger on the part of God for the sins of the house of Ahab, and more particularly, of Jezebel. It seems that Ahab's son as well as Ahab himself were included in the sentence which associated the ruin of their house with the vineyard of Naboth. It was fell execution on the part of Jehu thus to despatch two kings in one day.

But the event of greatest interest is the execution of Jezebel. We can imagine nothing more impressively set forth than is the destruction of Jezebel in the simple words of this very plain and simple narrative. It has all the force and vivacity of a picture. I know not if any artist has fancied it for a subject. There is horror in it; but I conceive that the painted Jezebel from her upper window, and the looking out of the eunuchs, and the group of stormy invaders below, with Jehu at their head, would supply the materials of a most striking picture. Altogether there is much to interest the imagination in this chapter. One feels as if introduced by it into the familiar habitudes of these days, nay, into the very interior of their houses—as when Jehu was convivializing with his brother officers at Ramoth-gilead, or when he took possession of the palace at Jezreel. But the higher view to take of it is the example here given forth of retributive justice—of which there are often signal displays even in this world, but the conclusive triumph and settlement of which are reserved for the great judgment-day, when all secrets shall be manifested; and many who would shudder at the monstrosities of Jezebel shall, nevertheless, in virtue of their decent ungodliness, and a worldliness that characterizes thousands of respectable men, be thrown forth as the outcasts of an entire and irrevocable condemnation. Jehu could recognise the hand of the Lord, and do homage to the memory of Elijah his servant, yet became himself an idolater and a rebel.

II. KINGS X.

May, 1847.

Jehu had obviously in all these fell perpetrations an eye to his own interest, as well as to the authority and will of God. It is the general policy of usurpers to make off with the descendants of those whom they have dethroned, and this for the security of their own power. The question put by Jehu to the people, when the revolting spectacle of the baskets full of human heads was set before them, seems to have had this significancy in it— You may think it was I who slew Ahab, but who slew these ? It is the doing of the Lord ; and so he reconciles them not only to the executions that had already taken place, but prepares them for future ones : and so still in conformity with his own interest did he proceed further in this dire work of blood, to the slaughter of the remaining kinsfolk, as well as the adherents among the great, whether civil or ecclesiastical, of king Ahab. We do not see how his interest was in like manner bound up with the slaughter of Ahaziah's relatives, unless in so far as they were in friendship and alliance with Ahab. But beside this, there seems on these dread occasions to be a thirst excited for a further destruction of human life than was at first contemplated, or than is required by any consideration of prudence or policy—as in the sack of cities and the cruel ravages of a country lying open to the movements of a victorious army. Jehu in taking Jehonadab up to his chariot, meant that his further proceedings should be an exhibition to him of his zeal for the Lord. Still his slaughter of the priests of Baal was directly at one with the objects of his own selfishness—as he thereby cleared away a whole host of adherents to the policy and cause of his predecessor. Nevertheless it was all of God, who employs either the wrath of man or the policy of man as instruments for the fulfilment of His counsels. All was done if not singly because of, yet according to the saying of the Lord which he spake to Elijah—and this though there were artifice and guile in the performance of it. Still God did annex His sanction to this work of destruction; and let us not look so much to Jehu, the executioner of the sentence, as to the holy and avenging Judge who gave it forth.

And the Lord let loose His vengeance upon Israel from other quarters beside—and this too in fulfilment of what the Lord had said to this same Elijah. (1 Kings xix. 17.)

Jehu had a royal burial, and seems to have ended his eventful history in peace. He was not so reprobate as to go the length of idolatry to Baal; yet like all the other kings of Israel, he did that which was evil in the sight of the Lord.

II. KINGS XI.

This atrocious personage, the Lady Macbeth of the Jewish nation, holds out a dreadful picture of relentless and hardy ambition. The story is most graphically told, and so as to set forth its incidents with picturesque and powerful effect upon the mind. Jehoiada again was the stay of Judah at this period, the restorer and preserver of its legitimate monarchy. Nor must the services of Jehosheba be overlooked at this critical juncture in the history of the kingdom. Jehoiada though an ecclesiastic seems to have had great authority and influence over both the military and civil office-bearers at this period, joined together by the bond of a common abhorrence at the enormities and crimes of the foul usurper. He laid down the tactics of their most righteous conspiracy, which by the good providence of God was completely successful. The priest both armed and marshalled all the forces, and by the adjunction of the testimony to the coronation, he gave the same character of religious to the august ceremonial which is still preserved in our own day. He seems to have enacted the same, or at least a very similar part, with the Archbishop of Canterbury at the coronation of our own monarchs. Let the Church and the State, the civil and the ecclesiastical, be ever thus harmoniously blended, each in its own true place, and without jealousy or collision, mutually exchanging benefits the one with the other. The tragical death of Athaliah was altogether in keeping with her crimes. It bears a great resemblance to, but yet differs from the death of Jezebel—the one killed by precipitation from a height and the trampling of horses; the other, though in the way of horses too, killed by the sword. (verse 20.) Mark here the twofold covenant between God and the people, and between the king and the people. The fear of God takes precedency of honouring the king. (1 Pet. ii. 17.) O my God, guide and actuate me aright among all the ambiguities of the question when the civil and the ecclesiastical come into contact and threaten to come into conflict with each other. Let it be remarked that in pursuance of the engagement on which they had just entered, they proceeded to remove all the monuments of idolatry—and that this was idolatry in its most aggravated form, being that of the house of Ahab, or the worship of Baal, everywhere represented as of greater enormity than the worship of the calves in Bethel. Ahaziah walked in the way of Ahab's house, (ch. viii. 28); and Athaliah, Ahab's sister, would not fall behind in that way. Jezebel and Athaliah were sisters-in-law through Ahab. What names of infamy and horror!

END OF VOLUME FIFTH.

OTHER SOLID GROUND TITLES

In addition to *Sabbath Scripture Readings* we are pleased to reveal several other titles we are delighted to have brought back in print.

Biblical & Theological Studies: *Addresses to Commemorate the 100th Anniversary of Princeton Theological Seminary in 1912* by Allis, Machen, Wilson, Vos, Warfield and many more.

Notes on Galatians by J. Gresham Machen

The Origin of Paul's Religion by J. Gresham Machen

A Scientific Investigation of the Old Testament by R.D. Wilson

Theology on Fire: *Sermons from Joseph A. Alexander*

Evangelical Truth: *Sermons for the Family* by Archibald Alexander

A Shepherd's Heart: *Pastoral Sermons of James W. Alexander*

Grace & Glory: *Sermons from Princeton Chapel* by Geerhardus Vos

The Lord of Glory by Benjamin B. Warfield

The Person & Work of the Holy Spirit by Benjamin B. Warfield

The Power of God unto Salvation by Benjamin B. Warfield

Calvin Memorial Addresses by Warfield, Johnson, Orr, Webb...

The Five Points of Calvinism by Robert Lewis Dabney

Annals of the American Presbyterian Pulpit by W.B. Sprague

The Word & Prayer: *Classic Devotions from the Pen of John Calvin*

A Body of Divinity: *Sum and Substance of Christian Doctrine* by Ussher

The Collected Works of James H. Thornwell

A Puritan New Testament Commentary by John Trapp

Exposition of the Epistle to the Hebrews by William Gouge

Exposition of the Epistle of Jude by William Jenkyn

Lectures on the Book of Esther by Thomas M'Crie

Lectures on the Book of Acts by John Dick

To order any of our titles please contact us in one of three ways:

Call us at **1-866-789-7423**
Email us at sgcb@charter.net
Visit our website at www.solid-ground-books.com

www.ingramcontent.com/pod-product-compliance
Lightning Source LLC
Chambersburg PA
CBHW030329240426
43661CB00052B/1578